T0284870

Sports Illustrated™

THE FOOTBALL VAULT

Great Writing from the
Pages of *Sports Illustrated*

Library of Congress Cataloging-in-Publication Data available upon request

This book is available in quantity at special discounts for your group or organization. For further information, contact:

Triumph Books LLC
814 North Franklin Street
Chicago, Illinois 60610
(312) 337-0747
www.triumphbooks.com

Printed in U.S.A.
ISBN: 978-1-63727-539-9
Design by Patricia Frey

THE FOOTBALL VAULT

CONTENTS

ALL ACCESS

A DANGEROUS GAME

COLORFUL CHARACTERS

FAN-TASTIC

BETWEEN THE LINES

AFTER THE WHISTLE

UNDER CENTER

OCTOBER 17, 1966

The Sweet Life of Swinging Joe

Jet quarterback Joe Namath has closed the sports celebrity gap in New York with amiable enthusiasm, flushing foxes in the hip saloons and treading llama in his plush penthouse pad

BY DAN JENKINS

Stoop-shouldered and sinisterly handsome, he slouches against the wall of the saloon, a filter cigarette in his teeth, collar open, perfectly happy and self-assured, gazing through the uneven darkness to sort out the winners from the losers. As the girls come by wearing their miniskirts, net stockings, big false eyelashes, long pressed hair and soulless expressions, he grins approvingly and says, "Hey, hold it, man—foxes." It is Joe Willie Namath at play. Relaxing. Nighttiming. The boss mover studying the defensive tendencies of New York's off-duty secretaries, stewardesses, dancers, nurses, bunnies, actresses, shopgirls—all of the people who make life stimulating for a bachelor who can throw one of the best passes in pro football. He poses a question for us all: Would you rather be young, single, rich, famous, talented, energetic and happy—or President?

Joe Willie Namath is not to be fully understood by most of us, of course. We are ancient, being over 23, and perhaps a bit arthritic, seeing as how we can't do the Duck. We aren't comfortably tuned in to the Mamas and the Uncles—or whatever their names are. We have cuffs on our trousers and, freakiest of all, we have pockets we can get our hands into. But Joe is not pleading to be understood. He is youth, success, the clothes, the car, the penthouse, the big town, the girls, the autographs and the games on Sundays. He simply *is*, man. The best we can do is catch a slight glimpse of him as he speeds by us in this life, and hope that he will in some way help prepare us for the day when we elect public officials who wear beanies and have term themes to write.

Right now, this moment, whatever Joe means to himself behind his wisecracks, his dark, rugged good looks, and his flashy tailoring, he is mostly one thing—a big celebrity in a celebrity-conscious town. This adds up to a lot of things, some desirable, some not. It means a stack of autographs everywhere he goes ("Hey, Joe, for a friend of mine who's a priest, a little somethin' on the napkin, huh?"), a lot of TV and radio stuff, a lot of photography stills for ads and news and continual interviews with the press. Such things he handles with beautiful nonchalance, friendliness—and lip.

Then comes the good part. It means he gets to sit at one of those key tables in Toots Shor's—1 and 1A, the joke goes—the ones just beyond the partition from the big circular bar where everyone from Des Moines can watch him eat his prime rib. It means that when he hits P.J. Clarke's the maitre d' in the crowded back room, Frankie Ribando, will always find a place for him, while, out front, Waiter Tommy Joyce, one of New York's best celebrity-spotters, will tell everyone, "Joe's inside." It means he can crawl into the Pussy Cat during the late hours when the Copa girls and the bunnies are there having their after-work snacks, even though the line at the door may stretch from Second Avenue to the Triborough Bridge. It means he can get in just as easily at two of his other predawn haunts, Mister Laffs and Dudes'n Dolls, places long ago ruled impenetrable by earth people, or nonmembers of the Youth Cult.

Easing into the clubs and restaurants that he frequents, Joe Willie handles his role well. "Don't overdo it, man," he says. "I can hang around till 3 or 4 and still grab my seven or eight." He sits, he eats, he sips, he smokes, he talks, he looks, and maybe he scares up a female companion and maybe he doesn't. "I don't like to date so much as I just like to kind of, you know, run into somethin', man," he says.

Namath is unlike all of the super sports celebrities who came before him in New York—Babe Ruth, Joe DiMaggio and Sugar Ray Robinson, to name three of the more obvious. They were grown men when they achieved the status he now enjoys. Might even be wearing hats. They were less hip to their times and more or less aloof from the crowd. Joe thrusts himself into the middle of it. Their fame came more slowly—with the years of earning it. Joe Willie Namath was a happening.

He happened first when he was a sophomore passing whiz who made Alabama Coach Bear Bryant change his offense. He happened again as a junior when he proved to be such an away-from-the-field mover that Bryant had to kick him off the team for drinking and carousing before the last two games of the season. He happened again when he returned to take Alabama to the 1964 national championship on a gimpy leg. Then Sonny Werblin, the owner of the New York Jets, made him really happen when he gave him that $400,000 contract on the second day of 1965. No football player in history had ever been worth half that much. But this wasn't all. He quickly had to undergo an operation on his knee to have a torn cartilage removed and a loose ligament tied. And, thanks to those splendid satirists, Robert Benton and David Newman, the hip line in New York became, "Sorry I can't make your party, Sybil, but I'm going to the tapping of Joe Namath's knee."

He was already a celebrity then, but his image grew throughout 1965 when a certain amount of suspense built as to whether he would be drafted, or whether his knee would allow him to play any football at all for Werblin's $400,000. During it all, the wisecracks flowed like cocktails.

"I'd rather go to Vietnam than get married," he said as the draft board in his home town of Beaver Falls, Pa. requested that he appear for his physical.

Then after he flunked it and a lot of superpatriots bristled, as they did at Cassius Clay's attitude, Joe said with brutal honesty, "How can I win, man? If I say I'm glad, I'm a traitor, and if I say I'm sorry, I'm a fool."

Once when he was asked to point out the difference between Bear Bryant and Jet Coach Weeb Ewbank, Joe grinned and unwisely said, "Coach Bryant was always thinking about winning. Weeb is mainly concerned over what kind of publicity you get."

When a writer tried to tease him about his classes at Alabama, asking if he majored in basket-weaving, Joe Willie said, "Naw, man, journalism—it was easier."

When he was asked to explain the origin of the white shoes that he wore—and still wears—during a game (and now endorses commercially), he shot back, "Weeb ordered 'em. He thought it would save tape."

But all of this was a year ago. Now in this season as he goes about the business of proving that he is worth every cent of his contract (he has thrown nine touchdown passes and put the Jets in first place in the American Football League's Eastern Division through five games), he is becoming the quarterback that Werblin gambled he would be—a throwing artist who may eventually rank with the best—and he is still a swinger. Namath may be Johnny Unitas and Paul Hornung rolled into one; he may, in fact, be pro football's very own Beatle.

He lives in a penthouse on New York's upper East Side, one that features a huge white llama-skin rug, an Italian marble bar, an elaborate stereo hookup, an oval bed that seems to increase in size with each glance, a terrace, and a couple of roommates—Joe Hirsch, a writer for *The Morning Telegraph*, and Jet Defensive Back Ray Abruzzese, whom he knew at Alabama.

Of Hirsch, Joe Willie says, "I got my own handicapper." Of Abruzzese, he says, "I got my own bartender," referring to Abruzzese's onetime summer job tending bar at Dudes 'n Dolls. And of his apartment, he says proudly, "I had the same decorator that Sinatra had for his pad."

He whirls around the city in his gray Lincoln Continental convertible, the radio blaring, parking by fireplugs whenever possible, wearing tailor-made suits with tight pants and loud print linings, grabbing checks, laughing, enjoying life, spending maybe $25,000 a year ("On nuthin', man") and wondering why anyone should be offended.

"I believe in letting a guy live the way he wants to if he doesn't hurt anyone. I feel that everything I do is O.K. for me, and doesn't affect anybody else, including the girls I go out with," he says. "Look man, I live and let live. I like everybody. I don't care what a man is as long as he treats me right. He can be a gambler, a hustler, someone everybody else thinks is obnoxious, I don't care so long as he's straight with me and our dealings are fair. I like Cassius Clay, Bill Hartack, Doug Sanders and Hornung, all the controversial guys. They're too much. They're colorful, man. If I couldn't play football, I'd like to be a pro golfer. But I like everybody." Joe's eyes sparkle, as if he is getting ready to make a joke, and he says, "Why, I even like Howard Cosell."

Joe Willie's philosophy is more easily grasped when one realizes what he lifted himself up from in Beaver Falls. It is a picturesque but poor town in the hills about 30 miles outside of Pittsburgh. He was the youngest of five children, and his parents were divorced when he was in the sixth grade. His father was a mill worker. He lived with his mother, and there was little money, so Joe hustled. He shot pool, he shined shoes, he ran messages for bookies, he hustled; he got by. "Where I come from," he says today, "ain't nobody gonna hustle *me*, man."

As he prepared for his senior year of high school the idea of going to college was remote. An older brother, John, was a career man in the Army, a warrant officer now in Vietnam. Joe was set on joining the Air Force and making it a career. What stopped him was a lot of touchdown passes and offers from precisely 52 universities, including Notre Dame—but not Alabama.

"I wanted to go to Maryland because I was stupid enough to think it was down South," he says. "I didn't know from outside Pittsburgh, man. All I knew was that I wanted to go South. I think a lot of kids from the East and Midwest do because of the climate."

Namath took the college board exams and failed them at Maryland. "You needed 750 and I scored 745, right? They wanted me to take it again, but I said to hell with it." He thought next of Penn State, but Maryland had to play Penn State the next few seasons and didn't want to face Namath. Maryland's coaches promptly called Bear Bryant at Alabama, whom the Terps would not play, and Bear welcomed "the greatest athlete I've ever coached."

Despite his dismissal for the last two games of his junior season, Namath worships Alabama and his experiences and successes there. Bryant is the greatest man he has ever known, Joe even has the hint of a southern accent, his closest friends are from Alabama, and if there is anything that makes him mad today, it is the eastern press, which he calls "the northern press."

"There's only three things I'm touchy about," says Joe Willie, who naturally got that name down South. "No. 1, the northern press and how it ignores southern football when I'll guarantee you that a team like Louisiana Tech can beat about 80 of these lousy schools up here. Two is the publicity that Notre Dame gets. And three is a joke about a Hungarian."

One other tiny thing bothered him when he first went to the Jets after taking Alabama to three bowl games with seasons of 10–1, 9–2 and 10–1. He read a statement by a pro player who suggested that Joe might not want to "pay the price" with his big salary. "Can you believe that?" he said. "Why, you can't play for Bryant for four years and not know how to pay the price for what you get out of life."

Considering that the most money Joe ever had at one time before he signed the Jet contract was $600, which he got for peddling some Alabama game tickets, he might have been justified in blowing the whole stack on a car, a blonde and a diamond ring. He had a shrewd business consultant, however, in a Birmingham lawyer named Mike Bite. At Bite's bidding he learned to spread the money out as he would an evening on the town. He takes only $25,000 a year in salary, and will through 1968. He has $200,000 in bonuses working for him over the next 100 years or something like that. And he was generous enough to let members of his family in on the loot. Two brothers and a brother-in-law are on the Jets' scouting payroll at $10,000 a year.

Contrary to popular notion, Joe did give the St. Louis Cardinals, who drafted him in the NFL, some serious consideration. "And they weren't that far off in money," he says. "But they had it laid out wrong, like I had to do a radio show for part of my salary. I couldn't believe that. I said, man, I'm just a football player, and what I make will be for football only." He did guess that the Cardinals, who had an established passer in Charley Johnson, might be dealing for him on behalf of the New York Giants, who had nothing, and, one way or another, he wanted to "get to this town." Bear Bryant's only comment was that Ewbank had won a couple of championships at Baltimore and, if Joe was still interested in winning, he might give that some consideration.

He wasn't a winner right off, of course. The Jets' 5–8–1 record last season made New York the worst team Joe had ever played on. Admittedly, he didn't know the first thing about quarterbacking a pro team. He had the quickest delivery anyone had ever seen, and he got back into the Jets' exceedingly secure passing pocket, formed by Sherman Plunkett, Dave Herman, Sam DeLuca, and Winston Hill—his "bodyguards"—so fast that Kansas City's All-AFL lineman, Jerry Mays, said, "He makes the rush obsolete." But there was so much he had to learn.

At Alabama he had raced back only five yards and released the ball in approximately 1.3 seconds. Ewbank, however, demanded that he get eight yards deep and go 3.2 seconds before throwing. His firmly braced knee prevented him from using the threat of the run, which he had done so well for two and a half seasons in Tuscaloosa.

He had to learn how to read defenses, how to look for tips among the defensive backs, how to hit his receivers on the break, how to set up when he threw, how to call audibles and how to convince his Jet teammates that he could lead them.

"Last year," says Defensive End Gerry Philbin, "there was an undercurrent of resentment—nothing you could pinpoint, but it was there—about Joe's money and his publicity. That was at first. It disappeared when everybody found out what a great guy he is."

Curley Johnson, the punter, says, "Mainly we wanted to see how good he was. He really didn't throw the ball that damn well for a long time. Now, we know how good he is—the best."

Says the ace receiver, Don Maynard, "At first he'd knock us over on short patterns. Now he's slacked off. His timing is great, and he adjusts to situations like a veteran." To this, George Sauer Jr., another top Jet receiver, adds, "He never knew how to throw on the break last season. The ball was always early or late. Now it's there."

Not according to Joe Willie, though. "I haven't thrown well since Alabama," he says. "Maybe it's my leg. I don't know. If I knew, I'd throw better. You hear a lot about getting the ball up here by your ear, but that's junk. It doesn't matter how you deliver as long as the ball goes where you aim it and gets there when it's supposed to. I don't know how I throw the ball, and I don't remember anybody ever teaching me to throw it. But there's a lot I have found out."

For one thing, Joe says, the quarterback who has to call a pile of audibles (changing plays at the line of scrimmage) is a dumb one. "You're supposed to know what the defense will be when you're in the huddle. I'll only call five or six audibles a game now. Last year it was more. That's funny, too, because the public thinks it's a big deal if a quarterback can switch plays a lot at the scrimmage line. They think it makes him brainy. Man, most of the time it means he's stupid."

A simple thing it took Joe all last season to learn was that backs key on the mannerisms of a quarterback and cover their areas accordingly.

"For example," he says, "about 80% of the time when the quarterback takes the snap, turns and races back to set up with his back to the defense, he'll throw to the right. That's because it's easier, more natural, to plant your feet when you start that way. On the other hand, it's easier to throw left when you drop straight back, without turning around. There are defensive backs who'll play you for this and, of course, you have to cross 'em up."

Among the defenders that have Namath's highest respect are Oakland's speedy Dave Grayson and Miami's Jim Warren, who was with San Diego a year ago. "All you can say about 'em is they play you tight and cover you. To beat 'em, you have to run what we call progressive patterns, you know, something that goes out, slant, down and in. The whole game is trying to get the defensive man's feet turned wrong."

Strangely enough, Joe finds that the ball has a tendency to turn wrong on his home turf of Shea Stadium. "It's my unfavorite place to play," says he. "Somehow, the wind swirls in there, and I don't like what it does to the balls I throw. It could be some kind of fixation, I don't know, Like I have about throwing a night football. It's different, man, I swear. The coaches and the sporting-goods salesmen say it's the same ball, but it isn't. It goes different. So does the ball in Shea."

It certainly went differently in Namath's first home game of 1966. He passed for five touchdowns as the Jets humiliated the Houston Oilers 52–13. Joe's hottest streak of all so far came in the fourth quarter of a game at Boston, where he had to hit 14 of 23 passes for 205 yards and two touchdowns so the Jets could salvage a 24–24 tie. This sent the Jets into pure ecstasy. "He brought us back from a bad day in a real clutch situation," said Ewbank. And Publicity Man Frank Ramos, with his usual sharp eye on statistics, pointed out, "The papers are raving about Terry Hanratty at Notre Dame, but do you realize Joe hit as many passes in *one quarter* as Hanratty hit against Northwestern all day long? I think that's interesting."

The supertest for both Namath and the Jets came last Saturday night, however, and they were more than up to it. While Shea Stadium shook from the noise of 63,497 New Yorkers—an all-time AFL record crowd—who had come to cheer their town's only winning team against unbeaten San Diego, Joe Willie's arm was right when it had to be. He threw a touchdown pass to Matt Snell early that gave the Jets a 10–9 lead, which they carried into the last 10 minutes. Then, after San Diego pulled ahead 16–10, Namath rapidly fired three straight completions and whirled his team 66 yards to the winning touchdown and the final 17–16 score. He had shown once more that he could deliver in the clutch, and the Jets had the only defeatless record (4–0–1) in the AFL as proof.

If there is a single myth that Joe Willie would like to have destroyed about pro football, it is the widely held belief that the game's quarterbacks are pampered by opposing defensive linemen; that they are not "shot at," particularly himself because of his bad knee and what his drawing power means to the AFL.

"O.K.," he says, "How about the Houston exhibition in Birmingham in August? Don Floyd comes at me after the whistle, and I move to miss a shot and reinjure my knee. What's that? Of course, Don didn't mean to. He says he didn't hear the whistle, and I believe him. But he was comin' at me and I kind of think he'd of hit me if he could have. What about the Denver game? I still got a wrist bandage and a sore back from that one. Johnny Bramlett, one of their linebackers, is a buddy of mine—he played for Memphis State—and he had me over to dinner the night before the game. His wife cooked an Italian feast, plenty good, too. But the next day he was after me like a tiger, and he'd cuss me when he missed. He wanted to win, man. That's the way it is. I don't think any of our opponents are too interested in my health."

If he stays healthy, Joe Willie may achieve his deepest ambition, which is "to become known as a good quarterback, not a rich one." He may even become what Boston Owner Billy Sullivan says he is now: "The biggest thing in New York since Babe Ruth." Slowly, because trying to fathom youth is always a slow process, you get the impression that Joe is quite serious about it and, despite his hip ways, is working hard to make it. Beneath the gaudy surface there somehow beams through a genuine, considerate, sincere, wonderfully friendly and likeable young man. But he's going to be himself. He's going to do it his way, and nobody else's.

AUGUST 6–13, 1990

Born to Be a Quarterback

Schooled in the fundamentals from the time he could walk, Joe Montana showed early that he was a gifted passer, and football fans from Monongahela to San Francisco have marveled at his abilities ever since

BY PAUL ZIMMERMAN

Part 1

It's a normal minicamp lunch break at the San Francisco 49ers' training facility. The players are unwrapping their sandwiches in the locker room, and Joe Montana is giving an interview upstairs in p.r. director Jerry Walker's office. Well, most of Joe Montana is concentrating on the interview. His right hand is busy with something else, as if it has a life of its own, a mechanized life of autograph production.

A steady stream of objects appears on the table in front of him—hats, jerseys, photos, posters—and Montana's right hand automatically rises, then lowers, producing a large sweeping *J* and tailing off to an almost illegible *ana*. Then his hand rises again, and another item is moved into place. Secretaries, p.r. people, coaches, players all come to present offerings at this ritual.

"A book to sign," says Walker. "Two pictures," says tight end Jamie Williams. "A ball," says p.r. assistant Dave Rahn. "Make this one out to 'a Nevada sports fan,'" says defensive coordinator Bill McPherson, sliding in a picture.

Rise and fall, rise and fall; the big *J*, the scribbled *ana*. Most of the time Montana doesn't even look at what he's signing. You get the feeling that someone could slip in a small child, a hamburger bun, a fish. It's all the same. At 34, the world's most famous quarterback has turned into an autograph machine.

Secretary Darla Maeda brings a hat. Walker is back with a toy rabbit. Guard Guy McIntyre is next with a jersey.

"Oh, no, not you too," Montana says, rolling his eyes.

"Yeah, me." It's Norb Hecker, the team's senior administrator, and he has a poster showing a glowering Montana. "A beauty, huh?" he says.

"They name animals after him," Rahn says, producing a picture of a German shepherd. "They send in every piece of football equipment you can think of. The office is cluttered with stuff." There is a children's book from a woman in Hillsborough, Calif. "To Joe Montana, for your kids...let me know if you need extra copies," reads the accompanying letter. There are eight mail cartons filled with letters going back four months, letters from France, Ireland, Tokyo.

"He'll come up here once or twice a week to sign stuff," says p.r. assistant Al Barba. "We use the real Joe pictures until they run out, then we send the ones with the printed autograph. Everyone will get something—eventually."

Since he blistered the Denver Broncos in last January's Super Bowl, Montana is hot again, just as he was after the 49ers' Super Bowl victory in '82 and the one in '85, having been voted the game's Most Valuable Player each time. The first success represented the thrill of discovery, the potential star who blossomed, and it carried a healthy round of commercial endorsements with it. The second one reestablished him after Miami Dolphin quarterback Dan Marino had captured most of the headlines in '84. But then, in the 1985 season, the adulation for Montana cooled.

There were drug rumors, all unsubstantiated. Montana in his Ferrari reportedly stopped by police, even though the car was in his garage at the time. Montana seen in a bar, when he happened to be in a team meeting. In '86 there was the back operation two weeks into the season. Doctors said Montana might never play again. He was back in 55 days. The '87 season was his best statistically at that time, but the year ended with a disastrous loss to the Vikings in an NFC divisional playoff. When Montana was lifted for Steve Young in that game, it was the first time since he had reached football maturity that San Francisco coach Bill Walsh had given him the hook. The fans cheered when Young entered the game. Trade Joe now, they said, while you can still get something for him.

Walsh started Young a few times in '88, saying he was giving Montana time to get over nagging injuries and "general fatigue." Montana says it was a lack of confidence, tracing back to the end of '87. "It's tearing my guts out," Montana told his wife, Jennifer. But the exclamation point on the '88 season was the terrific 92-yard drive in the final minutes to beat Cincinnati in Super Bowl XXIII, and Montana came into '89 riding the crest. He put together a remarkable season, the best any quarterback has ever had, according to the NFL's rating system. And he was even better in the playoffs and Super Bowl XXIV, reaching a level of brilliance that had never been seen in postseason football. Which leaves only one question to ask about this remarkable 11-year veteran: Is he the greatest quarterback ever to play the game?

Wait, let's back off from that one for a minute. Greatest ever? What about Unitas, Baugh, Luckman, Graham? History's a serious business. Van Brocklin, Bradshaw, Tittle? When, in the long history of the NFL, was a quarterback in his prime called the greatest ever? The man in the most glamorous position in football going against the most famous names of the past? Does anyone point to a surgeon in Houston and say, "Yep, there's the greatest doctor ever"? How about Albert Schweitzer? It's rare ground we're treading on.

Montana's roots are in western Pennsylvania, the cradle of quarterbacks. Soft coal and quarterbacks. Steel mills and quarterbacks. Johnny Lujack from Connellsville, Joe Namath from Beaver Falls, George Blanda from Youngwood, Dan Marino from Pittsburgh, Montana from Monongahela, Tom Clements and Chuck Fusina from McKees Rocks, Arnold Galiffa from Donora, Terry Hanratty from Butler—he was Montana's idol as a kid. Terry Hanratty of Notre Dame, the Golden Domer. Montana would throw footballs through a swinging tire in the backyard, just like Terry did. Why? Why do so many of them come from western Pennsylvania? "Toughness, dedication, hard work and competitiveness; a no-nonsense, blue-collar background," says John Unitas, from Pittsburgh.

But there are a lot of no-nonsense, blue-collar places in the country. Why not Georgia or Texas, where the great running backs come from? Why not Michigan or Ohio, with all those fine linemen? What is it about western Pennsylvania and quarterbacks?

"Maybe it's the Iron City beer," says Montana.

The most logical answer is tradition—and focus. If you're a kid with athletic ability in western Pennsylvania, you've probably got a picture of Montana or Marino on your wall. Montana had the athletic gift. You could see it right away.

"He used to wreck his crib by standing up and rocking," his mother, Theresa, says. "Then he'd climb up on the side and jump to our bed. You'd hear a thump in the middle of the night and know he hit the bed and went on the floor."

And he had the focus, supplied by his father, Joseph Sr., who put a ball in his son's hands when the kid was big enough to walk and said, "Throw it."

"I played all sports in the service, but when I was a kid I never had anyone to take me in the backyard and throw a ball to me," says Joe Sr., who moved to California with his wife in '86. "Maybe that's why I got Joe started in sports. Once he got started, he was always waiting at the door with a ball when I came home from work. What I really wanted to do was make it fun for him. And I wanted to make sure he got the right fundamentals. I read books. You watch some quarterbacks, sometimes they need two steps to get away from the line of scrimmage. I felt the first step should be straight back, not to the side. We worked on techniques, sprint out, run right, run left, pivot and throw the ball.

"You know, I've been accused of pushing him. I don't think that's right. It's just that he loved it so much, and I loved watching him. And I wanted to make sure he learned the right way."

Joe Jr. was an only child, a pampered child, perhaps, but he didn't see it that way. The family lived in a two-story frame house in a middle-class neighborhood on Park Avenue, a house no better than the neighbors' and no worse. To Montana, his home was his strength, his support system. He was shy with strangers, outgoing at home. He had a few friends, neighborhood kids mostly, but no one was as close to him as his father—and his mother. His fondest childhood memory? Playing ball in the backyard with his dad, then coming into the kitchen, where his mother would have a steaming pot of ravioli on the stove. That was the best.

Montana started playing peewee football when he was eight, one year younger than the legal limit. His father listed his age as nine. His first coach on the Little Wildcats was Carl Crawley, a defensive lineman in college and now an NCAA referee.

"We ran a pro offense, with a lot of the stuff he's doing now, the underneath stuff," Crawley says. "Joe would roll out. If the cornerback came off, he'd dump it off; if he stayed back, he'd keep going and pick up five or six yards. He was an amazingly accurate passer for a kid."

Montana's favorite receiver was Mike Brantley, who caught his passes through junior high and high school. Brantley eventually made it as far as the Pittsburgh Steelers' training camp. "Joe throwing to Mike was like the right hand throwing to the left hand," Crawley says.

Crawley remembers Montana as an "exuberant kid who had stardom written all over him, but nobody ever resented it because it came so naturally. And there was no show-off in him. He wanted to win, and he'd do whatever it took, and that's another thing the kids liked about him. With Joe on the field, they knew they were never out of any game."

In the spring it was baseball, and Montana played all the positions. As a pitcher in Little League, he threw three perfect games. In the winter it was basketball, for which there was no organized program for kids until Joe Sr. started one. The team practiced and played in the local armory, and the kids paid a dollar apiece for a janitor to clean up after them. The practices were five nights a week, and there were always tournaments to play in. "Those were the most fun," Montana says. "The trips. We'd go anywhere. One night we played in a tournament in Bethel Park, Pennsylvania, then drove up to Niagara Falls for another one, then back to Bethel Park for the finals."

Montana has always said that his favorite sport, through Waverly Elementary and Finleyville Junior High and finally Ringgold High, was basketball. He loved the practices. "I could practice basketball all day," he says. Practicing football was work.

He came to Ringgold with a reputation for being something of a wunderkind. When coach Chuck Abramski took his first look at Montana on the football field, he saw an agile, 6-foot, 165-pound sophomore with a nice touch on the ball, but a kid who was too skinny and too immature to stand up to the rigors of western Pennsylvania Class AAA football. Abramski gave Montana a seat on the bench and told him to watch and learn. And to be sure to report to the summer weight program before his junior year. Montana had other ideas.

"For me, competing in sports was a 365-day-a-year thing," he says. "I was playing American Legion baseball, summer basketball. It was hard for Coach Abramski to accept that."

Last January, a week before the Super Bowl, a story appeared in the *Baltimore Sun* saying that, in Monongahela, Montana was regarded as a lesser god, a fact the rest of the world was dimly aware of. A number of old resentments surfaced in the story, but the worst quotes of all were from Abramski. "A lot of people in Monongahela hate Joe," was one of them. "If I was in a war, I wouldn't want Joe on my side...his dad would have to carry his gun for him," was another, and it was the one that bothered Montana most because it hit him where he lived. No one connected with football had ever questioned his courage.

"I called him about it," Montana says. "Three times now, I've seen those Abramski quotes around Super Bowl time, about why people hate me. I asked him why he kept saying those things, and he said, 'Well, you never sent me a picture, and you sent one to Jeff Petrucci, the quarterback coach.' I said, 'You never asked.' I mean, I don't send my picture around everywhere. We ended up yelling at each other. We had to put our wives on.

"Of course, I know what it was really about...that summer weight program. Chuck was a great coach in a lot of ways. He always tried to get the kids good equipment, he was always helping them get into college. I even wrote a letter of recommendation for him to go to another school after he left Ringgold. He was a fired-up, gung-ho coach, but he never got over the fact that I didn't take part in his summer weight program before my junior year. The man's all football."

Abramski, hard and wiry at 58, still lives in Monongahela, but he's out of football now. He sells real estate, just as Joe Montana Sr. does in the Bay Area. Abramski bounced around the western Pennsylvania high school circuit and held one college coaching job, at California University of Pennsylvania, under his old assistant at Ringgold, Petrucci. The problem was always the same: He was a great guy for developing a program, but school administrators found him impossible to deal with.

"I came from the south side of New Castle, the poor side," Abramski says. "My father was an alcoholic. My mother died of tuberculosis when I was 10. My grandmother raised me. There have been coaches with more brains, but nobody in the world worked harder at football than me. The year before I came to Ringgold, they lost every game and scored two touchdowns. They left me 14 players in uniform. Two years later, we had 100 kids out for football and we dressed 60, home and away. Three years later, Joe's senior year, we had one of the best teams in the eastern United States. We went 8–1 and then lost to Mt. Lebanon in the playoffs on a miserable, sleety night with three starters out. Before the season we scrimmaged South Moreland and scored 19 touchdowns. Nineteen touchdowns!"

The weight program was Abramski's baby, his joy. It was part of the toughening-up process. According to Abramski, Montana and only one other player, a halfback, didn't participate in his summer program. Petrucci says that about 20% to 30% of the squad didn't take part. Some former players say the number was higher. But here was Abramski's junior quarterback, a guy who had superstar written all over him—hell, everyone knew it—and he wasn't there. It ate Abramski up. When the season started, Montana was on the bench. "It's very painful now, when people say I harbored this hatred for Joe," Abramski says. "Hell, I loved the kid. I was doing what I thought was right for my squad."

"It's just an unfortunate thing," says Petrucci. "Here's a kid who never did anything wrong, never smoked or drank or broke curfew, never gave anyone a hard time, just a terrific kid. And on the other side, you've got a good coach who's stubborn."

People who were close to the situation feel that the real source of Abramski's resentment was not Joe but his father, who had worked with Joe for so long and taught him all the right habits. It was a matter of control, the fact that the father, not the coach, had had more to do with making a star out of the boy.

And now Abramski had benched that potential star, and his quarterback was 6'3", 215-pound Paul Timko, a big, rough youngster who splattered defenders when he ran the option play but had a throwing arm like a tackle's. In the scrimmages, Timko would line up at defensive end and take dead aim at Montana, the guy who was trying to take his job away. "Every day he just beat the hell out of me," Montana said. "I'd be dead when I came home. Football wasn't much fun at that point."

The Ringgold Rams were blown out by Elizabeth Forward 34–6 in the 1972 opener. They won the next two games by forfeit because of a teachers' strike, but lost the two practice games that were played to fill in the schedule. Timko wasn't the answer, obviously, especially with an away game coming up against mighty Monessen, the favorite to win the Big Ten league title. During the time of the forfeits Montana had moved up to become the starter. Timko was shifted to tight end. "Hell, I wanted to play there anyway," Timko says.

Keith Bassi, who was the Ringgold fullback, says the scene that night at Monessen was like nothing he has ever seen before or since. "You had to be there," he says. "I mean Monessen had some players—Bubba Holmes, who went to Minnesota; Tony Benjamin, who went to Duke. The rumor was that guys there had been held back a year in nursery school so they'd be more mature when they hit high school. We were doing our calisthenics, and there was this big roar, and here they came, 120 of them, in single file from the top of that concrete stadium, biggest stadium in the [Monongahela] Valley. It was like Custer's Last Stand."

The final score was 34–34, Holmes scoring for Monessen in the last moments. "We call it our 34–34 win," Bassi says. Montana's passing numbers read 12 for 22, 223 yards and four touchdowns, three of them to Timko, the new tight end.

Last April, Ringgold threw a welcome-home dinner for Montana at the New Eagle Fire Hall. The 1,000 tickets were sold out in three hours. Among the gifts presented to Montana was a set of videotapes of all his high school games. A month later Joe Ravasio, the current football coach at Ringgold, showed me the original game films in a storeroom off the boys' locker room.

The first pass Montana threw against Monessen was on a scramble to his right; he pulled up and hit Brantley, crossing underneath. The second was a sideline completion to Timko, neatly plunked between two defenders. The show was on. "They played a three-deep, where they give you the short stuff," said Frank Lawrence, who had been the offensive line coach. "Joe just killed 'em with timed patterns." It was an eerie feeling, watching Montana drop back from center, set and throw. All his 49er mechanics were there, the quick setup, the nifty glide to the outside, scrambling but under control, buying time, looking for a receiver underneath. It seemed as if he had been doing it all his life, and this was a kid in his first high school start. "Watch Joe now," Lawrence said as Ringgold scored on a one-yard plunge. "See that? He backpedals after the touchdown and throws his hands up. Same mannerisms as now."

There were some amazing athletic plays by Montana—a 10-yard bootleg to the one, having faked everyone; a 35-yard touchdown pass to Timko, a play on which he rolled left, corkscrewed his body, dodged a rusher and laid the ball into the hands of the tight end, who was surrounded by three defenders.

We watched it all, junior year and senior year. The somewhat slender kid was gradually filling out, standing taller in the pocket, almost 6'2" now, up to 180 pounds—the makings of a superstar. In the Laurel Highlands game his senior year (won by Ringgold 44–0), Montana rolled to his right, went up on his toes and pump-faked two defensive players out of position before he hit his receiver on a crossing pattern. But the most interesting thing was that the cameraman wasn't fooled. He kept the camera right on Montana. By then everyone knew what he was capable of.

He was all-everything his senior year—including Parade All-America as a quarterback—a gifted athlete who starred on a league championship basketball team ("He could stand flat-footed and dunk with two hands," says Fran LaMendola, his basketball coach), a baseball player good enough to get invited back to a major league tryout camp, a potential standout in sports in which he merely filled in—a victory in his only tennis match, an informal 6'9" high jump, a junior high record in his only attempt at the discus. He was a B student who could have done better if someone had figured out a way to get him indoors, in front of a book, a little longer. He was popular in school, easy to get to know, hard to get close to. His classmates elected him class vice-president his senior year; the Ringgold yearbook, *Flame '74*, lists him as a member of the choir as a senior. The photo that appears under "Sports Personalities" in the yearbook shows a thin kid with blond, floppy hair that is almost girlish-looking. He is leaning on the wall next to a trophy case; no waist or hips, string-bean legs in long bell-bottoms. "Joe Banana" was one of Abramski's nicknames for Montana.

North Carolina State offered him a basketball scholarship. Notre Dame basketball coach Digger Phelps said he would try to arrange it so Montana could play football and basketball. A few dozen college offers came in. Georgia assistant coach Sam Mrvos stood next to Montana's dad at one practice session, watched Joe throw a bullet while sprinting to his left and told Joe Sr., "We'll give him a scholarship right now." Georgia was one of the schools Montana visited, along with Boston College, Minnesota and Notre

Dame. His parents had taken him for a look around Penn State, and he had been to Pitt many times to watch the Panthers play.

It was all window dressing. His mind was already made up. It would be Notre Dame, where his idol, Hanratty, had played.

"In his senior year, the games at Legion Field were a happening," said Bob Osleger, the golf coach at Ringgold. "There was this flat bit of ground above the stadium, and Joe's father would stand there and watch the game, and all these college coaches and scouts would vie for position to stand near him. The whispers would start, about which college coaches were there that night, and I can see it so clearly now. Joe's dad would be standing there with his hands in his pockets and all these guys jockeying for position around him."

Sixteen and a half years later Montana was back, sitting on the dais at the dinner in the New Eagle Fire Hall, facing a roomful of people who had paid the cut rate of $20 a head, same price they paid for his first welcome-home dinner in '79. Earlier in the day he had given four speeches to a few thousand school kids—elementary, middle and high school—and there was a gleeful moment when six-year-old Anthony Vaccaro asked him, "Do you know who's living in your house?"

"No," Montana said.

"I am," Anthony said, "512 Park Avenue."

"Do you sleep in my bedroom?"

"Yes."

But there was also an edge to Montana's return that some kids couldn't quite understand. That day the *Pittsburgh Post-Gazette* ran a story that dredged up all the old resentments. Some people felt Montana had turned his back on the Mon Valley when he moved to San Francisco, and that his parents had done likewise when they followed him west. There was mention in the *Post-Gazette* of his infrequent visits home and how his name had been rejected in a newspaper phone-in poll on the naming of Ringgold's new stadium. Once again there was an old Abramski quote about all the people who hated him.

Montana read the piece on his way to Monongahela from the Pittsburgh airport, and his opening remarks to the Ringgold middle school students left a few kids scratching their heads. "What you hear about me, about my feelings, are totally false," he said. "When they say Joe Montana doesn't think of the Mon Valley as his home, well, you can tell whoever's saying it that he's full of it." It was a sentiment he would repeat to the high school kids, and at the dinner. His relatives in town knew only too well what he was talking about.

"My 14-year-old granddaughter, Jamie, was afraid to go to school that day," says Montana's aunt, Elinor Johnson. "She was afraid the kids were going to boo him."

"The kids were telling me he doesn't really care about Monongahela," Jamie says. "There's a picture of Joe on a locker in school that says, 'My Hero—Joke!' They don't know him. They hear what some people say. Sometimes I'll get upset, sometimes I'll walk away."

"You grew up working in a mill or a factory," says Pam Giordenango, Jamie's mother. "Now the mill's closed, the factory's closed. Heavy industry moved out of the Valley. People lost their jobs, lost their homes, lost their families. They're bitter. Whatever they read in the news gives them something to bitch about, other than the fact that they can't make their house payments, can't afford to put food on the table. Now here comes Joe, who's made a lot of money playing football. He's an easy target."

I am standing in front of the armory, the old place where Montana practiced basketball at night. It seems small, much too small to hold a basketball court. A blue Chevy pulls up and stops. "If you want to get inside, you have to get the key from the minister down the street," the woman in the car says. She seems friendly. On an impulse I ask her, "What do you think of Joe Montana?"

"I don't like him," she says.

"Why not?"

"Stillers," she says.

Stillers? A bitter family in town?

"Stillers, Pittsburgh Stillers," she says. "Joe should be a Stiller."

A youngster asked Montana the same question earlier in the day. How come you aren't a Steeler, if you like this town so much?

"The football draft is like the draft in the Army," Montana had said. "When they call you, you go."

"Hey, you're in Steeler country," Elinor Johnson says. "They don't want Joe to beat Terry Bradshaw's record. You can get your man in the street, your man in the bar, he'll tell you that."

There's more, of course, like the fact that Montana's parents worked for Civic Finance—his father was the manager, his mother a secretary—while the area was going through a financial crisis. "One person who defaulted on a loan can spread more bad news around town than 50 people can spread good news," says Carl Crawley. And then the fact that the Montanas left for California, to be with Joe and Jennifer. Joe Jr. had instigated the move in 1986. He had always been close to his parents, but how could you be close when you were 2,500 miles apart? "Joe said, 'Quit and come out here with

Jennifer and me,'" his father says. "It's hard, though, when you've lived somewhere all your life, when your roots are there."

There had also been a newspaper story about a financial mix-up, an accusation that Montana had billed a Monongahela group for speaking at a dinner held to honor him for being the '82 Super Bowl MVP. It was a bum rap. Montana was an infrequent public speaker in those days, and the few appearances he made were mostly unpaid charity work. There was no fee for his Monongahela appearance, only a guarantee of airfare, but when he put in an appearance at a second affair, in nearby Washington, Pa., there was a tap dance about who would pick up the expense for Montana's trip home. "I never knew a thing about it until I read all that stuff in the paper," Montana says.

As for the stadium that does not bear his name, the newspaper poll drew on a wide area, feeding on neighborhood rivalries and jealousies. None of the other local heroes was acceptable either, not Stan Musial, not Ken Griffey.

Perhaps the main cause of conflict is that Montana has always guarded his privacy. "We've come back to Monongahela four or five times in the last few years to visit relatives," Jennifer Montana says, "but people don't know that. What is he supposed to do, go down to the corner drugstore and hang out?"

That's probably what the people of Monongahela wanted. They wanted a superstar to act like one. But Montana's public persona had become a nightmare for him. "I love to eat out," he says, "but it's just no fun anymore. There's always a group of people coming by your table, always some guy just pulling up a chair and lighting a cigarette and starting to talk football."

He did what he had to do publicly—sign autographs and give interviews—but his privacy was his, and that included trips back home. In Monongahela, it was hard to understand. He was still Joey, the local kid. It's a complex area, the Mon Valley, fiercely loyal at times, but a place where it's easy to form resentments. And it's the area that Montana left in the fall of 1974 for a strange sojourn at Notre Dame that mirrored his entire athletic career—lows, moments of despair, followed by glorious highs.

He was 18 when he arrived in South Bend, still skinny, still shy with people he didn't know, a bit at sea so far away from his hometown and his parents. He had become engaged to his high school sweetheart, Kim Moses, from Monongahela Valley Catholic High. They would be married in the second semester of his freshman year and divorced less than three years later.

At Notre Dame he found himself amid an incredible collection of talent. He was a high school hotshot who was surrounded by hotshots, a hatchery fish in the deep ocean. Forty-six players who played for Notre Dame during the Montana years would be drafted by the NFL, eight in the first round. The Irish won a national championship under Ara Parseghian the year before Montana arrived in South Bend, and they would win another one, under Dan Devine, in '77, Montana's junior year.

Montana saw no varsity action his first year and got only minimal playing time in the freshman games. The eye-catching recruit was Gary Forystek, a big, strong, rocket-armed kid from Livonia, Mich. Montana? Well, he had that sleepy look about him. He missed home. He would call his dad three, four times a week. Joe Sr. told him to hang in. On a whim Montana once drove home in the middle of the night. Joe Sr. occasionally would make the eight-hour drive from Monongahela to watch Joe Jr. in an afternoon scrimmage, grab a bite to eat with his son, and then drive home to be at work the next day.

"His dad would sometimes show up in the middle of the night, and we'd all go out at 1 a.m. for a stack of pancakes," says Montana's freshman roommate, Nick DeCicco. "It was crazy."

"The fact is, his father was his best friend," says Steve Orsini, Montana's former teammate at Notre Dame. "The person Joe felt closest to was back in Monongahela."

Parseghian resigned suddenly, for health reasons, on Dec. 15, 1974, and the new coach was Devine, from the Green Bay Packers. "I asked the coaches about my quarterbacks when I first got there," Devine says. "No one said much about Joe. He'd been something like the seventh or eighth quarterback. Then he had a fine spring practice, really outstanding. I came home and told my wife, 'I'm gonna start Joe Montana in the final spring game,' and she said, 'Who's Joe Montana?' I said, 'He's the guy who's going to feed our family for the next few years.'"

It took a while in coming, until Montana came off the bench as a sophomore to pull out two games in the fourth quarter, and then did it again as a junior. The players couldn't figure out why it was taking the coach so long to grasp something they already knew, that this skinny, sleepy-eyed kid from Monongahela was the man, the guy who could get it done when he had to.

"Whenever he came on the field," says L.A. Raider noseguard Bob Golic, who played at Notre Dame with Montana, "the players knew they had a friend coming in."

"When the pressure came," says 49er free safety Dave Waymer, who started his Notre Dame career as a wideout, "we knew he was the guy who wouldn't overheat."

Montana started the season behind Rick Slager as a sophomore in '75, and behind Rusty Lisch in '77, Joe's year of junior eligibility after he had separated his shoulder and missed all of '76. The time Montana spent on the bench still bothers him; the resentment of Devine is still there. Waymer says the reason was that Montana was a Parseghian recruit and Devine favored his own guys, which really doesn't figure because Montana went nowhere under Parseghian.

Walsh, the former 49er coach, says there's something about Montana when you first see him on the practice field, "an almost blasé look, although actually he's anything but that. I could see a college coach being put off by the fact that he's not responding overtly, so he'd say, 'Well, this guy's not motivated, he's not with the program.'"

Devine says Montana simply wasn't ready to start at the beginning of his sophomore year. He said that he got him in "as soon as he had medical clearance to play" as a junior. Montana feels that there was something about him that Devine just didn't like.

The interesting thing is that Montana, who has been called extremely coachable by whoever has worked with him, has had three major coaches in his life—Abramski at Ringgold, Devine at Notre Dame and Walsh with the 49ers—and at one time he has held bitter feelings toward each one. And for the same reason: Why won't he play me?

"Yeah, I guess it's true.... I never thought of it," Montana says, "although with Bill it wasn't a major problem; it only lasted a few games. With Abramski I guess it was because no player had ever challenged him like I did. The Devine situation was a mystery to me. I mean I'd been demoted to third string the year after I got hurt. Other guys had gotten their positions back. I couldn't understand it. It hurt me."

Montana carried a B- over C+ average and eventually graduated with a degree in business administration and marketing. Dave Huffman, Montana's center at Notre Dame arid currently a guard with the Vikings, remembers him as "just a regular guy who wanted to play hoops, go drink a beer. We called him Joe Montanalow because he was the spitting image of Barry Manilow. In his senior year he moved into an apartment above a bar. When the bar closed down, we'd go upstairs to Joe's place. It was our after-hours joint."

There is a stat sheet compiled by the Notre Dame sports information department entitled "Joe Montana's Comeback Statistics," which lists six games. The Irish won five of those games in the fourth quarter, and they almost won the sixth—the 1978 game at Southern Cal in which Montana brought the Irish back from a 24–6 deficit to a 25–24 lead before USC pulled it out with a field goal at the end. At the top of the list is a game at North

Carolina in his sophomore season. The Irish were down 14–6 with 5:11 to play, when Montana came off the bench and pulled out a 21–14 win with 129 yards passing in his minute and two seconds on the field. That's the kind of list it is, and there probably isn't another one like it.

"[Athletic director] Moose Krause grabbed my hand in the locker room after the North Carolina game," Devine says, "and said, 'Fantastic. Greatest comeback I've ever seen. Better than the Ohio State game in '35.' Then Joe does it again next week against Air Force; comes off the bench and brings us back from 30–10 down in the fourth quarter to a 31–30 win. In the locker room Moose said, 'This one's better than last week.'"

The legend was born; Montana was the Comeback Kid. Then, kaboom! The big slide. Montana was hurt before his junior season, and when he returned a year later it was as the third-string quarterback, behind Lisch and Forystek.

"When we lost to Mississippi [20–13 in the second game of the season] with Joe on the bench, I thought, 'What a weird deal.'" says Ken MacAfee, an All-America tight end at Notre Dame who went on to play for the 49ers. "I mean we all knew he could do it, he knew he could do it, but he wasn't playing. He was really down. I remember going to his apartment one night and he said, 'I'm just sick of this crap, sick of the whole thing.'"

Devine says, "Joe probably doesn't remember this, but he hadn't been given medical clearance to play in those first two games." Montana says it's news to him. Devine says that on the following Wednesday he told him to be ready to play at Purdue. Lisch started, then he was yanked for Forystek. When Forystek tried to scramble on one play, Purdue linebacker Fred Arrington met him with a ferocious blow. Forystek went down with a broken vertebra, a broken collarbone and a severe concussion. His football career was over.

Devine came back with Lisch ("I didn't want to bring Joe in until he had the wind at his back"), and then finally Montana trotted onto the field. The Notre Dame players began waving their fists and cheering. The fans went crazy.

In the press box Purdue sports information director Tom Shupe turned to Notre Dame's S.I.D., Roger Valdiserri, and said, "What's everybody yelling for?"

"Because Joe Montana's in the game," Valdiserri said, "and you're in trouble."

It became comeback No. 3 on the list. Down 24–14 with 11 minutes to go, Montana threw for 154 yards and a touchdown, and the Irish won 31–24. The following year there were comebacks against Pitt and Southern Cal ("I have nightmares about Montana in that game," says L.A. Ram coach John

Robinson, who coached the Trojans. "I remember thinking, Isn't this guy ever gonna miss on one?"), and the famous Cotton Bowl win over Houston on Jan. 1, 1979.

But the game Devine has special memories of is the one at Clemson in 1977, one that didn't make the list. "I remember Joe driving us down the field to win it in the fourth quarter," he says, "and I remember him having something like a second-and-52 at one point and getting a first down out of it. But best of all I remember him taking off down the sidelines with two linebackers closing in on him, and I was yelling, 'Go out of bounds, Joe! Go out of bounds!' And there was this tremendous collision, and they went down in a heap and only one guy got up, and it was Joe. I said, 'My god, he's taking on the whole Clemson team.'"

It's strange, and maybe it's partly because of guilt feelings, but Devine has become one of Montana's biggest boosters. Montana still resents the fact that Devine didn't give him what he feels was his rightfully earned playing time, but the resentment has softened, and they have gotten together socially since their Notre Dame days. Devine says he handled Montana the best way he knew how, right or wrong, but he adds that there's no question in his mind that Montana is the greatest ever to play the game. Devine describes a scene in the 1989 Super Bowl, during which he was in the stands, when Cincinnati kicked a field goal to make the score 16–13 with 3:20 to go. Devine turned to the man next to him and said, "I'd have thought twice about kicking it. They've given Joe a shot."

The 1979 Cotton Bowl against Houston, the famous Chicken Soup game, was, of course, the one that put the capper on the Comeback Kid's collegiate career. A freak ice storm had hit Dallas, and "all you heard as you came in was, bam, bam, bam, people knocking ice off the seats," Waymer says. By the fourth quarter, Montana was in the locker room with hypothermia, his temperature down to 96°, and the medical staff was pumping bouillon into him (no, not chicken soup, bouillon; the team kept it on hand for cold-weather emergencies) to warm him up. Houston was building a 34–12 lead, while Montana lay in the locker room covered with blankets. Oh, yes, it's a story, all right.

"Rick Slager was in law school then, and he was a graduate assistant coach on the sidelines with me," Devine says. "His job was to run into the locker room every five minutes to see what Joe's temperature was. He'd come back and say, 'It's up to 97°,' and five minutes later I'd tell him to run in and find out again."

With 7:37 to go, Montana came running onto the field, and a mighty roar went up. "Uh, no, not exactly a mighty roar," recalls Huffman, the Notre Dame center. "More like a feeble, frozen roar, since there were only a few people left in the stands, and ice was falling out of their mouths. Actually, I didn't even know Joe was out there until I felt his hands taking the snap. I thought, Wait a minute, these are different hands."

With six seconds left, the Irish were down by six points. "I told Joe to run a 91, a quick out," Devine says, "and if it wasn't there, to throw it away. Kris Haines, our wideout, slipped, and Joe threw it away. Now there were two seconds left. I turned my back on the field. That meant Joe could call his own play. He called the 91 again, the noseguard came through, Haines broke to the flag, and with the noseguard staring him in the face Joe threw a perfect pass, low and outside, a bullet—under all that pressure, with terrible conditions. He was so calm. I swear to God he was no different than he would have been in practice."

Final score, 35–34, and six months later Notre Dame was marketing a promotional film called *Seven and a Half Minutes to Destiny*, "which," Devine says, "was really a Joe Montana film."

So you look for hints, for clues to help you understand Montana's ability to bring his team back from the brink. It would become his trademark in the NFL, too. Montana says that right until the end of his Notre Dame career he was filled with doubts about his ability. Even after the Houston game, he says, "I remained a skeptic, maybe because of the mind games Devine had been playing with me." Did any of his Notre Dame teammates have a feeling that Montana's career would take off the way it did, that they were in the presence of royalty?

"If I'd have known how famous he'd get, I'd have stayed in closer contact with him," Huffman says. "To us, he was just Joe Montanalow, a regular guy. If he wasn't so skinny, we'd have made him a lineman."

"Well, I knew he was going to be good, but I never knew he'd be that good," says MacAfee, now a dentist in the Philadelphia area. "The thing is, I don't think the guy ever feels pressure. The people around him feel it more than he does. I don't think he knows what it is. When he walks onto the field, he could be throwing to Dwight Clark or Jerry Rice or Kris Haines. He could be playing Navy, or the Jets in September, or Denver in the Super Bowl. I don't think there's any difference in his mind. To him it's just football. He doesn't change, it's just the aura that changes. At Notre Dame, I can't remember Joe ever missing a read. Even watching him on TV now, he knows the system so perfectly, he knows so well where everything's going to go. He could call everything himself, call it on the line. I don't even know why they send in plays for him."

When the 1979 draft was approaching and the Cotton Bowl glow had worn off, the NFL scouts got together and started putting down numbers for Montana. One combine gave him a grade of 6½ with 9 being the top of the scale and 1 the bottom. Washington State's Jack Thompson got the highest grade among the quarterbacks—8. Montana's arm was rated a 6, or average. "He can thread the needle," the report said, "but usually goes with his primary receiver and forces the ball to him even when he's in a crowd. He's a gutty, gambling, cocky type. Doesn't have great tools but could eventually start."

The dumb teams believed the report. The smart one has won four Super Bowls.

Part 2

Here's the thing about scouting college football players for the NFL draft. It's based on fear. Scouts cover their tracks. They hedge their bets. Their evaluations all read, "Yes..., but...." *Yes*, he can move the team down the field, *but* he doesn't have an NFL arm. If the player makes it, the scout will say, "Well, I told you he had potential," or if he's a bust, the scout will shake his head and say, "See, the arm didn't hold up, just like I said."

There are more negatives than positives in most scouting reports. It's a wonder the teams can find enough people to play. Intangibles, the look scouts see in a player's eye or a certain feeling about him, are for late-night, third-drink talk at the hotel bar. Unless a scout feels very secure in his employment, he won't load up his reports with intangibles. It's too easy to be wrong. And that's what terrorizes the scouts—the fear of being wrong all by themselves, the big error, the No. 1 pick that was a total bust. And on draft day 1979, a lot of scouts were wrong about Joe Montana.

Eighty-one choices were made before the San Francisco 49ers took him near the end of the third round. A lot of teams made a mistake. Thinking back, what were the negatives on Montana when he was coming out of college? Strength of arm? Sure, he couldn't knock down buildings. So what? The Hall of Fame is filled with quarterbacks who didn't have a cannon. But there was something else, an undercurrent. He had trouble with his coach at Notre Dame. Uh-oh, look out. A warning light went off.

"Trouble, what trouble?" Montana says. "I mean, I was unhappy that I didn't start when I thought I should have, and I was pretty upset when I opened my junior year as third string, but I never openly challenged Dan Devine, or missed practices or stuff like that."

"It's always bothered me that people felt we didn't get along," says Devine, who's now out of football and living in Arizona. "At the time, I did things I had to do, and I tried to explain them to him, and I know it must have been hard for a kid to understand that."

If the scouts had talked to some of the Notre Dame players about Montana—teammates like Ken MacAfee, Dave Huffman and Dave

Waymer—they might have gotten a different picture of the quarterback, not so much by what the players said but by the way they said it. There was a belief, almost mystical, among Montana's teammates that as long as Joe was on the field things would turn out right, no matter what the score was. Didn't he bring them back from 20 points down in the fourth quarter at Air Force, and from 22 down against Houston with 7:37 to play in the Cotton Bowl? Cool, unshakable, treats a bowl game the same as a practice. "The guys on the team knew who wouldn't overheat," was the way Waymer put it.

Look at the little decisions that might have changed the course of history. What if, for instance, the Pittsburgh Steelers had decided that neither Mike Kruczek nor Cliff Stoudt were the eventual successors to then 30-year-old Terry Bradshaw, and the team had drafted Montana? Instead of four Super Bowl victories by 1980, would the Steelers have gone on to win five? Six? Seven? Who knows?

Actually, there was a solid corps of quarterbacks in the NFL at the time of the '79 draft; only three teams had a crying need for one. In the first round, the New York Giants selected Phil Simms of Morehead State, which was not much of a surprise; Giants coach Ray Perkins had worked out Simms himself. Later in the first round, the Kansas City Chiefs took Clemson's Steve Fuller, whom Montana had outdueled as a junior in one of his six classic come-from-behind victories at Notre Dame. Fuller was 6'4", with a mighty arm; a safe pick. As for the Chicago Bears, they knew they weren't going to a Super Bowl with Bob Avellini or Mike Phipps at quarterback, and Vince Evans was a long shot. For a while the Bears were very close to drafting Montana.

"Notre Dame is right down the road, and my wife and children loved Joe Montana," Bears player personnel director Bill Tobin says. "When I left the house, I told them, 'If he's there on the third round, he's ours.'"

But while Tobin was in the draft room, things changed. Montana was there when the Bears picked in the third round, but the team took Willie McClendon, a running back out of Georgia. "I had a lot of explaining to do to three young kids and my wife," Tobin says. "But who knows, if he came here, that he would have had the career that he's had in San Francisco? That's true of any player."

"What if a Tampa Bay or a New Orleans would have taken him?" says Chuck Abramski, who was Montana's coach at Ringgold High in Monongahela, Pa. "What if, instead of having Bill Walsh to work with all those years in San Francisco, he had been in a system where he had to drop back seven steps and throw 50 yards downfield?"

Montana has reflected on that many times himself. "There's no coach I could have played for who would have been better for my career," he says. "Absolutely none."

There's one more *what if*. What if, when Walsh went to Los Angeles to work out UCLA wide receiver James Owens in the spring of '79, Montana hadn't dropped over to throw Owens some passes? Or so the legend goes.

"Now, that's not true," Walsh says. "We were coming off a 2–14 year. We were in dire straits everywhere. I investigated every viable college quarterback. I first became aware of Montana the previous year, my second year coaching at Stanford. We were so proud of our 25–22 comeback win over Georgia in the Bluebonnet Bowl, and then I looked in the paper and read about Notre Dame and Joe's even more spectacular comeback in the Cotton Bowl—under impossible conditions. That was just so impressive.

"Joe was the last quarterback we looked at. [Montana had graduated from Notre Dame in December and was living in Manhattan Beach, Calif.] I went down there specifically to look at him, and he worked out with Owens and Theotis Brown, the UCLA fullback who played for Seattle. Joe threw for an hour. The minute I saw him drop back—his quick movement, those quick, nimble, Joe Namath–type feet—I got very serious. As much as I wanted Steve Dils, who'd been my quarterback at Stanford, who knew my system, I knew I had to forgo that for Joe. Joe was bigger and quicker, and he threw better."

The 49ers, who had given up their first- and third-round choices in trades, used their second-round pick to take Owens, and they used a late third-round pick, acquired from Dallas, to select Montana. He signed a three-year contract that paid him a $50,000 signing bonus and a base salary of $50,000, $70,000 and $85,000 for the three years.

The first thing people noticed about Montana when he reported to 49er training camp was how skinny he was. The team's media guide listed him as 6'3", 200 pounds. (The guide has since dropped an inch off his height and five pounds from his weight.) Actually, he stood 6'2" and weighed barely 185.

"I was sitting next to him at the counter in Howard Johnson's," says Dwight Clark, a 10th-round pick who would become Montana's favorite receiver. "Long blond hair, Fu Manchu mustache, skinny legs. I thought, This guy must be a kicker. Then he introduced himself, and I couldn't believe this was the guy who brought Notre Dame back to beat us in the fourth quarter when I was at Clemson.

"Lord, we were so homesick. I thought it was only a matter of time until I got cut. Joe acted that way, too. Maybe he was just trying to make me feel better—he was a third-round pick—but we used to sneak in the back door at breakfast. The guy who did the cutting, the guy who told you, 'Coach wants to see you,' used to be in front—Max McCartney, Max the Axe."

Montana started one game in his rookie year, saw brief action in two games and made spot appearances in the other 13 games. Walsh, who had developed quarterbacks Ken Anderson at Cincinnati and Dan Fouts at San Diego, was in no hurry to push Montana. But Walsh closely monitored his progress.

"There were those in our organization who didn't think Joe would be an NFL starter," Walsh says. "That was never even a consideration his first year. I knew the stage he was going through. He was a little in awe of everything, like all first-year quarterbacks. If he hadn't broken out of it, it would have been a different story, but he did break out of it.

"When we looked at films of him in college, I said I also wanted to see his worst game. At his worst he played desperate. He'd throw late and beyond the receiver; never early, always late. It's as if he was waiting until the last moment to make something happen. At his best, and that's true today, when he was in sync, he had an intuitive, instinctive nature rarely equaled by any athlete in any sport. Magic Johnson has it.

"When he was first breaking in with us, whenever the thrust of what he was doing was by instinct, he played very well. Even watching Joe warm up, there was something hypnotic about him. That look when he was dropping back; he was poetic in his movements, almost sensuous, everything so fluid, so much under control. But you couldn't lose sight of the fact that he was still a young player, and in game situations every play is almost crisislike to a young player."

By 1980 the 49er offense was beginning to come into focus. The running game was nowhere; it wouldn't get healthy until Wendell Tyler arrived in '83. The short, controlled pass became much of the running game. Clark, who began to emerge as a serious midrange threat, had his own thing going with Montana, who started seven of the last 10 games that year.

"We'd stay out after practice and work on our own stuff," Clark says. "I don't know how much it helped him, but it helped me. I didn't have a clue about reading defenses, about making adjustments. That's the thing about Bill's system. You could do your own adjusting as long as it was in the parameter, the guidelines. A lot of times, say, I'd run a 10-yard hook. If the guy was inside me, I'd kind of push off and run a breakout. Joe could read that. He was good at it.

"Everyone said there was a chemistry between us. Joe once said in an interview, 'I can look all around the field. I can look away and still come back and find Dwight, that big, slow, loping receiver.' He could see me moving across the field. I didn't run out of his sight line. Joe's got a knack of being able to figure out your body English, of knowing by your position on the defensive guy what you're going to do at the end of your route. He had that with me, and he has that now with Jerry Rice.

"I remember one game against the Rams. I was running a clearing route, just clearing my guy out for the tight end underneath. I ran inside and broke it back out, and I thought, Damn, I wish Joe could see me. Next thing I knew, the ball was on its way to me. After the game I asked him, 'How the hell did you ever find me?' He just shrugged."

Steve DeBerg, who had shared the starting job with Montana, was traded before the '81 season. The defense, with three rookie backs and the addition of old pros Fred Dean and Hacksaw Reynolds, had potential. The running game was only a change of pace, maybe a power sweep or two to keep opponents guessing. No one had yet called Walsh a genius. Nothing had been written about Walsh's system, which is now the standard for offensive football. But it was coming into focus. He had had to go slowly with Montana. He couldn't give him the full package at first, but now he felt Montana was ready.

So much has been written about the system, but on the field there is no mystery to it. Anyone can figure out the attack just by studying a lot of film—underneath crossing patterns, flood an area and put pressure on the linebackers, optional reads by the receivers and breakout patterns at the end of the route.

"Three-man patterns to a side off different combinations. Joe knows that in his sleep," says L.A. Raider managing general partner Al Davis.

The thing that makes the system unique is the way it is coached, the subtleties and nuances. The "teaching," as Walsh calls it, is the key, starting at the top and filtering down through the quarterback coach. There never was a title of offensive coordinator under Walsh; quarterback coach Mike Holmgren was awarded the designation under George Seifert last year.

The two predecessors to Holmgren on Walsh's staff had been outstanding quarterbacks. Sam Wyche was a nine-year NFL veteran with four years under Walsh at Cincinnati. Paul Hackett was a record-breaking passer at UC Davis.

"There was a lot of time spent studying," Montana says. "Sam helped me a lot with the little keys, the knowledge of what a defense was or was not capable of in a certain situation—prereads we call it, knowing where not to go before the ball is even snapped. You'd learn to work on individuals. We'd see a film, and Sam would say, 'See, this guy can't cover that far, but he tries to.' Bill's system works only if the guy running routes is able to read. Most of our routes have a lot of options built in, according to zone or man coverage. Everyone has to be on the same page. We never want to be at the point where one defense can cover a route completely."

When Walsh talks about offensive football, he eventually mentions the "quick, slashing strokes" of attack. He'll use analogies with tennis and boxing, even warfare, which was why he was so taken with Montana's nimble feet. A quick, slashing attack needs a quick-footed quarterback. The players Walsh brought in to back up Montana were also mostly guys who could move—Bryan Clark, Matt Cavanaugh, Jeff Kemp, Steve Young. The statuesque quarterback who can throw the ball 60 yards downfield has never been Walsh's type. And when he refined his offense to blend with Montana's skills, Walsh introduced the x factor, which was the great escape talent of his quarterback—elusiveness, body control, the ability to throw while in the grasp of an opponent.

"A lot of our offense was play-action," Walsh says, "and I learned through my experience that on a play-pass you have to expect an unblocked man just when you're trying to throw the ball. Your linemen have blocked aggressively. You can't expect them to hold their guys. Joe had to understand that. You're going to fool somebody downfield, but also you're going to have someone unblocked bearing right down on you. Here he comes. If you can throw and take the hit—TD. If you can avoid him, so much the better. We were on the cutting edge of Joe's ability. He was gifted at avoiding and throwing.

"We practiced the scrambling, off-balance throw. It wasn't accidental when he did it. It was a carefully practiced thing. I'd tell him, 'Timed pattern to the first receiver. If he's covered, move and look for the second. Then scramble and throw off balance, and jerk it to the third. By the time you're reading the third receiver, someone's got hold of you.' And that's what we'd practice. I'd tell him, 'I never want you to throw to the third receiver on balance.'"

Finally it all came into focus in the '81 postseason, in one momentous play, the last-minute touchdown pass to Clark that buried Dallas in the NFC championship. The play will always be known as The Catch—Montana scrambling to his right, with three Cowboys clutching at him; the off-balance throw; and finally Clark, on a breakoff route, ducking inside, then cutting back—just the way he and Joe had practiced on their own so many times in camp.

"On the touchdown play my concentration level was never so high," Montana says. "I remember pump-faking to get those guys chasing me off the ground, just like when I was playing basketball with my dad. I remember trying to get the ball to Dwight high, so no one else could get it. I never saw the catch. I heard the crowd roar."

The Super Bowl was an anticlimax. Montana was facing the consensus All-Pro quarterback, Ken Anderson of the Bengals, and one pregame angle explored by the media was that Walsh had coached both of them. Montana was asked how he felt he would play against Anderson, and he gave the traditional answer that you don't play against a quarterback, you go against the defense. The 49ers beat the Bengals 26–21, with Montana taking MVP honors. In each of the 49ers' next two Super Bowls, he again was matched with a consensus All-Pro, Dan Marino of Miami in '85 and Boomer Esiason of Cincinnati in '89. Montana had gone in as the second-best quarterback each time and won. By the time of the 49ers' fourth Super Bowl, in '90, everyone had learned, and the question was only how badly would Montana and the 49ers beat John Elway and the Denver Broncos?

The first talk of Montana being the greatest of all came in Bay Area circles after the '82 Super Bowl, as put forth by a couple of old 49er quarterbacks. John Brodie said it, flat out, and people laughed. Frankie Albert said, "At 25, he's ahead of Unitas, Van Brocklin, Waterfield...all the immortals." That was a little more modest. People didn't bother to look up the records of those three quarterbacks at age 25. If they had, they would have discovered that each of them also had won a championship at 25. So did Joe Namath, Otto Graham and Sid Luckman. Twenty-five, it seems, is a magical age for quarterbacks.

Montana was rewarded with a four-year contract worth more than $1.7 million, and he was flooded with endorsements in the off-season. The demand on his time became a sore point with some people, who saw it as one of the reasons for the 49ers' collapse in '82, the strike year. Montana said it was a bum rap, because most of the commercials and appearances were one-shot deals. He would leave town on Monday night, spend the off-day Tuesday making the commercial and be back at practice Wednesday morning. What was the big deal? Nevertheless, he cut down on his appearances the following season.

The '83 season was a good year statistically for Montana, even though the 49ers lost to the Washington Redskins in the NFC Championship Game, but '84 was his best up to that point. In that season he received his highest NFL quarterback rating (102.9), his second Pro Bowl selection and the MVP award for leading San Francisco to a crushing 38–16 victory over the Miami Dolphins in the Super Bowl. Only one thing was better. It was also the year he met Jennifer Wallace, whom he would marry in February 1985.

Montana had been through two marriages. He was gun-shy. Then, in the off-season, he went to New York to do a Schick razor commercial. Jennifer was the Schick Sheriff, who always gets her man. Joe was, well, the shtick in Schick. By the next summer, he was sweating out how to propose. He finally hit on the idea of hiring a plane with a streamer reading: JEN WILL YOU MARRY ME? JOE. It cost him $600. He took her to their favorite park in San Francisco, the Marina Green. Finally, the plane flew overhead.

"I looked up, and the streamer was backwards," Montana says. "I said, 'Oh God.' We were on the wrong side of it. I started maneuvering her around. She said, 'Joe, what are you doing?' Finally she saw it. She said, 'Yes,' right away. I was ready for her to say no. Then she said, 'What took you so long?'"

For a while everything was fine. The newlyweds settled in Palos Verdes, Calif., but soon they were building a home in Redwood City. Montana was earning $900,000 in the second year of a new six-year contract worth $6.3 million. Jennifer got him off junk foods, shaped up his eating habits. They worked out together, did everything together. Their first baby was on the way when, suddenly, in November 1985, the drug stories hit.

There were rumors spreading around the Bay Area that Montana had been arrested for speeding in his red Ferrari (which happened to be in his garage at the time he was said to have been stopped) and "a controlled substance" was found in the car, but the San Francisco police had let him off. Another rumor placed the incident in Atlanta (he had been in a team meeting preparing for the Falcons when the arrest was supposed to have occurred). Someone called the San Francisco Examiner and said, "We heard that Joe Montana has been admitted to a drug rehab center"—and this was during the season.

The rumors were never substantiated. They weren't even reported in the media until Walsh and Montana issued public denials. But the rumors wouldn't die. "I remember watching the six o'clock news with Joe one night," Jennifer says. "They flashed his face on the screen, and underneath was the word DRUGS. Then they went to a commercial. I can remember Joe's eyes welling up. It was just so untrue, but what could we do?"

"The absolute low point came after a trip to Detroit," Montana says. "We'd lost to the Lions, we were 3–4, and I came back with the flu. Our baby, Alexandra, had caught it, and I was getting in the car to take her to the hospital, holding her in my arms, and I couldn't get out of my driveway. A bus was blocking it, and the driver, a woman, was sitting there making faces at me and turning thumbs down, and all the people on the bus were staring. I just sat there thinking, Please go away. That was the worst."

The 49ers were bruised and banged up when they faced the New York Giants at Giants Stadium in the NFC wild-card game. San Francisco lost 17–3. Montana injured a shoulder on a blind-side hit by Lawrence Taylor after an interception, but he remained in the game. It was a preview of things to come.

In the '86 season opener at Tampa Bay, Montana twisted in the air while throwing a pass, and his back went out. An examination showed a ruptured disk and, worse than that, a congenital narrowing of the spinal cavity. He would need an operation. Doctors told Montana he might play again, but he would be crazy if he tried it.

Crazy? His whole life had been football. He was 30 and at the peak of his game. After two marriages, the first to hometown sweetheart Kim Moses in college and the second to flight attendant Cass Castillo from 1981 to '84, he had found a woman he could be happy with. He was still bugged by a lack of privacy—clumps of fans followed him every time he stepped out of the house—but he viewed that as an occupational hazard. Football had brought him to the absolute crest, and now doctors were telling him to give it up?

"I thought he was finished," his mother, Theresa, says. "I was in his hospital room the day after the operation. They wheeled him in, sat him up, or at least tried to. I could see the pain in his eyes. I wanted to cry, but not in front of him. Ronnie Lott was in the room, Dwight Clark, Wendell Tyler. They couldn't hold the tears back. A day later I asked him, 'What do you want to do?' He said, 'I want to play football again.' The next day he was up doing exercises, the day after that he was working with weights, small stuff mostly, but at least he was doing something."

Montana was out of action for 55 days. The 49ers were 5–3–1 when he returned, but he led them to five victories in the last seven games and into the playoffs. They faced the Giants in Giants Stadium again, and lost again, 49–3. Montana was knocked out in the second quarter when noseguard Jim Burt buried his helmet under Montana's chin. But the back held up.

The 49ers were the sweethearts of the NFL in '87, going 13–2 in the regular season, and Montana had a career high for touchdown passes (31), all of which made it tough for everyone to take when Minnesota beat them 36–24 in an NFC divisional playoff in San Francisco. By the third quarter of that game it was clear that the 49er offense was going nowhere, and Montana was benched for Young. That's all the fans and the media needed to start talk of trading Montana, who would be 32 that June. Young was 26. Now there was the future.

In '88, Young started three times and came off the bench to play in eight other games as Montana was slowed by nagging injuries to his elbow, ribs, back and knees. Montana said he could have played; he was bitter about Walsh's not playing him. "One bad pass, one bad series, and I'm out of there," he said. He and Jennifer started looking around for teams that might want him.

Montana has looked back on the '88 season many times, thinking about what Walsh has meant to his career and about the bad time they went through, and he has a feeling it's time to set things straight. "We played golf the other day," Montana said in May. "I didn't even know Bill knew how to play. I've dropped by his office a few times. I will again. I'm sure we'll talk about all this, but that's for later on. We're just getting used to each other, because I'd never really spoken about my feelings to Bill."

"I had to almost calculate the things I did," says Walsh, who now works as an NBC analyst. "I had to follow my own ethical code in coaching, such as pulling Joe from a game. You struggle with things like sentiment and loyalty. Should I stay with him or not? Then you do what you have to do as a coach. And you have to decide it quickly. There were times when I'd be driving away from the stadium and I'd wonder in my heart, Did I really do my job as coach?"

The '89 Super Bowl, the final drive against the Bengals—92 yards to win it 20–16 with 34 seconds left (actually 102 yards if you count an ineligible receiver penalty)—cured everything. It was the 19th time as a pro that Montana had brought his team from behind and led it to victory in the fourth quarter. There were four more in the '89 season. Has any quarterback had more? Does anyone keep track of those things? Add six as a collegian, one more in the Big 33 Pennsylvania-Ohio high school all-star game, and Montana has a total of 30. Is it a record? Who knows? But it's pretty impressive.

That last drive against the Bengals in the '89 Super Bowl has been well documented. Montana completed eight of nine passes for 97 yards en route to the winning throw.

"I was kind of wild on the sidelines before we took the field for that drive," says right tackle Harris Barton. "I was worried about the penalty on the kickoff that set us back to the eight. I was yelling at somebody, can't remember who. Joe came over to me and said, 'Hey, check it out.'

"I said, 'Check what out?'

"He said, 'There in the stands, standing near the exit ramp, there's John Candy.' I looked. Sure enough, it was him. I grabbed John Frank, our tight end. 'Hey, John,' I said. 'There's John Candy.' Then I got hold of myself. What the hell was I doing? Fifteen seconds later we're in the huddle and Joe's clapping his hands and saying, 'Hey, you guys want it? Let's go.'"

The scariest moment in the drive came with a minute and a half left, first-and-10 on the Bengal 35. Montana had been yelling, calling signals, and he began to hyperventilate. He couldn't catch his breath.

"He signaled to me that he wanted a timeout," Walsh says. "He didn't know if he could go on. I waved it off. I didn't realize what was happening to him. He came up to the line, and the next pass he threw went over Jerry Rice's hand. It was his only incomplete of the drive. Later he said he threw it away because he didn't want to risk an interception.

"He told me that as he was coming to the line he felt himself getting his breath back. He didn't panic. Now you take your strutting quarterback, and he couldn't function like that. But the thing was that Joe functioned in a clearheaded manner, even in distress. He didn't lose it. It's like the soldier taking two in the belly and still finishing in charge."

Based on the NFL quarterback rating system, Montana's '89 season was simply the best anyone has ever had—the highest rating (112.4) and third-highest completion percentage (70.2) in history. But those are just numbers. The 49ers swept through the playoffs and Super Bowl like a broom, trouncing Denver 55–10 to repeat as NFL champions. Their efficiency was frightening, and Montana was the master. If you want to highlight one game during the season, try the game in Philadelphia on Sept. 24. Some people call it the finest Montana has ever played.

For three quarters the 49er offense was falling apart. Montana had been sacked seven times, with one more to come. He had tripped twice while setting up and had fallen down in the end zone for a safety. The Eagles were coming at him like crazy, and the 49ers were down 21–10 with 10 seconds gone in the fourth quarter. Then Montana threw four touchdown passes into the teeth of the Eagle rush to pull out a 38–28 victory. His fourth-quarter stats read 11 completions in 12 pass attempts for 227 yards, and he scrambled for 19 more.

"Worried? Oh, hell, yes, we were worried," Barton says of the Eagle assault on Montana. "Joe gets that glazed look in his eyes, and you know he's been shellacked. Then three guys try to help him up. That's the first thing you think of. Let's get him on his feet right away, then maybe everyone will miss what happened.

"It wasn't a good situation to be in. We'd get to the sidelines and Joe would say, 'O.K., let's get this thing settled down.' I was just amazed that he could line up at all after getting smacked in the head by [Eagle end] Reggie White."

If you want to make a case for Montana as the greatest quarterback who ever played the game, there it is. Toughness. The great ones all had it—Unitas, Graham, Baugh, Waterfield, Tittle, Bradshaw. When you add Montana's finesse, the sensuous and fluid qualities that Walsh saw at the beginning, plus his uncanny accuracy—no one has ever thrown the short crossing pattern with a better touch—you've got a special package.

The numbers declare him the best of all time: highest career quarterback rating (94.0), highest career completion percentage (63.9; no one else is above 60), second to Bernie Kosar of the Cleveland Browns in lowest lifetime interception rate. Here are a few more. Among quarterbacks with a minimum of 1,500 passes, Montana is the only one to have thrown twice as many career touchdowns (216) as interceptions (107). In the 150 games in which he has thrown at least one pass, including the playoffs, his completion percentage has been under .500 only five times, and he once went five seasons (1980–84) without having a sub-.500 game. In three playoff games after the '89 season, he threw 11 touchdown passes and no interceptions. Had enough? The best stat of all, of course, is his feat of 23 fourth-quarter, comeback NFL victories.

Teammates and coaches have talked about Montana's almost mystical calmness in the midst of turmoil, when everything's on the line in the fourth quarter. How does he describe it, this ability to elevate his performance? "I don't really know," he says. "It seems like your concentration level goes up and things get a little clearer because of that."

Concentration level? Come on, that's a coach's phrase.

"Well, you think of little things," he says. "You want to make sure you get enough depth in your drops. You want to go through every situation ahead of time. When you're behind, the idea is to do something, but not everything. You want to get a flow going, then you can take a chance."

Montana pauses. He is not interested in self-evaluation. It's almost impossible for him to put himself in a historical context. Football to him is playing the game. You go out and do it. You don't tie it up with a bunch of numbers. Questions about his all-time rating make him nervous; it's too much like an obituary.

"Maybe it's because ever since I was little I was involved in pressure situations, plus winning traditions," he says of his days as an athletic wunderkind growing up in Monongahela and starring at Ringgold High. "You knew you had to win. Those basketball tournaments we played in—Niagara Falls one night, Bethel Park the next night. You learned to deal with it.

"What I want is the chance to play, to compete. When a coach would sit you down, when you knew you'd get yanked if you didn't do well, well, that was real pressure. Once you know you can play no matter what, once you can get in your flow, then the pressure is only what you create for yourself."

Everyone who has come into contact with Montana has tried to figure out the source of his greatness. Wyche said that no quarterback ever reacted as fast to changing situations, no one ever absorbed coaching so readily and immediately put it into execution. "When I'd tell him something," Wyche says, "it was almost like he'd lean in and pull the words out of my mouth."

According to Clark, now a marketing consultant with the team, everyone's performance on the 49ers is elevated because of Montana's presence. "The receivers can go into their patterns with confidence because they know Joe's never going to put them in a bad position," he says. "That's why you see so many of his short passes break for 80 or 90 yards, because the guys are fearless going in there."

"Joe presented all of his linemen with gold Rolex Presidential watches this year," Barton says. "It's us that should be giving him the watch. The success of this organization, how we've been treated, how we travel, how much we make, it's a tribute to Joe, the guy who wears number 16."

Perhaps Jeff Petrucci, Montana's high school quarterback coach, has the best answer to the secret of Montana's greatness. "Joe was born to be a quarterback," Petrucci says. "You saw it in the midget leagues, in high school, even in the Big 33 all-star game—the electricity in the huddle when he was in there. How many people are there in the world, three billion? And how many guys are there who can do what he can do? Him, maybe Marino on a good day. Perhaps God had a hand in this thing."

So is he the greatest quarterback of all time or not? A large body of players and coaches, including Walsh, votes yes. The ones who say no point to the new era of football, the freer passing lanes, the bump-and-run restrictions, the elimination of head-slapping by defensive linemen. They say that a Johnny Unitas or a Norm Van Brocklin playing in this era would do the same things Montana does.

"Yeah, I know. I've heard it," Petrucci says. "How would Joe do in the other era? How would he do against the Steelers in that two-deep zone, when they'd roll their corners up and it was over? Well, in my mind, he'd be the greatest in any era because he's the ultimate winner. Somehow he finds a way to get it done."

My opinion? The eras are dissimilar. Quarterbacks like Unitas had to face things that Montana never saw, such as his receivers getting mugged downfield. So I'll give you my two greatest quarterbacks: Unitas of the bump-and-run era, Montana of today. Sorry to cop out, but it's rough, messing with idols.

Perhaps the secret to Montana's great surge while in his early 30s is that his life finally has some harmony. He has severely limited his endorsements and outside speaking engagements, but he is financially secure thanks to his new four-year, $13 million contract. His greatest enjoyment is finding a place to escape to for a vacation with Jennifer, four-year-old Alexandra, three-year-old Elizabeth and 10-month-old Nathaniel. His family has become his strength.

"There are two sides to Joe, the one people see on the field and the one we see at home," says Jennifer. "Dwight Clark once told me, 'You'd never recognize Joe out there.' I've asked Joe, 'What do you feel when you are under all that pressure? How can you stay so calm?' He says, 'I really don't know.'

"What makes him comfortable is his home and his kids and everyday life, not being put on a pedestal, not being called a hero every five minutes."

How long will Montana play? "Forever," says Al Davis. "He'll be able to play until he's 40, like George Blanda did, unless he gets hurt. That's if they use him right, rest him for some games that don't matter, maybe play him in only eight or nine games a year when he's 40 years old."

"What about the other seven?" Montana says with a twinkle in his eye. "Sure, I'd like to play until I'm 40, but I don't think Jennifer would let me."

Well, what would he like to be doing at 40? Coaching? "Maybe," he says, "but not at the professional level. I'd like to work with kids, like my dad did.

"I'll tell you what I'd really like to do. I'd like to go up to the northern California wine country, Napa or Sonoma, and settle down there. Open a little Italian restaurant with seven or eight or 10 tables and a big wine list. I'd like to own some vineyard land, grow my own grapes, make wine."

We are sitting next to the swimming pool at the Meadowood Resort Hotel in St. Helena, Calif. Montana is watching Jennifer and the kids splash around. Three hundred yards away the annual Napa Valley Wine Auction is taking place, and next to the auction tent a display table has been set up with 100 or so of the Valley's finest. Montana says he "wouldn't mind dropping over to taste a few cabernet sauvignons or merlots, but you know, that would be impossible."

He is well known in the wine country. "I remember coming out of the office when one of the regular tours was going on," says Bruce Neyers, vice-president and marketing director of Joseph Phelps Vineyards in St. Helena, "and there were Joe and Jennifer, standing in line at the end of the tour, waiting to pay for a couple of cases of wine.

"I went over to him and said, 'Hey, why didn't you tell us you were here? I'll take you around.' He said, 'Nope, we're in a hurry. The regular tour was fine.'"

"He must have spent an hour with me in my smokehouse," says Michael Chiarello, the young chef at Tra Vigne, the innovative Italian restaurant in St. Helena. "He wanted to know all about how I cured my prosciutto and smoked my meats. The guy really knows food; he has a real interest. I said, 'Hey, Joe, you going to open a restaurant and drive me out of business?' He said, 'You never can tell.'"

"Food and wine," Montana says. "Not a bad life."

Raise your glasses, folks. He's the greatest of our era.

SEPTEMBER 23, 2002

The Best There Ever Was

For the author—a Baltimore native and future sportswriter—the Colts' quarterback was more than a boyhood hero. He was an inspiration for the entire city

BY FRANK DEFORD

Sometimes, even if it was only yesterday, or even if it just feels like it was only yesterday....

Sometimes, no matter how detailed the historical accounts, no matter how many the eyewitnesses, no matter how complete the statistics, no matter how vivid the film....

Sometimes, I'm sorry, but....

Sometimes, you just had to be there.

That was the way it was with Johnny Unitas in the prime of his life, when he played for the Baltimore Colts and changed a team and a city and a league. Johnny U was an American original, a piece of work like none other, excepting maybe Paul Bunyan and Horatio Alger.

Part of it was that he came out of nowhere, like Athena springing forth full-grown from the brow of Zeus, or like Shoeless Joe Hardy from Hannibal, Mo., magically joining the Senators, compliments of the devil. But that was myth, and that was fiction. Johnny U was real, before our eyes.

Nowadays, of course, flesh peddlers and scouting services identify the best athletes when they are still in junior high. Prospects are not allowed to sneak up on us. But back then, 1956, was a quaint time when we still could be pleasantly surprised. Unitas just surfaced there on the roster, showing up one day after a tryout. The new number 19 was identified as "YOU-ni-tass" when he first appeared in an exhibition, and only later did we learn that he had played, somewhere between obscurity and anonymity, at Louisville and then, for six bucks a game, on the dusty Pittsburgh sandlots. His was a story out of legend, if not, indeed, out of religious tradition: the unlikely savior come out of nowhere.

The quarterback for the Colts then was George Shaw, the very first pick in the NFL draft the year before, the man ordained to lead a team that was coalescing into a contender. Didn't we wish, in Baltimore! Didn't we dream! The Colts had Alan (the Horse) Ameche and Lenny (Spats) Moore and L.G. (Long Gone) Dupre to carry the ball and Raymond Berry and Jim Mutscheller to catch it and Artie Donovan and Big Daddy Lipscomb and Gino Marchetti to manhandle the other fellows when they had the pigskin. Then one day, as it is written, Shaw got hurt in a game, and YOU-ni-tass came in, hunched of shoulder, trotting kind of funny. He looked crooked, is how I always thought of him. Jagged. Sort of a gridiron Abraham Lincoln.

And on the first play the rookie threw a pass that went for a long touchdown. Only it was an interception; the touchdown went the other way.

For those of us in Baltimore, this seemed like the cruelest fate (however likely). Finally Baltimore was going to amount to something, and then, wouldn't you know it, Shaw gets taken from us. It seemed so terribly unfair, if perhaps exactly what we could expect for our workingman's town, where the swells passed through, without stopping, on their way to Washington or New York.

But then, there couldn't have been a mother's son anywhere who knew exactly what Unitas had in store for us. Marchetti, apparently, was the first one to understand. It was a couple of weeks later, and he was lying on the training table when the equipment manager, Fred Schubach, wondered out loud when Shaw might come back. Marchetti raised up a bit and said, "It doesn't matter. Unitas is the quarterback now."

Evidently all the other Colts nodded; they'd just been waiting for someone to dare express what they were beginning to sense. Marchetti had fought in the Battle of the Bulge when he was a teenager and thus, apparently, had developed a keen appreciation for things larger than life.

Of course, no matter who John Constantine Unitas had played football for, it would've been Katie-bar-the-door. But perhaps never has greatness found such a fitting address. It wasn't only that Baltimore had such an inferiority complex, an awareness that all that the stuck-up outlanders knew of our fair city was that we had crabs and white marble steps in profusion and a dandy red-light district, the Block. Since H.L. Mencken (he who had declared, "I hate all sports as rabidly as a person who likes sports hates common sense") had died, the most famous Baltimorean was a stripper, Blaze Starr. The city hadn't had a winner since the Old Orioles of a century past. For that matter, until very recently Baltimore hadn't even *had* a major league team in the 1900s. Before the Colts arrived in 1947, the best athlete in town was a woman duckpin bowler named Toots Barger. Football? The biggest games in Baltimore had been when Johns Hopkins took on Susquehanna or Franklin & Marshall at homecoming.

But no mother ever took her children to her breast as old Bawlmer, Merlin (as we pronounced it), embraced the Colts. It wasn't just that they played on Sundays and thus finally made us "big league" in the eyes of the rest of a republic that was rapidly becoming coaxial-cabled together. No, the Colts were just folks, all around town, at crab feasts and bull roasts and what-have-you. Why, I knew I could go a few blocks to Moses' Sunoco station on York Road and see a bunch of Colts there, hanging out, kicking tires. Had I had a good enough fake I.D., I could've even gotten into Sweeney's, up Greenmount Avenue, and drunk beer with them. The Colts were real people, so we loved them even more as they went on their merry way to becoming champions of the world.

With each passing game, though, Unitas elevated above the others until, on Dec. 28, 1958, he entered the pantheon of gods. 'Twas then, of course, in Yankee Stadium itself, that he led us from behind to an overtime victory over the despised New Yorkers in the Greatest Game Ever Played. Yet even as we deified him, we still had it on the best authority that he remained one of the boys. Just because he was quarterback, he wasn't some glamour-puss.

Certainly he didn't look the part of a hero. This is how his teammate Alex Hawkins described Unitas when Hawkins first saw him in the locker room: "Here was a total mystery. [Unitas] was from Pennsylvania, but he looked so much like a Mississippi farmhand that I looked around for a mule. He had stooped shoulders, a chicken breast, thin bowed legs and long, dangling arms with crooked, mangled fingers."

Unitas didn't even have a quarterback's name. All by himself he redrew the profile of the quarterback. Always, before, it had been men of Old Stock who qualified to lead the pros. Baugh and Albert and Van Brocklin and Layne and Graham. (All right, Luckman was a Jew, but he was schooled in the WASP-y Ivy League.) Unitas was some hardscrabble Lithuanian, so what he did made a difference, because even if we'd never met a Lithuanian before, we knew that he was as smart a sonuvabitch as he was tough. Dammit, he was our Lithuanian.

They didn't have coaches with headphones and Polaroids and fax machines then, sitting on high, telling quarterbacks what plays to call. In those halcyon days, quarterbacks were field generals, not field lieutenants.

And there was Unitas after he called a play (and probably checked off and called another play when he saw what the ruffians across the line were up to), shuffling back into the pocket, unfazed by the violent turbulence all around him, standing there in his hightops, waiting, looking, poised. I never saw war, so that is still my vision of manhood: Unitas standing courageously in the pocket, his left arm flung out in a diagonal to the upper deck, his right cocked for the business of passing, down amidst the mortals. Lock and load.

There, to Berry at the sideline. Or Moore. Or Jimmy Orr real long. Lenny Lyles. John Mackey. Hawkins. Ameche out of the backfield. My boyhood memory tells me Johnny U never threw an incompletion, let alone an interception, after that single debut mistake. Spoilsports who keep the numbers dispute that recollection, but they also assure me that he threw touchdown passes in 47 straight games. That figure has been threatened less seriously than even DiMaggio's sacred 56. Yes, I know there've been wonderful quarterbacks since Unitas hung up his hightops. I admit I'm prejudiced. But the best quarterback ever? The best player? Let me put it this way: If there were one game scheduled, Earth versus the Klingons, with the fate of the universe on the line, any person with his wits about him would have Johnny U calling the signals in the huddle, up under the center, back in the pocket.

I've always wondered how people in olden times connected back to their childhoods. After all, we have hooks with the past. When most of us from the 20th century reminisce about growing up, we right away remember the songs and the athletes of any particular moment. Right?

A few years ago I saw Danny and the Juniors performing at a club, and all anybody wanted them to sing was *At the Hop*, which was their No. 1 smash back in 1958, the year Unitas led the Colts to that first, fabled championship. About a year after I saw Danny, I read that he had committed suicide. I always assumed it was because no matter how many years had passed, nobody would let him escape from singing *At the Hop*, exactly as he did in 1958.

Unlike songs, athletes, inconveniently, get on. They grow old. Johnny U couldn't keep on throwing passes. He aged. He even let his crew cut grow out. Luckily for me, after I grew up (as it were) and became a sportswriter, I never covered him. Oh, I went to his restaurant, and I saw him on TV, and I surely never forgot him. Whenever Walter Iooss, the photographer, and I would get together, we would talk about Johnny U the way most men talk about caressing beautiful women. But I never had anything to do with Unitas professionally. That was good. I could keep my boy's memories unsullied.

Then, about five years ago, I finally met him for real, at a party. When we were introduced he said, "It's nice to meet you, Mr. Deford." That threw me into a tailspin. *No, no, no. Don't you understand? I'm not Mr. Deford. You're Mr. Unitas. You're Johnny U. You're my boyhood idol. I can't ever be Mr. Deford with you, because you have to always be number 19, so I can always be a kid.* But I didn't explain that to him. I was afraid he would think I was too sappy. I just said, "It's nice to meet you, too, Mr. Unitas," and shook his crippled hand.

A couple of years later I went down to Baltimore and gave a speech for a charity. What they gave me as a thank-you present was a football, autographed by Himself. When you're not a child anymore and you write about athletes, you tend to take 'em as run-of-the-mill human beings. Anyway, I do. I have only one other athlete's autograph, from Bill Russell, who, along with Unitas, is the other great star of the '50s who changed his sport all by himself.

After I got that autographed Unitas football, every now and then I'd pick it up and fondle it. I still do, too, even though Johnny Unitas is dead now, and I can't be a boy anymore. Ultimately, you see, what he conveyed to his teammates and to Baltimore and to a wider world was the utter faith that he could do it. He could make it work. Somehow, he could win. He *would* win. It almost didn't matter when he actually couldn't. The point was that with Johnny U, it always seemed possible. You so very seldom get that, even with the best of them. Johnny U's talents were his own. The belief he gave us was his gift.

DECEMBER 6, 2010

Where He Belongs

Saints quarterback Drew Brees brought a Lombardi Trophy to New Orleans—just one of the countless ways he has contributed to the rebirth of a great American city

BY TIM LAYDEN

The little hired bus rumbles north across Lake Pontchartrain on the longest bridge in the U.S., 24 miles of roadway sucked up underneath the front of the vehicle and spit out the back in a monotonous sound track of tires against expansion joints. *Thumpthumpthumpthumpthump.* New Orleans fading in the distance, northern suburbs ahead on the far shore, water everywhere else. Drew Brees, quarterback of the Super Bowl champion New Orleans Saints, sits idly in a hard seat. When he came to Louisiana five years ago, so much of this was foreign. Now it is deeply familiar. "New Orleans surprised me so much," says Brees. "People told me it was like the Vegas of the South. That's so wrong. This place is in people's blood, and they want you to feel that too." It is the Thursday morning of the Saints' bye week, and players have scattered in a precious escape from the routine and the violence. Brees remains behind for two extra days because there is more to his work than throwing touchdown passes.

Here the bus comes to a stop in front of Magnolia Trace Elementary School, in Mandeville, where Brees will speak to the students as part of an NFL-sponsored community program. Shrieks of joy rise from the sidewalk, where excited children and swooning teachers have gathered to greet their celebrity guest. Brees bounces out of his seat, pulls a black number 9 game jersey over his head and steams toward the front of the bus, clenching both fists. "The kids are pumped!" he shouts. He signs a small collection of memorabilia in the principal's office and then hustles down the pristine hallways of the school. Cafeteria worker Julia Collins of nearby Lacombe sticks her hand in Brees's path; he slaps it emphatically, and Collins runs back to work squealing. Teacher Laura Cangiamilla, seven months pregnant, poses for a photo with Brees. "This is Baby Drew," she says, pointing to the belly stretching her Saints jersey.

Now Brees stands on a stage in the school's gymnasium, and more than 400 students are spread across the tiled floor. He leads them in the Saints' traditional cheer. "Every time I say, 'One, two, three,' you say, 'Who Dat!'" implores Brees. He shouts it half a dozen times or more, cupping his hand next to his ear, and the response is ever louder. Then he asks for quiet, pressing his palms downward against air as if trying to suppress the noise with his hands. There are questions from the kids. What is the greatest challenge of your career? Is it easy to work as a team? Did you do a dance in the locker room after the Super Bowl? This one Brees turns back on the students. "Everybody who thinks they can dance," he shouts, "stand up and give me your best Super Bowl touchdown dance!" Instantly the floor is a beehive of jumping, gyrating, spinning kids, filling the air with celebratory screams. Brees watches like a proud father, or a mischievous co-conspirator.

Then there is another question. A little girl stands and reads nervously from a slip of yellow paper while a teacher holds the microphone. "What is your empowering word?" she asks, then timidly casts her eyes to the floor.

On the stage Brees, 31, raises a microphone to his mouth. Not laughing now. "My empowering word," he says, "is *faith*."

It is a word that in modern times can polarize—or politicize—an audience, ingratiating some listeners and repelling others. (Not this audience, the adult portion of which gasps in approval.) It's a word that the children have been taught but can't yet fully understand. For Brees the word is more than religion and spirituality, although it has been both of those, increasingly, through the years. Faith is more than Brees's empowering word. It is the central force in his life, slicing across family, football and community, carrying him to the top of his profession and to an iconic status in a still-wounded city that he has helped lift from despair.

When Brees blew out a knee in 11th grade and college recruiters largely abandoned him, it took faith to believe he would someday play college football. When the entire NFL passed on him in the first round of the 2001 draft, when the San Diego Chargers benched him four times and then brought in a young quarterback to replace him, when he tore up his shoulder in December '05, it took faith to believe he would be a star in professional football and lead a team to a Lombardi Trophy. When only

New Orleans—the doormat franchise and the ravaged city—believed in him, he believed in New Orleans. When his estranged mother ended her life in the summer of 2009, it took faith for Brees to embrace and understand the complicated and sometimes fleeting power of a family's love. When he rises every weekday at 5:15 a.m., it takes faith to look a cynical public in the eye and nakedly embrace the earnest values of fidelity, fatherhood, service, selflessness and sportsmanship, knowing that the slightest error in behavior will bring a furious blowback.

Yet is faith not also the essence of sport? A fan's unwavering faith in the home team. A player's faith in the workaday value of practice done hard and right to extract the most from his physical gifts. A team's faith that its members can do more together than each could do alone. On the night of Feb. 7, 2010, Drew Brees led the New Orleans Saints to the first Super Bowl championship in the franchise's star-crossed history, a 31–17 victory over the Indianapolis Colts in Miami. He completed 32 of 39 passes for 228 yards and two touchdowns, did not throw an interception and was named the game's most valuable player. For Brees it was the culmination of a four-year climb to a place among the best quarterbacks in football, and for the Saints the crowning moment in a 44-year romance with their home. For that city, nearly lost to a terrible storm, it was a critical step on a very long and ongoing path to recovery. "I needed New Orleans just as much as New Orleans needed me," says Brees. "People in New Orleans needed somebody to care about them. And it was the one place that cared about me."

And cares deeply still, every day. "People come up to Drew and don't say, 'Congratulations,'" says Saints veteran tackle Jon Stinchcomb. "They say, 'Thank you. Thank you for coming here.'"

When the Super Bowl was finished late on that Sunday night, Brees grabbed his one-year-old son, Baylen, and hoisted him skyward into the shower of confetti. The little boy's head was framed by oversized headphones to protect his eardrums from the noise. (He wears them for every game he attends.) Nearby stood Brees's wife, Brittany, unknowingly pregnant with their second child, another boy, Bowen, who would be born in October. And here were a city, a team and a man all reborn, new life reflected in the innocent eyes of a child.

It is for his vital role in that rebirth, for his willingness to immerse himself in New Orleans's recovery while relentlessly pursuing his own, that Drew Brees is SPORTS ILLUSTRATED's 2010 Sportsman of the Year. It is the 57th such honor the magazine has bestowed since its founding in 1954, and in the truest spirit of the award his influence reaches far beyond the walls of the stadium.

It is not a good time to be anyone's hero. Not with the gaping maw of endless news cycles, cellphone camera photos, social media and gotcha blogs, all lying in wait for the Tiger Moment that reveals the lie and exposes the hypocrisy. And the higher the pedestal, the harder the fall. Brees is acutely aware of this reality but unafraid. "People are waiting, if not to catch you doing something bad," he says, "then to catch you doing something that can be twisted into something that looks bad. But I'm aware of my position. Kids hang on your every word and action. You have an influence on their lives. And I believe this is who I am. It comes pretty naturally to me. I mean, I don't avoid using drugs because kids are watching me; I avoid doing drugs because it's not a good idea to use drugs." In Brees's best-selling memoir, *Coming Back Stronger*, published last July, he wrote of his marriage to the former Brittany Dudchenko, 34, whom he met in 1999 when both were students at Purdue, "...when I put the ring on Brittany's finger, I said, 'For better or for worse, till death do us part.' Period. No matter how bad it could possibly get, I am committed. It's not about happiness. It's not about a feeling. I committed myself to her for the rest of my life, and I promise *never* to walk away."

Maybe the idolization of athletes has always been a lousy idea, but the concept will not die soon or easily. It is very much alive on Halloween in New Orleans, where the Saints will play the Steelers in a Sunday-night game at the Superdome (another symbol of the city's climb back from the horror of Hurricane Katrina). By mid-afternoon the streets are bustling with costumed revelers—vampires, superheroes and villains, political figures, Troy Polamalu. But the most ubiquitous costume, by far, is a number 9 football jersey. There are slender women wearing number 9 in tight-fitting pink and gigantic men wearing number 9 in the size of parachutes. There are little children in snuggly number 9s. There is retro number 9, Pro Bowl number 9 and camouflage number 9. There is a cluster of young women with matching T-shirts that say KREWE DU DREW on the back, above a little gold, sequined number 9.

Part of this is organic: Fans wear jerseys to football games, and a lot of them wear the star quarterback's jersey. And while any city with an NFL franchise claims some degree of connection to the team that plays there on Sundays, there is a special bond between the Saints and New Orleans that predates Super Bowl victories and devastating storms. It goes back to the early days of the franchise, born in the fall of 1967, when veteran players like Billy Kilmer and Doug Atkins would stumble down the beer-and-bourbon-soaked streets and share with the townsfolk in the futility that comes from playing the first 20 years of existence without a winning season. Plus it is Halloween. Yet none of this fully explains the number 9 revolution in the city on game day. Says NFL commissioner Roger Goodell, "It's hard to point to a relationship in our league, between a player and a city, that's more meaningful than the Saints and Drew Brees."

New Orleans proper is nearly 70% black, and, says Ronald Markham, the 32-year-old African-American CEO of the New Orleans Jazz Orchestra, "It is a city with many schisms." Yet African-American fans wear number 9 too. "I'll say this: Drew is definitely an honorary brother," says Troy Henry, 50, a black businessman who finished a distant second to Mitch Landrieu in the mayor's race just before this year's Super Bowl. "He transcends race, and he does it with class and dignity."

On a French Quarter side street, Tom Church, a lifelong Saints fan from Jennings, La., is wearing number 9 in black. "It's because of what he did for the city just by coming here," says Church. "And the way he conducts himself. Can you imagine if Ben Roethlisberger lived here? A guy like that would go crazy in this town." Over on Royal Street, one block south of Bourbon, Kelly Hale of New Orleans rocks her shiny gold number 9 jersey. "He's a good family guy," says Hale. "He seems like a nice person. That means a lot."

This love between quarterback and city took root unexpectedly in the winter of 2006. Brees had suffered a catastrophic injury to his throwing shoulder while playing for the Chargers, who had selected him with the first pick of the second round of the 2001 NFL draft. San Diego, which had acquired the rights to Philip Rivers in a draft-day move in 2004, effectively jettisoned the rehabbing Brees by offering him a contract that guaranteed only $2 million. Backup money. The Miami Dolphins showed interest but lowballed Brees when team doctors were skeptical about his chances of coming back.

The Saints, meanwhile, threw themselves at Drew and Brittany Brees. Their courtship was both skilled (a dinner in the chef's kitchen at Emeril's and a film session in which coach Sean Payton promised to tailor his wide-open offense to Brees's strengths) and clumsy (an accidental tour through the parts of the city left most damaged by Katrina barely six months earlier, devastation from which the Saints had hoped to shield Brees). Yet Brees felt something familiar. As a child he had attended weekly Baptist church services; like most of his peers he was there largely from habit rather than devotion. One Sunday at age 17 he felt something stronger, as if the scripture were speaking to him, giving him purpose. Now in 2006, with only the Saints and their bludgeoned home showing belief in him, he sensed that purpose again. "As those few days went by," says Brittany, "Drew and I felt that maybe we were being called to New Orleans for a reason."

The central reason was for Brees to play quarterback, which he has done surpassingly well. That first season he threw for a league-high 4,418 yards and led the Saints on a surprise run to the NFC title game. Two years later he became just the second quarterback in NFL history (after Dan Marino) to throw for 5,000 yards in a season (5,069, to be exact), and in 2009, the Super Bowl season, he completed 70.62% of his throws' the most accurate season ever by an NFL quarterback. "He always had unbelievable instincts, great athletic feet, the whole skill set," says New York Jets offensive coordinator Brian Schottenheimer, Brees's quarterbacks coach for four years in San Diego and still a close friend. "Now, with experience and age, he's just mastered his craft."

Solid quarterbacking alone might have been enough to deify Brees in New Orleans, so beaten was the city after Katrina and so in need of a rallying force. But it is Brees the person who has earned the lasting trust and love of New Orleanians.

Consider: Late in the afternoon of Wednesday, Nov. 10, as Brees was running through a long checklist of bye-week obligations, he detoured to the Lusher Charter School, not far from his home in Uptown New Orleans. The four-story, 77-year-old brick building, previously a traditional high school, was vacant when flooded by Katrina and had slouched into a rotting, mold-choked shelter for displaced residents. In the storm's aftermath New Orleans educators, including Lusher CEO Kathy Hurstell Riedlinger, reopened the building as a charter high school. During the renovation they were contacted by The Brees Dream Foundation, which helped raise $671,000 to restore the school's athletic field, scoreboard and running track. In October 2009 those facilities were christened the Brees Family Field. Drew wrote a $38,000 personal check to rebuild the weight room.

Here Brees jumps from his Mercedes into the middle of the Lusher Lions' football practice. Coach Louis Landrum's team, in its second year of varsity competition, had won four of 10 games and qualified for the Louisiana state playoffs against powerhouse Evangel Christian of Shreveport. Brees calls the players into a circle and animatedly recounts to them the story of David and Goliath before breaking the huddle with a shout. "They've got a tough game," Brees says after leaving the school. "They could lose 70–0 to that team. I wanted to get them fired up." (In fact, Lusher would lose by the relatively respectable margin of 47–6 to a school with multiple Division I prospects.)

In the nearly eight years since The Brees Dream Foundation was established to support cancer research and the care and education of children in need, it has contributed or committed more than $6 million in Louisiana, San Diego and West Lafayette, Ind., home of Purdue. In addition to its work with the Lusher school, the foundation is in the final stages of completing $1 million in funding for the American Cancer Society's Patrick F. Taylor Hope Lodge in New Orleans, a residential facility for patients undergoing chemotherapy, and $100,000 for completion of G.W. Carver High's Field of Dreams in the Ninth Ward.

In total the foundation has worked with nearly 50 New Orleans schools and organizations, providing $300,000 to New Orleans Outreach for after-school assistance; $127,550 to the New Orleans Recreation Department to help with initial costs in the restoration of Pontchartrain Park; $78,000 to Best Buddies Louisiana, which facilitates one-to-one friendships for adults with intellectual disabilities; and $74,000 to the Greater New Orleans Rebuild Child Care Collaborative, to restore child-care facilities lost to Katrina. "A lot of people have a foundation just to have a foundation," says Mark Brunell, an NFL warhorse who was Brees's backup with the Saints in 2008 and '09 and now plays behind Mark Sanchez with the Jets. "Drew has a foundation that does all kinds of things. The guy cares. He's genuine."

From the high school practice in Uptown, Brees stops briefly at home to swap a Saints golf shirt for a dress shirt and sport coat, and then rushes off to Brennan's restaurant in the French Quarter for a meeting of what he calls his Quarterback Club, a group of nine New Orleans businessmen brought together by Brees to pool their creativity and wealth. (Each man commits at least $25,000 a year to Brees's foundation.) "In times of crisis, communities look for leaders, and Drew has become one of those leaders," says club member John Payne, a Caesars Entertainment Corp. executive. "Drew's day job is a high-pressure, full-time job, but he believes passionately that it's part of his role to stay energized and stay involved. He looks at it as a responsibility."

That infectious sincerity is why future Hall of Fame running back LaDainian Tomlinson found himself uncommonly engaged while watching Super Bowl XLIV on television. He met Brees in 1997 when they played together on a high school all-star team in Texas—Brees from Austin, Tomlinson from Waco. "The guy's work ethic stood out from the jump," says Tomlinson. "He was smart, he was a leader. You could just see he was going to be special." In April 2001 the Chargers took Tomlinson with the fifth selection in the draft (Michael Vick went first, to the Falcons, with a pick the Chargers had traded to Atlanta) and chose Brees 27 spots later. The two played together for five seasons; when Brees needed a throwing partner on an off-season afternoon, it was often Tomlinson he'd call. So on that February night in Miami, when Brees took a knee to finish the Super Bowl, Tomlinson felt a deep kinship. "I was screaming," says LT. "It's like I was right there with him. I called him and told him, 'I'm proud of you, man.'"

That sincerity is also why Billy Miller, who played tight end with Brees for four years in New Orleans, and Miller's wife, Rachael, rewrote their will. If the couple were to die or otherwise be incapacitated, the care of their children—sons Caine, 13, and Jaden, 8, and daughter Celeste, 5—would be entrusted to Drew and Brittany Brees. "There is nobody in the world we trust more," says Billy, who now operates the Elite Performance Factory, a gym in Southern California. "Our values line up perfectly."

Miller came to know Brees best not in the locker room or on the field but during USO trips the two have taken together. Brees has been on five such NFL-sponsored trips in the last five years, visiting troops in Afghanistan, Dubai, Guantanamo Bay, Iraq, Kuwait and Japan. His admiration for the military springs from his relationship with his 85-year-old grandfather, Ray Akins, a legendary Texas high school football coach who fought on Okinawa in World War II and still works 100 head of cattle on a ranch in New Baden, Texas. But Brees's appreciation for soldiers goes beyond his family's legacy. "Think of the sacrifices they make," says Brees. "I'm away from my son for a day, and I can't wait to see him. Some of those guys are gone for 15 months."

Brees has also flown in fighter jets a handful of times, once pulling 9.2 G's in an Air Force F-16 with the Thunderbirds. "It gives those guys a chance to promote what they do," Brees says of the rides, "and they appreciate that you're interested." It's also yet another chance to compete. On a tour of Iraq in 2008, Goodell, Brees and Giants defensive end Osi Umenyiora were roommates in Saddam Hussein's former guest palace, where the commissioner got a sense of Brees's fire. So when Goodell flew with the Thunderbirds during Super Bowl week in 2009, he told his pilot, "I've got to do 9 G's, and I can't pass out or throw up, or Drew Brees will never let me hear the end of it." (Goodell made it through fine.)

Perhaps it should be mentioned—just for balance—that Brees is not perfect. Back in eighth grade at St. Andrew's Episcopal School in Austin, young Drew took the occasion of a class party on Lake Austin to moon his classmates from the dock as he jumped into the water. The school suspended him, and worse, his parents held him out of the season-opening flag football game against his team's biggest rival. "It crushed me," says Brees. "And it took me a long time to get over that." Saints legend has it that Brees helped engineer an epic locker room prank so diabolical that nary a teammate will spill the details. And while he's unfailingly cordial with autograph-seekers under most circumstances, don't approach him during private time with his family.

Yet Brees's foibles are rare and refreshingly harmless. "If a father gives his kid a number 9 Saints jersey," says Stinchcomb, "he's probably never going to have to do any explaining about the guy who wears that jersey."

A week into football practice at Purdue in 1997, first-year coach Joe Tiller had grown impatient. His three returning quarterbacks, upperclassmen Billy Dicken and John Reeves and redshirt freshman Clay Walters, were making a mess of the spread passing offense that Tiller intended to unleash on the unsuspecting, plodding Big Ten. Three true freshmen QBs—Drew Brees from Texas, Jim Mitchell from Missouri and Ben Smith from Nebraska—were watching from behind the huddle when Tiller shouted, "Give me one of those young guys to run with the [first team]!"

Smith says, "I took two steps back and was trying to find somewhere to hide, because I sure didn't want to hop out there. It was a very stressful moment—I mean it was intense. Then just as I stepped back, Drew stepped up. He moved right in, took control of the huddle, brought the offense up to the line of scrimmage and ran the play. I remember it was a Four-Go route, and he threw to one of the outside go receivers, and he just put the ball right on the money. I was thinking right there: I'm going to have to find another position." (Epilogue: Smith became not only a starting safety at Purdue but also one of Brees's roommates and, to this day, one of his best friends.)

In retrospect it doesn't seem shocking that Brees was the player who stepped forward and stamped himself on the Purdue program. One year earlier his team at Austin's Westlake High had gone 16–0 and won the Texas 5A state championship game with a 55–15 squeaker over Abilene's Cooper High, and Brees was named the state large-school offensive MVP. But there were issues: He had torn his left ACL in a state playoff game in December of his junior year—scaring off college recruiters—and he was just barely six feet tall. By the middle of Brees's senior season Purdue was the only major program offering a scholarship. (When an SI writer profiled Brees in 1999, his friends chided Brees with the names of quarterbacks recruited by colleges in his home state, including Matt Schobel at Texas A&M and Major Applewhite at Texas.) It was to become a recurring theme in Brees's life: swimming upstream against the collective wisdom.

Brees backed up Dicken that first year and started for the next three. As a senior he led Purdue to its first Rose Bowl in 34 years, and he still holds Big Ten career records for passing yards (11,792) and touchdowns (90). He left behind the indelible memory of a 1998 game against Wisconsin in which he completed 55 of an NCAA-record 83 passes. "There's an It factor in sports," says Greg Olson, who was Brees's quarterbacks coach at Purdue and is now the offensive coordinator for the Tampa Bay Buccaneers. "It's a hard thing to pinpoint. But I'll tell you what: Drew had it."

Evaluators at the next level were skeptical. NFL scouts endlessly debated Brees's height (again), his arm strength and the possible skewing effect of playing in Tiller's wide-open offense (which would be pedestrian by today's standards, just a decade later). At a poke-and-prod for scouts before the 2001 Hula Bowl in Maui, Brees was measured and announced by a stentorian clerk as "five-eleven-seven!" or 5'11⅞". Brees refused to leave the stage until he was remeasured and announced as "six even!" to applause from the scouts. A month later he flopped at the NFL scouting combine in Indianapolis when coaches supervising drills dulled Brees's enthusiasm by telling him to simply complete throws at three quarters speed rather than passing in a game-speed rhythm. At one point Brees one-hopped a five-yard square-out. In the stands Brian Schottenheimer, who had seen Brees tear up the Big Ten, said out loud, "Who is this guy?"

On a long ride home to Purdue that night, through the mid-winter darkness on I-65, Brees said to a writer in his company, "Now I have to prove myself all over again."

With the Chargers he sat behind Doug Flutie as a rookie, then beat out Flutie in '02, but that only put him on a roller coaster that included four benchings in two seasons. Schottenheimer, whose father, Marty, was the head coach, recalls, "Every time Drew got benched, he would stand on the sideline with his helmet on, chinstrap buckled, ready to go. Sometimes for the whole game. Pretty powerful."

Slowly Brees made himself better. Sean Payton bristles when Brees is described as an overachiever. "He's an amazing athlete," says the Saints' coach. "Quick feet, explosiveness, anticipation." Yet Brees has the mind of an overachiever. He had always been hypercompetitive, but that was no longer enough. Following the 2002 season he began working out extensively with trainer Todd Durkin at Durkin's private gym in San Diego. A year later Brees met with former major league pitcher Tom House, now 63, a pitching coach at USC with a Ph.D. in performance psychology. House helped Brees minimally with throwing mechanics and significantly with the underpinnings of leadership. "Drew wants to please people," says House. "He cares too much. He needed to learn that you can't be everything to all people." What Brees took from the sessions was this: "I was too nice a guy, as a leader. I had this tendency that if people were doing things wrong, I would try to make up for it instead of calling them out. And that will burn you out."

The new Brees kept Rivers at bay for two years; then in the last game of the 2005 season Brees was trying to recover his own fumble when he was driven into the turf by Broncos defensive tackle Gerard Warren. Dr. James Andrews, who operated on Brees's shoulder, called it "one of the most unique injuries of any athlete I've ever treated," a rare 360-degree labrum tear with associated rotator-cuff damage. Andrews repaired the joint with 11 surgical anchors—three or four is common. Brees awoke from surgery right where he was as a senior in high school, as a senior in college and as a fourth-year pro: doubted.

Sean Payton leans forward in his chair, looks at the huge flat-screen wall monitor he uses to watch game tape in his office and begins punching his remote. "I want to show you something," says Payton. "This is amazing. Watch." He cues up the Saints' 34–3 victory over the Carolina Panthers on Nov. 7 and moves ahead to a second-and-five for the Saints from the Carolina 19-yard line with just under three minutes to play in the first half. The play call is Bunch right tear, fake slash 37, weak F, naked right, Z escape, Y boiler. Brees will take a snap, feign a handoff to running back Julius Jones, turn and roll on a bootleg to his right and then make a rapid series of reads before choosing a target and throwing. Three receivers—Robert Meachem, David Thomas and Heath Evans—are "bunched" at the right side of the formation; rookie tight end Jimmy Graham is alone outside on the left.

At the snap the Panthers blitz three men from the right side of the offense and none are effectively blocked, bringing immediate heat on Brees. After Brees fakes to Jones—"With his back to the blitz," says Payton, no small detail—he turns and shuffles right, looking at Meachem, Thomas and Evans. Abruptly Brees switches direction, backpedaling parallel to the line of scrimmage. He plants his right foot, swivels his head to the left and throws across the field to Graham for a touchdown. "You know how people say a quarterback reads A, B, C, D?" says Payton. "That was, like, G. Or H. It blew my mind. We've never even talked about throwing back to Jimmy Graham on that play."

What Brees saw, even before the snap, was that the 6'6" Graham was going to be single-covered by 5'11" cornerback Richard Marshall. Brees was still willing to throw outside to Meachem, except that as soon as Brees snapped his head around from the run fake he saw that the front-side corner was jumping Meachem and that three pass rushers were coming free. "He processed all that in about two seconds," says Payton. "A lot of quarterbacks would have thrown an incompletion toward Meachem or thrown a pick. I still hadn't sorted it all out when Drew got to the sideline. I said, 'How did you get to Graham?' You know how many quarterbacks in the league make that play? Three? Maybe four?"

It was just one play, but one play can reveal a man. The Brees who went under Andrews's scope in 2006 was broken. The Brees who now leads a team and a city is whole. His initial rehab was stunning. "The most remarkable of any patient I've ever treated," Andrews told SI in 2007. Brees's work ethic since has been inspirational. "Follow him around for a day," says Payton. "You'll just go, 'Wow.'" Last July, on the morning after winning four ESPY

Awards in Los Angeles and attending parties afterward, Brees met Durkin for a 7 a.m. workout at USC. "We could have done it at nine or 10, or we could have waited until later in the day back in San Diego," says Durkin, "but Drew wants an edge. 'I'm doing it and they're not.'" During the season he continues to do a full set of light-weight, high-rep shoulder exercises four days a week, always thinking back to 2005.

It's Brees who formulates the Saints' raucous pregame chants and leads them like a middle linebacker. It's Brees who stays after practice every day, grooming the Saints' receiving corps, building the communal faith that makes a modern passing offense work. "The biggest thing Drew ever said to me," says slot receiver Lance Moore, an undrafted free agent out of Toledo who has caught 169 passes in five seasons with Brees, "is, 'I trust you.' When Drew trusts you, you can get the ball anytime." Marques Colston, a seventh-round pick out of Hofstra, arrived in New Orleans the same year as Brees, and through endless repetition the two have become arguably the most effective back-shoulder combo in NFL history. "Just being around that great a player, a guy who works so hard," says Colston, "it makes you feel like you have to raise the level of your game."

For precisely that reason Tampa Bay's Olson arranged for his second-year quarterback, Josh Freeman, to spend a week with Brees last summer in San Diego, soaking up the effort (but not discussing schemes, since they play in the same division). Likewise Brian Schottenheimer put Mark Sanchez on the phone with Brees during the off-season. Miller says he gets a steady stream of 5'11" high school clients at his gym who say they want to be the next Drew Brees. "I have to tell them there's a little more to it than being short," says Miller.

Brees juggles the roles of franchise quarterback and local hero by dividing his day into sections and dealing only with the task at hand. Friends have seen it before. "At Purdue we would all study in front of the TV," says Jason Loerzel, a former Purdue linebacker and roommate of Brees's who now lives in New Orleans. "Drew couldn't do it. If the TV was on he had to watch the TV. You couldn't even talk to him." Brees holds rigorously to routine. "He controls every aspect of his life," says Stinchcomb. For instance: Last summer Brees's family moved from one vacation home in San Diego to another, and Brees insisted on renting a U-Haul and doing the job himself. Wiser heads prevailed before Brees started putting couches on his back but not until he had transferred three loads of smaller items.

In the fall of '06 Payton left his office shortly after noon on the bye-week Sunday, and as he climbed into his car, he noticed a solitary figure on the practice field in gray shorts and gray practice T-shirt. It was Brees, dropping back, throwing on air, jogging up the field to the next imaginary line of scrimmage and throwing again.

"What are you doing?" said Payton, incredulous.

"We usually play on Sunday, so I don't want to mess up the routine," said Brees.

"Are we winning or losing?" Payton asked.

"We're winning," said Brees.

Last February in the biggest game of his life, Brees outplayed his surefire Hall of Fame counterpart, the Colts' Peyton Manning. Brees's 82% completion rate was the second best in Super Bowl history. With the game on the line it was Manning, not Brees, who threw a killing pick. And long after the end, Brees rode Saints bus No. 1 back to the team hotel, sitting up front with Payton and assistant coaches Joe Vitt, Greg McMahon, Pete Carmichael and Joe Lombardi, whose grandfather's name was etched into the sterling silver trophy they passed around. "What a special moment," says Brees. "I wished it would never end." It might not, yet. After a 4–3 start the Saints have won four straight, including Thursday's 30–27 comeback win at Dallas, and are battling for a return trip to the Super Bowl.

It is clearly victory that drives Brees, and service that moves him. He is a richly compensated professional with more than 20 sponsorship deals beyond his football contract. Yet it is family that fulfills him. Late on a bye-week afternoon he rushed to Danneel Park, a half mile from the Breeses' Uptown home. The new playground at the west end of the park was alive with small children—climbing, running, falling and rising again to play more in that indomitable way that only children can. It was a spectacular autumn day in the city, warm without humidity, windless and clear. Brees walked to where Brittany stood over three-week-old Bowen's stroller. The little guy was blissfully asleep. Brees kissed his wife and then darted off to find Baylen; soon the Saints' franchise quarterback was climbing up the side of a playscape, the biggest kid in the park. "Oh, no," said Brittany. "Drew is going to hurt himself. We better walk over there. I don't want to make that call to Sean Payton."

Part of Brees's rigid daily schedule includes getting home each Monday through Thursday night (NFL players are usually free on Fridays) at 7:30 to read books to Baylen and put him to sleep before resuming tape study. If Brees is delayed at the team's facility, 15 minutes away in suburban Metairie, Brittany brings the boys to see their father before bedtime. (During the reporting of this story, Brees sent an e-mail saying, "Balance in my life is so important with my four priorities: Faith, Family, Football, Philanthropy. The four F's. LOL.") He is collecting game balls for his boys, five so far for

Baylen, one for Bowen, painted and inscribed with their names as if they shared in the wins. Brees says he would like to play long enough in the NFL for his sons to see him in action and remember it.

Brees's own childhood was less than idyllic. His parents, Chip and Mina Brees, both successful lawyers in Austin, divorced when Drew was seven years old and his brother, Reid, was nearly five. (The brothers have a sister, Audrey, a 21-year-old junior at Georgia, from Chip's second marriage.) After the divorce the parents agreed that Drew and Reid would split time between their parents' houses. In the spring of 1999 Drew, then a college sophomore, told SI that the arrangement, while palpably delicate even to an interloper, was acceptable. "My parents get along," he said. He now admits they did not. "The situation was challenging, going back and forth like they did," Chip says. "If I could go back in time and do things differently, I would. But I can't."

Lacking a single household, the boys leaned on each other. "He was a great brother and a great friend for me," says Reid, now 29 and a medical-equipment sales rep in Colorado. "He let me hang with his friends. He beat on me a lot, but in a fun way, and he looked out for me. That's Drew. He looks out for other people."

Last February, two days after the Super Bowl, Brittany took a home pregnancy test, confirming that she was expecting. Bowen was born on Oct. 19, a Tuesday, serendipitously the slowest day of the week for NFL players. Drew was there for the delivery. "There's a saying that the greatest gift you can give a boy is a younger brother," says Drew. "We'd like to have more. We'd like to have a big family."

There is a tragic symmetry to his family's growth. Mina Brees died in Granby, Colo., on Aug. 7, 2009, from a prescription drug overdose; her death was ruled a suicide. Brees's relationship with his mother had been intensely complicated. They were clearly close once: During an SI writer's visit to Austin in 1999, Drew played a spirited tennis match with Mina at her private club and ate brunch with her afterward. They had shared a love of sports; Ray Akins is Mina's dad, and Marty Akins, a former quarterback at Texas, is her brother. Yet Drew and Mina grew apart in the intervening years, over a succession of emotional disagreements. In 2006 Drew publicly asked his mother to stop using his image in advertisements for her judgeship campaign. The episode was sad and unseemly. In his book Brees writes extensively of his efforts to understand their conflict and concludes, in part, "The full truth is that my mom and I had a toxic relationship." He suggests that his mother might have suffered from mental illness.

Brees and his mother barely spoke for the last eight years of Mina's life, but when Brittany became pregnant with Baylen, mother and son began to communicate again. “Things were in the process of getting better,” says Brees. “Once Baylen was born, I really hoped she could be a part of his life. We had been communicating back and forth about when that first meeting would be, and then all of sudden she was gone.”

Their last exchange, however, had not been uplifting. “Drew and my mother, they never really got back on a good note,” says Reid. “I knew Drew felt very bad about that. I'm pretty sure he felt some blame.”

But it is part of Brees's spirit that he has grown stronger and more passionate from the loss. And here is faith again, building greater love from tragedy. “I've learned never to take anything for granted,” he says, “whether it's a relationship, an opportunity or something in your personal or professional life. I just value little things more. Being with Brittany and my two boys. Time goes by too fast.”

Now the quarterback is standing next to a dusty circle in the park, where two little girls slap at a yellow tetherball. Brees is holding Bowen in his arms; the little boy's brown fleece sleeper with bear ears is unzipped in the warm air. The sun is falling and casting long autumn shadows across the earth. The Saints are winning, the city is alive, the family grows. The father drops his head, closes his eyes and softly kisses the son on the forehead. Everything is sweet. Everything is right.

DISTANT REPLAY

SEPTEMBER 4, 1985

Was He the Greatest of All Time?

You would never get Red Grange himself to say it, but there's a strong case to be made for the Galloping Ghost

BY JOHN UNDERWOOD

Incontestably, it was the perfect nickname. You could make a case that it was the best nickname in the history of American sport, although good nicknaming, like legible handwriting and jitterbugging, has pretty much become a lost art. But his was perfect because it compressed into imagery a style and a talent so wonderful that even now, more than half a century later, just saying it evokes heroic images.

The weekly newsreel clips that made the rounds of the movie houses in those days took the images to millions and enhanced them. In black and white, fluttering at 16 to 18 frames a second, they stoked the illusion of speed and made even more impressive the other eerie components of his long touchdown runs: the sublime shifts and feints, the paralyzing stiff-arms, the breathtaking bursts of speed. Reviewing those reels now, you get the impression that if Red Grange were not, indeed, a Galloping Ghost, he surely must have just seen one.

Still photographs taken at the time pinned down the image and put a face to it, but even in those Grange looked ghostlike. Beneath the leather pancake of his headgear, his eyes, embedded in deep sockets, appeared in perpetual shadow and shone so brightly black that they seemed more like objects to be looked at than to look with. A protracted exposure to hard work—he had toted ice for wages during his hardscrabble boyhood in Wheaton, Ill.—had toughened him. He was ruggedly handsome, but he never seemed youthful. Even at 22, which he was in 1925 when he single handedly took professional football out of the dark ages, he had a face like a well-worn coin. It is ironic that today, when he is very old, he looks much younger than he is.

There remains but a handful of people who actually saw Grange play, and most recall him only after he had suffered the crushing knee injury that made him a straight-ahead runner as early as his second year as a professional. He played the remaining six years of his pro career in pain, and witnesses at the end recall a productive but less nimble ballcarrier, the way most modern observers remember Joe Namath after his knees were gone. Those who played with and against Grange, men like Bronko Nagurski, remember him almost as much for his defensive skills. In those days the rules did not permit a player to escape to the bench when the other team got the ball.

Could it be that Grange really was the greatest ever? Damon Runyon wrote about him, as did Westbrook Pegler and Paul Gallico. It was the Golden Age of Sport, and those three supplied much of the burnish. When Runyon saw Grange play for the first time, he said he was "three or four men and a horse rolled into one. He is Jack Dempsey, Babe Ruth, Al Jolson, Paavo Nurmi and Man o' War." Gallico called him a "touchdown factory."

On an October day in 1924 in Champaign, Ill., against a Michigan team that hadn't lost in 20 games, Grange scored touchdowns on runs of 95, 67, 56 and 45 yards—in the first 12 minutes of play. He added a fifth TD later and passed for a sixth, as Illinois won 39–14. Grantland Rice, who is generally credited with giving Grange his sobriquet (Warren Brown of the *Chicago Tribune* and Charlie Dunkley of AP are also given nods), was deeply moved. When Rice became moved, he summoned poetry:

A streak of fire, a breath of flame,
Eluding all who reach and clutch;
A gray ghost thrown into the game
That rival hands may rarely touch.

Rice never missed a chance to see Grange play after that.

A year later, in Philadelphia, Grange played 57 minutes in a stunning 24–2 defeat of heavily favored Pennsylvania. In ankle-deep mud, he amassed 363 yards and scored on runs of 56, 13 and 20 yards. Laurence Stallings, who had co-written *What Price Glory?*, worked the game for the *New York World* primarily to see Grange. He agonized over his portable as he considered the performance and finally said, "This story's too big for me. I can't write it."

That was Grange's senior season at Illinois. In the 20 games he played as an undergraduate, he scored 31 touchdowns, many on spectacular long runs, usually when they stood to mean the most to his team. A maddeningly humble man, Grange has always regarded this ability as a kind of celestial fluke, like a passing comet, and has given any recitation of it the kind of passion one might show in reading a train schedule. The reason may be that he was on such intimate terms with the end zone for so long. At Wheaton High he scored 75 touchdowns and was also a four-time state sprint champion and captain of the basketball team.

Two days after his last college game, a 14–9 victory over Ohio State in Columbus before 85,500 fans—college football's largest crowd up to that time—Grange did something extraordinary, as significant as any single event in the history of American football: He turned pro. Specifically, his colorful agent, C.C. (Cash and Carry) Pyle, made him an offer he and the Chicago Bears could not refuse: the chance for everybody to make a lot of money in a hurry.

To appreciate the impact of Grange's decision, you have to understand that in 1925 pro football was regarded as a dirty little business run by rogues and bargain-basement entrepreneurs. The Milwaukee franchise had to fold that year because it was using high school players. Tim Mara bought the year-old New York Giants for $500. The game was confined mainly to tank towns (Pottsville, Frankford, Providence, Rock Island, Green Bay) where gatherings—you couldn't call them "crowds"—numbered four or five hundred on a good day. People who patronized professional football were thought to be of a caliber you now associate with Roller Derby.

College officials wanted no part of the pro game. Besides being seedy, pro football posed an economic threat. So they were aghast that the mighty Grange would defect without at least waiting for graduation day. He was, after all, college football's jewel, a three-time Walter Camp All-America who had represented all the appropriate virtues. He didn't drink or smoke. He hadn't even had a date until he got to college, and once there he was a solid student. The only thing outrageous about him was his modesty. ("The Michigan game? I had great blocking.")

The *Chicago News* warned that a "living legend" would be wise not to "go and sully" his reputation. Fielding Yost, the Michigan coach, said, "Anything but that." Grange's own coach, Bob Zuppke, lobbied against it ("Stay away from professionalism, and you will be another Camp") and criticized him pointedly at a banquet they attended. "Zup," said Grange, a pragmatist awakening, "you coach for money. Why isn't it O.K. to play for money?" They didn't speak for two years.

Grange played his final game for Illinois on a Saturday, announced his intentions at the Bears game in Chicago on Sunday (he was mobbed by ecstatic fans), signed what amounted to a personal-services contract with the Bears on Monday, practiced two days and played his first pro game on Thanksgiving Thursday. What followed were the 17 days that made pro football.

A hybrid schedule—part regular season, part exhibition, all barnstorm—had been doodled up by Pyle and approved by George Halas, the Bears' owner, coach and starting right end. It called for a miracle of endurance: 10 games in 17 days, seven of them within a nine-day period. Grange was expected to perform in every game. For that, he was guaranteed a 50-50 split of all gate receipts, with Pyle getting 40% of Grange's share.

The first game matched the Bears against the Chicago (now St. Louis) Cardinals. Accustomed to attracting crowds of less than 5,000, Halas was not prepared for the demand. The 20,000 tickets he had printed were sold in three hours. More had to be ordered. A standing-room-only crowd of 36,000 jammed into Cubs Park (now known as Wrigley Field) on a snowy day. No NFL game had drawn near that number. Halas was said to have cried while counting the receipts.

St. Louis, Washington, Boston, Pittsburgh...the trains carrying the Galloping Ghost and his supporting cast of 17 mortal Bears rumbled across the East and Midwest, and wherever they went, it was the same. Grange was an event, a happening so stupendous that the curiosity to see him seemed insatiable. The Bears played before an NFL-record 40,000 fans in Philadelphia in a steady downpour, and Grange scored the game's only two touchdowns. The next day, wearing the same muddy jerseys, the Bears were cheered by 73,000 fans at the Polo Grounds in New York as Chicago beat the Giants 19–7. The $130,000 take saved Mara from financial ruin. "My worries," he said, "are over."

More than 125 reporters covered that game. Rice, Pegler, Runyon and Ford Frick joined the merry group for the remainder of the tour. The Bears were hurried along like artificially ripened fruit to take advantage of the market. At every stop, Halas passed out press releases he had written himself. The Bears traveled in Pullmans and used the ladies' washroom as a training room. Although there were a lot of injuries—the trainer had to suit up for a couple of games—the converts kept coming.

The gate at one stop was $200,000. A Chicago writer noted, "All of a sudden some people around the country think that pro football might be a good investment." In Detroit, nursing a torn muscle and a blood clot in his left arm, and bone tired from the killing pace ("Deep lines showed about Red's face," wrote Frick), Grange could not play. More than 20,000 fans demanded refunds. That game and the next one the following day in Chicago were his only no-shows. "In those days," Grange said later, "you were taken off the field only if you could not walk or breathe."

To keep the trip, in perspective, a Chicago newspaper printed a gleeful running box score of Grange's cumulative earnings. They came to roughly $300 an hour. By the end of the tour, Grange was in pitiful shape, but he rallied when he saw Pyle. "Make me feel good. Tell me how much I'm up to now," he said. Grange's share, with endorsements, came to more than $100,000. Pyle had made deals for Grange's name to go on sportswear, soft drinks, shoes, a doll, pictures, peanuts, a chocolate-nut candy bar—even a meat loaf. When Pyle brought in an offer from a cigarette company, Grange demurred. "I don't smoke," he said.

"You only have to say you like the aroma," said Pyle. Grange relented.

By now Grange occupied a room in the annals of sport that no football player had ever entered. *The New York Times* called him "the most famous, the most talked of and written about, the most photographed and most picturesque player the game has ever produced." Wrote the enraptured Rice:

There are two shapes now moving,
Two ghosts that drift and glide,
And which of them to tackle
Each rival must decide;
They shift with spectral swiftness
Across the swarded range,
And one of them's a shadow,
And one of them is Grange.

The Ghost was allowed eight days to recuperate before Pyle had him and the Bears off on a second barnstorming tour. This one lasted nine games, beginning on Christmas Day in Miami and moving across the South to the Far West. In Los Angeles, Brother Pyle's Traveling Football Salvation Show drew 75,000 spectators, another pro record.

By the time the Bears hit the finish line in Seattle on Jan. 31, they had played 19 games in 17 cities in 66 days, or about two games a week. Grange went home to Wheaton bruised and battered, but driving a new $5,500 Lincoln Phaeton and wearing a $500 raccoon coat. That spring the Wheaton Iceman (his other enduring nickname) wore the coat on his rounds. His old benefactor at the icehouse, Luke Thompson, asked him please not to park the Phaeton out front. "It confuses me as to who is working for whom," said Thompson.

From then on, football was no longer Grange's game; it was his entrée. There followed the second phase of his celebrity, that of the slightly flawed but increasingly beloved swashbuckler seeking any hedge against his own mortality. "Ten years from now," he said with uncanny imperception, "no one will know or care what Red Grange did or who he was." With Cash and Carry's assistance, he began storing up for the inevitable downside.

When Halas rebuffed their bid to buy a piece of the Bears for the 1926 season, Grange and Pyle went to New York and started their own American Football League. (Fancy that.) When the league bombed, Grange and his New York Yankees joined the NFL in 1927. That season, in the third game, against–of all teams–the Bears, he collided heavily with Chicago's huge center, George Trafton. As they fell, Grange's cleats grabbed in the turf, and Trafton landed on Grange's twisted knee.

Grange tried to come back sooner than he should have, reinjured the knee and missed the entire 1928 season. The damage was permanent. When he rejoined the Bears in 1929, he was no longer a breakaway runner, but he would play through the 1934 season. He had, however, found other open fields in which to maneuver.

Pegler once countered an editorialist's suggestion that Grange should shun pro football and "try to write or act in the movies" by saying, "To be an imitation writer or a fake movie actor would surely be less virtuous than becoming a real football player." Ironically, by becoming a "real football player," Grange assumed those other roles as well. He made movies. He helped write a book on Zuppke, with whom he had a reconciliation, and, much later, a column of college football picks for this magazine. He appeared on the cover of *Variety* and had a brief stint in a vaudeville act called C'mon Red.

In 1928, Pyle staged a transcontinental 3,422-mile footrace and accompanying sideshow that became known as the Bunion Derby. Grange rode along in a specially outfitted $25,000 bus to help in the promotion. The Bunion Derby, like Grange's one-man review, was a reach. The thousands who were expected to flock to those towns the runners passed through didn't materialize, and Pyle's sideshow, which included a fire-eater, a wrestling bear, a mummified human cadaver and a five-legged pig, was a flop. In Conway, Mo., citizens egged the bus.

Grange's movie career, like that of most athletes who try Hollywood while their names are hot, was a shooting star. Pyle made a deal with Joseph P. Kennedy during that first barnstorming season. Afterward Cash and Carry flashed a $300,000 check that the guileless Grange immediately identified as phony. "One of Charlie's crazy stunts," he said. Nonetheless, Grange did make two films (*One Minute to Play* and *Racing Romeo*) and a serial (*The Galloping Ghost*) for Kennedy. Each was as unsensational as the next, and

Grange complained that it was "hard work." After 1929 he didn't make any more movies.

As his football abilities waned, his involvement in the game changed. In the '40s, he was briefly named president of the proposed United States Football League (fancy *that*), but resigned before it got airborne. He went into broadcasting, and his sometimes unique use of the language gave critics the impression he was self-educated. Still, he was in great demand. He did the Bears games on radio and TV for 14 years and teamed with Lindsey Nelson on network telecasts of college games.

Nelson recalls that Grange was never beguiled by his own importance ("He was incapable of taking himself seriously") and suffered his detractors with good humor. Nitpickers in Chicago were not relentless, but they were pointed. "It is considered a masterpiece of achievement," wrote one, "when Grange has the right team in possession of the ball."

Athletes to Grange were "atha-letes," and sometimes an atha-lete played "right side rinebacker." He had trouble with the collective noun. "The Army team," he would say, "now have four first downs to Navy's three." A staunch defender of Grange, Nelson told a complaining NCAA television executive, "That's the way they do it in England."

"Dammit, Lindsey," said the executive, "Red didn't go to Oxford. He went to Illinois!"

Nelson recalls that Grange once said his greatest achievement was the success he made of an insurance business in Chicago, "because he felt he did that by himself. Everything else was God-given and teamwork." However, Grange gave up the business after a mild coronary in 1951. By then, no doubt, he realized that his apotheosis as a sports hero was going to carry him through after all. When Grange talked, people queued up to listen, and he was not so much a sweetheart that he qualified everything he said. He was, for example, adamant in his futile support of a pension plan for those who had played pro ball when he did and were not as well off as he was. But he always made his case politely.

Says Nelson, "Red had such a wonderful way of handling things that he could make the worst of situations seem O.K. A waitress dropped a bowl of Roquefort dressing on my new blue suit in Chicago one night. I hopped up and was dancing around, all excited, and there sat Red, looking at me ever so sweetly. 'I thought you ordered Thousand Island,' he said."

Sixty years is actually a short bridge in time when a hero is being defined or on his way to being better defined. Instead of dissipating, the testimonials to Grange's preeminence have accumulated over the years. Halas said over and over again that Grange's signing in 1925 was an event "comparable to the national televising of games" in bringing pro football to power. Nagurski called him "the greatest running back I ever saw." Bulldog Turner said he was "the greatest name football ever had." To commemorate college football's 100th anniversary in 1969, the Football Writers Association of America chose an alltime All-America team. Grange alone was a unanimous choice. O.J. Simpson made the second team.

Unlike those modern-day cads and bores who make millions from their sports without exhibiting a redeeming social grace, Grange was a much-loved figure, partly because he was easy to love. The effusive Sid Luckman said that just meeting him was "one of the greatest honors I've received in sports." Upon meeting Grange socially, the Giants' All-Pro center/linebacker Mel Hein called him "the nicest, dearest man I ever met." Hein had first met him on the field at the end of "a stiff-arm so strong it knocked me over."

"The most modest hero who ever lived," said baseball Hall of Famer Ralph Kiner when he met Grange. "An absolute peach," said Nelson. "You couldn't get him mad at you if you tried."

Eventually, Grange left football altogether, but as the years rolled by, he surfaced now and again, usually at the business end of a comment about the passing scene. Asked what it had been like as "the first Herschel Walker" to quit college to go pro, he said he couldn't have been better received "if I'd announced I was joining the Capone mob." Asked about the rigors of playing 10 games in 17 days, he said, "It beat practicing." Asked about the millions of dollars agents were demanding for their players, he said, "I'd have to have an agent, too, because I couldn't keep from laughing if I asked for that kind of money to play football."

In 1980 his age coincided with his old number, 77, which had become so familiar that it turned into a golfing term. "I shot a Red Grange today." The predictable birthday columns reviewed his achievements. He conducted the interviews by telephone from his home near Lake Wales, Fla., where his wife, Muggs, would say, "He'd rather do it that way. He really doesn't care one way or the other if anybody writes about him anymore."

Then, two years ago, Jack Dempsey died and again Grange was sought out, except on a more melancholy note. All the great heroes of the Golden Age had finally passed from the scene—Ruth and Cobb from baseball, Jones from golf, Tilden from tennis, Dempsey from boxing. Only Grange was left. He is the last of those national treasures, and though it isn't so grand to be a grand old man of 82, he is holding on. To what? To what dreams, and to what memories? What could he be thinking now about his game and the part he played in making it? It was to that end that a man with a notebook recently went to Florida.

The town of Lake Wales is one of those fortresses of underdevelopment around which time did not pass as much as it got rerouted. The thundering interstates that allow one to race from Miami to Disney World to Tampa without seeing anything else were plotted well to either side, and not even a Holiday Inn can be found within the city limits. The only prominent landmark is a 10-story apartment house that was in its heyday the Seminole Hotel. Like the town itself, the building is a faded, peeling relic, protruding from the flat terrain like an impaired thumb.

Route 60, an old, thin zipper that slants across the state below Orlando, penetrates Lake Wales in four lanes from the west and squeezes out the other side in two. The land boom that was anticipated years ago never detonated. Except for the voracious discount chain stores and the inevitable Century 21 real-estate office, enterprise to the east of town has a tentative, distrustful quality about it, like the struggling motels there that promise shelter but don't risk putting phones in the rooms.

Farther east, a silica-mining firm has opened the earth right next to where fruit lies spoiled on the ground in a frost-devastated orange grove. The central Florida winters have become more drastic and threaten to shove the citrus industry deeper down the peninsula. A sign advertises five acres for $9,900, NO MONEY DOWN! A new shopping center, with an appositeness undoubtedly lost on its clientele, features a Kash & Karry grocery.

Exactly 20 miles out, a brown and yellow billboard introduces Indian Lake Estates, a "country club community." Passersby are welcomed to "inspect our model homes," although the "estates," half an acre apiece, were carved out of the palmetto patches, sectioned off and grabbed up years ago by speculators hoping to make a bundle selling them to older people looking for perpetual warmth. That was a more optimistic time. Many of the lots have been resold more than once without development. Long stretches of the neatly cut paved roads are devoid of housing. FOR SALE signs dominate the landscape. Indian Lake Estates is a resort that never quite made it.

The star inhabitant, who did, lives on Amaryllis Drive, three blocks from the sticky, blue-black waters of Lake Weohyakapka and half a mile from the golf course he no longer patronizes. Grange is mostly untouched by celebrity now, and that's fine with him. When he moved in 25 years ago, Grange figured he would fish a lot and play golf. He bought two boats. "It's amazing how little the earth seems to move when you're sitting in a boat," he says.

After a while, though, he didn't fish anymore. He didn't mind the fishing, he said. It was the catching and the cleaning. He golfed until recently, but he found that the game lacked something. "It's like kicking field goals," he says. "You don't have to be a football player to kick field goals; you just have to be precise." Golf, he said, would be all right "if somebody came up from behind and tackled you when you were swinging."

He doesn't travel anymore either, "if I can get out of it." He reads. "Baseball books, mainly," he says. "I'm more of a baseball fan than anything. I got footballed to death after it became a job." And he mows his lawn and feeds a sandhill crane that flies in regularly. But "mainly I do nothing, if that's what I want to do. It's what happens when you have enough dough. Muggs and I can have 20 people in for dinner tonight, or go a month without seeing anybody." When strangers inquire if he might be "the guy who played football," Grange tells them, "That was my uncle."

He was in the driveway of the sprawling, airy green-and-white concrete-block house when the visitor drove up. Grange had a bag of birdseed out and was making a large, neat mound on the concrete. High on a nearby telephone wire, the huge crane waited for his friend to finish serving. Grange straightened effortlessly upon seeing the car and waved. That simple act seemed to make him young again—trim and pink-faced and smiling warmly. From head to toe, he was impeccably coordinated: a chocolate brown Ban-Lon shirt, matching knit trousers, a light cream-colored jacket and brown running shoes that looked untested. Although his hair was white as tissue, it showed tints of red when the sun hit it right. Indeed, he looked as if he could be some older man's nephew.

He admired the visitor's rented Thunderbird, running his fingertips along the top of the car door. Once, he said, he bought four cars at the same time—Auburns for his brother and father and two Stutz Bearcats. "We were car nutty," he said. "The Stutz had a sphinx head on the radiator cap, and the overdrive would go *whirrrrrr*!" He enjoyed the image of his former auto whirring along the back roads of Illinois. "It was the first car I had that could do 100 miles an hour." In his garage now were a pair of worn-looking Pontiacs.

Inside the ranch-style dwelling, each room seemed to broaden into another. Muggs, a handsome, stringy, bright-eyed woman with a golfer's tan, said Red had designed the house "to take advantage of every inch." It has no halls, and the windows and sliding glass patio doors open onto the screen-enclosed pool so that the breezes can cool even the hottest days. There are some signs of disrepair, but in middle age it remains a comfortable house.

Muggs and Red have been married 44 years. She was a stewardess, and they met on a plane. They have no children. They share quarters with a waddling dachshund named Rusty and a mellowing hoard of memories. They have only memories now, said Muggs, because except for the oil Zuppke painted of Red in his wool jersey and leather helmet, which hangs over the bar, "Everything else has been shipped to the Hall of Fame. Red got tired of me polishin' every time we had company."

Red and the visitor passed a white brick fireplace and a formidable television set on the way to the patio. Red said, yes, he still watches football, "especially if it's a good college game," but "there's so many of them on TV now, and with all the time-outs they just go on forever. Football can't be so important that you'd sit and watch five or six hours of it a day. I get up and go for a beer, or go mow the lawn. I used to mow the hell out of that lawn on a Sunday afternoon."

The trouble with television, he said, "is that they try to sensationalize everything. Hell, a guy hits a home run, that's what he's supposed to do. That's why he gets all that money. When the fans realize it's not that sensational, they get bored. The media makes the Super Bowl seem like it's going to be World War III, and then after you watch it you realize it's not, and you feel cheated."

Grange sat straight in the aluminum patio chair, his posture so erect that his visitor instinctively straightened. The visitor was pleased—delighted, actually—to have found Grange so spry. The legend recounted his feats with no wasted words, as one might give a prepared speech. When the subject demanded it, he skillfully grafted the present to the past. As legends go, the Galloping Ghost had endured the march of time remarkably well.

"Football hasn't changed that much, really," Grange said, "except for the shape of the ball. The ball in the '20s and '30s was fat like a basketball, and on a windy day it was like throwing a balloon. The longer, narrower ball opened up the passing game, no question. But it took away the dropkick. An old dropkicker could kick a field goal inside the 50 with no trouble." He laughed, enjoying the irony. He said there were many ironies.

"The equipment got better and better," he said. "In one of those old helmets I'd get kicked in the head and I'd be dingy the rest of the game. Everything we wore was heavy except the helmets. But then they started making 'em so hard and heavy that coaches started using 'em like spears, getting guys hurt, so that wasn't much of an improvement.

"I don't think coaches are necessarily better today; there are just more of them. We had a coach for the line and one for the backs. Now they've got a coach for everything. It makes the game better to watch because you can specialize. But it still all boils down to blocking and tackling. You get a bunch of guys who'll do that—not can do it, but will do it—and you win."

He had tried coaching the Bears' backfield after he quit playing, but he didn't last past the third season because "it wasn't going to be my lifestyle. I didn't want to work that hard at it. Halas was the coach, and he had us in there from 8 a.m. to midnight, which wasn't my idea of a normal working day. Besides, I didn't want to have to kick some kid in the pants to make him play."

The visitor said he had seen the old film clips and had been amazed at Grange's running. "It was God-given; I couldn't take any credit," he said. "Other guys could make 90s and 100s in chemistry. I could run fast. It's the way God distributes things. I don't remember ever losing a footrace as a kid. I'd go to those church picnics and I'd win a baseball, and then my father would give me a quarter every time I won. Hell, I was a pro when I was in the sixth grade!"

He smiled, one side of his mouth rising above the other and the skin gathering around his glistening, impenetrable black eyes. "My best day in sports happened when I was 15 or 16," he said. "I'd been on the ice wagon all morning, and I went to this track meet in the middle of the day. I won six first places. Then I went back and finished my rounds and put the ice truck away."

But that didn't explain his style, the visitor said. "People say you ran with the football in a way no one ever has. How do you account for it?"

"I don't know if I can," said Grange. "It's not something you're taught. You throw a football to 10 kids and tell 'em to run at a defense, they'll do it 10 different ways. Hey, would you like a beer? Muggs, how about a couple beers?"

"They used to write about the ice wagon being good training for you," said the visitor.

"I only thought of it that way afterward, because there's no doubt it made me stronger. But I did it for the money. I was 15 or 16 when I started, and I'll never forget that first check—the unheard-of amount of $37.50. Mr. Thompson used to come by with the wagon, and we'd chase it for ice chips. One day he said he'd give any of us a dollar if we could take the tongs and carry a 75-pound block of ice on our shoulders. We all tried it, and it always slid off. None of us could do it, so I practiced. There's a knack to it; you have to hold the ice tongs so they don't come apart, and balance the block on your shoulder. When I got so I could do it he gave me the dollar and said, 'You want to work for me?'"

"The ice tongs are in the Hall of Fame now, chrome-plated," said Muggs, returning with the beer. "We'll have lunch soon," she said. "A typical Red Grange lunch."

Grange unbuttoned his jacket and leaned back in his chair. He seemed to be enjoying himself, despite Muggs's warning that he really didn't care "one way or the other" about these things anymore. "You can come," she had told the visitor, "but it won't matter to him either way."

"I'd go into the icehouse at 5 a.m.," Red said, "and I'd deliver until seven at night. I got to know so many wonderful people, going in the back door. 'Harold, are you hungry?' and I'd get a piece of sausage. I could have weighed 300 pounds. But every summer I'd save the three or four hundred bucks it took to pay for another semester at Illinois."

"You had no financial help?"

"There were no scholarships then, and I wouldn't have taken one if it had been offered. We were taught to earn those things. My father didn't have anything. He'd been a lumberjack as a young man back in Forkville, Pennsylvania, where I was born. When he moved to Wheaton, he became a policeman and was a one-man force for about 30 years. The toughest man I ever knew, my father. I'll tell you, when the drunks got off the Chicago Aurora & Elgin, they'd all run for home instead of raising Cain downtown. I don't think anything in the world scared my father. I was always afraid he'd get shot, he was so fearless. He did, once, in the foot.

"But he didn't have the money to send me to school. My mother had died when I was five, and Dad had to leave my two sisters back East for an aunt to raise. He took my younger brother, Garland, and me to Wheaton. Wheaton was a railroad town of about 4,000 people then, and probably 80 percent of them worked in Chicago. I got to be such a White Sox nut that I'd take the train in on school days, catch the 10:30 to the Wells Street station downtown, then the elevated to Comiskey Park. I didn't fool anybody. One of my teachers said, 'Harold, how'd the White Sox do yesterday?'

"They did fine, until the [1919 World Series] scandal, of course. I loved to watch Cicotte pitch, putting that glove up there like he was loading up for a spitball, and he probably didn't throw one in a hundred. And Collins and Weaver in the infield, and Joe Jackson—what a hitter. He could put it over the fence with one hand. There might have been better teams, but I never saw one."

"Had your father been an athlete?" the visitor asked.

"He could have been, he was so big and strong. He lived to 86, and he never missed a football or basketball game. He knew more about my career than I did. He hated anybody who got cocky about success. If I'd gotten cocky, he would have paddled me. But he was like everybody else in town when it came to athletics—they had an interest in you. The merchants would stop you in the street and ask what happened Saturday. Everybody was involved, in a supportive way. It was great because it made you feel like you were part of something."

The visitor asked how heavily Illinois had recruited him.

"The only time Zuppke spoke to me was when I went to Champaign for the state track meet, representing Wheaton. I won the 100 and 220, and he came and put his arm around me and said, 'If you come down, I think you have a chance of making our team.' That's the only selling job he did. Anything more than that was beneath his dignity."

"Do you think recruiting is beneath a coach's dignity?"

"Most of it. Ninety percent of the kids I knew went to Illinois because they wanted to be there. It was a matter of pride and loyalty. Also, for me, it was cheaper. But I know the Michigan kids wanted to go to Michigan, the Iowa kids went to Iowa, not because they were sweet-talked into it. I think scholarships ruined that. I don't think they should give them except when a kid can't afford school any other way, and then they should be equally available whether you play football or play in the band.

"When they started giving scholarships, they made athletes pros. What's the difference if you give a kid a scholarship or the money? What's the difference between a $5,000 scholarship and $5,000 cash? I think most of the trouble they're having now stems from that and from the alumni getting involved. It makes football too big. When football gets more important than the college, they should just forget college and form a league and play football."

"So you didn't get anything in college?"

"I didn't, and I didn't expect it. Not 10 cents. Hell, I didn't even plan to play football until I got there and my fraternity brothers made me."

"Made you?"

Grange laughed. "I was pledging Zeta Psi, and in those days they'd line you up and say, 'What sport you going out for?' I said, 'Basketball.' I always thought I was a better basketball player than anything. They said, 'You play four years of football in high school?' 'Yeah.' 'Football's bigger at Illinois than basketball. You go out for football.'

"So I went out, and about 120 guys were there trying out for the freshman team. When I saw how big they were, I didn't even check out a uniform. I came back and said, 'They're too big.' And then they got the paddle out and made me bend over. And I said, 'Football makes a lot of sense to me.'

"As it turned out, that was probably the best freshman team anybody ever had. We beat the varsity regularly, and three of us went on to make All-America our sophomore year—except that Moon Baker made it at Northwestern and Frank Wickhorst at Navy after they transferred. Earl Britton should have made it. What a player—our fullback for three years, the best blocker I ever saw. He gave me my biggest thrill in football."

"What was that?"

"The field goal against Iowa our sophomore year. It was our first big game before a big crowd, at Iowa City, 35 or 40 thousand people. I held for him, and I just sat there watching the ball go, 52 or 53 yards, as I remember. I knew immediately he had it. We won the game nine to six." Typically, Grange didn't mention that the Illini were losing 6–3 until he scored the winning touchdown with two minutes to play.

If Iowa was his biggest thrill, what about Michigan?

"What I remember about the Michigan game was the blocking. We outblocked 'em, that's all. And I remember afterward being so hungry. I went back to the fraternity, and a lot of people were partying. So a friend and I ducked out through the kitchen and went for something to eat. Then we went to a movie and went to bed."

"How'd you get number 77?"

"The guy in front of me got 76; the guy in back got 78."

"You didn't graduate, which I suppose at the time was perceived as a bad thing for college sport," the visitor said. "Do you regret it?"

"Well, I never had anybody ask me for my diploma, if that's what you mean. But I suppose I resent it a little that people mistake a lack of a diploma for a lack of brains. I was a good student. Hell, I had all kinds of trigonometry. A lot of people think if you play football you're dumb, but if you play golf or tennis you're smart.

"The thing is, I had a chance to make some money, a lot of money for me. When Herschel Walker got his chance, I couldn't blame him. I don't see how you can turn down four or five million dollars, no matter what anybody thinks. Ten or 15 years from now there'll be new Herschel Walkers. Herschel Walker has to take care of himself."

Muggs returned, holding up a pair of old football pants. They were the color of dead leaves, and beneath the stark weave of their canvas skin the mysterious bulges of protection stood out like large welts. The pants had a formidable, inviolate look, as if they were capable of sweating on their own. The old man sitting in the chair smiled and turned over the belt for the visitor to see the inscription sewn inside: RED GRANGE MODEL. "I never wore these," he said. "They were sent to us by an Indian in Oklahoma."

"They were one of your endorsements?"

"I endorsed everything there for a while."

"Tell me about Cash and Carry Pyle," the visitor said.

"Dapper, that's the first word that comes to mind. He went to the barbershop every day of his life, and he was immaculate. He wore that derby and spats and carried a cane, and he had that neat little mustache. The greatest ladies' man you ever saw. He was married five times, three times to the same woman, and despite everything you might have read, he was one of the most honest men I ever knew.

"Charlie had more good ideas than any 10 men about how to make a buck. He'd made and lost a million three or four times. If he were active today, there'd be no end to the money he'd make. But he was straight with me from the start. He owned two theaters in Champaign. One night I was in there and the usher said, 'Mr. Pyle wants to see you.' I thought he was going to give me a couple of passes.

"I went into his office and he said, 'How'd you like to make $100,000?' I said, 'You've got the wrong guy. I don't do things like that.' He said, 'I'm talking about playing pro football. I'll guarantee you that much.' I said, 'Well, I'm interested.' I was only with Charlie for about three years, but I got everything he said I'd get, and more."

What you have to remember about the times, Grange said, "was that there just didn't seem to be a future in football. Now, of course, the game gives so many atha-letes a chance, and that's good. There's money in it, and when you're at your prime you should be able to pursue it. I told Zuppke, 'I've played three years [at Illinois]. I've got more than three years left. I've got my life ahead of me. Are you going to take care of me until I'm 60?'

"We had some terrific arguments in his kitchen. He'd close the door and keep Mrs. Zuppke out. I said, 'You teach football, I'll take care of Grange.' I just couldn't accept the fact that it was all right for him to coach football for his life and not for me to play it. But most people take care of themselves first, and that's what he was doing. The colleges were scared to death that the pros would lure away their players with money.

"That's why I did it, of course. Football itself wasn't that important to me. But I went from having nothing to owning two or three cars at a time. I bought my father a $25,000 house, which was an expensive house in those days. I spent money like it was going out of circulation, until I learned better. I was a big shot. I drank Dom Perignon champagne. I wore a raccoon coat. I'd go into a restaurant and order from the right side of the menu. After I became a pro, if something I ordered didn't cost $20, I didn't want it.

"It was fun, but I don't think it was a good phase of my life. I noticed one thing that still seems to apply. Once you start getting paid to play, the crowds treat you differently. I got booed for the first time as a pro. It was a new feeling. I can understand it, though. They expect you to play up to what you're being paid. When we made that tour, the crowds only cared that I produced. They didn't care if I was tired or beat-up. I can't blame them. But it made football different for me.

"I don't have any complaints. I've lived the way I wanted, done what I wanted. I don't owe anybody. I couldn't be this way if it weren't for football.

But I wonder now and then how the other guys are doing, guys who helped make the pro game, guys who played even after I did.

"Pro ball in the early days got two or three inches on the third page. After we made those tours, it was getting top headlines. We spread the NFL across the country, taking it to towns that never saw a pro game, doing anything to push the product. We played in Memphis one year, and after the game started, we were driving for a touchdown when the promoter came running on the field and told everybody we'd have to start over. The backer of the game was the founder of the Piggly Wiggly stores, Clarence Saunders, and he'd gotten caught in traffic and missed the kickoff. So we started over.

"They're benefiting today because of the things we did. And isn't it too bad that the NFL never took care of those early players? I complained a few times, because we had guys in hospitals, guys who had had amputations because of football injuries. Guys who had problems. I thought the game could have done something for them, but it never did. As far as I know, pro football hasn't done anything for anybody except lately, and that's mostly for itself. I never made a real stink about it, but I was sad for the oldtimers."

Muggs returned with lunch—homemade soup, finger-size crackers coated with cheese, and fresh grapes. "That's the way we like to eat," she said. "Simple but to the point." Grange didn't finish his soup. Later, Muggs went to a dental appointment, and Grange and the visitor moved into the kitchen for coffee. Rusty rested on a plaid cushion under the table.

"How did you like Hollywood?" the visitor asked.

Grange said it was fun, that he had been flattered and petted by a lot of important people. "I went to the parties and had some interesting dates," he said. "I played poker with Adolphe Menjou and Andy Devine, and Mr. Kennedy was wonderful to me. But it was the hardest job I ever had. The best part was the blood-and-thunder stuff—the fights, the chases. I did a lot of the stunts myself, riding a motorcycle in some scenes. My dad taught me when he was a cop, and I was a pretty good motorcycle rider. But I didn't want to work that hard."

"What about television? You worked hard at that for a long time."

"Well, it's so demanding. You say the wrong word, people make a big thing out of it. Make a mistake in football, you can cover it up. If it's on TV, it's out. It can make you nervous. I actually didn't talk too much when I did television. Now these color guys hold a clinic after every play to let you know how much they know about the game. They're wrong half the time."

He said he could understand the complaints about his grammar, "although we all make those mistakes. The part I didn't like was when they wanted us to harp on the bad things. I think a lot of guys do it—criticize atha-letes, criticize coaches—to make themselves look good, but it doesn't. When I saw a mistake, I didn't make a big deal, because I didn't want to hurt a guy's feelings. There isn't anything in life where mistakes aren't made."

He said all the celebrated atha-letes he had met had finally come to a live-and-let-live outlook on life. "Babe Ruth came to my room that first year in New York. He called from the lobby. I'd never met him, so I asked him to come up. He said, 'Kid, I want to give you two pieces of advice: Don't pay any attention to what they say or write about you. And don't pick up too many checks.'"

The real book on Ruth, though, he said, was that "when I was with him, I couldn't spend a dime. He picked up checks quicker than anybody. He'd say, 'I'll take that, kid.' There was never a more down-to-earth guy than Babe Ruth."

What about the other starry lights in his constellation who now, in retrospect, shine so brightly? Did he realize how golden the Golden Age was? "No, I don't think so," said Grange. "It's something you accept as the way things are supposed to be. I can't think of a reason for it, except maybe the atha-letes knew the details of their games better in those days. You never stopped learning the details. Coaches would spend hour after hour drilling you. At Illinois we took batting practice, and then we took more batting practice [yes, he played baseball, too]. We never complained because we liked it."

What about Dempsey. Did he know Dempsey?

"I met Jack at a party in New York, one of those 'How are you, Mr. Dempsey,' 'Nice to meet you, Mr. Grange,' and you shake hands. After that I'd go around to his restaurant on Broadway in Manhattan, and we'd sit and talk. The trouble was I didn't know anything about boxing, and he didn't know anything about football.

"Bobby Jones I met at a banquet in Atlanta, and I thought, 'What a smart man and a nice man.' But I couldn't really talk golf with him, because golf was too financial for me. I could appreciate tennis a little more because it was easy to see that it took a good atha-lete to play it well. Pyle introduced me to Bill Tilden at a match at the old Madison Square Garden. Must have been 1928 because I was living in New York then. What I remember about Tilden was his quickness. He had those long arms and legs, and you couldn't get a ball past him. But his quickness was the thing—something all the great atha-letes have in one form or another. That and good legs. Even golfers have to have good legs."

But most of those star crossings, Grange said, were only that—brief encounters: "I met Cobb through a boxer friend in Wheaton. He took me around to the Tiger bench before a game at Comiskey Park, and Cobb said hello. I remember I was glad to see him lose to the White Sox. Jim Thorpe, of course, was my No. 1 guy in football. I played against him in a couple of those exhibitions when he was past 40 and out of shape. I never saw him in his prime, but Halas did and he said he lived up to his clippings.

"The thing I remember about Thorpe was that he wanted to borrow everything from you—your helmet, your shoes. Otherwise, he didn't have a lot to say. He'd let you carry the conversation. I guess there was just so much inside him, being an Indian in a white man's world. He was fiercely proud of that, and he wouldn't take any stuff about Indians. But you'd never hear him say, 'I scored four touchdowns that game.' You'd have to ask. Once you asked him about anything or anybody, though, he'd give it to you straight—'I think so-and-so was horse manure.'

"I remember the first time we had a drink together. He said, 'Are you sure you want this? I know I do, but are you sure you do?' Drinking wasn't something Thorpe was scared of; he was pretty familiar with it. In those days, though, atha-letes weren't supposed to touch the stuff, and he was concerned about me. I said, 'I guess I'll pass.'"

It must have been an exciting time, the visitor said, "and to be so well known."

"Well, something always happens to keep you in line. When Pyle took us to Washington, Senator McKinley of Illinois sent a car around to take Halas and me to the White House to meet President Coolidge. He said, 'Mr. President, this is Mr. Grange and Mr. Halas. They're with the Chicago Bears.' Mr. Coolidge said, 'Glad to meet you fellows. I always did like animal acts.' He didn't know anything about football, which is maybe the way it ought to be."

Finally, the visitor got up to leave. Grange seemed sorry to see him go and invited him to come back "anytime." As they walked to the rented car, the visitor noted that the birdseed was all gone. He recalled what Zuppke had said about Grange. Zuppke had once seen a deer bound by in a national park, and he stopped his car and exclaimed aloud, "There goes Red Grange!"

The visitor recited the story for Grange and told how Zuppke, years later, had remarked, "They can argue all they want about the greatest football player who ever lived. I was satisfied I had him when I had Red Grange."

The Galloping Ghost laughed. "I played football the only way I knew how," he said. "If you have the football and 11 guys are after you, if you're smart, you'll run. It was no big deal."

JANUARY 13, 1997

Frozen in Time

The Packers are reborn, but their hallowed home remains as it was when Vince Lombardi stalked the sidelines

BY JOHNETTE HOWARD

There was a time when the Green Bay Packers' Lambeau Field wasn't the quaint anomaly it is today. Everyone played football on grass, and there were no Teflon roofs to shut out the midday sun, no domes to block the late-autumn wind. When mud-spattered linemen Forrest Gregg and Jerry Kramer hoisted coach Vince Lombardi on their shoulders in 1961 for his first NFL title ride, only God's gray sky hung overhead.

Franchise free agency didn't exist back then either. There was no threat of the Packers' being wooed away by some Sun Belt city offering a percentage of the revenue generated from the sale of personal seat licenses. Why, the world hadn't even heard of turf toe when Lombardi stalked Lambeau's frozen sidelines in his trademark overcoat, shrieking, "Hey! Whaddaya doin' out there?" in his best Brooklynese. "With Lombardi it was never cold here," says former All-Pro Fuzzy Thurston, who played guard for Green Bay from 1959 to '67. "Before games he'd just say something like, 'Men, it's a little blustery out there today.' Blustery, see? Then he'd say, 'It's our kind of day. Now get out there and strut around like it's the middle of July.'"

The Packers were a league power then, as they are now, and Lambeau Field was the NFL's answer to Boston Garden or Yankee Stadium—hallowed ground where dynasties were born. During Lombardi's nine-year stay the Packers won five league championships, including the first two Super Bowls. Twenty-nine winters have passed since Green Bay last had a championship team, yet within the magical space of Lambeau Field it still seems to be 1967.

Once the ball is kicked off and pads start to clatter, the Titletown past and the promising present almost become one on the floor of the old stadium. The sight of defensive end Reggie White barreling into an opponent's backfield conjures up memories of Hall of Famer Willie Davis. Quarterback Brett Favre's 1992 burst from anonymity—he led the Packers to an electrifying, come-from-behind victory over the Cincinnati Bengals in relief of starter Don Majkowski during coach Mike Holmgren's first season—wasn't all that different from Bart Starr's midseason ascension in 1959, Lombardi's first year.

Visitors from far and wide still stop by Lambeau and ask to be shown the spot in the south end zone where, in the 1967 NFL championship game, better known as the Ice Bowl, Starr made the one-yard touchdown plunge that gave the Pack a 21–17 win over the Dallas Cowboys. Grainy black-and-white photos show Starr burrowing across the goal line with 13 seconds to play, his arms hugging the football as if he were protecting a newborn from the -46° windchill.

For four decades Lambeau Field has been a landmark moored on the southwest edge of Green Bay, its underside sunk into a gently sloping hill, making it look like a ship run aground, never to leave. But, says Packers president and chief executive officer Bob Harlan, "it's not so much what the stadium looks like; it's what happened here that makes this place unique. A story like this will never happen in professional sports again."

Football history isn't learned in Green Bay as much as it's lived and touched and felt. Linebacker Ray Nitschke, who played from 1958 to '72, isn't just one of the 19 members of the Pro Football Hall of Fame whose names form a ring at skybox level around the inside of Lambeau: Nitschke is in the Green Bay phone book, and he still attends home games, often eschewing a skybox for a seat in the stands. Call Nitschke at home and ask for an audience, and he's likely to reply, "Let's talk over the phone. I might scare ya in person."

Starr and Kramer still come back to Lambeau for the Packers' annual fantasy camp, and numerous players return for alumni day and the opportunity to walk along the hash marks one more time as applause rains down, as it always has. Thurston, who has survived throat cancer and two hip replacements, still owns and operates Shenanigan's, a neighborhood bar on the southeast fringe of town. On one wall he has begun a collection of mostly out-of-state license plates given to him by patrons; all are vanity plates bearing some expression of support for the Packers (GO PACK, for example, or GBP FAN) "Forget Dallas," Thurston says. "The Green Bay Packers are America's Team."

Martha's Coffee Club, a feisty group of 40 or so fans, some of whom have been meeting since 1947, convenes in a diner near Lambeau at 9 a.m. every weekday year-round to discuss the Packers' fortunes. In accordance with a set of arcane rules the club levies 25-cent fines for transgressions such as talking about something other than football, and the members roll dice to see who picks up the check—visitors not excepted.

When the Packers return from an important road game, win or lose, townspeople leave their porch lights on as a show of support. When a heavy snowfall hits the area in the days leading up to a game, the front office puts an announcement in the *Green Bay Press-Gazette* asking fans to show up at Lambeau, shovel in hand. For six dollars an hour citizens come by the dozens to clear the stands. (More than 150 people showed up the weekend before Christmas after a storm dumped 10 inches of snow on Green Bay.) "It's like a time warp here," says Packers wideout Robert Brooks, who has been with the Packers since 1992. "There's an aura, and you can feel it when you're in the stadium. It's almost like you're still back when Lombardi was here. It's just that the names on the jerseys have changed."

The oft-told story of the good old championship days when the NFL's smallest city (current population: 96,466) boasted a team good enough to tweak its big-city rivals is being replayed now that the Packers, 8–0 in playoff games at Lambeau and winners of 27 of their last 28 there overall, are one home victory away from finally getting back to the Super Bowl. And it's made all the sweeter for Packers fans because the more things change in the rest of pro sports, the more things remain blissfully the same in Green Bay.

In this era of extortionist owners, Packers fans needn't worry about getting jilted. "We're a nonprofit, public corporation whose only business is football," Harlan says. The owners of the team are 1,915 stockholders from all walks of life, most of whom live in Wisconsin. (However, there are stockholders from all 50 states and three foreign countries.) When the team, which was founded in 1919, was on the brink of bankruptcy in 1950, about 5,000 shares of stock were offered to the public at $25 apiece. No dividends have ever been paid; all profits have been plowed back into the franchise. According to the Packers' bylaws, anyone wishing to sell shares must first turn them over to the executive committee of the team's board of directors, who then decide to either reissue the shares or buy them back. No individual can own more than 200 shares, and if the shareholders ever vote to sell their investment (the Packers' estimated worth is $166 million), the profits will go to the Sullivan-Wallen American Legion Post on Sal Street in Green Bay.

The Packers, who draw from all around Wisconsin and are sold out on a season-ticket basis, have played before 175 consecutive sellouts at Lambeau, dating back to 1960. A Lambeau-record crowd of 60,787 witnessed last Saturday's 35–14 divisional playoff win over the San Francisco 49ers. There were all of three no-shows. This season a game-day scalping zone was established one block from the stadium, and the action there has been fierce: A $28 end-zone seat goes for between $125 and $200, depending on the opponent. The waiting list for season tickets stands at more than 28,000, and only eight people from last year's list received tickets for this season. In 1985, when the Pack announced plans to construct 72 skyboxes, the suites were all leased within 24 hours. Lambeau now has 198 skyboxes, and the waiting list for them exceeds 230.

The easiest way to get season tickets is through the death of an immediate family member who leaves the prized objects behind in his or her will. Green Bay ticket manager Mark Wagner admits he has heard every ruse in his 19 years on the job—sob stories, bald-faced lies, even offers of bribes—from Packers fans determined to get season seats. Inevitably, some impatient fans suspect that others have come by their tickets by less-than-ethical means, even though the transfer of the title to tickets requires notarization. Some fans have even blown the whistle on others who have renewed the tickets of a relative who died without bequeathing the tickets to them. And then? "Well," Wagner says, "then we have to call them and, well, you know." Ask them why they're not dead? "Yeah," he says with a laugh.

People go out of their way to stop at Lambeau, even when it's empty. In 1996 more than 29,000 visitors took the 90-minute tour of the place. President Clinton dropped in after a Labor Day campaign speech in nearby De Pere. Harlan recalls leaving work one day last August when a van bearing Kansas plates pulled into a stadium parking lot. The driver jumped out, fell to his knees and began bowing with his arms outstretched while his passengers laughed and snapped pictures. "Pilgrimages, that's what they are," says Char Sievert, a tour guide who has had season tickets since 1956, the year she graduated from high school. "Last year a man on one of my tours said, 'I saw the Colosseum in Rome last year. Now this!'"

Many Packers say there's nowhere they'd rather play than in Green Bay. When more than 4,000 fans showed up for a training-camp workout last summer, awestruck rookie center Mike Flanagan asked a teammate, "Doesn't anybody in Green Bay have a job?" Wideout Don Beebe spent six years playing before the rabid fans of the Buffalo Bills, yet he says, "I'd give a little edge to the people here. I mean, we had 45,000 people in the stadium for our first intrasquad scrimmage this year. It was unbelievable."

Brooks popularized the Lambeau Leap, the ritual in which a Packer who scores a TD vaults into the end-zone stands like a salmon swimming upstream. He says the idea came to him before the 1995 season. Sterling Sharpe, Green Bay's career receptions leader, had been forced into retirement with a neck injury, and Brooks was entering his first year as Sharpe's replacement. Rather than slink onto center stage, Brooks says he wanted to ingratiate himself with the Lambeau crowd by doing something "crazy, out of the ordinary, to get the fans' confidence." He remembered how safety LeRoy Butler had tried to leap into the seats after returning a fumble for a touchdown in a December '93 victory over the Los Angeles Raiders, which clinched a playoff spot for Green Bay. "Except LeRoy didn't get all the way in," Brooks says with a chuckle. "He stuck to the wall like Velcro. I said, When I score at Lambeau, I'm jumping all the way in."

Which is exactly what Brooks did on Sept. 17, 1995, after catching a 19-yard touchdown pass from Favre during the second quarter of a 14–6 win over the New York Giants. The fans loved it. By the end of last season most of the Packers' scorers were jubilantly mimicking him. "The first time I did it and saw the TV highlights, I thought, Man, that is so much fun! It's just the best," Brooks says. "You can dance and do all that other stuff in the end zone. But this, it's like you're a rock star, and you're trusting your fans completely, and you dive off the stage, and they throw you back on. It's the best feeling in the world. And I don't think you could do it anywhere but here."

The irony? For all the memories that Lambeau has provided, it's not much to look at. Its beauty is in its throwback simplicity. There are no flourishes, certainly nothing like the grand pillars that adorn Chicago's 73-year-old Soldier Field. Lambeau's exterior is a serviceable skin of steel sheeting painted in the Packers' colors of forest green and stoplight yellow.

Steve Sabol, president of NFL Films, has been coming to Green Bay for 30 years, or ever since he and his dad, Ed, used to preview their work for Lombardi on a bedsheet hung on the basement wall of Lombardi's house. While Sabol agrees that Lambeau is the "holy ground of the NFL," he adds, "When I think of NFL stadiums, there are so many other more eccentric places that come to mind.

"At Giants Stadium you've got the Hawk—that terrible wind. And Phil Simms can tell you how three-fourths of his touchdown passes there came in the north end zone, where Jimmy Hoffa is supposedly buried. Texas Stadium has its shadows. Al Davis used to always complain that his Oakland

Raiders could never beat those great Pittsburgh Steelers teams at Three Rivers because the sidelines freeze before the middle of the field, so Cliff Branch could never get open deep. To me, those are the stadiums that have a sense of mystery. Lambeau is just a nice, friendly, intimate place to watch a game."

It was built on a shoestring budget of $960,000 and opened at the start of the 1957 season. The Packers had outgrown their previous home—City Stadium, a 25,000-seat bandbox so primitive that it didn't have women's rest rooms and players used the facilities at adjacent East High for locker rooms. At a rally the weekend before the balloting on whether to build a stadium, George Halas, the legendary owner and coach of the rival Chicago Bears, told Green Bay voters that the only way the Packers could continue to compete in the NFL was with a new facility. The bond issue passed by a 2-to-1 margin.

A game-day walk around Lambeau's main concourse reveals no-frills concession stands, cinder-block rest rooms and metal framing that supports the grandstands. Over the past 15 years Green Bay has poured $40 million into stadium updates such as skyboxes, club seating and JumboTron replay boards. Seating has been expanded seven times since 1961, increasing Lambeau's capacity from the original 32,150 to 60,790. All of the outdoor seats are backless aluminum bleachers. Lambeau's single-level, bowl-shaped configuration assures that there are no obstructed views.

Inside the home locker room there's no cracking Naugahyde sofa on which notorious playboy halfback Paul Hornung might've slept off a hangover, no battered oak desk on which Lombardi could've propped up his cleats. Instead there's the usual wall-to-wall carpet, walk-in dressing cubicles and players-only lounge with a mammoth TV. Action photos line the walls of the Green Bay executive offices, and the Packers celebrate their 11 title seasons by listing the years in the southeast corner of Lambeau, at the same level as the names of the Hall of Famers.

And there aren't any claims of helpful gremlins blowing field goal attempts wide right or ghosts haunting Lambeau—though it has been pointed out that many fans have asked the Packers if their ashes could be scattered on the field after they die. "We always say no," says head groundskeeper Todd Edlebeck, "but, you know, it could've happened. Some mornings you can just tell someone's been on the field overnight. Carts that we left out will be moved. Equipment has been handled."

Lambeau's most famous feature—the Frozen Tundra—isn't all that it's cracked up to be. In the summer of 1967 Lombardi had the field equipped with a then newfangled underground heating system, which works something like an electric blanket. About 14 miles of plastic-covered cables, spaced one foot apart, run sideline to sideline and are buried six inches beneath the surface. A General Electric press release touting the system promised "September-like playing conditions throughout the season. Instead of a frozen field, the Wisconsin contests will be played on a green, soft, frost-free turf."

Meaning the Frozen Tundra isn't really frozen? "Well, the system doesn't do much good when the air temperature drops below 20," Edlebeck says. "But the field's not frozen nearly as often as it's said to be. I guess it sounds cute to say *frozen tundra*. And at least when ESPN's Chris Berman says it, he says it as a joke. What bugs you is when TV announcers say it's a frozen tundra and they haven't even been on the field. My mother used to watch all the games on TV, and, you know, that really used to burn her up."

It has been 40 years since quarterback Babe Parilli and tight end Gary Knafelc made opening day (Sept. 29, 1957) at Lambeau a success for the Packers, combining on a fourth-quarter touchdown pass that clinched a 21–17 win over the Bears. It has been 32 years since the name of the facility was changed from City Stadium to honor team founder and longtime coach Curly Lambeau, the bon vivant who won seven championships during his 31 seasons in Green Bay, married three times and in 1922 paid the club's $250 league entry fee with money he got from the sale of a friend's car.

Just as the 1967 championship game is rarely called anything but the Ice Bowl, some other games have been so compelling that Packers fans have slapped titles on them, too. The Snow Bowl was an '85 game against the Tampa Bay Buccaneers; a 16-inch snowfall blanketed the city, and many fans drove their snowmobiles to the stadium, where, predictably, the Packers whipped their warm-weather opponents 21–0. The Instant Replay Game? That was the one in '89 during which Bears coach Mike Ditka went ballistic after officials reversed themselves and announced that Majkowski hadn't been over the line of scrimmage after all when on the last play of the game he'd tossed a game-winning touchdown pass to Sharpe. The hard feelings run so deep that the Chicago media guide still carries an asterisk next to the result of that game.

From 1973 through '92 the Packers languished, qualifying for the playoffs only in the 1982 strike-shortened season. But Green Bay fans still laugh about the 1980 season opener at Lambeau in which the Bears blocked Chester Marcol's overtime field goal attempt, only to see Marcol catch the ricochet and scoot 25 yards for the winning score. Marcol looked like an accountant in his thick, black-frame glasses, and he ran as if he had pails on his feet.

Nitschke's finest Lambeau moment came in the 1965 NFL title game against the Cleveland Browns. He was assigned to shadow the great Jim Brown, who finished with just 50 yards rushing on 12 carries, and his diving, fingertip deflection of a sure touchdown pass intended for Brown sealed the Packers' 23–12 win. Hornung outdid Brown with a scintillating 105-yard performance. After scoring a third-quarter touchdown, Hornung ran to the sidelines shouting, "It's just like the good old days!" That led Lombardi to crow, "Did you hear that? Just like the good old days, boys!"

When Harlan, a member of the Packers' front office since 1971, looks at the sports world today, he notes that the Bears are talking about abandoning Soldier Field, that Boston Garden is no more and that if George Steinbrenner has his way, Yankee Stadium may soon follow. "Every time I see another old ballpark bite the dust, I think, That's too bad," Harlan says. "There will never be another Yankee Stadium. Regardless of what you name the new one, it will never be *the* Yankee Stadium. It's the same with Lambeau Field. There have been just too many world championships and glory times here. I think for the NFL to lose a story like the Green Bay Packers would be a disaster."

But Harlan says it could happen—if the NFL ever changes some of the fundamental ways it does business, especially revenue sharing. No less than 86% of the Packers' revenue comes from shared sources—63% from the league's television contract and another 23% from ticket receipts, licensing agreements and other income that the NFL divides among its teams. Right now, business is booming. The Packers have a rainy-day fund of $21 million. Beginning last year they picked up an additional $2.5 million in annual skybox revenue by dropping an arrangement under which they played three games a season at Milwaukee County Stadium. For the first time since 1932 the Packers played all their home games in Green Bay. There's talk of boosting revenue from Lambeau by staging concerts there, increasing sales of stadium advertising, opening concourse restaurants and raising by $5,000 the prices on the bargain-basement skyboxes, which go for $19,000 to $25,000 per season.

However, Lambeau's structure won't support further expansion. Green Bay has the second-lowest average ticket prices in the league, and even with the long waiting list, Harlan doesn't believe the market can bear an increase. And what if when the collective bargaining agreement expires after the 2002 season, there is no longer a salary cap and teams have no restraints in pursuing free agents? "We know there could come a time when, first, we just won't have the money to stay competitive," Harlan says. "And, well, I can't sit here and say that for 10, 15 or 20 years this stadium is going to be fine. Because I'm not sure it is."

In the 1970s some businessmen approached the Packers' board of directors with plans for a dome. Smiling bemusedly, Harlan says, "The idea didn't go over very well." And he doubts it would now. "When you go out in our stadium and sit in the stands for a game, you just get the feeling this is football the way it's supposed to be played," he says. "Somehow those voices just sound louder in that terrible chill."

When Thurston is asked what Lombardi would think of playing in a dome, his eyebrows arch like those of a startled cat. He smirks. "Lombardi would say, 'No dome—no, no, no,'" he says, his chin jutting out. "He'd say, 'Football is meant to be played outdoors. Now and forever.'"

OCTOBER 12, 2009

The NFL's Jackie Robinson

He broke professional football's color barrier in 1946, yet even though he played alongside Robinson in college, few people remember the great running back Kenny Washington or the shameful history of segregation in the NFL

BY ALEXANDER WOLFF

The actors took their marks, director Stanley Kubrick stood at the ready, and Woody Strode turned on the 100-yard stare he had deployed so effectively a decade earlier on the football field. By then, in late 1959, Strode had largely moved on from the frustration of his single season in the NFL. He and Kenny Washington, his teammate at UCLA, had broken the league's color barrier with the Los Angeles Rams in 1946, and since then Strode had cashed in on the physique that once made Leni Riefenstahl beg him to model for her. He had gone to Canada and won a Grey Cup and spent off-seasons barnstorming as a good-guy pro wrestler. Now he was in the movies, preparing for the scene in *Spartacus* in which he and Kirk Douglas are ordered to fight to the death. Suddenly Strode heard the voice of another actor in the cast.

"Woody Strode!" said Laurence Olivier.

"Yes, sir?"

"I'm a fan of yours and Kenny Washington's."

"I don't know what I'm doing here in your business," Strode said.

"What you're about to do," Olivier replied, "I could never do."

What Strode does in *Spartacus*—he subdues a fellow slave in one of cinema's epic one-on-one battles but refuses to kill him and is instead finished off by a Roman general, played by Olivier—emblemizes the ferocious, tragic grace with which Strode and Washington made history. Today those feats go essentially unremembered. Their NFL careers were brief and, in Strode's case, personally unfulfilling; both men had passed their primes when the league finally admitted them. But together they were to the NFL what their UCLA football teammate Jackie Robinson would be to major league baseball one year later: pulling guards in the sweep of history.

Baseball, bless its pastoral soul, offers a tidy and reassuring desegregation narrative. It's a story that reflects how we like to think of ourselves, as a society forever improving if not perfecting itself, and it offers ennobling roles for whites as well as blacks. We know the archetypes: commissioner Kenesaw Mountain Landis, overtaken symbol of the bigoted past; Brooklyn Dodgers general manager Branch Rickey, patron of a new day; Robinson, who fulfills his potential once given the chance. Robinson is one of the first men we see when we visit Cooperstown, at the very portals of the Hall of Fame, in life-sized bronze paired with the words CHARACTER and COURAGE.

By rights the NFL should be able to celebrate a history of abiding enlightenment. Whereas organized baseball began excluding African-Americans in 1898 and kept them out for the next five decades, pro football's Shelby (Ohio) Athletic Club paid a black man, Charles Follis, to play for it in 1904. In 1920 the Akron Pros' black quarterback, Fritz Pollard, was the first great star of the league that would two years later rename itself the NFL, and he even served as his team's player-coach. (Not just a black NFL quarterback, not just a black NFL coach, but *both at the same time!*) At the peak of African-American participation, in 1923, six players suited up in the NFL. But as the pro game grew in popularity, the ranks thinned to just two in 1933. The following year the league began a stretch of 12 all-white seasons that, Arthur Ashe writes in his survey of the African-American athlete, *A Hard Road to Glory*, has to be "one of the blackest spots on the record of American professional sports.... All NFL records should properly show asterisks beside any records made during this era."

How did the league come to bleach itself white? No single explanation entirely satisfies. Pro football had no strong commissioner like Landis, who categorically barred blacks. But in 1933 the NFL restructured itself into two divisions of five teams each, with a season-ending title game, which led to more media attention and presumably a desire to emulate baseball and its commercially successful formula of large markets and all-white rosters.

Paul Schissler coached the Chicago Cardinals' Joe Lillard, one of the last two blacks to play before the ban, and after the 1933 season Schissler told the *Brooklyn Eagle* that the Cardinals had let Lillard go in the best interests of both club and player. "He was a marked man, and I don't mean that just the Southern boys took it out on him either," the coach said. "After a while whole teams, Northern and Southern alike, would give Joe the works." But Ashe and others speculate that owners were just as likely favoring white players in a shrinking labor market. The NFL had shed franchises as the Depression wore on, and surviving teams carried fewer and fewer players.

Whatever the reasons, the period from 1934 to '46 is a stain on the names of the NFL's founding families. "Among the NFL's decision makers during those 12 years were some of the most storied individuals in the history of the game," writes Andy Piascik in his recently released book, *Gridiron Gauntlet*. "Their commitment to apartheid was seemingly stronger than their commitment to winning championships. The Bears under [George] Halas did not employ a single black player in their first 32 seasons. The Giants began play in 1925 and did not sign any blacks until 1948. The Steelers were all-white from the day Ray Kemp was released [in 1933] until 1952." As for George Preston Marshall, owner of the Washington Redskins, Piascik writes: "He at least did not pretend there were no blacks good enough to make his team. Unlike the others, he was honest enough to admit that he simply didn't want them around."

Halas claimed to journalist Myron Cope in 1970 that "no great black players were in the colleges then," but such protestations are disingenuous and even slanderous. During the period of the NFL's segregation, a time when it was hard for them to win the favor of white selectors, no fewer than nine black players earned All-America honors, and not one got an NFL tryout. Northwestern coach Dick Hanley called Ozzie Simmons, a back at Iowa from 1934 to '36, "the best I've ever seen." In 1937 Grantland Rice named Jerome (Brud) Holland of Cornell a first-team All-America end. Other African-American stars included Julius Franks, a guard at Michigan; Bernie Jefferson, a running back at Northwestern; and Wilmeth Sidat-Singh, a quarterback at Syracuse. Scores more played in obscurity at historically black colleges.

The league instituted a 20-round draft in 1939, yet no team chose an African-American until 1949. Even with the advent of World War II, when the NFL was so shorthanded that a desperate Halas coaxed Bronko Nagurski out of a five-year retirement and owners considered signing high school players, blacks needed not apply.

The snubbing of Kenny Washington indicts the football establishment more than any other exclusion. Though he led the nation in total offense as a senior in 1939, and played 580 of a possible 600 minutes by doubling as the anchor of the defensive secondary, Washington was relegated to second-team All-America by Hearst, the AP, the UP and Grantland Rice, while the East-West Shrine Game passed him over entirely. Yet when *Liberty* magazine polled more than 1,600 collegians on the best player they had faced on the field, Washington was the lone man named on the ballot of everyone he played against. It is only fitting that Washington—of whom former UCLA teammate Ray Bartlett once said, "He could smile when his lip was bleeding"—gouged the first bricks out of the NFL's all-whites wall.

The story of the NFL's integration offers no comfort to the league, which would prove notoriously slow to trust blacks with the positions of greatest responsibility, on the field, along the sideline or in the front office. Nor does the story offer the angels or redemptive moments we'd like or expect. "Integrating the NFL was the low point of my life," Strode told SI in an unpublished interview before his death. "There was nothing nice about it. History doesn't know who we are. Kenny was one of the greatest backs in the history of the game, and kids today have no idea who he is.

"If I have to integrate heaven, I don't want to go."

Woody Strode grew up not far from the L.A. Coliseum, in what's now known as South Central Los Angeles but was then called the East Side. Just as he entered Jefferson High, his father, a mason with Native American blood, moved the family to Central Avenue, which ran like a high-tension line through the black community. As a high school freshman Woody spread only 130 pounds over a 6'1" frame, but he soon filled out enough for the *Los Angeles Examiner* to rave, "He haunts his end like a departed spirit, taking out four men on one play if need be."

Kenny Washington hailed from Lincoln Heights, where his was the rare black family among mostly working-class Italians. A woman who lived next door would regularly drag six-year-old Kenny to early-morning mass. His father, Edgar (Blue) Washington, was a rolling stone, playing Negro leagues baseball between intermittent jobs in Hollywood. He would collect from a studio, then disappear until his pockets went light. Kenny would write him out of his life and credit two others with raising him: his grandmother Susie, a grammar school custodian beloved for vetting the suitors of the daughters of her Italian neighbors; and his uncle Rocky, who would become the first black uniformed lieutenant in the Los Angeles Police Department.

"I had a black principal in my grammar school when I was a kid," Strode would recall. "On the Pacific Coast there wasn't anything we couldn't do. As we got out of the L.A. area we found these racial tensions. Hell, we thought we *were* white."

The two met in 1936 as freshmen at UCLA, which welcomed black football players. In the idiom acceptable at the time, a local sportswriter called them the Goal Dust Twins, a play on the two black children featured on the box of Fairbank's Gold Dust, a popular soap powder. "When I met Kenny, I swear he was nothing but a nice Italian kid," Strode wrote in his 1990 memoir, *Goal Dust*. "He had an accent that was half-Italian."

Washington—a.k.a. the Kingfish, after a character in the radio comedy series *Amos 'n' Andy*—stood astride the Westwood campus. During two seasons of varsity baseball he hit .454 and .350, far better than Robinson. Rod Dedeaux, the longtime USC baseball coach who scouted for the Dodgers, believed that Washington also had a better arm, more power and more agility than Robinson.

Though pigeon-toed and knock-kneed, Washington ran with power and a prodigious straight-arm. "He had a crazy gait, like he had two broken legs," Tom Harmon, a teammate with the Rams, told SI before his death in 1990. "He'd be coming at you straight, and it would look like he was going sideways." As a tailback in the single wing, Washington passed as much as he ran. In 1937, with five minutes to play and the Bruins trailing USC 19–0, he threw for two touchdowns in 29 seconds, then added what could have been the winner if Strode had held on to his pass at the one-yard line. The first scoring pass traveled 62 yards in the air. Afterward UCLA coach Bill Spaulding went by the USC locker room to congratulate his counterpart, Howard Jones. "It's all right to come out now," Spaulding called through the door. "Kenny's stopped passing!"

When the Washington State coach taunted him from the sideline with the n word, Washington went after him. Opposing players would sometimes pile-drive Washington's face into the lime used to line the fields; Strode and other Bruins would take names and settle scores on subsequent plays. But Strode remembered Washington's reluctance to play the same game: "If Kenny knocked a guy down, he'd pick him up after the play was over."

As the wingback in motion during Washington's senior season, Robinson helped free up Washington, who led the Bruins to an undefeated 6–0–4 season, including a scoreless tie with USC, which ended as UCLA's final drive stalled inside the Trojans' four-yard line. Years later it would be easy to read a pattern into both those dramatic games with USC: They seemed to prefigure a fate in which Washington would fall just short or lose out to the clock. When he left the Coliseum field as a Bruin for the final time, Washington received an ovation that sounded, as Strode put it, as if "the pope of Rome had come out."

Robinson, writing for *Gridiron* magazine in 1971, called Washington "the greatest football player I have ever seen.... I'm sure he had a deep hurt over the fact that he never had become a national figure in professional sports. Many blacks who were great athletes years ago grow old with this hurt."

Anticipating the snubs that would inflame the black press, *Pittsburgh Courier* columnist Wendell Smith wrote, "When the All-American teams are selected this year, the one with Washington's name missing can be called the 'un-American' team." Washington did play in the College All-Star Game at Soldier Field, scoring a touchdown, and afterward Halas asked him to stick around Chicago, saying he would "see what he could do," Washington recalled. A week later the Bears owner told Washington that he couldn't use him.

Similarly, New York *Daily News* columnist Jimmy Powers appealed to Giants founder Tim Mara and Brooklyn (football) Dodgers co-owner Dan Topping to sign him. Yet Washington went unselected in the NFL draft, prompting NBC Radio commentator Sam Balter to blast league executives in a broadcast *j'accuse*: "You know ... he would be the greatest sensation in pro league history with any one of your ball clubs ... [yet] *none* of you chose him."

Washington spent the next year coaching the UCLA freshmen and finishing up his degree, then joined the LAPD. As undergraduates he and Strode had earned spending money as porters on Warner Brothers movie sets, and Washington picked up several film roles. In the meantime Strode took a job serving subpoenas and escorting prisoners for the L.A. County DA's office, and after Pearl Harbor he joined an Army football team at March Field in Riverside, Calif. When they could, Washington and Strode played in a pro league that would have them, the Pacific Coast Football League (PCFL).

Washington never failed to earn all-league recognition during his four minor league seasons, despite several knee injuries, including one in 1941 that kept him out of the service. Legend had it that he once stood in one end zone of Hollywood's Gilmore Stadium and heaved a football clear to the other. ("It was really 93 yards," Washington would confess.) By 1945, when he and Strode played for the Hollywood Bears, Washington found his former Bruins teammate with a touchdown pass that covered 62 yards, and he surpassed that with 65- and 67-yard strikes to another black NFL *refusé*, Ezzrett (Sugarfoot) Anderson. "You'd have thought it was a revival for black people," Brad Pye Jr., the longtime sports editor of the *Los Angeles Sentinel*, says of those PCFL games. "People would come on Sundays after church, all dressed up. Thirty to forty percent in attendance were black. Kenny was like a god. He did everything, and Sugarfoot Anderson could catch anything Kenny put up."

By the end of 1945 the future of the Hollywood Bears—indeed, the fate of the entire PCFL—hung on two developments. One was a vow by the fledgling All-American Football Conference (AAFC) to plant a flag in Los Angeles with a team owned by actor Don Ameche and called the Dons. The other factor was the decision by NFL owners, eager to checkmate the new league, to grant Cleveland owner Dan Reeves permission to move his Rams to L.A.

That city, however, was no longer the one Washington and Strode had known upon leaving Westwood. The war had fed the East Side's growth as blacks poured into Southern California to work in the defense industries that FDR barred from discriminatory hiring. Restrictive covenants kept blacks from settling in much of the L.A. basin, but the Double V campaign waged by the *Courier*—"victory over fascism abroad and segregation at home"—elevated expectations, especially among returning African-American troops.

Meanwhile, policies barring blacks from downtown hotels and Hollywood clubs had touched off a flowering along Central Avenue. Film stars lit out for the 4200 block, which included the Dunbar Hotel, the Club Alabam and the Last Word Café, to drink in the music and the vibe. "They had to come down there because we couldn't go over *there*," jazz pianist Gerald Wiggins would recall in 1993, savoring the irony. One night Stepin Fetchit pulled up in front of the Dunbar in a yellow Rolls-Royce with Mae West riding shotgun. Swing had given way to bebop, and the result was an empowering headiness among black Angelenos.

Operating along "the black Sunset Strip," as Central Avenue was known, L.A.'s African-American reporters now worked to secure the second V, targeting whites-only unions and bigoted housing policies. Edward (Abie) Robinson of the *Sentinel* and later the *California Eagle* was one of the most prominent of these crusaders. Herman Hill, West Coast bureau chief of the *Courier*, could count some two million readers of 13 editions nationwide. But the most fearless, outspoken and tenacious of all was a former pro athlete who served as sports editor of the *Los Angeles Tribune*.

William Claire (Halley) Harding wrote in a voice that jumped off the page. Sarcastic, conversational, self-congratulatory and self-aggrandizing, he never lacked for an opinion or a provocation. Harding called his *Tribune* column SO WHAT?, and the contrariness in the title captures him perfectly. "He was a loudmouth," remembers the *Sentinel*'s Pye, who as a junior high schooler in 1946 made pocket change emptying wastebaskets in the *Courier*'s West Coast bureau. "I used to pass by [his] office and hear him through the door. There was a boxing gym down the street and a pool hall around the corner—I could always hear him in there too. With 90,000 people in the Coliseum you could still hear Halley Harding."

As a kid in Rock Island, Ill., Harding would have known of Robert (Rube) Marshall, the second black pro footballer, who played for the local team, the Independents, as would two other pioneers, Sol Butler and Fred (Duke) Slater. Harding himself played football at historically black colleges Wilberforce, Wiley and Fisk. At Wiley he overlapped with Melvin B. Tolson, the renowned

English professor and debate coach—played by Denzel Washington in the 2007 film *The Great Debaters*—whose team memorably defeated national debate champion USC in 1935. Tolson served as an assistant coach of the Wiley football team, which went 8–0–1 in 1928 with Harding at quarterback.

Through the late '20s and '30s, Harding was a kind of black sports Zelig, playing Negro leagues baseball after the college football season ended and basketball for Abe Saperstein's Savoy Big Five, the Chicago-based forerunner of the Globetrotters. When the NFL drew the color line, all-Negro pro football teams popped up, and Harding spent the mid-'30s with Pollard's Chicago Black Hawks and New York Brown Bombers. By the end of the decade he had landed in Los Angeles. In 1939 and 1940 he appeared in a couple of films with all-black casts, including *Gang War*, in which he throws a mean right cross during a barroom brawl.

On the afternoon of Jan. 15, 1946, representatives of the Rams and the Dons appeared before the L.A. Memorial Coliseum Commission to lobby for leases to a stadium that had never before hosted pro football. Commission president Leonard Roach, an L.A. County supervisor who enjoyed broad black support, had tipped off the black press that the meeting was open to the public. Just off a plane from Cleveland, Rams G.M. Charles (Chile) Walsh surely had no idea what the black man seated beside him had in store.

While minutes of the Coliseum Commission note that "Hally Hardin [*sic*], representing 30 colored newspapers," was present and delivered one of a number of "short talks" that day, they don't record exactly what he said. But from surviving accounts we do know that Harding set his sarcasm aside and stood and delivered like a Wiley College debater. He walked the commissioners through the NFL's early, integrated history. He highlighted pioneers like his old teammate Pollard. He invoked the Double V campaign and the contributions of black soldiers during World War II. He fingered Marshall as the handmaiden of Jim Crow pro football and appealed to Southern Californians' tradition of tolerance. And he declared it "singularly strange" that no NFL team had signed Kenny Washington.

After Harding sat down, the *Sentinel*'s Abie Robinson told Ron Bishop, a Drexel communications professor, in 2002, "You could have heard a rat piss on cotton."

"Walsh was really shook up," the *Courier*'s Hill later reported. "He turned pale and started to stutter. He denied any racial prejudice on the part of the Rams or the NFL. He even went to the league's rulebook. Halley and I answered by charging [that the rule barring blacks] was *unwritten*. The old supervisor [and commission member] Roger Jessup got up and asked whether the Rams would dare bar Kenny Washington."

"Of course not," said Walsh.

"I just want you to know," Jessup said, "if *our* Kenny Washington can't play, there will be no pro football in the L.A. Coliseum."

Attorney Lloyd Wright, representing the Rams, pledged at length that Washington or any other qualified African-American could play with the Rams. Roach urged the Rams and the black newsmen to further discuss the issue on their own. So a week later Walsh and Rams publicity man Maxwell Stiles ventured to Central Avenue to the Last Word, where at least a dozen black journalists lay in wait. Here the names of Washington and several other Hollywood Bears came up, but Walsh expressed concern that they were all under contract to the PCFL club. Harding replied that if the Bears wouldn't stand in their way, what impediment could possibly remain? The Rams conceded as much. Walsh promised to try to sign Washington and also expressed interest in Strode and another Bears end, Chuck Anderson.

Most historical accounts say the Coliseum Commission forced integration on the Rams. But in her forthcoming book, *The Lost Championship Season*, historian Gretchen Atwood makes the case that Harding deserves the primary credit. "Harding pushes Roach to put in writing the promise not to discriminate, and Roach does," Atwood says. "Both in the commission meeting and at the Last Word, every time Walsh says something vague like, 'We'll try out all qualified players regardless of race,' Harding responds with a demand for specifics, such as, 'O.K., when will Washington's tryout be?' Then when the Dons don't hire any blacks, Harding goes back to the commission and asks it to enforce the written nondiscrimination agreement. Roach isn't at this meeting, but the commission now says it has no record of any such agreement and won't tell a team who it can or can't hire. If it was the Coliseum Commission that forced the Rams to integrate, then how do you explain that the Dons had a lease in 1946 when they hadn't even given a black player a tryout? So in sports terms, Harding gets the goal and Roach the assist, not the other way around."

Atwood believes a comment made years later by Rams backfield coach Bob Snyder—that the team signed Washington at the insistence of the Coliseum Commission—is a convenient official story. "I think Snyder believed that, but I also think Chile Walsh was sick of Harding's constant pressure. And because of the public statements Roach and Jessup made against racial bias, Walsh and the Rams could pass the buck if anyone objected to the signing—basically, shrug and tell other NFL owners, 'Hey, our hands were tied, we needed the lease to the stadium.'"

The Rams' press release on March 21, 1946, announcing Washington's signing includes this disclaimer: "The National [Football] League has never had a rule against the use of Negro players and no precedent is being set in the signing of Washington." But that's belied by the reaction of other NFL owners. "All hell broke loose," Snyder told Mike Rathet and Don R. Smith, authors of *The Pro Football Hall of Fame Presents: Their Deeds and Dogged Faith*, in 1984. "There was objection to it—you can bet your butt on that."

The *Tribune* gloried in the news of Washington's signing. One article exulted, "Yesterday *Tribune* sports editor Halley Harding's one-man crusade against the National Football League's patent, if unwritten, law against Negro players paid off in full."

In his column Harding wrote, "Of course Kenny hasn't got a whole lot of years on the gridiron ahead of him, but we'll string along with him for our money's worth, never having been robbed yet. Another Negro is about to sign on the dotted line in the same office, but while the details are being worked out, mum's the word."

That other black player, Strode, came to terms a couple of months later. The Rams had asked Washington to choose someone to room with on the road, and he nominated his old running mate. The Rams grumbled about Strode's marriage to Luana Kalaeola, a descendant of Hawaiian royalty, Strode said later, "but Kenny had power at that point, and he said, 'I want my buddy.'"

Kenny Washington had already undergone five knee operations when he made his NFL debut at age 28. Now a running back on a T formation team, he could no longer mystify defenses as a tailback who might run or pass. He fared best in the second of his three seasons, when he finished fourth in the NFL in rushing yardage, led the league with 7.4 yards per carry and ran 92 yards from scrimmage for a score shortly after being knocked unconscious by a Chicago Cardinals linebacker.

"Kenny was just a shell of himself when he played for the Rams," says the *Sentinel*'s Pye. "If you could have seen him with the Hollywood Bears...." Angelenos seemed to know that. Upon his retirement in 1948, the 80,000 fans who came out for a tribute did so to honor his entire career.

When the Rams hit the road that first season, management checked the white players into one hotel and peeled off a hundred dollars for each of the black players to find lodging elsewhere. This wasn't always because of Jim Crow; Washington and Strode liked the autonomy. "In the black section of Chicago, we'd never seen so many black people in our whole lives," Strode recalled. "Bob Waterfield and about five players came down looking for us because they'd made arrangements for us to move back to their hotel. We're in a cellar [of the Persian Hotel] where Count Basie's playing, it's integrated and all the white people are having a ball. We're sipping Tom Collinses, and Waterfield said, 'You sons of bitches!' The team was too embarrassed to bed check us because we'd been shoved out of the family. And when the white players came to get us, we said, 'No way, we're gonna stay segregated.' That's why I say it was never [an issue among] the athletes."

On offense, Strode, then 32, played only enough to catch four passes; on defense, he was put "in the butcher shop on the defensive line at 200 pounds," Strode said. "It was a joke."

Harmon, his old teammate, confirmed this. "Woody was one of the greatest defensive ends I ever saw, but he never got a chance to prove it because of that fool coaching staff. In practice you could never get near him. You never saw a man in better shape."

Strode learned of his release while lying in bed one morning, when several of Washington's mob-connected friends from Lincoln Heights came by with the news. One of the wise guys—"the biggest bookie in Hollywood," Strode said—reported overhearing Reeves and Snyder in a bar on Sunset Boulevard ("drunk on their asses," in Strode's telling) bragging about how they'd let Strode go. "[The bookie] said, 'We don't like the way they did it. We want to know if you want to fight it.' I could have started a war."

Both Chile Walsh and his brother Adam, the L.A. coach, resigned after the Rams, NFL champions in 1945, went 6–4–1 in 1946. But even if the season had been a disappointment on the West Coast, to a man watching from Brooklyn it had been a triumph. As a teammate of Charles Follis's with the Shelby Athletic Club at the turn of the century, Branch Rickey had been impressed by Follis's even temper in the face of taunts and cheap shots. Now, Rickey said to himself, if blacks and whites could play a game of violent collisions in close quarters without major incident, the Dodgers could surely call up Jackie Robinson to the majors. Robinson made his debut with the Dodgers the following season.

Strode went on to play two seasons in Canada and spent five years in Italy doing spaghetti Westerns and action films. On screen he exuded an equipoise that one critic praised as "an effective counterpoint to the noise and confusion around him." By the time he died of lung cancer in 1994, he had made more than 100 movies, including *Sergeant Rutledge* and *The Man Who Shot Liberty Valance*. His last film, *The Quick and the Dead*, was released in 1995.

After retiring, Washington worked as a distributor for a grocery chain and a whiskey distillery. He served as a part-time scout for the Dodgers, in whose system his son, Kenny Jr., played several seasons. In 1971, after Washington became ill with congestive-heart and lung problems, Strode hurried back from Italy to his old friend's hospital room in the UCLA Medical Center. He wanted to take Washington to Rome, to show him a place full of people like the neighbors back in Lincoln Heights. But Washington was too far gone and knew he was best left to contemplate the Bruins' football practice field, which he could see from his window.

Washington was 52 when he died. In his obituary in the *Los Angeles Times*, Waterfield said, "If he had come into the National Football League directly from UCLA, he would have been, in my opinion, the best the NFL had ever seen."

In what kind of peace is that supposed to leave a man? Pastor L.L. White addressed the question in his eulogy, invoking St. Paul's Epistle to the Philippians: "You live in a world of crooked and mean people. You must shine among them like stars lighting up the sky."

Pete Fierle oversees education programs for the Pro Football Hall of Fame in Canton, Ohio. He knows well the obscurity that shrouds the story of the game's reintegration in the modern era. "My 11-year-old son could tell you Jackie Robinson's name but not Kenny Washington's or Marion Motley's," Fierle says. Thus, the Hall hangs most of the tale of pro football's desegregation on Paul Brown's addition of Motley and Bill Willis to the Browns in 1946. Those events came after the Rams' signings of Washington and Strode, but they are stories of principle, vision and courage. It's a narrative more in the Rickey-Robinson mold and, Fierle points out, easier for visitors to get a handle on.

Problem is, Motley and Willis didn't integrate the NFL. They integrated the AAFC. Washington and Strode integrated the NFL. League owners remained reliably reactionary even after the NFL champion Minnesota Vikings lost Super Bowl IV to the AFL's Kansas City Chiefs, who fielded more black starters than white. Not until Doug Williams led the Redskins to a Super Bowl title in 1988 did a starting black NFL quarterback become less than remarkable. And not until a renegade owner, Oakland's Al Davis, hired Art Shell in 1989 did the NFL get its first black head coach since Pollard.

The sad fact is, the NFL's journey to integration didn't have to take place at all. If only the league had left well enough alone, its history would be a proud one. Instead those 13 years of segregation—ended only when the NFL gave ground grudgingly to a howling sportswriter and a public servant—diminish the league to a level of a small-minded steward of some waiting room or lunch counter.

That gracelessness wasn't lost on the key players. "They didn't take Kenny because of his ability," Strode said. "They didn't take me on my ability. It was shoved down their throats."

NOVEMBER 24, 2003

Black Sunday

Forty years ago this weekend, as America grieved for President John F. Kennedy, stunned NFL players were told to take the field

BY CHARLES P. PIERCE

The ice spread out of a brilliantly blue Southern sky. It suffused the air. You took it in with every breath, and it got into your blood and spread to your deepest places. It made the world fragile, and you with it, until it seemed that you might shatter at the slightest sound, and all the world shatter around you. On the morning of Nov. 22, 1963, there were things that the United States believed about itself, and those things were solid and basic and seemed as permanent as granite. By midday, as the ice spread through them, those fundamental things became delicate and crystalline. Anything loud seemed dangerous.

Cheering was loud. There had been cheering in Dallas, along the streets and on either side of that long, slow—too damned slow—turn from Houston down onto Elm Street past the book warehouse. Some of the cheering was so loud that the gunfire drowned in it. After that, for the next three days, the country breathed shallowly. It spoke to itself only in chapel whispers. Football, by contrast, is loud, and therefore it seemed a perilous thing.

On that Friday at noon, the Washington Redskins were beginning an ordinary practice in the middle of a season that was going nowhere. They'd lost seven games in a row. Their game that weekend was in Philadelphia, against the Eagles, who were even more woeful than the Redskins. Philadelphia was in a long slide in which it would lose eight of its last nine games and finish 2–10–2, slightly worse than Washington's 3–11.

Amid this hopeless flotsam, the Redskins' Bobby Mitchell was having a good season. He was on his way to 69 catches and seven touchdowns. In Philadelphia, Tommy McDonald would end 1963 with 41 catches and eight touchdowns, but neither man had any illusions about his team. "We were pretty terrible," recalls McDonald. "It wasn't the best year, anyway, before all this happened."

The players heard the news, like the country did, in a thousand ways. Raymond Berry and the Baltimore Colts heard it on their airplane, at 30,000 feet, on their way to Los Angeles for a game with the Rams. Sam Huff, the New York Giants linebacker who'd campaigned for John F. Kennedy in 1960 before the pivotal primary in Huff's home state, West Virginia, heard it on his car radio in the middle of the Triborough Bridge. McDonald found out after practice.

In Washington, coach Bill McPeak called the Redskins together in the middle of the field outside D.C. Stadium. Mitchell was baffled. McPeak, an unemotional organization man, told everyone to take a knee and pray because the president was dead.

"The first thing I thought was, God, Mr. Marshall died," Mitchell says, referring to Redskins president George Preston Marshall. His teammates sank to the ground around him, and then he knew. "It never occurred to me," Mitchell says. "I mean, that somebody would shoot the president of the United States? It took me a couple of seconds to realize that was what he meant."

Mitchell had gone to Washington in 1962, two years after the Kennedy Administration began. He'd become close friends with Robert Kennedy, the president's brother and the attorney general, and had met President Kennedy several times, once at a state dinner at the White House. Mitchell had even gone to Robert Kennedy's home in Virginia to play touch football with that boisterous and ever-expanding family. Now, as he fell to his knees on the hardening earth of autumn, Mitchell thought mostly about his friend.

"I was frozen there for a minute because I'd really fallen in love with Bobby," Mitchell says. "My thoughts turned to him, and I thought, Damn, this is going to kill Bobby."

The Redskins practiced anyway, and it was terrible, and McPeak finally gave up and sent the team home. The streets of Washington were a shadow play. Cars disappeared almost entirely. Black crape began to appear in shop windows. Mitchell saw people on the sidewalk, still and weeping, as though they were afraid to move. He felt cold and numb too. He felt close to breaking.

"It was just silence," he says. "That's what I remember. Even the playgrounds were empty and quiet. I felt, I don't know, slow, somehow, and like everything had slowed down around me."

On the way home through the stunned and silent streets, the last thing Mitchell thought about was the game in Philadelphia two days later. It had been a forgettable piece of business anyway, and now it seemed unspeakable. Why did we even practice? he wondered. He was home that evening, glued to his television like the rest of his frozen and fragile country, when *Air Force One* came back from Dallas.

Football was what they played on the New Frontier. Oh, they paid the usual obeisance to baseball, the ritual national pastime. But football ran deep in the Kennedy family mystique. All four Kennedy brothers had played the game at Harvard. John was a halfback undersized even by the standards of the Ivy League in the 1930s, but young Edward once scored a touchdown in the Yale game. Football was an integral part of Joseph Kennedy's grand plan—a demonstration of muscular Americanism that would help break down the prejudices his children would face for being rich, Irish and Catholic.

"Politics is like football," JFK once noted. "If you see daylight, go through the hole." And photographs of John Kennedy hauling in passes from his brothers helped camouflage his myriad health problems, some of which have only recently come to light.

Moreover, the touch football games at the compound in Hyannis Port, Mass., were part of the glamour of the Kennedy White House, as much as Jacqueline Kennedy's horses and the iconic PT-109 tie clips. There was a tyranny of the new at work, stretching from outer space to Southeast Asia. Football was a part of all that.

By 1963 Pete Rozelle and his National Football League already were well on their way to developing a new national pastime, changing the way Americans watched their sports, much as the Kennedy campaign had changed the way Americans elected their presidents. Both were perfect creatures of television, a medium just then coming into the fullness of its power. Rozelle tailored his games to TV the way that Kennedy tailored his press conferences to it. Both the NFL and the Kennedy Administration were pure products of the brawling, confident America that had been built by the generation that had fought World War II.

The year had not been the easiest for Rozelle. In April he'd indefinitely suspended two star players, Alex Karras of the Detroit Lions and Paul Hornung of the Green Bay Packers, for gambling on their teams' games, and a bidding war for college players still raged because the renegade American

Football League had stubbornly refused to fold. But on Nov. 22 Rozelle was confronted with a decision that seemed to render all the others he'd made that year trivial.

There was no blueprint for what to do on the weekend that a president is being buried on national television. In Wisconsin more than 100 high school basketball games were played on the night of the assassination. Pimlico Race Course in Baltimore ran all weekend, and games were played in both the NBA and the NHL. In college football Nebraska and Oklahoma played each other, but all four games in the Big Ten were rescheduled, and Iowa and Notre Dame canceled their game. The AFL wiped out its entire slate of games, but Rozelle had made Sunday afternoons the property of the NFL, and because of that he was on the hook.

He called his college friend Pierre Salinger, who was Kennedy's press secretary. Speaking from the Honolulu airport, shell-shocked by the events of the day, Salinger gave Rozelle what amounted to the dead president's permission to play. "Football," Rozelle said in making the announcement, "was Mr. Kennedy's game."

The reaction very nearly undid Rozelle. At least two owners called and begged him to reconsider. Cleveland's Art Modell wound up paying for extra security to guard the Dallas Cowboys, who were in town that weekend to play the Browns. In Philadelphia, Eagles owner Frank McNamee announced that he would miss his first game in 15 years and Mayor James H.J. Tate, who'd shared a platform at Independence Hall with President Kennedy a year earlier on July 4, tried to get a court to stop the Eagles-Redskins game.

It also became clear that Rozelle's golden touch with the media had deserted him. He was barbecued for going ahead with the schedule. In the *New York Herald-Tribune*, Red Smith all but called Rozelle a heartless mercenary, and Melvin Durslag of the Los Angeles *Herald Examiner* called the games that weekend "a sick joke." In *The Philadelphia Inquirer*, Sandy Grady wrote, "I am ashamed of this fatuous dreamland."

Perhaps the most significant thing of all was that players around the league began to rebel, in their hearts if not on the field. "Nobody wanted to play," says McDonald. "There wasn't anything you could do about it, but there was no way anybody wanted to go out and play a game that weekend. I'm a guy who wears his emotions on his sleeve, and I couldn't stop crying.

"It was bad enough playing, but that weekend, to be playing the Redskins, from Washington, where the president lived, that was just another reason to be upset."

For his part, Mitchell felt strange leaving Washington. "Everywhere you looked, down along the street, people would just start crying," he says. "It didn't seem like the time to leave." The Redskins drove the three hours to

Philadelphia and checked into their hotel. Across town, at the Sheraton on Chestnut Street, where the Eagles always stayed before home games, the team was falling apart.

The Eagles had decided to collect money for the family of Dallas policeman J.D. Tippitt, who'd been shot to death on Friday afternoon, allegedly by Lee Harvey Oswald. A team meeting, which also reportedly dealt with the Eagles' feelings about playing the game the next day, ended with a fistfight between defensive back Ben Scotti and defensive lineman John Mellekas. The two went behind closed doors to finish it, and both wound up in the hospital that night, Scotti with a broken hand and Mellekas with severe facial cuts. In his room, McDonald watched TV and never heard a thing.

That Sunday dawned cold and surreal. In their hotels, caught up in what became the first national news miniseries of the television age, the template for CNN and Fox and for the Watergate hearings and the O.J. trial and everything that came after, the players were drowning in the coverage, and how strangely that strangest of Sundays began depended vitally on where you were playing that weekend.

Kickoff was at 1 p.m. Eastern standard time. Some players around the league were at stadiums and some were in their hotels, but wherever they were, many of them were watching television at 12:21 p.m. EST when the Dallas police were transferring Oswald to the county jail and Jack Ruby gunned him down. "That was the last thing that weekend that I couldn't believe," says McDonald.

Then people showed up to watch football. That was the remarkable thing. There were 60,671 fans at Franklin Field to see the Eagles and the Redskins play a game that didn't matter on a weekend on which almost everything else seemed to matter. There was no pregame hoo-ha; Rozelle, at least, had drawn the line at that. There were no player introductions. The Eagles and the Redskins simply walked out to midfield and joined hands. A bugler blew *Taps*, which nearly finished McDonald on the spot. Then the whole stadium sang the national anthem a cappella.

After that the stadium was as silent as a football stadium can be, as if tearing themselves away from the extended obsequies on television had used all the energy the fans had left. McDonald was bawling when he went back to receive the opening kickoff, and Mitchell noticed that even his coaches' words seemed hollow. "Before the game there was a lot of what you could tell was false chatter," Mitchell says. "Coaches are always over there saying, '*Grr*, let's go get 'em.' And me, I gave them a weak yell."

He made plays. So did McDonald. They each caught four passes in the game. Once, while running down the sideline for a pass, Mitchell felt the game dissolve around him. "I was there, looking up, concentrating on the ball spiraling in the air, like you're supposed to, and then I started thinking about everything that was going on in Washington," he recalls. The ball sailed over his head.

Redskins quarterback Norm Snead had a hot hand. He pushed his team out to a 13–0 lead at halftime, hitting on 12 of his first 17 passes for 192 yards. Late in the second quarter he found Dick James for a 31-yard touchdown. The game, however, seemed to be played in a virtual vacuum. "You didn't hear anything," Mitchell says. "I don't remember any noise from the stands, and in the pileups, where guys are always shouting and jiving, there was none of that. It was one play after another, trying to get the game done. To this day, sometimes I can't believe that I played that game. I still think I was out there in slow motion."

It wasn't a day for coming from behind. It looked for a long while as though Washington was on its way to its first shutout since 1958. However, playing with a stiff wind behind them in the fourth quarter, the Eagles mustered 10 points, highlighted by a 25-yard touchdown pass from Sonny Jurgensen to Timmy Brown. But on Philadelphia's final drive McDonald let a pass go through his hands, and Mike Clark missed a 16-yard field goal that would have tied the game. The Redskins won 13–10.

Out in the players' parking lot, Eagles backup quarterback King Hill discovered that all the windows in his car had been shattered. The car had Texas plates.

That night, when he got home, Mitchell was struck for the last time that weekend by how quiet the streets of Washington had become. It was the strangest game any of the players had ever played and, in some ways, the most dangerous. Football is best (and most safely) played with heedless emotion, and everyone on the field seemed to be holding back. They played like men who had become aware of some unfamiliar fragility deep in themselves—far beneath muscle and bone, ligament and tendon, where they hadn't noticed any before.

Bobby Mitchell avoided Bobby Kennedy for as long as he could. Finally, about a month after the Philadelphia game, somebody from the Justice Department called Mitchell and told him that Kennedy wanted him to help dedicate the John F. Kennedy Playground on Seventh Street in the Washington ghetto. Mitchell went, distractedly driving slowly around the block, again and again, until he realized what he was doing. He was looking at all the rooftops for someone with a gun.

At the playground Mitchell took a spot in the back of the crowd, hoping that Kennedy wouldn't see him. "I was afraid," he admits. "I didn't know what I'd say to him." Kennedy spotted him, though, and brought him up to the front of the crowd, near where they had already turned the cold earth for the groundbreaking.

Kennedy was gaunt, almost lifeless in the face. He gripped Mitchell as if with iron talons. "I don't think I can do this," he said, and he couldn't. His hands were shaking too hard to work the shovel. He handed it to Mitchell so they held it together.

"I was so nervous," Mitchell recalls, "I must've thrown that dirt 50 feet over my head behind me."

He's older now, telling his story in the lobby of the Willard, a great old history-laden pile on Pennsylvania Avenue, not far from the White House. Abraham Lincoln was taken there when he was smuggled into Washington before his first inauguration, and it was the Willard's lobby that reputedly inspired the word *lobbying* when people gathered there to ply and beg and otherwise try to sublet President Ulysses S. Grant.

History has more or less passed judgment on those three frozen days in November. Later in his life Rozelle wrote that the worst decision he ever made was to play the games that weekend. And history sits with Bobby Mitchell in the awful synchronicity of anniversaries: Every commemoration of John Kennedy's death follows a commemoration of Robert's. This week will mark the 40th anniversary of John's death, not long after the 35th of Robert's, and Mitchell knows that the ice is still there, deep within him.

"You're never sure how that kind of thing will affect you, or when," he says. "We all learned from it, I think. Back after 9/11, there wasn't any choice: Teams just didn't play. That was something we learned from that weekend in 1963."

And he leaves then, across the great lobby and out into the late autumn sunshine. Washington is alive with color as this November afternoon falls toward evening. Earlier that day, across the river in Arlington, down the hill from the gravesite and the eternal flame, drums were beating deep behind the golden trees, distant and muffled, like a heartbeat encased in something that can never melt but only shatter and reform, and then shatter again, over and over and over.

ALL ACCESS

SEPTEMBER 2, 1996

Bottom's Up

No wonder long snappers are the game's oddballs: The world they view between their legs is upside down

BY AUSTIN MURPHY

They are anonymous except in times of disaster, for which they are invariably blamed. They are paid to perform an act that gives them an upside-down perspective on the world and leaves them in an absurdly vulnerable position that cries out to opponents: Clobber me! Is it any wonder that there is an inordinately high incidence of strangeness among NFL long snappers?

Among their number we find a poet, a pilot, the owner of a boutique cookie business, a singer in a group called Toe Jam and a heavily tattooed heavy-metal junkie who has sported a Mohawk. And you thought kickers were flakes.

Our question for Trey Junkin is this: Does long-snapping lead to eccentricity, or are the eccentric drawn to long-snapping? Junkin, a 14-year veteran who returned to the Oakland Raiders in June after six seasons with the Seattle Seahawks, believes it is the latter. "Not every kid grows up and says, 'Mommy, I want to put my head between my legs and let other guys beat on me while I snap a football,'" he says.

When Junkin and Dave Binn of the San Diego Chargers got together in a hotel coffee shop to swap anecdotes and insights about long-snapping, it looked like a Hell's Angels' chapter meeting. Binn, who is entering his third NFL season, showed up with shoulder-length hair and a goatee; Junkin was sporting a goatee and a black leather jacket with a Harley-Davidson pin. Security eyed them nervously.

Tell us, guys. Has anyone tried to sabotage a long snap by putting a foreign substance on the ball?

"My rookie year a guy threw dirt on the ball," says Binn. "That wasn't too cool."

Junkin has a longer list: "I've had Stickum. I've had Vaseline, which some defensive linemen put under their arms, so you can't hold 'em. I've had packing grease on the ball. I've had guys spit on the ball. One time a guy spit on my hands while I was snapping the ball."

"How was the snap?" asks Binn.

"The snap was good," says Junkin, "but I got fined for punching the guy."

These two occupy opposite ends of the long-snapping spectrum. Binn was a walk-on at Cal who eventually received a scholarship to do nothing but long snap; in 1994 the Chargers signed him as a free agent solely to snap. Junkin didn't snap at all at Louisiana Tech, where he was a linebacker with 4.3 speed in the 40. The Buffalo Bills took him in the fourth round of the '83 draft. "That was 13 years and six knee operations ago," says Junkin, who doubles as a tight end. He took up long-snapping in 1990 to make himself more valuable. Smart move. For the last six or seven years long-snapping has paid the mortgage.

Only a few long snappers double as regular players. They don't *need* long-snapping. Those guys constitute a smug minority. Probably a quarter of NFL teams split the long-snapping duties: a deep snapper for punts and a short snapper for field goals and extra points.

Which is tougher? Though shorter, the snap-for-placement is often more pressure-packed, since points—and sometimes victory—are at stake. This explains why, according to Adam Schreiber, a 13-year vet who does both short- and deep-snapping for the New York Giants, "you find a lot of spitting in field goal situations."

The center on kick placements makes two adjustments: He has to take something off the ball—"You're not trying to knock the holder over," says Schreiber—and he has to "snap laces." That means the snapper must deliver the ball so that when the holder catches it his top hand is on the laces. "That way when he puts it down, the laces are facing the goalpost," Schreiber adds.

The punt snap is "more of an aggressive snap, with speed," says Schreiber. The ball must reach the punter in .8 of a second. How fast is that? Faster than his wife, Dalene, thought. At a picnic several summers ago, Adam felt "the itch to snap" and asked Dalene if she would catch a few. "What do I do?" she asked. "You say 'set,' and I snap the ball at my convenience," he replied.

"The first one was a nice, tight spiral," recalls Schreiber. "It wasn't high, but then again she's only about five foot four." The ball broke a couple of her fingernails.

Usually it is the snapper who absorbs the abuse. When Junkin thought a Cleveland Browns player was diving at his knees two years ago, he started brawling with him. Junkin was in turn set upon by his own teammate, Kevin Mawae, who, as he tried to save Junkin from being ejected, shouted, "I'm not snapping!" Mawae was Seattle's backup snapper.

In addition to dabbling in motorcycles and martial arts, Junkin writes poetry. The following minimalist, arbitrarily capitalized lines are from "The Snap":

Get a Look
Defense, Ball, Punter
Feel movement
Hear the call
Adjust the Ball
everything comes to
zero
stillness
you feel the Line
you to punter
15 yards
perfect snap
Block
Some can; some can't.

Some can appreciate timeless verse, some can't. After zipping through Junkin's poem, Binn merely says, "Cool."

To fill the uncomfortable silence, I compliment Junkin on his economical style. Junkin mentions that he has also tried to write haiku. "But that form, like Japanese society, is highly restrictive," he says.

So the poet laureate of long snappers has no snapping-related haiku for us. Emboldened by his example, I give it a whirl:

This jerk waits until
I'm helpless, then cleans my clock.
I hate the noseguard.

By the end of last season Junkin estimates that he had bent over the ball 1,040 times in succession without making a bad punt snap. When he reached the 1,000 mark last season, in a game against the New York Jets, play was not stopped; Cal Ripken–like festivities did not erupt. Junkin staged his own little celebration. "I ran down and snatched the ball from the official," he says. "The guy thought I'd lost my mind."

Ingratitude comes with the territory. As Brad Banta, who handles long-snapping duties for the Indianapolis Colts, says, "The more unnoticed you are, the better you must be doing."

Just because I'm anonymous at work doesn't mean I have to be anonymous in life. This seems to be the philosophy of many of today's deep snappers, none of whom enjoys a higher profile than Minnesota Viking Mike Morris, who stands 6'7" when his Mohawk has been teased to its full height. No long snapper has cultivated his minor celebrity more assiduously or shrewdly than Morris, who last season got several minutes of face time on *Six Days to Sunday*, a TNT documentary about a week in the life of two pro football teams. He co-hosts a sports talk radio show and has his own fan club, which Morris fondly describes as "my rednecks–a bunch of biker-slash-taxidermists in black T-shirts. They love ball, and they've chosen me as their leader."

Morris acts as a kind of self-appointed shop steward of long snappers. Don't use the expression "long-snapping chores" around him. "Do you hear people calling them 'the quarterbacking chores'?" he says. This reminds him of another slight: "They ought to take a long snapper to the Pro Bowl. They bring a return man, they even bring some goofball who blows up the wedge on kickoffs. But they don't take a long snapper. That's a lot of money out of someone's pocket."

Your pocket, Mike? "Hey, I'll take my name off the list," he says. "That's how strongly I feel about this."

One man doesn't buy it. "If self-promotion was an art, he'd be Michelangelo," Junkin says.

In issuing the following warning to his fellow snappers, the martial artist echoes the wisdom of Master Po, the blind Shaolin sage from the *Kung Fu* TV series. "You've got to be a little strange–that's part of the job description," Junkin says. "But you can't be weird when you're *doing* the job. If you miss a block or roll one back there, you've hurt the team, and it's time for you to leave."

It's also time to meet the press. Long snappers do not get interviewed unless something has gone badly awry. The Atlanta Falcons' Harper Le Bel recalls a game in which he triggered a "jailbreak–snapper-speak for the anarchy that ensues when the ball sails over the punter's head. After the game reporters crowded around his locker. Feigning compassion but looking for blood, they asked, "What happened?"

"I wanted to say, 'What does it look like happened? I snapped it over his head!'" says Le Bel. Instead he explained, as if to a group of second-graders, "I...held...on...to...the...ball...too...long."

Not all NFL snappers bend over and peer back at an upside-down punter. Junkin is one of the few who snap "blind." Another is Trevor Matich of the Washington Redskins. The advantage of this technique is that it enables the center to pick up a rusher more easily. As a result, says Redskins special teams coach Pete Rodriguez, "a lot of teams don't even bother trying to pressure us." The skill is even more impressive considering that Matich, a licensed pilot, did not start snapping until 1990, his sixth season in the league. It was easy to pick it up, he says, "because I didn't have a paradigm to unlearn."

We'll take your word for that, Trevor.

When he was with the Arizona Cardinals, Rodriguez once coached another blind snapper, a Hawaiian named Kani Kauahi. In 10 NFL seasons Kauahi earned a reputation as one of the league's finest snappers. Unfortunately he stuck around for an 11th.

Kauahi played one game in 1993, and Rodriguez remembers it well. Kauahi's first snap in the opener, in Philadelphia, was a peach. "But Kani blocked the wrong way," says Rodriguez, "and the kick was almost blocked." His next snap was somewhere over the rainbow. The play resulted in a safety. Kauahi bounced the next snap to punter Rich Camarillo, who kicked the ball sideways. "Kani almost put *another* one over Rich's head," says Rodriguez. "All of a sudden Kani couldn't snap, and he knew it. That was his last game in the NFL."

We feel a haiku coming on:

The punter should not
need an eight-foot stepladder.
Good luck on waivers.

How does a deep snapper go off the deep end? When does a long snapper... snap? "You get the mental spins," says Adam Lingner, a 13-year long-snapping veteran who retired from the Bills last spring. "You're thinking, Should I snap it now? Yes—no! Don't! I'm not ready. Once you start thinking over the ball, you're doomed. That's why I used to crack jokes at the line of scrimmage. To keep myself from thinking."

A bad back, rather than the mental spins, forced the retirement of Lingner, who attributes the first poor snap of his career—it came in 1989, during his seventh NFL season—to his inability to come up with a timely put-down. "We were playing the Jets, and [New York's] Troy Benson looks across at John Davis, our tackle, and says, 'Hey, John, nice gut.'

"I was trying to think of a snappy retort when John Kidd, who is holding for the extra point, gives me the signal to snap. I wasn't ready, and I put it over his head."

So why volunteer for such unappreciated duty? Because it is the best way for a mediocre athlete to sneak into the NFL. Do great athletes gravitate to long-snapping? Dale Hellestrae of the Dallas Cowboys thinks not. Hellestrae, who owns and operates a Cookie Bouquet in Phoenix, has survived for 12 years in the league primarily as a long snapper and special-teamer. "If you're a pretty good athlete in ninth, 10th, 11th grade, you're thinking, Why would I ever want to do that?" he says.

As a 10-year-old, Greg Truitt came to that realization too late. One day at a practice for a traveling all-star team in Sarasota, Fla., the coach was auditioning long snappers. The word had spread among the boys: If you don't want to do it, just hike the ball over the punter's head.

"But I'd already gone," says Truitt, "so I got the job." His skill eventually earned him a scholarship to Penn State, and he handled the deep-snapping during the Nittany Lions' 14–10 Fiesta Bowl upset of Miami at the end of the 1986 season. That was his junior year. Truitt took the next season off. "I was disillusioned with the reality of life," he says. Spoken like a true long snapper.

After working two years as a restaurant manager Truitt grew disillusioned with the reality of the job. So he made a crude long-snapping video and sent it to a few NFL teams. To eat, he drove a limo, waited tables, mowed lawns.

He tried out with the Redskins and the Miami Dolphins. Zilch. His agent, Brett Senior, suggested Truitt head to State College, Pa., during the week that the scouts would be on the Penn State campus. "I went to a corner of the field house and started long-snapping," he says. He caught the eye of a Cincinnati Bengals scout; the team offered him a tryout and, soon thereafter, a contract.

While negotiating the two-year deal, Senior had the temerity to ask about a signing bonus. As Truitt recalls, "They said, 'The guy's been out of football for six years!'"

Thus in 1994 did Truitt become, at 28, the oldest rookie to play in the NFL in 48 years. Last season he made $150,000. He has teamed up with the Bengals' kicking specialists to form an a cappella group called Toe Jam. Truitt says that he feels blessed, but not lucky. "Everyone has the same opportunity," he says. "It's just a matter of who wants to take it."

As a poet of our acquaintance once wrote: Some can, some can't.

OCTOBER 8, 2012

American Zebra

Folk hero, two-time Super Bowl ref, owner of the most famous guns in the NFL. Then along came the lockout and Ed Hochuli became something else, at least in the Twittersphere: the most important man in football

BY STEVE RUSHIN

I sing of arms and a man, a man obscured by his celebrated arms, biceps bulging from his tightly tailored referee's shirt. "Tailored?" says Ed Hochuli, the impossibly fit NFL official of whom we sing. "There's no need for tailoring when you buy your shirts at Gap Kids."

And then he beams, revealing the laugh lines of a 61-year-old man whose 10 grandchildren call him Papa Touchdown.

It is Tuesday in Phoenix, the Tuesday after the *Monday Night Football* game in Seattle, the one that became the nation's top news story and led the President of the United States to request the return of "our refs."

Hochuli won't talk about the labor dispute that locked out the zebras for the first three weeks of the season, but he seems startled by Barack Obama's remark and wonders whether Iran's nuclear program might not be a more pressing issue. What Hochuli doesn't realize is that he himself has become a matter of national security—our national security blanket, a football referee in whose massive arms we suddenly feel safe and warm.

"Ed has captured the nation with his physique and presentation," says Jerry Markbreit, an NFL official from 1976 to '98. "When he steps on the field you know you're in good hands."

Many players feel the same way. "Godspeed, Ed Hochuli," Texans running back Arian Foster wrote that Monday night on Twitter, where the hashtag #FreeEdHochuli had taken hold.

Hochuli is huge on Twitter, despite his never having tweeted. "He's flabbergasted by his fame; he doesn't understand where it comes from," says Shawn Hochuli, a Pac-12 referee and the fourth of Hochuli's six children. "But he's well-respected and looks the part with the guns."

As the Packers were playing the Seahawks that Monday night, Hochuli was in the living room of his Phoenix home, its curio cabinets filled with ceramic zebras ("People give me zebras"), gold Super Bowl whistles ("We don't actually use those") and silver commemorative coins from a lifetime of coin flips. At Super Bowl XXXVIII, between the Patriots and the Panthers, 77-year-old ceremonial captain Y.A. Tittle asked for the coin to give to his granddaughter. Hochuli was under orders to hand it over to the Hall of Fame afterward, but, he says, "I thought Y.A. Tittle's granddaughter should have it." It was his easiest call of the evening: He dug out his own silver dollar for the flip and gave that to Tittle's granddaughter; the Hall got the (unused) commemorative coin.

As the rest of America watched the Seahawks-Packers game play to its shambolic denouement, Hochuli was on his sectional sofa, watching the Diamondbacks play the Rockies in Denver, as is the prerogative of a man who had already taken in 15 hours of NFL action that week. "I don't watch a lot of football for fun," Hochuli would say the next morning behind his desk at the Phoenix law firm of Jones, Skelton & Hochuli, where he works 50 hours per week as a trial lawyer. "I've tried, but I'm always looking to see if the left tackle is holding."

In preparing for a game, Hochuli might watch a 90-minute montage of nothing but left tackles holding, which even he concedes is a pretty perverted DVD. He devotes roughly as much time to refereeing as he does to the law, studying 15 hours of video a week, moderating a Tuesday teleconference for the league's other 120 officials and making certain that he (and they) are prepared for any possibility, no matter how remote.

If a team fakes a punt and passes instead—as he'll tell you with much greater enthusiasm than is warranted—defensive pass interference is no longer a foul. Or it isn't a foul in theory, because a fake-punt-turned-pass-followed-by-pass-interference play had never actually occurred in Hochuli's lifetime of officiating, which now includes more than 450 NFL games. That scenario was just an intriguing concept, like time travel, until it happened in a game he was working in San Diego last season.

"We were almost giddy," Hochuli says of his seven-man crew. "We were saying to each other, 'It happened! It finally happened! And we got it right!'"Getting it right is Hochuli's joy and his mission, though getting it wrong is also part of his purview, most famously in 2008 when he ruled that a fumble by then Broncos quarterback Jay Cutler was an incomplete pass, a blown call that cost the Chargers a victory. Hochuli apologized profusely, for several days, both publicly and personally, to anyone who e-mailed him, though doing so soon became impossible. It is a measure of football's place in American life that there were 150 e-mails on his work Blackberry when he boarded a postgame flight to LAX; 1,100 when he deplaned a short time later; and 25,000 after six days, at which time the server at Jones, Skelton & Hochuli finally cried uncle.

This same level of care has made him one of the league's top-rated officials, worker of two Super Bowls and an alternate for three more. "He's the bellwether of officiating," says Markbreit, who now trains league referees. "Among the best of the best ever. He's got charisma, he's a deep-feeling guy, he's a wonderful human being. And he's Hercules. If I had his physique, I'd still be refereeing."

To some football fans, Hochuli or Hercules—he is sometimes called Hochules—is a two-dimensional cartoon, the Venus de Milo inverted, a pair of arms and nothing else.

"The guns thing?" Hochuli says, walking into a gleaming health club in Tempe for the two-hour workout he does four times a week. "I think it started with Phil Simms. At least that's what I always tell him. He was calling a blowout and there was nothing else to talk about, so he drew two circles around my arms with the telestrator and said, 'Look at this guy's biceps.'"Now players flex in his presence, demanding to compare pythons. "Which is ridiculous," Hochuli says, "because every one of their arms is the size of my thigh."

In college, at UTEP, where he played linebacker, Hochuli benched 370 pounds. But he spent the next 20 years ducking the weight room in favor of running marathons. By 1990, when he became an NFL back judge, he weighed a buck-seventy-five.

That's when he started lifting again. "I think it's important to look like an athlete," says Hochuli, who now weighs 210. "Athletes themselves respect you more. I tell [other officials] to look good, to look professional. I'm also vain enough that I want to look good. I work for a law firm—which is a conglomeration of egomaniacs—and as an NFL referee, where you also find a lot of big egos."

Self-deprecation endears Hochuli to people but is squarely at odds with his professional obligations. "As an official, you try to project confidence without arrogance," he says. He sometimes emerges from under the replay hood having reviewed a decision that is obstinately ambiguous, only to get a signal from the television crew that it's time to announce his verdict to the nation. "You gotta sell it," he says.

This is a problem on those days when you can't compose a simple declarative sentence. It took Hochuli 56 seconds to explain the new overtime rules before the fifth quarter of last year's NFC title game in San Francisco, leaving viewers more confused than they had been beforehand. "An overtime broke out in the middle of Hochuli's explanation," jokes Hochuli himself, whose three decades as a trial lawyer and extemporaneous speaker occasionally abandon him when he switches on his field mike. "Sometimes I open my mouth and don't know how the sentence is going to end," he says. "I can't tell you how many times I start to say something and realize halfway through, This is going to be on YouTube, isn't it?"

In that same NFC title game last January, Hochuli's tongue could not locate the word *indisputable*, as in *indisputable video evidence*. He finally settled on a rarefied legal term—"uncontroverted"—that sent a nation to its law dictionaries and the video, of course, to YouTube.

All of which makes Hochuli endearingly human in a way that Hochules never could be. He likes to walk the dogs with Cathie, his wife of 2½ years. ("That's an old-guy thing to do, isn't it?" he sighs.) Asked what kind of dogs he has, he is tempted to go off the record: "I should have two Dobermans, right? We have two little lapdogs. Shih Tzus. Sadie and Sophie."

"He's a total science-fiction nerd who goes to Comic-Con every year, listens to science fiction podcasts and waited in line overnight to [attend a panel discussion by the cast members of *Lost*]," says Shawn Hochuli, laughing but not kidding. "I'm surprised he didn't tell you any of this."

So let's sing of a man and the arms, in that order. For it's the man who radiates through the television screen a sense of justice and fair play. As a lawyer, Hochuli still goes to trial three or four times a year, and prospective jurors are always asked if they have any knowledge of his other profession. One man confessed that he was so certain of Hochuli's integrity as a ref that he'd be inclined to believe anything that Hochuli said in the courtroom. That juror was duly dismissed—which might have been his goal all along—but still: On a football field Hochuli exudes righteous impartiality. His unusual surname, after all, derives from Switzerland, land of neutrality.

Through no doing of his own, but rather through a deep national longing, Hochuli became the human face of locked-out officials, "more famous for not working than he ever was for working," as Markbreit says. When the lockout ended last week, 49ers receiver Randy Moss tweeted,

"Just found out Ed Hochuli and the boys are back!" Years ago, a fan approached him at Phoenix's Sky Harbor Airport and asked, "Are you Ed Hochuli?" Hochuli shook hands with Charles Barkley.

All Ed Hochuli ever wanted to be was a lawyer, he says, just like his dad, Walter, who moved the five Hochuli children from Milwaukee to Tucson when Ed was eight. "I was never a kid who pretended he was Babe Ruth," he says. "I never said, 'I want to be famous; I know what I'll do: I'll referee Pop Warner football games—that'll get me trending on Twitter.'"Forty years ago, a high school coach in Tucson named Dean Metz told a recent college graduate that refereeing was a great way to stay involved in football and also to earn some extra cash. The young man, newly married, started reffing four Pop Warner games every Saturday morning for 50 bucks a week. "I was instantly hooked," Hochuli says. "It was the internal challenge to be right."

Pop Warner led to high school, which led to junior college, which led to a back-judge job in the Pac-10. Finally, in the spring of 1990, after a league psychologist interviewed him for five hours, Hochuli had a job in the NFL.

In his first game, in Green Bay, he was, like every new official, astonished by the speed of professional players. That preseason night at Lambeau Field, Hochuli threw his first NFL flag, for pass interference. While the hankie was still tracing its majestic yellow arc, the rookie back judge had a terrible epiphany: That isn't pass interference in the NFL. Unable to catch the flag, he pretended it was never thrown, retrieving the marker and stuffing it back into his pocket like an airbag that had accidentally deployed.

Within a few years he was promoted to referee, having never even held that position in college. He still doesn't know why he was given the white hat. "I'm a far better referee than I was a back judge," he says. "The most important aspect of being a referee is leadership. Officiating is so much bigger than the sum of the pieces. You take care of each other. I'm in no way comparing officiating to war, but you have an esprit de corps when everyone is mad at you."

Of course, everyone is happy with Hochuli and his fellow officials now. When fans gave the real refs a standing ovation in Baltimore last Thursday night, before their first game back, 77-year-old Jerry Markbreit sat in his den in Skokie, Ill., and shed a tear.

"It'll last a week," Hochuli says of this strange honeymoon, which last week saw him get his own taped TV introduction on CBS ("Ed Hochuli, University of Texas–El Paso....") before he called a Jaguars-Bengals game in Jacksonville. Soon enough, the fans' focus will return to its rightful place, the players, for whom he has a profound respect. "They're real people—fun guys with great personalities," he says. "I am so impressed with them. We have a very superficial relationship, but the number of times I have seen a player drag himself up in agony, just killing himself for this job, and then stay in the game to do it again...."

He remembers Brett Favre rolling right and reversing left toward a blindside hit from Warren Sapp and thinking, They're gonna bring out the ambulance. But Favre popped up instantly, smacked his face mask against Sapp's and screamed, "Is that the hardest you can hit, you [polysyllabic profanity]?!"

To witness their talent up close is a privilege. "Half a dozen times a game," he admits, "I still say, Wow!"

On rare occasions one of these athletes will pancake Papa Touchdown. Junior Seau sped late to a tackle in one game and leaped over the pile to avoid piling on, breaking his fall on Hochuli. Like a London pedestrian, the referee apologized for getting hit. "You were in my blind spot," he told Seau.

"You mean I got you in the eyes?" Seau replied.

Hochuli howls. Aspersions on his eyesight are a game-day leitmotif. Former Falcons coach Jerry Glanville once said something unprintable to him, and Hochuli replied, "What did you say?" Glanville turned to an assistant and said, "Hear that? He's not just blind, he's deaf too."

He's less blind than blond. "He definitely has his blond moments," says Shawn. Like the time Hochuli forgot his uniform for a game in Green Bay. "I couldn't go to Foot Locker," he says. "Different stripes." A colleague sent his jersey up from Milwaukee, and the Packers' seamstress sewed on an 85.

But far more often Hochuli is wildly overprepared. He carries the same silver dollar all season for coin flips but still makes a member of his crew carry a spare, which Hochuli asks to see three or four times every game.

To summon his fullest concentration, he says out loud before each snap, "Lock and load." It's a mantra he repeats every single time the quarterback goes under center. He is a movie and baseball buff, and he recalls the film *For Love of the Game*, in which Kevin Costner played an aging Tigers pitcher who blocks out hostile crowd noise with a mantra of his own, Clear the mechanism.

"Your concentration level has to be so high for so long," he says—there are roughly 160 plays in every game—"and you're mentally exhausted when it ends. But it's hard to get off that high. It's like a mainline IV of adrenaline in my arm. I love that 50 million people are waiting for me to be right or wrong. It outweighs all the garbage—standing in a security line at the airport. The NFL spends eight hours reviewing every official in every game, and as long as my grades are solid, I would love to stay long enough to work with my son Shawn."

Shawn, a financial adviser in Newport Beach, Calif., resisted officiating at first. When he finally started, he reffed for two years without telling his father. He wanted to make it entirely on his own—a welcome effort in a profession where charges of nepotism are known to divide the ranks—and only ever used his first name when introducing himself to other refs in the Arena League, in NFL Europe and in the WAC and Big 12 conferences. But he is still his father's biggest fan as well as his acolyte. "My dad is my hero," Shawn said before refereeing the Cal–Arizona State game last Saturday. "He's my idol."

Ed Hochuli was standing on a corner in downtown Phoenix one day when he saw a guide dog lead a blind man across the street. As the pair safely reached the other side, the man pulled a biscuit from his pocket and fed it to the dog.

Hochuli couldn't help himself. "Excuse me, sir," he said to the man. "This is probably none of my business, but your dog just crossed against the light. You might not want to reward him for that."

To which the blind man said, "I'm just finding where his mouth is so I can kick him in the ass."

The transformative power of a kick in the ass is not lost on Hochuli, who was divorced from Bonnie, the mother of his first five children, 20 years ago. "I failed," he says, growing very quiet. "It was a very dark period, and...." He pauses, gathering himself to go on.

"My son Aaron was eight years old at the time," he continues. "And for the next four years—I'm sorry, it will be hard to get through this—but for the next four years he didn't speak to me or even look at me. For four years I kept showing up: 'Great practice today, Aaron.' And he'd walk right past me without looking." The tears are now coming, and his square jaw is going. "I'm sorry," Hochuli says, "but it tears me up."

He takes a deep breath and says, "When you fail, you have to kick yourself in the ass and go on. A lot of times we feel sorry for ourselves and let the defeats define us." Instead, he just kept showing up to see the boy who wouldn't see him back, until one day Aaron returned his gaze.

There's a picture on Hochuli's office wall, taken in 2004, of his children—Heather, Scott, Jennie, Shawn, Aaron and Rachel—and various spouses and grandchildren outside of Reliant Stadium in Houston before Super Bowl XXXVIII. All of these Hochulii wear number 85 referee jerseys, even the babies. During warmups, Hochuli spotted them in their seats, a herd of zebras in a sea of Patriots and Panthers jerseys. “The best moment of my career,” he says, “was looking up and seeing that.”

Aaron calls his dad “a big softie with a big heart, a great guy who’d do anything for his kids and grandkids.” The boy is 28 now, with two children of his own. On Friday nights he referees high school football games in Arizona, in unspoken homage to his father, Papa Touchdown, who was once broken and then repaired, and who has now returned to where he belongs: behind the glass panel of our flat-screen TVs, the ceramic zebra in our national curio cabinet.

OCTOBER 29, 2007

Shadow Warriors

Like their brethren across the league, the Detroit Lions' practice squad players live in a world of blurred lines and constant uncertainty, one step removed from the NFL dream—or from football oblivion

BY LEE JENKINS

They look like NFL players. They hit like NFL players. They dress with NFL players and watch film with them. From Monday through Friday they are a crucial part of every NFL team. But come Sunday, the only day in the league that really matters, they wear jeans and polo shirts. They are the anti–Allen Iversons. They just practice.

On Sunday, as the Detroit Lions hosted the Tampa Bay Buccaneers at Ford Field, Detroit's practice squad players were sitting in leather lounge chairs high above the action, munching on quesadillas and chicken tenders, watching their teammates from a luxury suite. It is one of the few luxuries of the job.In addition to the 53 players on the active roster, every NFL team has an eight- or nine-man practice squad—a unit made up of players who fulfill a critical role but are not full-fledged team members. Practice squad players are paid a minimum of $4,700 per week, but their salaries are not guaranteed beyond today. They're eligible neither for long-term benefits nor for an NFL pension. If their team wins the Super Bowl, they're entitled to championship rings—but not necessarily ones with real diamonds. In a league of bling, the practice squad is cubic zirconium.

The Lions' nine-player practice squad is diverse but not atypical. Ron Bellamy, a former Michigan standout, has one career NFL reception. Ben

Noll, a former stockbroker, has one career start. Brandon Middleton, a former substitute teacher, has played in one NFL game. Jon Dunn, a former chef, has never gotten onto the field. These are the veterans of the group. None of them is older than26.

While those players are trying to sustain NFL dreams, the younger ones are just embarking on theirs. Rudy Sylvan is an undrafted rookie free agent; LaMarcus Hicks, an undrafted second-year free agent; Buster Davis, a third-round pick in the 2007 draft; Ramzee Robinson, the last player drafted this year; and Salomon Solano, a free agent from Mexico who is part of the NFL's international development program.

They are not tackling dummies. The squad includes linemen who weigh in at 300 pounds and receivers who run a 4.4 40-yard dash. They come from such football powers as Florida State, Alabama and Virginia Tech. All were legitimate NFL prospects. Many of them still are.

But when they are on the practice squad, their names are listed below the 53-man roster, below the injured list, below the inactive list, not even on the depth chart. At this time a year ago none of the Detroit nine was in the NFL. Six were not playing organized football. Their career options included the Arena league, Canadian football and other fields altogether. "Look how far we've come," says Bellamy, 25. "Now we're just one play away."

One Play Away–it is the mantra of practice squad players everywhere. They are indeed that close to making the active roster. But they are also one misplay away from losing whatever shot they had. One blown assignment in practice and they may be gone for good. Pro Bowlers and first-round draft picks cannot fathom the anxiety.

"It eats at your guts," says Middleton, 26. "It has to be the hardest job in the NFL."

On Monday the practice squad players study tape of a game they did not play in. On Tuesday they study tape of an opponent they will not play against. On Wednesday, Thursday and Friday, in practice, they pretend to be people they're not. And on Saturday, when the other players go to a hotel, the practice squad players go home, to one-bedroom apartments with month-to-month leases. They have the weekend off. But they would rather be working.

"I've seen it take the love away from a lot of guys," says Dunn, 25, a three-year starter at tackle for Virginia Tech (2002–04). "That's the secret to doing this: No matter what happens, you can't ever let it take the love away."

Dunn's devotion was tested last month. He was watching NFL games on his couch in Virginia Beach, monitoring injury lists. Practice squad players do not like to acknowledge the obvious: For their chance to arise, someone usually has to get hurt. One Play Away can be a euphemism for One Injury Away.

Dunn was among the Cleveland Browns' final cuts in 2006 and the New York Giants' final cuts this summer. A skilled chef, he thought about opening his own restaurant if football didn't work out. But before he could begin devising a menu, the Lions called. Two of their offensive linemen had suffered rib injuries against the Philadelphia Eagles on Sept. 23. Detroit needed another big body.

Dunn is 6'7" and 324 pounds, so wherever he goes people ask him if he plays in the NFL. "Yes," he tells them. "I play for the Lions." Then they ask if they'll see him on television on Sunday. "Not exactly," he explains. "I'm practice squad."

That really confuses them.

Practice squads were instituted by the NFL in 1989 as a way to give teams a pool of extra bodies to draw from in practice or in the event of injury. At the time the squads comprised five players per team, but in 2004 they were expanded to eight. The Lions carry a ninth player as one of 11 teams participating in the league's international program, which is intended to cultivate new talent and grow the game outside the U.S.

Solano, 22, is a novelty on the practice squad, a player whose job is guaranteed through the season. He was a defensive tackle at the University of Tamaulipas in Mexico—several dozen Mexican colleges play American football—and hopes eventually to play in the NFL. More likely he'll end up as the defensive coordinator back at Tamaulipas. He has already taught the Lions' scheme at his alma mater. "The pressure on the other guys in the practice squad is a lot more," Solano says.

Lions coach Rod Marinelli views his squad as a farm system, a kind of football Triple A. Before their Week 3 game against Philly, the Lions called up Sylvan to fill in at tight end for the injured Dan Campbell. Then they sent Sylvan back down. Before the fourth game, as first-round pick Calvin Johnson nursed a bruised lower back, they elevated Middleton to the active roster. After the game they sent him down too.

Neither player had performed poorly. In fact, Middleton, who set Conference USA records for receiving yards and touchdown receptions as a senior at Houston in 2004,returned three kicks for a total of 70 yards and forced a fumble on special teams in a 37–27 win over the Chicago Bears. But when Johnson healed, the Lions needed a roster spot for him. Middleton had to go.

For just a moment Middleton missed Hightower High, outside Houston. At this time last fall he was a substitute teacher at Hightower. He stopped working out. He played football on weekends. When he told his students he used to be on the St. Louis Rams' practice squad, they didn't believe him. After they Googled his name, they accused him of creating a fake website with his picture and bio. "I had to call some former teammates and put them on speaker," says Middleton, 26. "After that I could feel a lot more respect in the classroom."

Something unexpected happened to Middleton during his time away: He enjoyed it. He knew his next paycheck was coming. He knew he could see his young daughter, Brielle, after work. And he knew, when the phone rang, it was not a coach calling to inform him of his release. "For the first time in my life I had stability," he says. "I wasn't waking up in the morning thinking, Is this it? Is this going to be my last day?"

He was done with football, but football wasn't done with him. Last winter NFL Europa called, and Middleton could not bring himself to hang up the phone. He played well enough with the Frankfurt Galaxy for the Lions to invite him to training camp. "I wanted somebody to just come out and tell me I wasn't talented enough to play in the NFL," Middleton says, "but nobody ever told me that."

When Middleton is losing hope, he need only look across the locker room at another former teacher. Jon Kitna started his professional career in the classroom, before joining the Seattle Seahawks' practice squad in 1996. Now he is the Lions' starting quarterback and an 11-year NFL veteran. "I know a lot of guys think the practice squad is a waste," Kitna says, "but it's the best thing I could have gone through."

They've all taken fairly circuitous routes to Detroit. For instance, Lions scouts found Noll at the football factory known as Northwestern Mutual Financial Network.

An all–Ivy League offensive lineman at Penn as a senior in 2003, Noll studied business and finance at the prestigious Wharton School. While his friends moved on to six-figure jobs as stock traders, he left Penn early to try to make it in the NFL. During the 2004 season he played in four games at guard for the Dallas Cowboys and started one, opening holes in a game in which Julius Jones scampered for 149 yards.

After Noll was waived by the Cowboys and then the Rams, he landed a job as a trader at Northwestern Mutual. He bought suits and ties. Then last December the Lions offered him a spot on their practice squad, and he put the finery back in the closet. "Nothing in the world compares to playing football," Noll says.

He is the rare NFL player who studies for forensic anthropology exams in the locker room. Noll is taking Internet courses toward his bachelor's degree from Penn. Last week he had a midterm. Next week he'll begin writing an essay on the fall of the Romanov dynasty during the Russian revolution. "I'm just like any other student," Noll says.

Except that his course load includes both the Bolsheviks and the Buccaneers. Every week the practice squad is required to learn everything about the opposing team. An offensive player such as Noll has to know the opposing defense in case he's suddenly activated. And he has to know the opposing offense in order to mimic it in practice.

The practice squad's primary role is to work on the scout team, giving the starters an accurate representation of what they'll see from the opposition on Sunday. Coaches call this representation the Look. Marinelli sometimes refers to the scout team as the Look Squads.

During practice last week Middleton and Buster Davis were supplying two of the most important looks. Middleton was pretending to be Joey Galloway, the Bucs' No. 1 receiver. Davis was pretending to be Derrick Brooks, Tampa Bay's Pro Bowl linebacker. Doing this every week can cause an identity crisis.

Davis wants to be the next Derrick Brooks, not his scout-team doppelganger. Like Brooks, he was a star linebacker at Florida State. He started 37 consecutive games, earned second-team All-America honors in 2006 and was drafted in the third round, 69th overall, by the Arizona Cardinals last April.

But during training camp the Cardinals saw a player who was uninspired and overweight. They wanted to send Davis to their practice squad, but he refused the assignment. Arizona released him before the season began, swallowing his $610,000 signing bonus.

Davis nevertheless ended up exactly where he didn't want to be—on an NFL practice squad. But in Detroit he has come to appreciate the role. "I'm not mad," he says. "It's a teaching tool. Ten or 15 years from now I'll be glad things weren't given to me." He pauses for a moment. "But I'll be up there this season."

Up there is on the active roster. Rookies make a minimum of $16,700 a week, with benefits. If they play three or more games, they get insurance in the off-season and earn a year toward their pensions. And they get to play football on Sunday.

Ramzee Robinson had no reason to think he would be *up there* this season. As the last player taken in the draft, No. 255 overall, he was dubbed Mr. Irrelevant—the perfect title for a practice squad player. It appeared that the highlight of his year would be the trip he took in June to Newport Beach,

Calif., where he was the guest of honor at the annual Irrelevant Week and received the traditional Lowman Trophy.

When Robinson did not make the Lions' active roster out of training camp, he wondered how he could support his family in Alabama. So he applied for a second job, flipping hamburgers at a Red Robin. The restaurant manager thought it was a prank—why would a Lions defensive back want to be a fry cook?—and rejected the application. He told Robinson to concentrate on football full time.

The advice paid off last week. Two Lions cornerbacks went down with injuries, and Robinson prepared for his call-up. But on the Wednesday before the game, the club signed Dovonte Edwards, a corner who'd last played for the Vikings in 2005. Robinson fumed. "Doing this job," he says, "you're always playing with fire." He could have packed up and left. Just as practice squad players can be released at any time, they can also sign to join another team's active roster if they get an offer. But Robinson stayed, and during practices last week it became apparent to the coaches that he was ready to play. He knew the system. Edwards was still learning it. On Saturday afternoon Lions player personnel director Sheldon White informed Robinson that he was going to make his NFL debut.

Robinson stayed up late Saturday night studying his playbook. He called family members, but they didn't have enough time to fly to Detroit. They had to rush just to buy the DirecTV package.

At 1 p.m. on Sunday, when the Lions lined up to kick off against the Bucs, Robinson was on the field. Mark Jones was back deep for Tampa Bay. As the ball was booted, Robinson sprinted down the sideline. Jones brought it out, and Robinson darted toward the middle. At the 22-yard line he dived at Jones's legs and spun him to the turf. First NFL play, first NFL tackle.

Robinson hopped out of the scrum, pumping his fists and yelling, like a guy who had just been set free. In fact, he had been set free—from the practice squad. "The way I reacted right there," he said afterward, "was an illustration of everything you go through."

In the luxury box the guys were rooting for their own. All around, it was a good day for the practice squad. Not only did Robinson see significant time on special teams, but Sylvan also made the active roster, started and played extensively; Marinelli said afterward that both had performed well. The Lions beat the Bucs, improving their record to 4–2, and the squad played a subtle but significant role in the victory. Its members clearly had given all the right looks during the week.

"Sitting up there, I root for the Lions like I've been here my whole life," says Dunn, the offensive tackle. "This is my team. They've got me to the end."

But what if another team—say, one that needs an extra offensive tackle and has an open spot on the active roster—calls tomorrow? "Oh," says Dunn. "Then I guess I'd have to root for them."

As for Robinson, he found out just how fleeting freedom can be. On Monday the Lions waived him, standard NFL procedure for a player moving off the active roster. Once Robinson cleared waivers, 24 hours later, the Lions expected to re-sign him, to the practice squad once more.

OCTOBER 27, 2008

Go Strong or Get Toasted

To cut it as an NFL cornerback requires the ability to read minds, eyes and hips; the tools to match up with wideouts half a foot taller; and above all the ego to bounce back from regular doses of abject—and very public—humiliation

BY SELENA ROBERTS

A lightning round of charades is unfolding on the edge of the field. The man doing the guessing is the cornerback, perched on the line of scrimmage—or, as he sees it, on a limb. He must distill the clues: The animated Peyton Manning is doing the hokeypokey behind center, picking his left foot up, putting his left foot down, and then, as if scratching an itch, he flicks the skin on his arm. Skin rash? No, skinny-post route. "He touches his arm, and the guy is going to run that route," says third-year Titans cornerback Cortland Finnegan, who faces Manning and the Colts twice a season in the AFC South. "Some quarterbacks tap their heads, and that means a go route." In the next instant a cornerback must apply split-screen vision, one eye still on the quarterback—a three-step drop indicates a quick route; a five-step portends deep trouble—and another on the receiver.

An intense hand of poker plays out. The Patriots' Randy Moss is breaking downfield in cornerback Quentin Jammer's shadow. In lockstep with Moss, the Chargers' Jammer is focused on the receiver's narrow hips. Don't bite on shimmies. Don't be a sucker for shakes. Hips are the directional arrows. Besides, Moss possesses more clever deceptions as a player gifted with height, agility and robotic eyes: He can make lids, lashes and sockets resist natural reflex. His eyes never widen at the sight of a spiral, eliminating a tip cornerbacks crave in determining when to turn and look for the pass. "Randy's really good at it," says veteran Green Bay cornerback Al Harris. Moss keeps gliding downfield as if on casters, with a strategically bored expression on his face. He gives up nothing, won't even lift a finger. Instead of raising his hands for the catch, another red flag for a defender, Moss lets the ball find him, allowing the pass to materialize in his grip, as if he has just plucked it from behind the cornerback's ear hole. "You can't panic," says Jammer, who confronted this scenario against Moss in a game on Oct. 12. "All you can do is make a play on the ball in his hands. I poked it out." Touchdown saved. Humiliation avoided.

Somewhere, a sportscaster, with clichés in the pocket of his tweed blazer and Ted Baxter in his voice, will have to tuck away his go-to nicknames for the poor, beaten cornerback: Toast, Grilled Cheese, Baked Alaska are popular. Anything charred, broiled or fried might be used to describe a position that is picked apart more than ever in the high-flying NFL. Embarrassment is part of the job description. Perhaps no corner has suffered more ignominy than the Saints' recently retired Fred Thomas, the hapless star of a YouTube clip entitled *Worst Cornerback Ever*. The four-minute, 35-second montage has drawn more than 135,000 views of Thomas flailing on at least 35 big pass plays. T.O., Ocho Cinco, Plaxico—he gets skunked by them all, as Iron Maiden's *Man on the Edge*, with its refrain "falling down, falling down," plays in the background.

That's just so wrong. HeHateMe isn't only for Rod Smart's jersey anymore. The conspiracy against cornerbacks isn't simply a viral phenomenon on the Internet; it's a contagion within the NFL rules, which, for the sake of fan-lovin' offense, have given receivers room to roam. No contact after five yards. No grabbing jersey fibers on a catch. The laws have been on the books for years, but only in 2004—after a leaguewide slump in offense, after Indianapolis complained about New England's clutching Marvin Harrison until he wrinkled in the AFC title game—did the NFL begin to enforce them strictly. Flag the culprits, the NFL declared. The persecuted cornerback was left with no other choice but to kill the zebras...with kindness. "I stroke them before the game," Harris explains with a laugh. "I go talk to them. You know, 'Hey, ref, how you doing; how's it going to be today?' And he'll say, 'I'm all right, Al, but I'm calling it tight.' They always do."

Receiver freedom has been a boon for offensive coordinators with deep thoughts. In 2003 the Colts led the NFL with 261.2 passing yards per game; after Week 7 this season Drew Brees had the Saints on a magic carpet, passing for 318 yards per game. In 2003 two QBs threw for more than 4,000 yards; last year the number was seven, which might seem unlucky for the cornerback until you consider how the pay and prestige has escalated with the job hazard. In '07 the 49ers set the market for top corners, signing free agent Nate Clements to an eight-year, $80 million contract. Since then the Eagles' Asante Samuels and the Raiders' Nnamdi Asomugha and DeAngelo Hall also signed for around $10 million a season. "Now it's just as valuable having a great corner as a great receiver," says Rod Woodson, the 11-time Pro Bowl defensive back who retired in 2004. "I think you'll start seeing more kids want to play corner. Kids say, 'I want to be a quarterback' or 'I want to be Jerry Rice.' Those are the limelight positions. But cornerbacks have risen to a level where they're getting recognized. They're on TV just as much."

More than a few cornerbacks possess the ham gene handed down by Deion Sanders to a generation of showmen who embrace the heightened scrutiny. The attention makes some want to put on their dancing shoes after a big hit or interception or incomplete pass. Neon Deion, a nine-time All-Pro from 1991 through '99, made coverage cool as he played the role of barnacle, and then Barnum. He was an act to be followed. So some cornerbacks juke, others moonwalk—and one recently pole danced. On Oct. 6 against New Orleans, the Vikings' Antoine Winfield picked up a blocked field goal, darted 59 yards for a touchdown, then celebrated by sliding down the goalpost. The NFL fined him $10,000. "A lot of [corners] have swagger," Winfield says. "It's confidence."

A healthy self-esteem provides a shield for every touchdown given up, for each missed open-field tackle, for the high rate of failure. "You're more exposed than anyone else," Winfield says. "It's always the cornerback's fault." Every man who plays this most vulnerable position longs to be known as a shutdown corner. Clements's website, lockdown22.com, features his image next to a padlocked chain. Harris's depicts him unveiling his full Rastafarian 'do as he yells into a lens next to the headline FEAR THE DREADS.

Some cornerbacks are less disciples of Deion than of Denver's Champ Bailey, noted for his quiet consistency. He is solid, strong and 6 feet tall on thick soles. Finnegan, who like a lot of corners stands shy of 6 feet, is packed with muscle, giving his body the look of a stocking stuffed with rolls of quarters. He didn't aspire to a stage, though he grew up in north Florida, not far from Florida State, where Sanders received his Prime Time start. The Seminoles didn't recruit Finnegan; no elite program did. He was playing mostly safety at quaint Samford, in Alabama, when the Titans drafted him in the seventh round in 2006 and changed his career track. "I remember saying to myself, I definitely don't want to be a cornerback. They don't tackle," Finnegan says. "But now I get to blitz. Now I thrive on challenges."

Hubris can make a cornerback feel a half-foot taller, a mental victory given the common height differential between corners and wide receivers.

Jammer gave up four inches to Moss if you believe the rosters, six inches if you believe your eyes, but few cornerbacks suffer a Napoleon complex. They are a secure bunch. "You've got to gamble," Finnegan says. "You gaze back into that receiver's eyes, and you bring it." Cornerbacks have a pool shark's mentality. They see angles; they take risks; they hone tricks. "I cheat a little bit," says Winfield. "If you show me something on film, trust me, the next week I'm going to play that route. If you do something different, well, I'll get beat." Of all the players on the field, the cornerback is arguably the most fearless, because he has the most to lose with each decision.

It doesn't matter if the defense is in man-to-man, Cover Two or Cover Three; it's always a catch-me-if-you-can matchup as the cornerback and receiver fly down the field, close enough to hear each other grunt, to sense each other's anxiety. In the lead-up to Super Bowl XLII, Moss suggested he could see fear in the eyes of a defensive back. Winfield senses it too when he watches his peers. "You can see fear by a cornerback's body language, if he's standing too far off a receiver, giving up too much cushion," Winfield says. "You can tell when a guy is afraid to play. You can see it."

Cornerbacks are human motion detectors. They notice nuance. When Terrell Owens leans on a defensive back's body, it means he's about to dash the opposite way, a good reason why cornerbacks cannot afford wasted movement. "One little hop, and that's three inches," Woodson says. "And that's a ball going over your hand for a catch." Cornerbacks are film students of human patterns. They know Chad Johnson can wiggle or circle his way to just about any route. "The best [wide receiver] I've covered is Chad," says second-year Jets cornerback Darrelle Revis. "In Cincinnati's offense he has the freedom to make any move he wants to." Some routes are more easily defended, but the timing patterns induce night sweats, particularly the fade to the corner of the end zone, when a pass arches over the receiver's back shoulder, landing in a spot unreachable to anyone but the quarterback's target.

The skinny post is devious, too. Just because a cornerback knows it's coming—Manning might flick his skin all day long—doesn't mean he can stop a play one cornerback calls "a bitch to cover." As the receiver plants downfield and breaks inside, the ball is already whistling past the cornerback's head. Clairvoyance is the only defense. "First time I played against the Colts, I was on the field before the game," Harris says of watching Indy run the route in warmups. "And my teammate in Philly, Troy Vincent, well, Troy never went out pregame. He stayed in the locker room and did his prayer. But I'm like, 'T, come on out here, you've got to see this play.'"

Not every pass play requires decoding. Some moments are just as they seem: "If your man is running like dogs are chasing him...you know the ball is coming, and it's going deep," Winfield says. "If a receiver is jogging, I pretty much relax." Receivers, if you ask a cornerback, treat contact like cooties. Really, how many crossing patterns does Moss run? But then there is Ravens receiver Derrick Mason, human projectile. "I mean to tell you, I could have slept for two days and gone into hibernation after playing him," says Finnegan. "On run plays he'd want to lock up every single time. And the whole game, he was just talking. It was talk-talk-talk, block-block-block. He'd say, 'I'm going to wear you out all day.' It was constant. All you can do is just smile and chuckle, and when you get a good hit on him, you just smile a little bigger."

Comeuppance can soothe a cornerback's weary body and mind. These are moments to indulge in because so many others—all the mistakes that cry out for a highlight film—wind up on an endless loop on *SportsCenter*, for everyone to witness. Friends see the clip and text a few jabs. Family members watch the goof and deliver jokes at Thanksgiving. "I have a 12-year-old son who's a corner," says Harris. "He's been doing drills since he was two. He'll see a highlight and say, 'Daddy, you didn't get a jump on that one, did you?' And I'll say, 'Let's turn off that TV.' Personally, I can't watch it."

What about the other cornerback highlight? The big hit that turns a game around, the strip of a ball that leads to a turnover, the interception to prevent a score? "Oh, that one? Oh, I can watch that all day long," Harris says, laughing. "I'm like, Hey, when's the next *SportsCenter*? Keep that TV on."

Don't touch that dial. Can't the cornerback—a.k.a. Fried Shrimp and Scorched Earth—get a little love?

A DANGEROUS GAME

SEPTEMBER 6, 1993

Concrete Charlie

Chuck Bednarik, the last of the 60-minute men, was a stalwart at both linebacker and center for the 1960 NFL champion Philadelphia Eagles

BY JOHN SCHULIAN

He went down hard, left in a heap by a crackback block as naked as it was vicious. Pro football was like that in 1960, a gang fight in shoulder pads, devoid of the high-tech veneer its violence has taken on today. The crackback was legal, and all the Philadelphia Eagles could do about it that Sunday in Cleveland was carry a linebacker named Bob Pellegrini off on his shield.

Buck Shaw, a gentleman coach in this ruffian's pastime, watched for as long as he could, then he started searching the Eagle sideline for someone to throw into the breach. His first choice was already banged up, and after that the standard 38-man NFL roster felt as tight as a hangman's noose. Looking back, you realize that Shaw had only one choice all along.

"Chuck," he said, "get in there."

And Charles Philip Bednarik, who already had a full-time job as Philadelphia's offensive center and a part-time job selling concrete after practice, headed onto the field without a word. Just the way his father had marched off to the open-hearth furnaces at Bethlehem Steel on so many heartless mornings. Just the way Bednarik himself had climbed behind the machine gun in a B-24 for 30 missions as a teenager fighting in World War II. It was a family tradition: Duty called, you answered.

Chuck Bednarik was 35 years old, still imposing at 6'3" and 235 pounds, but also the father of one daughter too many to be what he really had in mind—retired. Jackie's birth the previous February gave him five children, all girls, and more bills than he thought he could handle without football. So here he was in his 12th NFL season, telling himself he was taking it easy on his creaky legs by playing center after all those years as an All-Pro linebacker. The only time he intended to move back to defense was in practice, when he wanted to work up a little extra sweat.

And now, five games into the season, this: Jim Brown over there in the Cleveland huddle, waiting to trample some fresh meat, and Bednarik trying to decipher the defensive terminology the Eagles had installed in the two years since he was their middle linebacker. Chuck Weber had his old job now, and Bednarik found himself asking what the left outside linebacker was supposed to do on passing plays. "Take the second man out of the backfield," Weber said. That was as fancy as it would get. Everything else would be about putting the wood to Jim Brown.

Bednarik nodded and turned to face a destiny that went far beyond emergency duty at linebacker. He was taking his first step toward a place in NFL history as the kind of player they don't make anymore.

The kids start at about 7 a.m. and don't stop until fatigue slips them a Mickey after dark. For 20 months it has been this way, three grandchildren roaring around like gnats with turbo-chargers, and Bednarik feeling every one of his years. And hating the feeling. And letting the kids know about it.

Get to be 68 and you deserve to turn the volume on your life as low as you want it. That's what Bednarik thinks, not without justification. But life has been even more unfair to the kids than it has been to him. The girl is eight, the boys are six and five, and they live with Bednarik and his wife in Coopersburg, Pa., because of a marriage gone bad. The kids' mother, Donna, is there too, trying to put her life back together, flinching every time her father's anger erupts. "I can't help it," Bednarik says plaintively. "It's the way I am."

The explanation means nothing to the kids warily eyeing this big man with the flattened nose and the gnarled fingers and the faded tattoos on his right arm. He is one more question in a world that seemingly exists to deny them answers. Only with the passage of time will they realize they were yelled at by Concrete Charlie, the toughest Philadelphia Eagle there ever was.

But for the moment, football makes no more sense to the kids than does anything else about their grandfather. "I'm not *one* of the last 60-minute players," they hear him say. "I am *the* last." Then he barks at them to stop making so much noise and to clean up the mess they made in the family room, where trophies, photographs and game balls form a mosaic of the best days of his life. The kids scamper out of sight, years from comprehending the significance of what Bednarik is saying.

He really was the last of a breed. For 58½ minutes in the NFL's 1960 championship game, he held his ground in the middle of Philly's Franklin Field, a force of nature determined to postpone the christening of the Green Bay Packers' dynasty. "I didn't run down on kickoff's, that's all," Bednarik says. The rest of that frosty Dec. 26, on both offense and defense, he played with the passion that crested when he wrestled Packer fullback Jim Taylor to the ground one last time and held him there until the final gun punctuated the Eagles' 17–13 victory.

Philadelphia hasn't ruled pro football in the 33 years since then, and pro football hasn't produced a player with the combination of talent, hunger and opportunity to duplicate what Bednarik did. It is a far different game now, of course, its complexities seeming to increase exponentially every year, but the athletes playing it are so much bigger and faster than Bednarik and his contemporaries that surely someone with the ability to go both ways must dwell among them.

Two-sport athletes are something else again, physical marvels driven by boundless egos. Yet neither Bo Jackson nor Deion Sanders, for all their storied shuttling between football and baseball, ever played what Bednarik calls "the whole schmear." And don't try to make a case for Sanders by bringing up the turn he took at wide receiver last season. Bednarik has heard that kind of noise before.

"This writer in St. Louis calls me a few years back and starts talking about some guy out there, some wide receiver," he says, making no attempt to hide his disdain for both the position and the player. "Yeah, Roy Green, that was his name. This writer's talking about how the guy would catch passes and then go in on the Cardinals' umbrella defense, and I tell him, 'Don't give me that b.s. You've got to play *every* down.'"

Had Green come along 30 years earlier, he might have been turned loose to meet Bednarik's high standards. It is just as easy to imagine Walter Payton having shifted from running back to safety, or Lawrence Taylor moving from linebacker to tight end and Keith Jackson from tight end to linebacker. But that day is long past, for the NFL of the '90s is a monument to specialization.

There are running backs who block but don't run, others who run but only from inside the five-yard line and still others who exist for no other reason than to catch passes. Some linebackers can't play the run, and some can't play the pass, and there are monsters on the defensive line who dream of decapitating quarterbacks but resemble the Maiden Surprised when they come face mask to face mask with a pulling guard.

"No way in hell any of them can go both ways," Bednarik insists. "They don't want to. They're afraid they'll get hurt. And the money's too big, that's another thing. They'd just say, 'Forget it, I'm already making enough.'"

The sentiment is what you might expect from someone who signed with the Eagles for $10,000 when he left the University of Pennsylvania for the 1949 season and who was pulling down only 17 grand when he made sure they were champions 11 years later. Seventeen grand, and Reggie White fled Philadelphia for Green Bay over the winter for what, $4 million a year? "If he gets that much," Bednarik says, "I should be in the same class." But at least White has already proved that someday he will be taking his place alongside Concrete Charlie in the Hall of Fame. At least he isn't a runny-nosed quarterback like Drew Bledsoe, signing a long-term deal for $14.5 million before he has ever taken a snap for the New England Patriots. "When I read about that," Bednarik says, "I wanted to regurgitate."

He nurtures the resentment he is sure every star of his era shares, feeding it with the dollar figures he sees in the sports pages every day, priming it with the memory that his fattest contract with the Eagles paid him $25,000, in 1962, his farewell season. "People laugh when they hear what I made," he says. "I tell them, 'Hey, don't laugh at me. I could do everything but eat a football.'" Even when he was in his 50s, brought back by then coach Dick Vermeil to show the struggling Eagles what a champion looked like, Bednarik was something to behold. He walked into training camp, bent over the first ball he saw and whistled a strike back through his legs to a punter unused to such service from the team's long snappers. "And you know the amazing thing?" Vermeil says. "Chuck didn't look."

He was born for the game, a physical giant among his generation's linebackers, and so versatile that he occasionally got the call to punt and kick off. "This guy was a football athlete," says Nick Skorich, an Eagle assistant and head coach for six years. "He was a very strong blocker at center and quick as a cat off the ball." He had to be, because week in, week out he was tangling with Sam Huff or Joe Schmidt, Bill George or Les Richter, the best middle linebackers of the day. Bednarik more than held his own against them, or so we are told, which is the problem with judging the performance of any center. Who the hell knows what's happening in that pile of humanity?

It is different with linebackers. Linebackers are out there in the open for all to see, and that was where Bednarik was always at his best. He could intercept a pass with a single meat hook and tackle with the cold-blooded efficiency of a sniper. "Dick Butkus was the one who manhandled people," says Tom Brookshier, the loquacious former Eagle cornerback. "Chuck just snapped them down like rag dolls."

It was a style that left Frank Gifford for dead, and New York seething, in 1960, and it made people everywhere forget that Concrete Charlie, for all his love of collisions, played the game in a way that went beyond the purely physical. "He was probably the most instinctive football player I've ever seen," says Maxie Baughan, a rookie linebacker with the Eagles in Bednarik's whole-schmear season. Bednarik could see a guard inching one foot backward in preparation for a sweep or a tight end setting up just a little farther from the tackle than normal for a pass play. Most important, he could think along with the best coaches in the business.

And the coaches didn't appreciate that, which may explain the rude goodbye that the Dallas Cowboys' Tom Landry tried to give Bednarik in '62. First the Cowboys ran a trap, pulling a guard and running a back through the hole. "Chuck was standing right there," Brookshier says. "Almost killed the guy." Next the Cowboys ran a sweep behind that same pulling guard, only to have Bednarik catch the ballcarrier from behind. "Almost beheaded the guy," Brookshier says. Finally the Cowboys pulled the guard, faked the sweep and threw a screen pass. Bednarik turned it into a two-yard loss. "He had such a sense for the game," Brookshier says. "You could do all that shifting and put all those men in motion, and Chuck still went right where the ball was."

Three decades later Bednarik is in his family room watching a tape from NFL Films that validates what all the fuss was about. The grandchildren have been shooed off to another part of the house, and he has found the strange peace that comes from seeing himself saying on the TV screen, "All you can think of is 'Kill, kill, kill.'" He laughs about what a ham he was back then, but the footage that follows his admission proves that it was no joke. Bednarik sinks deep in his easy chair. "This movie," he says, "turns me on even now."

Suddenly the spell is broken by a chorus of voices and a stampede through the kitchen. The grandchildren again, thundering out to the backyard.

"Hey, how many times I have to tell you?" Bednarik shouts. "Close the door!"

The pass was behind Gifford. It was a bad delivery under the best of circumstances, life-threatening where he was now, crossing over the middle. But Gifford was too much the pro not to reach back and grab the ball. He tucked it under his arm and turned back in the right direction, all in the same motion—and then Bednarik hit him like a lifetime supply of bad news.

Thirty-three years later there are still people reeling from the Tackle, none of them named Gifford or Bednarik. In New York somebody always seems to be coming up to old number 16 of the Giants and telling him they were there the day he got starched in the Polo Grounds (it was Yankee Stadium). Other times they say that everything could have been avoided if Charlie Conerly had thrown the ball where he was supposed to (George Shaw was the guilty Giant quarterback).

And then there was Howard Cosell, who sat beside Gifford on *Monday Night Football* for 14 years and seemed to bring up Bednarik whenever he was stuck for something to say. One week Cosell would accuse Bednarik of blindsiding Gifford, the next he would blame Bednarik for knocking Gifford out of football. Both were classic examples of telling it like it wasn't.

But it is too late to undo any of the above, for the Tackle has taken on a life of its own. So Gifford plays along by telling what sounds like an apocryphal story about one of his early dates with the woman who would become his third wife. "Kathie Lee," he told her, "one word you're going to hear a lot of around me is Bednarik." And Kathie Lee supposedly said, "What's that, a pasta?"

For all the laughing Gifford does when he spins that yarn, there was nothing funny about Nov. 20, 1960, the day Bednarik handed him his lunch. The Eagles, who complemented Concrete Charlie and Hall of Fame quarterback Norm Van Brocklin with a roster full of tough, resourceful John Does, blew into New York intent on knocking the Giants on their media-fed reputation. Philadelphia was leading 17–10 with under two minutes to play, but the Giants kept slashing and pounding, smelling one of those comeback victories that were supposed to be the Eagles' specialty. Then Gifford caught that pass.

"I ran through him right up here," Bednarik says, slapping himself on the chest hard enough to break something. "*Right here*." And this time he pops the passenger in his van on the chest. "It was like when you hit a home run; you say, 'Jeez, I didn't even feel it hit the bat.'"

Huff would later call it "the greatest tackle I've ever seen," but at the time it happened his emotion was utter despair. Gifford fell backward, the ball flew forward. When Weber pounced on it, Bednarik started dancing as if St. Vitus had taken possession of him. And as he danced, he yelled at Gifford, "This game is over!" But Gifford couldn't hear him.

"He didn't hurt me," Gifford insists. "When he hit me, I landed on my ass and then my head snapped back. That was what put me out—the whiplash, not Bednarik."

Whatever the cause, Gifford looked like he was past tense as he lay there motionless. A funereal silence fell over the crowd, and Bednarik rejoiced no more. He has never been given to regret, but in that moment he almost changed his ways. Maybe he actually would have repented if he had been next to the first Mrs. Gifford after her husband had been carried off on a stretcher. She was standing outside the Giants' dressing room when the team physician stuck his head out the door and said, "I'm afraid he's dead." Only after she stopped wobbling did Mrs. Gifford learn that the doctor was talking about a security guard who had suffered a heart attack during the game.

Even so, Gifford didn't get off lightly. He had a concussion that kept him out for the rest of the season and all of 1961. But in '62 he returned as a flanker and played with honor for three more seasons. He would also have the good grace to invite Bednarik to play golf with him, and he would never, ever whine about the Tackle. "It was perfectly legal," Gifford says. "If I'd had the chance, I would have done the same thing to Chuck."

But all that came later. In the week after the Tackle, with a Giant-Eagle rematch looming, Gifford got back at Bednarik the only way he could, by refusing to take his calls or to acknowledge the flowers and fruit he sent to the hospital. Naturally there was talk that Gifford's teammates would try to break Concrete Charlie into little pieces, especially since Conerly kept calling him a cheap-shot artist in the papers. But talk was all it turned out to be. The Eagles, on the other hand, didn't run their mouths until after they had whipped the Giants a second time. Bednarik hasn't stopped talking since then.

"This is a true story," he says. "They're having a charity roast for Gifford in Parsippany, N.J., a couple of years ago, and I'm one of the roasters. I ask the manager of this place if he'll do me a favor. Then, when it's my turn to talk, the lights go down and it's dark for five or six seconds. Nobody knows what the hell's going on until I tell them, 'Now you know how Frank Gilford felt when I hit him.'"

He grew up poor, and poor boys fight the wars for this country. He never thought anything of it back then. All he knew was that every other guy from the south side of Bethlehem, Pa., was in a uniform, and he figured he should be in a uniform too. So he enlisted without finishing his senior year at Liberty High School. It was a special program they had; your mother picked up your diploma while you went off to kill or be killed.

Bednarik didn't take anything with him but the memories of the place he called *Betlam* until the speech teachers at Penn classed up his pronunciation. Betlam was where his father emigrated from Czechoslovakia and worked all those years in the steel mill without making foreman because he couldn't read or write English. It was where his mother gave birth to him and his three brothers and two sisters, then shepherded them through the Depression with potato soup and second-hand clothes. It was where he made 90 cents a round caddying at Saucon Valley Country Club and $2 a day toiling on a farm at the foot of South Mountain, and gave every penny to his mother. It was where he fought in the streets and scaled the wall at the old Lehigh University stadium to play until the guards chased him off. "It was," he says, "the greatest place in the world to be a kid."

The worst place was in the sky over Europe, just him and a bunch of other kids in an Army Air Corps bomber with the Nazis down below trying to incinerate them. "The antiaircraft fire would be all around us," Bednarik says. "It was so thick you could walk on it. And you could hear it penetrating. *Ping! Ping! Ping!* Here you are, this wild, dumb kid, you didn't think you were afraid of anything, and now, every time you take off, you're convinced this is it, you're gonna be ashes."

Thirty times he went through that behind his .50-caliber machine gun. He still has the pieces of paper on which he neatly wrote each target, each date. It started with Berlin on Aug. 27, 1944, and ended with Zwiesel on April 20, 1945. He looks at those names now and remembers the base in England that he flew out of, the wake-ups at four o'clock in the morning, the big breakfasts he ate in case one of them turned out to be his last meal, the rain and fog that made just getting off the ground a dance with death. "We'd have to scratch missions because our planes kept banging together," he says. "These guys were knocking each other off."

Bednarik almost bought it himself when his plane, crippled by flak, skidded off the runway on landing and crashed. To escape he kicked out a window and jumped 20 feet to the ground. Then he did what he did after every mission, good or bad. He lit a cigarette and headed for the briefing room, where there was always a bottle on the table. "I was 18, 19 years old," he says, "and I was drinking that damn whiskey straight."

The passing of time does nothing to help him forget, because the war comes back to him whenever he looks at the tattoo on his right forearm. It isn't like the CPB monogram that adorns his right biceps, a souvenir from a night on some Army town. The tattoo on his forearm shows a flower blossoming to reveal the word MOTHER. He got it in case his plane was shot down and his arm was all that remained of him to identify.

There were only two things the Eagles didn't get from Bednarik in 1960: the color TV and the $1,000 that had been their gifts to him when he said he was retiring at the end of the previous season. The Eagles didn't ask for them back, and Bednarik didn't offer to return them. If he ever felt sheepish about it, that ended when he started going both ways.

For no player could do more for his team than Bednarik did as pro football began evolving into a game of specialists. He risked old bones that could just as easily have been out of harm's way, and even though he never missed a game that season—and only three in his entire career—every step hurt like the dickens.

Bednarik doesn't talk about it, which is surprising because, as Dick Vermeil says, "it usually takes about 20 seconds to find out what's on Chuck's mind." But this is different. This is about the code he lived by as a player, one that treated the mere thought of calling in sick as a betrayal of his manhood. "There's a difference between pain and injury," Maxie Baughan says, "and Chuck showed everybody on our team what it was."

His brave front collapsed in front of only one person, the former Emma Margetich, who married Bednarik in 1948 and went on to reward him with five daughters. It was Emma who pulled him out of bed when he couldn't make it on his own, who kneaded his aching muscles, who held his hand until he could settle into the hot bath she had drawn for him.

"Why are you doing this?" she kept asking. "They're not paying you for it." And every time, his voice little more than a whisper, he would reply, "Because we have to win."

Nobody in Philadelphia felt that need more than Bednarik did, maybe because in the increasingly distant past he had been the town's biggest winner. It started when he took his high school coach's advice and became the least likely Ivy Leaguer that Penn has ever seen, a hard case who had every opponent he put a dent in screaming for the Quakers to live up to their nickname and de-emphasize football.

Next came the 1949 NFL champion Eagles, with halfback Steve Van Buren and end Pete Pihos lighting the way with their Hall of Fame greatness, and the rookie Bednarik ready to go elsewhere after warming the bench for all of his first two regular-season games.

On the train home from a victory in Detroit, he took a deep breath and went to see the head coach, who refused to fly and had one of those names you don't find anymore, Earle (Greasy) Neale. "I told him, 'Coach Neale, I want to be traded, I want to go somewhere I can play,'" Bednarik says. "And after that I started every week—he had me flip-flopping between center and linebacker—and I never sat down for the next 14 years. That's a true story."

He got a tie clasp and a $1,100 winner's share for being part of that championship season, and then it seemed that he would never be treated so royally again. Some years before their return to glory, the Eagles were plug-ugly, others they managed to maintain their dignity, but the team's best always fell short of Bednarik's. From 1950 to '56 and in '60 he was an All-Pro linebacker. In the '54 Pro Bowl he punted in place of the injured Charlie

Trippi and spent the rest of the game winning the MVP award by recovering three fumbles and running an interception back for a touchdown. But Bednarik did not return to the winner's circle until Van Brocklin hit town.

As far as everybody else in the league was concerned, when the Los Angeles Rams traded the Dutchman to Philadelphia months before the opening of the '58 season, it just meant one more Eagle with a tainted reputation. Tommy McDonald was being accused of making up his pass patterns as he went along, Brookshier was deemed too slow to play cornerback, and end Pete Retzlaff bore the taint of having been cut twice by Detroit. And now they had Van Brocklin, a long-in-the-tooth quarterback with the disposition of an unfed doberman.

In Philly, however, he was able to do what he hadn't done in L.A. He won. And winning rendered his personality deficiencies secondary. So McDonald had to take it when Van Brocklin told him that a separated shoulder wasn't reason enough to leave a game, and Brookshier, fearing he had been paralyzed after making a tackle, had to grit his teeth when the Dutchman ordered his carcass dragged off the field. "Actually Van Brocklin was a lot like me," Bednarik says. "We both had that heavy temperament."

But once you got past Dutch's mouth, he didn't weigh much. The Eagles knew for a fact that Van Brocklin wasn't one to stand and fight, having seen him hightail it away from a postgame beef with Bob Pellegrini in Los Angeles. Concrete Charlie, on the other hand, was as two-fisted as they came. He decked a teammate who was clowning around during calisthenics just as readily as he tried to punch the face off a Pittsburgh Steeler guard named Chuck Noll.

Somehow, though, Bednarik was even tougher on himself. In '61, for example, he tore his right biceps so terribly that it wound up in a lump by his elbow. "He just pushed the muscle back where it was supposed to be and wrapped an Ace bandage around it," says Skorich, who had ascended to head coach by then. "He hardly missed a down, and I know for a fact he's never let a doctor touch his arm." That was the kind of man it took to go both ways in an era when the species was all but extinct.

The San Francisco 49ers were reluctant to ask Leo Nomellini to play offensive tackle, preferring that he pour all his energy into defense, and the Giants no longer let Gifford wear himself out at defensive back. In the early days of the American Football League the Kansas City Chiefs had linebacker E.J. Holub double-dipping at center until his ravaged knees put him on offense permanently. But none of them ever carried the load that Bednarik did. When Buck Shaw kept asking him to go both ways, there was a championship riding on it.

"Give it up, old man," Paul Brown said when Bednarik got knocked out of bounds and landed at his feet in that championship season. Bednarik responded by calling the patriarch of the Browns a 10-letter obscenity. Damned if he would give anything up.

All five times the Eagles needed him to be an iron man that season, they won. Even when they tried to take it easy on him by playing him on only one side of the ball, he still wound up doing double duty the way he did the day he nailed Gifford. A rookie took his place at center just long enough to be overmatched by the Giants' blitzes. In came Bednarik, and on the first play he knocked the red-dogging Huff on his dime. "That's all for you, Sam," Bednarik said. "The big guys are in now."

And that was how the season went, right up to the day after Christmas and what Bednarik calls "the greatest game I ever played." It was the Eagles and Green Bay for the NFL championship at Franklin Field, where Bednarik had played his college ball, and there would be no coming out, save for the kickoffs. It didn't look like there would be any losing either, after Bednarik nearly yanked Packer sweep artist Paul Hornung's arm out of its socket.

But there was no quit in Vince Lombardi's Pack. By the game's final moments, they had the Eagles clinging to a 17–13 lead, and Bart Starr was throwing a screen pass to that raging bull Jim Taylor at the Philadelphia 23. Baughan had the first shot at him, but Taylor cut back and broke Baughan's tackle. Then he ran through safety Don Burroughs. And then it was just Taylor and Bednarik at the 10.

In another season, with another set of circumstances, Taylor might have been stopped by no man. But this was the coronation of Concrete Charlie. Taylor didn't have a chance as Bednarik dragged him to the ground and the other Eagles piled on. He kicked and cussed and struggled to break free, but Bednarik kept him pinned where he was while precious seconds ticked off the clock, a maneuver that NFL rulemakers would later outlaw. Only when the final gun sounded did Bednarik roll off him and say, "O.K., you can get up now."

It was a play they will always remember in Philadelphia, on a day they will always remember in Philadelphia. When Bednarik floated off the field, he hardly paid attention to the news that Van Brocklin had been named the game's most valuable player. For nine-of-20 passing that produced one touchdown—an ordinary performance, but also his last one as a player—the Dutchman drove off in the sports car that the award earned him. Sometime later Bednarik caught a ride to Atlantic City with Retzlaff and halfway there blurted out that he felt like Paul Revere's horse.

"What do you mean by that?" the startled Retzlaff asked.

"The horse did all the work," Bednarik said, "but Paul Revere got all the credit."

In the mornings he will pick up his accordion and play the sweet, sad "etnik" music he loves so much. As his football-warped fingers thump up and down the keyboard, he often wishes he and Emma and the girls had a family band, the kind Emma's father had that summer night he met her at the Croatian Hall in Bethlehem. Not what you might expect, but then Bednarik is a man of contradictions. Like his not moving any farther than his easy chair to watch the Eagles anymore. Like his going to 8 a.m. Mass every Sunday and saying the Rosary daily with the industrial-strength beads that Cardinal Krol of Philadelphia gave him. "I'm a very religious person, I believe in prayer," Bednarik says, "but I've got this violent temper."

Sixty-eight years old and there is still no telling when he will chase some joker who cut him off in traffic or gave him the finger for winning the race to a parking place. If anybody ever thought he would mellow, Bednarik put that idea to rest a few years back when he tangled with a bulldozer operator almost 40 years his junior. As evening fell the guy was still leveling some nearby farmland for housing sites, so Bednarik broke away from his cocktail hour to put in a profane request for a little peace and quiet. One verb led to another, and the next thing Bednarik knew, he thought the guy was going to push a tree over on him. He reacted in classic Concrete Charlie fashion and got a fine that sounded like it came from the World Wrestling Federation instead of the local justice of the peace: $250 for choking.

That wouldn't change him, though. It slowed him down, made him hope that when he dies, people will find it in their hearts to say he was a good egg despite all his hard edges. But it couldn't stop him from becoming as gnarly as ever the instant a stranger asked whether he, Chuck Bednarik, the last of the 60-minute men, could have played in today's NFL. "I wasn't rude or anything," he says, "but inside I was thinking: I'd like to punch this guy in the mouth."

Of course. He is Concrete Charlie. "You know, people still call me that," he says, "and I love it." So he does everything he can to live up to the nickname, helping to oversee boxing in Pennsylvania for the state athletic commission, getting enough exercise to stay six pounds under his final playing weight of 242, golfing in every celebrity tournament that will invite Emma along with him, refusing to give ground to the artificial knee he got last December. "It's supposed to take older people a year to get through the rehab," he says. "I was done in four months." Of course. He is the toughest Philadelphia Eagle there ever was.

But every time he looks in the mirror, he wonders how much longer that will last. Not so many years ago he would flex his muscles and roar, "I'm never gonna die!" Now he studies the age in his eyes and whispers, "Whoa, go back, go back." But he can't do it. He thinks instead of the six teammates from the 1960 Eagles who have died. And when he sees a picture of himself with six other Hall of Fame inductees from 1967, he realizes he is the only one still living.

It is at such a moment that he digs out the letter he got from Greasy Neale, his first coach with the Eagles, shortly after he made it to the Hall. "Here, read this out loud," Bednarik says, thrusting the letter at a visitor. "I want to hear it."

There is no point in asking how many times he has done this before. He is already looking at the far wall in the family room, waiting to hear words so heartfelt that the unsteady hand with which they were written just makes them seem that much more sincere.

Neale thought he hadn't given Bednarik the kind of introduction he deserved at the Hall, and the letter was the old coach's apology. In it he talked about Bednarik's ability, his range, his desire—all the things Neale would have praised if his role as the day's first speaker hadn't prevented him from knowing how long everybody else was going to carry on.

"If I had it to do over again," he wrote in closing, "I would give you as great a send-off as the others received. You deserve anything I could have said about you, Chuck. You were the greatest."

Then the room is filled with a silence that is louder than Bednarik's grandchildren have ever been. It will stay that way until Concrete Charlie can blink back the tears welling in his eyes.

MAY 7, 2001

The Wrecking Yard

As they limp into the sunset, retired NFL players struggle with the game's grim legacy: a lifetime of disability and pain

BY WILLIAM NACK

When I came to my first NFL camp, it was like I was a tall, cold can of beer. They popped the top, and all that energy and desire and ability poured out. I gave of myself with the same passion that I had in high school and college. When I was empty, when I had no more to give, they just crumpled me up and threw me on the garbage heap. Then they grabbed another new can and popped him open, and he flowed out until he was empty.

—CURT MARSH, NFL LINEMAN 1981-86

They are the wincing, hobbling wounded: the men who played professional football, a notoriously joint-shearing, disk-popping, nerve-numbing exercise that has grown only more dangerous since Curt Marsh last crashed into a defensive lineman as a Los Angeles Raider.

"If you go to a retired players' convention, there are older retirees who walk around like Maryland crabs," says Miki Yaras-Davis, director of benefits for the NFL Players Association. "It's an orthopedic surgeon's dream. I'm surprised the doctors aren't standing outside the door handing out their cards. Hardly one [former player] you see doesn't need a hip replacement. Everybody comes out of pro football with some injury. It's only the degree that separates them."

A 1990 Ball State study, commissioned by the NFLPA and covering the previous 50 years of league history, revealed that among 870 former players responding to a survey, 65% had suffered a "major injury" while playing—that is, an injury that either required surgery or forced them to miss at least eight games. The study also reported that the percentage of players incurring such injuries had increased alarmingly: from 42% before 1959 to 72% in the 1980s, after many stadiums had switched from grass to artificial turf. Two of every three former players disclosed that their football injuries had limited their ability to participate in sports and other recreation in retirement, and more than half of them also had a curtailed ability to do physical labor. Of those who played during the '70s and '80s, nearly half (50% and 48%, respectively) reported that they had retired because of injury—up from 30% in the years before 1959.

There's little doubt, based on a follow-up survey in 1994 and on considerable anecdotal evidence, that injuries in the NFL are becoming more serious and frequent as the colliding bodies grow bigger and stronger. The 300-pound-plus Sira-goosed lineman, a rarity 40 years ago, is today as common as the soccer-style kicker. James Andrews, a leading orthopedic surgeon who has been operating on pro football players for almost 30 years, sees a correlation between the worsening of injuries and the size and power of the modern player. In fact, Andrews, who works out of the HealthSouth Medical Center in Birmingham, is witnessing the rise of a phenomenon that was almost unheard of only 15 years ago.

"The incidence of serious, *noncontact* knee injuries is much higher than it used to be," he says. Artificial turf is only part of the problem. "These athletes are bigger, stronger and running faster, and they're tearing up knees from cutting, changing direction on a dime," Andrews says. "In fact, the incidence of anterior cruciate ligament injuries is higher from noncontact than contact. I've seen guys get significant injuries just falling on the football. It's like a big tree falling."

Indeed, among the most notable casualties of noncontact incidents are two gifted running backs: Jamal Anderson and Ki-Jana Carter. Anderson, of the Atlanta Falcons, missed all but two games in 1999 after tearing the ACL in his right knee during a *Monday Night Football* game on artificial turf; his foot got snagged in the rug, and Anderson went one way as his popping knee went another. Carter, the top pick in the 1995 draft, tore his left ACL in his rookie year by simply "twisting" the knee, says Andrews. The former Penn State star was cut by the Cincinnati Bengals last June and hasn't been picked up by another team.

As for the New Age tyrannosaurs battling in the trenches, they have become so large and powerful that injuries have risen alarmingly in their hand-to-hand combat. "They are exerting forces strong enough to dislocate their elbows and shoulders forward and backward," Andrews says. "With the blocking techniques we're seeing, there's an increased incidence of offensive linemen's shoulders being dislocated."

Some players have quit rather than court more pain. A teary-eyed John Elway, claiming he still had a passion for the game at age 38, retired two years ago because his body could no longer take the punishment. Minnesota Vikings running back Robert Smith, 28, an unrestricted free agent at the height of his game, astounded the NFL in February by retiring without explanation, turning his back on what was expected to be a lively bidding war, with offers likely to exceed $30 million for five years. Smith had already had three knee surgeries, and while his agent, Neil Cornrich, denied that the on-the-job pounding played any part in the running back's decision to leave the game, Smith had implied as much to reporters. (Another running back, Curtis Enis, retired last week at 24 because of a degenerative condition in his left knee. Enis, the No. 5 pick in the 1998 draft, tore a ligament in that knee during his rookie season, with the Chicago Bears.)

No matter how young they are when they retire, a great many NFL players face a visit in middle age from that most pernicious of postfootball afflictions, degenerative arthritis. An athlete who suffers an injury to a major weight-bearing joint, such as the hip or knee, is five to seven times more likely to develop degenerative arthritis than an average member of the population. Repeated pounding and jarring of the joints—even in the absence of injury—all but guarantee that former players will be caught in the ganglia of serious and chronic pain. The 1994 NFLPA–Ball State survey said that arthritis is the most commonly reported health problem among retired players, affecting 47% of respondents.

"A lot of ex-players with terribly arthritic spines say, 'But I never had a back injury!'" Andrews says. "That doesn't matter. There's no way to heal those cartilage lesions. They heal with scar tissue and are never as good again. What you end up with is a bunch of ex-NFL players, in their 40s and 50s, who shouldn't have arthritis but have degenerated knees and need total replacement done at an early age."

This, then, is not about a few casualties wandering off the playing field into retirement, their bells rung and still chiming in their heads, but rather about a whole society of broken men hounded through their lives by pain and injury, and all the psychological problems that often attend them.

Johnny Unitas once owned the most dangerous right arm in the NFL. Today he barely has use of the hand attached to it. Unitas, who is considered by many to be the greatest field general to play the game, is still paying for a hit he took more than three decades ago as a Baltimore Colt. That day in 1968, Unitas was drawing back his arm to throw a pass when a Dallas

Cowboy mashed the inside of his elbow. Unitas came back to play again—the arm seemed fine up through his retirement in 1974—but by the mid-1990s he was having problems with the nerves that controlled his hand and fingers. He lost strength and feeling in the hand and became unable to rotate the thumb back and grasp objects. The symptoms only got worse. Now Unitas cannot close the hand that made Raymond Berry famous.

Unitas's two knee replacements work perfectly well—cartilage and ligaments in the right knee were torn in a collision with two Bears in 1963, while the left wore out from years of favoring the right—but when he plays golf, which is about all the exercise he can get with those knees, he has to use his left hand to close the fingers of his gloved right hand around the grip, then strap the hand to the shaft with a Velcro strip. He goes through this tedium on every shot. "I do it putting, too," says Johnny U, who's 68.

Forty years ago Unitas was the toughest and smartest quarterback in the game, calling the plays and running the show in a way that inspired both fear and awe among teammates and opponents alike. Mentally, he always seemed a step ahead of everyone else. If a situation looked ripe for a pass, Unitas would signal a run; if it called for a run, he'd throw a pass. If it called for a pass and his opponents, trying to outguess him, set up for a run, he'd throw. Unitas perfected the two-minute drill, and no one since—not Montana, not Elway—has run it better.

Setting an NFL record that seems as unassailable as Joe DiMaggio's 56-game hitting streak, Unitas threw a touchdown pass in 47 consecutive games between 1956 and 1960. In the years since, only Dan Marino has come anywhere close to that mark, throwing scoring passes in 30 straight games from 1985 to '87.

Unitas has demanded disability compensation from the league but says he has been turned down for various reasons, among them that he didn't apply by age 55—though his right hand didn't fail him until he was 60—and that the league pays him a pension of $4,000 a month. The NFL adds that, in its opinion, Unitas is not "totally and permanently disabled."

Meanwhile, of that magical hand that spun footballs like strands of gold, Unitas says, "I have no strength in the fingers. I can't use a hammer or saw around the house. I can't button buttons. I can't use zippers. Very difficult to tie shoes. I can't brush my teeth with it, because I can't hold a brush. I can't hold a fork with the right hand. I can't pick this phone up.... You give me a full cup of coffee, and I can't hold it. I can't comb my hair."

Bill Stanfill never thought it would come to this. Never conceived, through all his years as a rampaging defensive end for the Miami Dolphins, that he would be reduced to what he is now. Never imagined that at 54, he would be navigating his house in Georgia with a metal walker—step-shuffle, step-shuffle—as he recovered from hip-replacement surgery. Or still feeling the consequences of that near-fatal injury he suffered when, during a preseason game against the Bengals in 1975, he cracked heads with teammate Vern Den Herder and almost severed his spinal cord between vertebrae C-4 and C-3.

It was like nothing he had ever felt. "I'd had stingers, but this was entirely different," Stanfill recalls. "I just numbed up. Could not move my arms or feel myself breathing." Stanfill had subluxed the joint in his cervical spine; that is, a disk and the surrounding bone had slipped nearly far enough to damage the cord. Stanfill would never be the same player again, and by the end of the next year he would be out of football. Two decades later, in the mid-'90s, the disks began herniating, and he has had four vertebrae fused in his cervical spine.

"I can't tip my head back at all," says Stanfill, an avid bird hunter, "so I can't shoot dove anymore. I feel like I swallowed a Viagra pill and it got stuck in my throat. My neck is stiff as hell. The neurosurgeons have told me that if another disk goes [in my cervical spine], I will be totally disabled."

Stanfill was an old-fashioned football gladiator, a 6'5½", 255-pound country boy who won the Outland Trophy, as the college game's best interior lineman, in his senior year at Georgia; helped Miami win two Super Bowls, after the 1972 and '73 seasons; and was named to four Pro Bowls. He relished the battle in the trenches, mano a mano. "All I wanted to do was play," he says.

All those wars left all those scars, however, and not only to his spine. In late January, while sitting next to the fireplace in his five-bedroom redbrick house outside Albany, Ga., Stanfill pointed out a glass jar sitting on the mantel. At the bottom of the jar, immersed in a clear solution, was a mysterious white ball. "I'm gonna see if I can donate it for auction," he said. "'Who wants a piece of Bill Stanfill?' That's part of me. The price I paid for playing pro football."

It was the ball of his left hip, and it had been sawed off his skeleton three weeks earlier. Stanfill had been suffering from avascular necrosis (AVN)—in which blood circulation is cut off to the hip bone, causing it to die—because of repeated trauma and, possibly, repeated injection of the anti-inflammatory drug cortisone when he was in pro ball. ("I was like a pincushion," he says.) Stanfill sells agricultural real estate, but he has worked little since March 2000, when a disk in his lower back ruptured. Doctors have told him that his right hip also has AVN and will have to be replaced.

Stanfill's football days have left him a physical wreck, making him wonder what his life will be like in five years. Still, he expresses neither rancor nor self-pity. "Just wish I'd made some of the money they're making today," he says wryly. "It would make this a lot easier to live with."

Earl Campbell has a dazzling assortment of rings that were given to him in honor of his storied accomplishments as a college and pro running back: the Heisman Trophy ring, the NFL Rookie of the Year ring, one MVP ring (though he was MVP three times) and the NFL Hall of Fame ring, but he wears none of them because of arthritis in both his hands, the ones that he used to push away pursuing tacklers. "Jim Brown and I were the best at the stiff-arm," says Campbell. "Now I can barely close my left fist—the arthritis and the soreness and the pain."

Campbell was a complete force as a running back, fast enough to turn the corner and race upfield, strong enough to crash through the line. He always seemed to be running out of his clothes; it was as if he invented the tear-away jersey. The abiding memory of Campbell is that of a man charging down the field with three defenders clinging to his back. It was easy to imagine him in the end zone dressed in nothing more than his jockstrap and shoulder pads, standing there with a quizzical smile on his face and various large bodies scattered behind him, each clutching a remnant of his uniform. As his Houston Oilers coach, Bum Phillips, said, "Earl Campbell may not be in a class by himself, but whatever class he's in, it doesn't take long to call roll."

Now 46 and the owner of a barbecue restaurant and a sausage-making business in Austin, Campbell winces at more than his swollen digits. His knees and back ache ceaselessly. He also has a condition called drop foot: As a result of nerve damage to his legs, he cannot raise the front of his feet when he lifts them off the ground to take a step. The feet flop along loosely when he walks. To use the bathroom upstairs from his home office, Campbell—unable to grip with his hands or bend his knees—must lean his forearms on the railings and drag himself up the eight or 10 steps. The process is as painful to watch as it must be for Campbell to complete.

"I realize that every time you get something in life, you've got to give up something," he says. He likes to hunt deer and wild boar in south Texas, and he is reminded of what he gave the game whenever he is home on the range. "Sometimes it gets to the point that I can't stand the pain, like when I've got to walk a lot," he says. "Thank God I'm with people who understand me: 'Take all the time you need.' It's embarrassing when I've got to hop onto the back of a pickup and I need help. Or I need help climbing into deer blinds.

"Sometimes I tell my wife, 'Shoot, if I knew it was going to hurt like this, I don't know if I'd have [played football].' It's a hell of a price to pay."

For most NFL players, especially linemen, weight training is as much a part of the daily regimen as stretching exercises—and the weight room works its own form of wickedness. Hoisting iron, players rupture the patella tendons in their knees, put enormous strain on their lower backs and cause ligament injuries to the lumbar spine. They even damage their shoulders by doing something the joint was not designed to do: bench-pressing huge weights.

Joe Jacoby, a former Washington Redskins offensive lineman, was a habitue of the Skins' weight room, squat lifting his afternoons away. He dare not lift weights anymore, for fear it will accelerate the deterioration of his ankles, knees, wrists, elbows and back. Jacoby still feels the echoes of years spent snatching iron and leaning his sequoia body into snot-blowing defensive linemen who drove shuddering forces down his spine and onto his lower joints.

At 6'7", 305 pounds, Jacoby was a giant among the Hogs, a 13-year veteran who retired in 1993, the year he collapsed in his bathroom at home and could not get up. "My lower back went out," he says. "I dropped to my knees on the floor. The pain was that sharp. I crawled out of the bathroom to the bed." Like Stanfill, imbued with the ethic to play in pain, Jacoby played again later that year. Then, against the Kansas City Chiefs, his back went out again. He ended up spending three days in a hospital.

"I never wanted to go out that way," says Jacoby, 41. "I wanted to keep playing, even though I was hurting. I felt like I was letting down the team. You've been brought up that way since high school. It's *ingrained* in you. I had a wife. I had a family. A business I was starting. But I kept hearing those little things in the back of my mind: *You're letting your team down.*" He was in traction, shot up with cortisone, when the thought finally struck him: I can't keep doing this. I have a life to live after this.

Jacoby had blown out his left knee earlier in his career, when his leg got wrenched in a pileup during a field goal attempt. "The kneecap was way over on the side of the knee," he recalls. "I still hear the crunching and popping." Another old wound—vintage for linemen, who are forever getting their fingers caught and dislocated in face masks and shoulder pads—is the busted knuckle on Jacoby's wedding-band finger, as gnarled as a tree root. He has won many wagers in bars, claiming he can get the ring over that knuckle. His wife, Irene, had the band made with a clasp, so he can take it off like a bracelet.

Jacoby owns an auto dealership in Warrenton, Va. He and Irene had the sinks in the kitchen and master bathroom of their house installed higher than normal, "so he doesn't have to bend down," she says. He often walks about sockless in loafers. "It's too painful for him to bend over and put on socks or lace up shoes," Irene says.

Jacoby walks stiffly on his damaged ankles, but he endures the discomforts with stoic grace. He still remembers vividly the pounding he took year after year, through 170 games, including four Super Bowls—a career that left him unable to do any exercise other than walking. "Some days the back gets unbearable," he says. "It's really deep in the lower back and goes down to my left buttock and hamstring. Sometimes it gets so bad it hurts my nuts. There's pain down my left leg now. My left foot has been numb for two months. The bone's pressing on the nerve. Too many years of abuse, using the back to block."

Like so many other hobbled former players, Jacoby says he would do it all again if he had the chance. He knew what he was getting into. "Football players know the risk and the consequences," he says. "They know they will pay for it later in life. If they don't, they are misleading themselves."

As much as Jacoby has gone through, he looks fortunate when compared with Chris Washington. Only 39, Washington seems old beyond his years. He was an NFL linebacker for seven seasons, most of them with the Tampa Bay Buccaneers, and he has had 21 operations. He suffers from severe arthritis in both knees—he has had six surgeries on the right, five on the left—and his right thigh and calf are atrophying. He endures his days with help from a pharmacopia in a kitchen cabinet: one pill for sleep, two for pain (including double-strength codeine) and two to reduce inflammation.

Washington was a zealous weightlifter, but now his home looks like a Gold's Gym after closing, with everything racked and idle: the stationary bike, the treadmill, the stair-climber and tons of barbells. He won't use any of them for fear of inflaming his diseased joints. Not only is he virtually crippled by ailing knees, but he also suffers hand tremors from pinched nerves; he shakes too much to fasten a necklace around his wife's neck. Although he has upper arms like ham shanks, he experiences periodic loss of strength in the right one and has back spasms as well. Washington carries his 10-month-old daughter, Taylor, in a Snugli, but not simply for convenience. He fears he will be seized by a shooting pain in his back or arm or suffer the sudden collapse of a knee and drop her—or, worse, fall on her.

Washington, who has worked as an insurance salesman and a data-entry clerk after retiring from the NFL in 1992, has been unable to hold a job since 1996. He draws disability payments to help support his family and is seeing his worst fears slide before his eyes. "Not being able to run around and play with my daughter," he says, giving one example. "I tried coaching [as a volunteer at the high school level], but my body couldn't take it; I can't stay on my feet that long. What kind of an example am I setting for kids if

I'm walking around with a cane? I don't go to a lot of NFL functions. I would like to hang out with those guys, but I don't want them to see me like this."

None of this comes in the tone of a complaint. Washington wishes only that when he played he had known more about what he was doing to his body and had taken better care of it. He wishes that he had not allowed himself to be shot up with painkillers and cortisone so he could play hurt. Like the other former players who have been down that tortuous road, he assumes his share of the blame. "It was my choice to do what I did," he says. "I guess I didn't expect to be in this kind of shape."

Nor did Harry Carson, for 13 years a crushing, headfirst inside linebacker of the New York Giants. Carson's injury is to a human organ that is still little understood. By his own count he suffered at least 15 concussions while playing pro football, from 1976 to '88, and he is afflicted by what Yaras-Davis, of the NFLPA, believes is one of the most common and troublesome maladies among former players: postconcussion syndrome, which is marked by headaches, forgetfulness, blurred vision and difficulty tracking mentally.

Former Cowboys quarterback Troy Aikman and former San Francisco 49ers quarterback Steve Young, each of whom has suffered repeated bell-ringers on the field, are the players most closely associated with concussions. Carson, however, was one of the first former players to go public with the debilitating aftershocks of concussions, in an attempt to broaden understanding of the problem. Carson had his share of other injuries, but none quite as stunning as the concussion he suffered in 1985 when he crashed head-on into his favorite opponent, Redskins fullback John Riggins. "It was pretty much my power against his power," Carson says. "I remember hitting John and going back to the huddle...everything faded to black. I was literally out on my feet."

Carson would find that such blows had long-term effects. In 1991, three years after he retired, he wrote in his journal, "I don't think as clearly as I used to. Nor is my speech, diction, selection of vocabulary as good as it used to be, and I don't know why." As a TV broadcaster with the MSG Network in New York City, he would occasionally misspeak. "I would mispronounce words and lose my train of thought," he says. "Things would happen, and I'd think I was going crazy. I'd go to the store to get something and forget what."

Like Yaras-Davis, Carson believes the syndrome is far more common than is generally thought. "One problem is that a lot of players who suffer from it have no clue what they're dealing with," says Carson, who still appears on a weekly show, *Giants GamePlan*, for MSG. "I've talked to players I've played with and against. Once I went public with this concussion thing, they were looking at me as being sort of brain-damaged, drooling and all this stuff. But it is an injury just like one to your knee or hip."

What ails Curt Marsh is far less elusive. The 41-year-old former offensive lineman for the Raiders could serve as a poster boy for crippled veterans who ache in all the usual NFL places: neck, back, knees, hips, ankles. Bone by bone, Marsh's body is gradually being replaced. He has had more than 20 operations, including one in '96 to replace his left hip, which had developed AVN, and he expects soon to undergo surgery to replace his right hip, which also has been damaged by AVN.

Like Stanfill, Marsh allowed team doctors to shoot him up repeatedly with painkillers and cortisone. By the time he retired, after seven years in the league, Marsh had a scoped knee, bulging disks and a right ankle that had been destroyed when the Raiders' team physician, Robert Rosenfeld, who died in 1994, apparently misdiagnosed and mistreated a broken talus bone. By 1994, after the 13th operation on it, the ankle was a hopeless ruin, and doctors cut off Marsh's leg eight inches below the knee.

Marsh is not shy about being an amputee. While attending a 1998 hearing of the California Senate's Industrial Relations Committee in Sacramento, Marsh, all 350 pounds of him, heard one agitated senator, Ross Johnson of Irvine, excoriate pro athletes who had taken advantage of the state's generous workers' compensation laws by filing their claims there, even if they lived in other states and had played only road games in California. Johnson, backing a bill that would have limited workers' comp payments for pro athletes, declared that he was "outraged" that "professional athletes, who earn huge sums of money, wind up abusing a system that was created for the benefit of average working men and women."

Moments later Marsh, in a move as memorable as any he ever made with the Raiders, pounced on Johnson, saying he was "offended" to see athletes being treated "as if they were a piece of meat" because they were well paid for their labors. "And that makes [what happens to them] O.K.? That really bothers me. We have families that go through the pain. We have...."

Here Marsh reached both hands down to his right leg, pressed a button on the side of his black boot and, to gasps from the audience, removed the prosthesis from his stump and raised it in the air. "Fact of the matter is, you cannot pay me enough money to make this worth my while," he said, holding the boot aloft. "This is a *real* issue.... Seventy times a game you run into a human being as big as you are. They say that's like a traffic accident.... What is that, 1,400 traffic accidents a year? And we're gonna say it's O.K. because we pay 'em a lot of money...but they don't deserve to get the same thing that we give everyone else?"

The bill was never enacted.

For all that he has been through, Marsh is remarkably free of bitterness, even though he believes his amputation was the result of poor medical care. "I'm not looking for pity," he says. "That's just the way it is." For him and for countless other veterans of pro football's trench warfare.

A whole battalion of Curt Marshes and Chris Washingtons and Earl Campbells is out there, enough to fill an NFL Old Soldiers' Home, doddering arthritically around the grounds. Busted knees, numb and bulbous ankles, sawed-off hips and all.

NOVEMBER 1, 2010

The Damage Done

While concussive hits dominate the debate, a groundbreaking new study suggests that minor blows—and there can be hundreds each game—are just as traumatic

BY DAVID EPSTEIN

You wouldn't guess that Jefferson High football players Joel Ripke and Brandon Stumph are part of a scientific breakthrough. Purdue researchers who put sensors in the helmets of the seniors from Lafayette, Ind., certainly didn't. Ripke, a mountainous 17-year-old at 6'6" and 260 pounds, is the Bronchos' starting right tackle. His buddy Stumph, a starter at defensive end, is a more mundane 6'1" and 190 pounds, but with a thirst for contact. His black helmet looks like one of those chipped and gouged bowling balls that hasn't beaten a straight path in years.

Despite their easy camaraderie and Penn-and-Teller size difference, Ripke and Stumph line up across from each other in practice and get after it, with Stumph breaking out every duck, dodge, chop or bull rush he knows to get past Ripke's forklift arms and Frisbee-sized mitts. "If I'm not bigger than the dude, I like to hit him with my helmet," Stumph says, "and then use a move so I can get his hands off me." Nor does Ripke shy away from putting hat on hat. He's been taught that effective run blocking requires three points of contact on the defender: hand, hand, helmet.

Despite their frequent bell-ringings and clock-cleanings, neither Ripke nor Stumph has suffered a concussion in practice or in a game. That would be unequivocally gratifying news, except that the Purdue researchers' data, to be published in the *Journal of Neurotrauma*, tell a far more troubling story. The findings suggest that while the NFL is going to unprecedented lengths to control the violent collisions that produce concussions, brain trauma in football may start much earlier, and much less conspicuously, with hits that never raise an eyebrow, much less a penalty flag.

Before the 2009 football season the group of Purdue engineering professors, athletic trainers and graduate students fitted 23 of the Bronchos' helmets with accelerometers and gave players both the ImPACT test—a computerized neurocognitive exam that tests memory and concentration—and tests of working memory while their brains were monitored with magnetic resonance imaging (MRI). The idea was to establish a baseline for each player against which he could be reexamined after a concussion. Says Thomas Talavage, a Purdue associate professor of biomedical engineering and electrical and computer engineering, "We were looking to understand what kinds of hits cause a concussion and what the consequences are."

Using NFL-sponsored studies as a guide, the researchers figured that hits in excess of 80 times the force of gravity (heading a soccer ball produces around 20 Gs) would cause concussions. So the Purdue researchers were stunned when, on the first day of full-contact practice, they started seeing hits of 100 Gs or more. "I thought, Oh, my god, we're going to be carrying these kids off the field," says Eric Nauman, associate professor of mechanical and biomedical engineering.

It turned out, however, that no particular magnitude of hit correlated with a concussion. One player holding the line on an extra-point attempt took 289 Gs to the helmet from a converging pair of would-be kick blockers. "You could hear the hit in the subdivision next door," says Evan Breedlove, a biomedical engineering grad student and member of the study team. But the lineman was fine. In fact, three weeks into the season the Purdue team had just one concussion for its study. (There were concussions among Bronchos players who were not part of the test.) So the researchers had players from the study who had never suffered concussions retake the ImPACT test and get their brains scanned with functional MRIs (fMRI), which image cerebral blood flow to pinpoint active areas in the brain. The players were meant to serve as a control group for later comparison to concussed teammates. But the first lineman who came in as an ostensible control subject surprised the researchers when, compared with the preseason, he scored 20% lower on the visual memory section of the ImPACT test, which requires rapid identification of recurring patterns. The player had no trouble with the verbal section, though, and Talavage began to think there might be something wrong with the test itself, which is used by the NFL and many college and high school teams to gauge whether a player has recovered from a concussion.

A few concussions did arise as the season went on, but the researchers continued to bring in nonconcussed players for ImPACT tests and fMRIs. And then they saw it again: Another kid who had never suffered a concussion flubbed the visual memory section of the ImPACT test. Of 11 players who took midseason testing, three had suffered concussions during the season and eight had never had concussions. Of those eight, four nevertheless showed significant declines in visual memory. In fact, the players with the most impaired visual memory skills were not coming from the concussed group but from a group that in the week preceding the test had taken a large numbers of hits—around 150—mostly in the 40 to 80 G range.

If the test scores were accurate, the researchers had inadvertently documented, in real time, a new classification of high school athlete: a player who was never concussed, was not verbally impaired and was asymptomatic even as far as his parents could tell, but whose visual memory was more impaired than his amnesic, headachy, light-sensitive, concussed teammates.

Says Talavage, "We started having weekly meetings to debate whether we were seeing something real."

And then they looked at the fMRIs. Those brain snapshots had been done while players took two versions of a working memory test. In the first version a subject must click a button each time a flashing letter repeats in sequence. D, A, B, B—*click*. The second version requires more brainpower: React when the letter that flashed two characters ago repeats. A, J, F, J—*click*.

All of the players were able to complete the test with relative accuracy, but the brain activity of the four players who took a lot of middling hits—but suffered no concussions—changed dramatically. When each one took the harder version of the test, there was an unmistakable decline in activity in an area of the brain just behind the forehead called the dorsolateral prefrontal cortex, which is critical to visual memory. "It's like a horse race," says Talavage. "When the brain starts a task, it starts all the horses running, and one wins, or gets the task done. But when the brain is already taxed, it prevents some of those horses from starting. There are fewer resources available."

Talavage has seen an interesting parallel in an unrelated study that compares gifted children with reading-impaired and average children. The gifted kids show relatively low brain activity on a reading test, presumably because they aren't challenged and need not summon all their mental horsepower. The average children start all the horses. But the reading-impaired subjects, like the gifted children, keep some of the starting gates closed—not because the task is too easy but because it is too difficult. A single week of 150 hits turned the four "functionally impaired" Jefferson High players, as the Purdue team calls them, into equivalents of the reading-impaired children, except that the damage was to visual memory.

Yet every method of sideline diagnosis for concussions relies on self-reported symptoms like headaches or dizziness, in addition to tests of verbal—not visual—memory. The NFL, for example, now mandates that a concussed player is done for the day if, after a hit, he can't carry on a coherent conversation or remember the last play or his gap assignment. The four functionally impaired Bronchos, however, showed absolutely nothing that would be categorized as a symptom. "You wouldn't even know to examine them," says Larry Leverenz, an athletic trainer and Purdue clinical professor of health and kinesiology who is on the study team. "There's nothing until you give them an fMRI or test the visual memory."

Even in the gladiator culture of football, the growing awareness of brain injury has transformed the act of hiding a concussion from one signifying bravery to one of stupidity. The functionally impaired four didn't hide symptoms; they never knew they had any.

Beyond the fact that the best predictor of impaired visual memory was not concussions but the number of hits absorbed in the previous week, one other bit of data jumped out at the Purdue researchers. While the players who were diagnosed with concussions tended to take heavy hits on the side of the helmet, the functionally impaired four tended to get hit on the front, essentially in the upper forehead, which houses the dorsolateral prefrontal cortex—where linemen get hit, play in and play out. It wasn't the rare, excessively violent collision between the wide receiver and the free safety, the Patriot missile intercepting the Scud, that mattered most, but rather the milder, more frequent kind of hits that replicated two adolescent rams knocking heads.

Consider this: Concussions as we know them involve a hit that rattles a part of the brain involved in language processing or motor skills. Hits to the forehead that might be every bit as damaging hide their nefarious effects in the frontal lobe, a part of the brain primarily involved in visual memory, planning and cognition, rather than motor or sensory function, and thus not taxed by sideline concussion exams. Indeed, it's possible that all along, while brain trauma questions have focused on concussions, the real damage is being inflicted by minor impacts that chip away at the brain. A 2009 study by researchers including Ann McKee, the Boston University neurologist who has autopsied the damaged brains of deceased former NFL players, noted that long-term brain deterioration did not strictly correspond to the history of concussions.

Randall Benson, a neurologist at Wayne State in Detroit who has studied former NFL players suffering from cognitive impairment and depression, says that some of them never suffered a concussion. Benson thinks the Purdue researchers may have taken a real-time snapshot of the early stages of the corrosive creep that wears away the frontal lobe, a part of the brain involved in navigating social situations. Too much erosion and victims reach a breaking point—like former Steelers offensive lineman Terry Long, who died in 2005 from drinking antifreeze. "It's an insidious progression," Benson says, "and it's not obvious when you talk to [players]." Benson has seen MRIs that show the brain drifting in the head with a movement as routine as a twisting of the neck. "It would defy the laws of physics if the brain didn't have a shearing injury when you stick your face into a 275-pound defensive lineman," he says.

But what if it doesn't take a 275-pound lineman? What if it takes only a 190-pound Brandon Stumph, the likes of whom many of the 1.1 million high school football players will encounter regularly on the field? Or what if it doesn't take even that? What if it just takes a one-pound soccer ball? In a 2003 study from the Florida Institute of Technology, subjects were briefly shown a design and directed to redraw it. Only one of 12 non-soccer-playing control subjects scored below the normal range, compared with seven of 21 soccer players who had a history of frequent headers. That cohort also scored worse on an IQ test than the control group, and lower than players who did not head the ball as frequently.

The mounting evidence suggests that some people—perhaps a lot—simply cannot play these games without being damaged, concussion or no concussion. "You can break something by hitting it hard once," says Katie Morigaki, a Purdue graduate assistant athletic trainer who worked on the study, "or you can break it by hitting it softer many times."

And now the good news. "There are issues we can address without changing football or racking up costs," says Nauman. If it's simply the number of hits that predict whether a player will suffer brain damage, then, like pitch counts, that can be managed. Instead of full-contact practice on Tuesdays and Wednesdays, high schools could take a cue from the pros. "If a school can't afford all this stuff"—like fMRI, which they invariably can't—"if they hit one fewer day a week, they're probably in better shape," Nauman says. Even simpler would be a cultural shift from the head-butt back to the high-five. The Purdue team found the Jefferson players' celebratory helmet-knocks registered 80 to 100 Gs near the frontal lobe.

More good news: Though the Bronchos were not told their test results, several, like Ripke and Stumph, figured out that they were in the high-hits group by virtue of getting called in for more fMRIs than their teammates. The Purdue researchers say one Jefferson High player who was in the impaired group last season seems to have figured that out and has played with better, heads-up technique this season, reducing the number of hits he's taken on the forehead.

And the best news: After nine months off from football, the functionally impaired players who were back for the 2010 season (one had graduated) returned to their baseline ImPACT scores. So perhaps the youthful brain is able to completely heal itself, or at least make up for any deficit.

Critical chronological windows are known to exist for recovery from particular brain injuries. For example, in the rare case when a very young child has a stroke and loses the ability to speak, a different part of the brain is able to take over speech, and the child invariably recovers full language ability. But if the stroke occurs after the age of nine, the brain is not as flexible, and the recovery may be longer and less complete. If it occurs after puberty, some symptoms will be permanent.

The Purdue study is continuing this fall at Jefferson High, with 32 Bronchos players now taking part, and it shortly will expand by adding the reigning Indiana Class 3A state champion West Lafayette High. Researchers hope to track players through high school and even college—Ripke hopes to play at the next level—to see at what point deficits become irreversible. That is, if they are not already looking at it. "Are these kids really coming all the way back to baseline?" Leverenz asks. "Or are they just a little bit off one year, and just a little bit off the next year, and pretty soon it's significant?"

Let's hope for good news.

COLORFUL CHARACTERS

NOVEMBER 26, 1990

Busman's Holiday

Coast-to-coast commuter John Madden likes what he sees as he rolls across America in his suite on wheels

BY PETER KING

When I was very young and the urge to be someplace else was on me, I was assured by mature people that maturity would cure this itch. When years described me as mature, the remedy prescribed was middle age. In middle age I was assured that greater age would calm my fever and now that I am fifty-eight perhaps senility will do the job. Nothing has worked.... I fear the disease is incurable.

—JOHN STEINBECK, *TRAVELS WITH CHARLEY*

John Madden, 54, has a job most of us would love to have. He sleeps as late as he wants and wears whatever clothes he wants almost every day of his life. He eats what he wants, when he wants. He *has* to be somewhere, with a tie on, for only three hours a week. He makes much more than a million dollars a year. To do this job, he crisscrosses the U.S. six months a year in the greatest bus you've ever seen. It is a hotel suite on wheels.

Madden, the CBS-TV color analyst who along with Pat Summerall forms the preeminent NFL broadcast team, is a big, friendly, surprisingly tranquil lug of a guy who sees his country as few other Americans do—from the ground floor. "People used to say to me, 'It must be great coaching and traveling and seeing all the things you do,'" says Madden, who piloted the Oakland Raiders for 10 years (1969 to '78) and to a Super Bowl championship. "Well, I'd get on the airplane, and then I'd get off the airplane, get on a bus and go to the hotel. Then the stadium, then the airplane again. I thought I'd traveled all over, but I hadn't seen anything. You've got to be on the ground to see things."

Madden is not talking about sightseeing. He's talking about being a witness to America—the land, the people, the lifestyles, the thoughts and the emotions that make up a society. He loved stopping at the Tastee-Freez in Sidney, Neb. (pop. 5,834), a few years ago to watch *Monday Night Football* on a small black-and-white TV, with a group of townspeople that included the coach and players of the local high school basketball team. He discovered great Mexican food in Van Horn, Texas (pop. 2,772), at a restaurant called Chuy's (pronounced CHEW-ees).

One fall he was walking through a Green Bay neighborhood and stopped to watch someone rake leaves; being a California guy, he had never raked leaves. While spending four days in Longboat Key, Fla. (pop. 8,000), between assignments last season, he was drawn every day to the Gulf Coast shoreline, where he watched the fishermen. You have to move around, overland, to see these things.

There have been circumstances in all of our lives that have placed us where we are today. There are reasons that Madden tours America on a bus. Twenty-eight years ago, as a myopic head coach at Allan Hancock College in Santa Maria, Calif., he read *Travels with Charley*, Steinbeck's rediscovery of America, and vowed one day to see the country. Madden tired of coaching after the '78 season and took a flier on a TV analyst gig with CBS in '79. Three attacks of claustrophobia while traveling to assignments forced Madden off airplanes and onto trains.

However, the Amtrak schedules weren't always convenient. The TV gig turned into a second career, one that has increased his wealth and fame more than he ever expected, and in '87 Greyhound offered to customize a bus for Madden and supply him with drivers for three years in return for promotional and speaking appearances. After three years, the bus would be his. It's now known as the Walker Advantage Muffler Madden Cruiser (a new sponsor, to cover expenses, you know), and Madden is one happy claustrophobic.

Sometime after dawn of every morning spent on the bus, while Madden sleeps soundly on a queen-sized, ultrafirm bed in the rear third of the vehicle, the driver stops to pick up a *USA Today* and whatever local paper is available. When Madden awakens, he picks up the intercom phone, calls one of his two drivers and asks, "Where are we?" And Dave Hahn or Willie Yarbrough might say, "In the middle of the Sierras, just past Reno," or, "Below Cleveland, almost into Pennsylvania."

Madden moves forward to the codriver's seat, puts his feet—in untied shoes, with no socks—on the railing near the windshield and digests the sports sections of the papers. During the day he eats, reads, talks and, for at least three or four hours, while sucking on an unlit Macanudo cigar, just peers through the front windshield and the huge side picture windows as America rolls past. He spends some time going over press releases and newspaper clippings about the teams playing in the game he'll be working that Sunday. Often he'll pick up the cellular phone and call his agent, Sandy Montag, in New York, or his wife, Virginia, in Blackhawk, Calif., or the coach of one of the teams in Sunday's game. At night he stops for dinner somewhere; rarely is it planned. Back on the bus he switches on one of his two 20-inch color TVs and pops a game tape into the VCR. He might watch two. Because it's his life, and he can do what he wants.

What follows is an account of his most recent coast-to-coast trip, from his house outside Oakland to his apartment on the Upper West Side of Manhattan. The Madden Cruiser left the East Bay area at noon on Wednesday, Sept. 26. It pulled in front of Madden's New York City apartment building at 10 p.m. on Friday, Sept. 28. I was on the bus with Hahn and Yarbrough, who split the nearly nonstop run into shifts; Madden's 25-year-old son, Joe, who is traveling with his dad this fall; and Madden's California neighbor, David Liskin, who was taking the long way to see family in Englewood Cliffs, N.J. The trip took 55 hours and covered 3,016 miles, but who's counting? Not Madden.

Day 1

Blackhawk, Calif., to the Nevada-Utah Border

We know so little of our own geography. Why, Maine extends northward almost to the mouth of the St. Lawrence, and its upper border is perhaps a hundred miles north of Quebec. And another thing I had conveniently forgotten was how incredibly huge America is.

—*TRAVELS WITH CHARLEY*

On the bus's digital temperature gauge, the outdoor reading is 79° and the indoor reading is 59°. No wonder Madden used to stalk the sidelines in shirtsleeves in December. The rules of the bus are made clear: "Don't wait for anyone, finish any bottle of water you start, drink right out of the bottle, and never take I-80 in or out of New York—there's always construction." Madden doesn't like the clutter of plastic bottles. One problem: The bottles each hold 50 ounces of water.

Soon the Madden Cruiser headed into the web of California freeways, turning onto I-580 and then onto I-205 in the San Joaquin Valley, where endless fields of vegetables were being irrigated. South of Stockton the bus picked up I-5, the freeway to Sacramento, which would connect with I-80, the highway Hahn and Yarbrough would drive for 53 hours. "Now, you don't think," Madden said, an hour from his front door. "You've got to turn off your brain for 50 hours."

On the right side, about mid-bus, is a table with two bench seats, and Madden, five deep slugs into his first bottle of water, sat on the bench facing the front. To his right were miles of fields. Straight ahead was road. He was the tour guide, and he relished the role. A passenger found out soon enough that one of Madden's favorite topics is America. He talked about its wide-open spaces with the same fervor he uses for a chalkboard description of a Lawrence Taylor sack. He is loquacious and engaging, but he doesn't burst through walls—as he was portrayed in the famous Lite beer commercials—and he doesn't wave his arms. That is Madden shtick. Madison Avenue Madden. This is the real Madden. On the whole trip, I counted only two booms, no whaps and no significant rise in his voice. You know, as in, "SeeTaylorcominginpastLacheyandBOOM!HelevelsBynerand-WHAP! Rypien'sdown!"

"If anything will impress you as you go across the country, it's how much space there is," he said. "This country, you'd think it was crowded, but you cross it, go for hours, and not see anything. You realize the only places that are truly congested are the big cities. Between congestions are just wide-open spaces. There's a hell of a lot more wide-open spaces than congested cities.

"That's why I've always said that before someone can be a congressman or a senator or president or vice-president, the person should ride across this country. Not drive, because you can't see when you drive. You have to ride, either like this or on a train. If you fly into Washington from New York, or from San Francisco or L.A. or Chicago, how the hell do you know? If a person can't see the country, how the hell can he represent it?"

He sounded like a father taking his seven-year-old son to see the Chicago Cubs play at Wrigley Field for the first time. "Wait until you see it all," he said.

Ninety miles outside of Reno, I asked the tour guide, "How did you get so interested in seeing the country?"

"*Travels with Charley* influenced me a lot," Madden said. "I always wanted to travel, because I'd never seen anything. He was a great storyteller, John Steinbeck. I read everything of his. What happened was, my wife was taking this class for her master's or something. It was a literature course, and she had to study an author. She picked Steinbeck. One of the things she had to do was go up to Monterey, where Cannery Row was, and I did the stuff with her. She'd read the books, and they were just lying around, so I'd read them.

The Monterey Peninsula, Cannery Row, is still my favorite place in the whole world.

"If the claustrophobia thing didn't happen, I wouldn't know what this country is, or what these people are like. I would have been like everybody else: run, run, run. Airport, airport, airport. Hotel, hotel, hotel. City, city, city. I wouldn't have found time to see things like I see them now."

The bus was climbing into the Sierras, and the temperature outside had dropped to 66°. "John Robinson and I were coaching together [with the Raiders in 1975] before he went to USC, and we used to ride to work together," said Madden. "He once said to me, 'You've changed. It's like you live in a tunnel. You don't have any idea what's going on in the world.' It was true. He thought I'd lost my sense of humor, my inquisitiveness. It got so I knew nothing other than football and the Raiders. I'm not criticizing that in myself; it's part of the job. You focus in so much, and you miss life."

In Nevada the bus sliced through mountains that were a mile and a half high. Yucca plants and paintbrush shrubs were the only things growing here, and Madden saw a solitary ranch about 500 yards off to the right. It consisted of a small house, two trailers, some farm machinery and about 600 head of cattle.

"What do they do at night?" he said, nodding toward the ranch. "No malls. No movies. No TV, it looks like. No neighbors. Where do they get groceries? If there's anything I'd really like to do, I'd like to pull into a place like that, knock on the door and say to the guy, 'What do you do? How do you live? God, I go to movies, restaurants, ball games, plays, the gas station, the market. You don't do any of those things. What do you do?'"

At about 5:30 p.m., he adjourned to his bedroom for a nap. When he returned an hour later, the sun was setting and the bus was passing through low clouds on a mountain pass. A voice on the CB piped up. "Breaker, breaker one-nine," a trucker said. "Is that the John Madden bus?"

"Affirmative," said Hahn.

"What game's he doing this weekend?"

"Giants-Cowboys in New York."

"Holy cow! That's a long way! Well, I enjoy listening to him."

We stopped for dinner in Elko, Nev., at a Red Lion Inn with a mini casino and sports book in the lobby. Madden walked through the casino, stopping at the sports book. The guy behind the counter was thrilled to see him. He started grilling Madden about who was going to win Sunday's games, and Madden, who doesn't gamble, kept telling the guy that he didn't know, that whatever he said would be only a guess—and he meant it.

"How can people bet on this stuff?" Madden would say later. "Nobody knows how these games are going to go."

Elko County is wider than Connecticut, and the town of Elko is the only place for 100 miles in either direction that has anything resembling shopping or something to do. It was 9:30 p.m., and Madden wanted to walk before eating. A shopping center was nearby, but most of the stores had already closed. The doughnut shop was still abuzz, and in the beauty shop a woman in a white uniform painted one last set of nails. Madden laughed. "God, are these things popular or what?" he said. "Every town in America has a nail shop, and somebody is always in 'em."

After Madden made a run through the Red Lion salad bar, the bus headed off into the night, and he broke out the tape of the Dallas-Washington game from the previous week. At 2 a.m., somewhere in the Great Salt Lake Desert, he turned off the TV and went to bed.

Day 2

Great Salt Lake Desert to Omaha

I discovered that I did not know my own country.... I knew the changes only from books and newspapers.

—*TRAVELS WITH CHARLEY*

At 6 a.m., Madden was still sleeping, but the sun was coming up over southern Wyoming. We had slept through Utah. Now the eastern horizon was slightly pink with wispy clouds. It was as if the horizon were a stage and the curtain was opening an inch a minute, revealing a work of art. "We see those things," Hahn said from the driver's seat, "but unless you mention them to me and Willie, they kind of go right by us. Now that you mention it, it's incredible, isn't it?"

We were near Rawlins, Wyo., more than a mile high, traversing the Rocky Mountains. But aside from a truck stop every 40 miles or so, nothing was out here except hills and rocks and mountains, which is why the surroundings are so pretty and so desolate at the same time. Through Bitter Creek, Table Rock, Wamsutter. So wide open. We had just left Sweetwater County. Delaware and Rhode Island together could fit in Sweetwater County. Delaware and Rhode Island have a combined population of 1.7 million. Sweetwater County has 42,347.

In the morning light Hahn pointed to antelope, 50 yards from the road, eating brush. Soon we saw deer and jackrabbits. Yarbrough woke up—drivers and guests slept on fold-out beds and shelves with mattresses—and went to the front of the bus in time to see a pack of wild horses grazing half a mile off the side of the road. "I remember John bringing a producer from New York on the trip once," Yarbrough said. "He'd lived in New York all his life. He gets out in this part of the country, and he says, 'Man, there's sky all over the place' We got a good laugh out of that."

After a 9:15 a.m. stop in Laramie, Wyo., so Madden could use a pay phone to do his daily five-minute spot for KSFO radio in San Francisco, he took his seat on the padded bench as the bus passed through the southeastern edge of Wyoming and headed for Nebraska. "Have you ever heard of whiteout?" Madden said. "Whiteout happens around here in the winter. It snows, and it blows so hard you can't see. Everything is white. If it's too bad, you can't drive." The Madden Cruiser was caught in a whiteout once. Hahn drove two miles an hour until he got through it.

We passed some tepees on a hill by the side of the road. "We're coming up to Pine Bluffs, Wyoming, now," Madden said. "That's where the missile silos are. Once we were coming through and stopped at a 7-Eleven or something, and we see all these things—not cars, I don't know what you'd call 'em."

"Armored personnel carriers?" someone said.

"Yeah, yeah. Well, [the troops] didn't come out of doors. They came out of holes in the roof of the carriers, and they climbed down on the side. And they go into the 7-Eleven for coffee. I was worried. I thought some gray-haired guy should be sitting at the controls, but these were just kids eating nachos in the morning in Pine Bluffs, Wyoming." Off to the right were the silos, built into the ground, with a lot of fence around them.

After another hour or so, we hit the cornfields of Nebraska. "We had to stop in Beaver Crossing, Nebraska [pop. 480] once, to use the phone for the radio show," Madden said. "It's near Lincoln. Some guy comes across the street from a gas station and introduces himself. Roger Hannon. He was the mayor, and it was his gas station. The next thing I know, we're in front of city hall, and the people start coming out, and they want to see the bus. One woman brought me a rhubarb pie. I didn't even know what rhubarb pie was, but it was great. The whole town came out. There were only about 10 of them, but they were the whole town. I remember asking them, 'What do houses sell for here?' They said the last house that sold was right down on the corner-three bedrooms, three baths, a picket fence, for $8,000."

Two days after Madden's visit to Beaver Crossing, the *Omaha World-Herald* ran a story on page 3 with the headline: MADDEN STOPS TO USE THE PHONE.

"Sometimes I just like to break up the trip, and Omaha's kind of halfway [across the country]," Madden said. "So I stayed in Omaha one night, and we went to see the minor league baseball team play. Anyway, they have a raffle for a case of pork and beans. It's the seventh inning, and everybody's excited. They pick the winner, and the guy's sitting right behind home plate. His name is Elmer something, and he's jumping up and down. To him it was like a trip to Hawaii or a new car or something. It was just a case of pork and beans. That was great."

He read all the press clips and new releases sent to him by the Cowboys, and then he looked out the window some more. When we saw some red wildflowers by the side of the road, Joe fetched a coffee-table book, *Wildflowers Across America*, to identify them. The book had been a gift from Joe to his father. How many former NFL coaches would be caught with a copy of *Wildflowers Across America* in the drawer next to the Giants media guide? Joe found the wildflower in the book: spotted knapweed.

In Brady, Neb., we saw the strangest sight of the trip. We pulled off the highway, emptied out of the bus and looked with the same fascination we would have if we had seen a UFO. It was an animal farm, with a long ranch-style house and a grazing pen that was home to one gray burro, two dozen deer, five dwarf ponies, five llamas, one crossbred deer-llama and several crossbred animals that resembled llamas with very thick necks.

"He looks like he's on steroids," Madden said of one thick-necked llama-lookalike. There were no signs, no explanation of what this farm was for. A man staring at us from the picture window of the house wouldn't come out to answer our questions.

Madden still hadn't gotten over the weird animals when we stopped for dinner at Grandpa's Steakhouse in Kearney, Neb. He asked a woman who had come to our table for his autograph if she knew why the animal farm was there. "I just think he has them for personal pleasure," she said.

While we were eating, the Kerry Kimple clan of Kearney collected near the bus, waiting for Madden. "Nebraska loves John Madden," said Kerry, whose son, Travis, 10, got Madden's autograph. "He's a common-sense, say-what-he-thinks guy."

Back on the bus, Madden watched the Giants-Dolphins game tape. Around midnight, somewhere just over the line into Iowa, he said, "We really saw a lot of stuff today, didn't we? Think of all the things we saw that we wouldn't see on a plane."

Day 3

Council Bluffs, Iowa, to New York City

There are customs, attitudes, myths and directions and changes that seem to be part of the structure of America.

—*TRAVELS WITH CHARLEY*

From some point just east of Des Moines to a rest stop south of Cleveland—a stretch of 640 miles traveled in 12 hours—Madden slept. He missed the early rush hour in the suburbs south of Chicago. He missed

South Bend, Ind., waking the echoes on a brand-new day. He missed the heart of the Rust Belt. He missed most of Ohio, including 19 consecutive American cars passing the bus in the westbound lane in Maumee, a Toledo suburb. He missed the colorful foliage of Sandusky County, Ohio. He missed Liskin, his amiable neighbor, talking about what a great time he had had seeing America.

"I don't want it to end," Liskin said. "I want it to keep going. I just called my brother in New York. He's an investment banker. His voice was so tense. He told me that with the Iraq situation, the world's going crazy. I told him, 'Not where I am. Everything seems fine here.' He told me, 'Ahhh, you don't understand reality.' I feel great now, like I just came back from Hawaii."

At 10 minutes past noon, with the bus pulling into the rest stop near Cleveland, Madden stirred. "Sleep," Madden said a few miles into Pennsylvania, "is the key to the whole thing. If you finish a trip and drag in like a washrag, it's not going to work. I sleep better on the bus than I do at home, I think. I've been on it so much, it truly is a home."

We stopped for lunch in Clarion, Pa. (pop. 6,664), and Madden strolled the sidewalks. Two men were sitting on a bench in the center of town when Madden passed. "That's the Ace Hardware guy," one said.

"No, he's the football announcer," the other replied.

Madden loved the sights, but he likes being invisible, so he doesn't walk the streets in small towns as much as he once did. When we were a few hours outside New York City, he was asked about the states he had slept through. "It seems that Iowa should be the capital of small-town America," said Madden. "Every town is so nice. Illinois is Chicago to me, Michigan Avenue—one of my favorite cities. Indiana is Notre Dame. Ohio is Youngstown. [San Francisco 49er owner] Eddie DeBartolo's from there, and he's always telling me, 'Stop by, come and eat, I'll cook for you.' Pennsylvania, trees. Look at this foliage. I mean, people pay money to take tour buses to see scenes like this."

We were in a long, deep canyon of red, green, yellow and brown, driving on a ridge just below the Moshannon State Forest in north central Pennsylvania. The trees looked like pom-poms.

Against his better judgment, Madden agreed to break one of his cardinal rules. He told Hahn and Yarbrough they could take I-80 all the way into New York City. Naturally, the highway was under construction in northeastern Pennsylvania, and the bus crawled for two hours. "No more of this ---- road, ever, into New York," said Madden before retiring for a quick nap.

When we reached the congestion of eastern New Jersey, it reminded Madden that he was closing in on his home away from home. He reflected on the trip and the country he had crossed. "I think we're in pretty good shape," he said. "The thing that's always amazed me is how it works. People who live on farms don't want to live in big cities. People who live in big cities don't want to be farmers. If everyone wanted the same thing, or wanted to live in the same place, the thing would never work. There are people who are as happy as hell living in Kearney, Nebraska, and eating at Grandpa's. There are people who are as happy as hell living in the middle of nowhere.

"Probably above that, what I've learned traveling around is this: People are nice. You go to a big city, and you hear the world is going to hell, but it's not true. Small parts of it are; the whole isn't. Hey, all we have to do is spread out a little bit, because we have a lot of space. You get out there, and it makes you feel better about America. The thing works."

From start to finish, I found no strangers.... These are my people and this is my country.

—*TRAVELS WITH CHARLEY*

SEPTEMBER 21, 1970

'Nobody Thinks I Can Talk'

He is the best of middle linebackers, he is the worst of middle linebackers

BY ROBERT F. JONES

Fill in the missing word: Dick Butkus is the ---- football player in the world.

Nastiest? Fiercest? Smartest? Strongest? Quickest? Angriest? Coolest? Roughest? Think about it for a while—maybe a moment or two. After all, Butkus thinks about it constantly.

O.K., time's up. According to those who know him most intimately—and you can count their bruises to determine the degree of intimacy—Dick Butkus is all of the above and perhaps a bit more. In a sense, he is his own missing word in the act of self-definition, though some may claim that he is merely the missing link. In a game as complex and specialized as pro football, where experts abound at everything from placekicking to face-masking, it is impossible to determine a "best player" in the overall sense. Yet if such a designation could be made, Butkus would come close to filling it.

Listen to Phil Bengtson, the Green Bay coach: "Butkus rates with any linebacker I've ever seen—Bulldog Turner, Joe Schmidt, Ray Nitschke, George Connor. He has as much enthusiasm as any player I've ever known, and you can always count on him being sharp."Joe Schmidt, who sort of invented the middle linebacker position during his playing days at Detroit, where he is now head coach, feels Lion MLB Mike Lucci is the best—good for you, Joe!—but even his grudging praise of Butkus cannot conceal the cast-iron truth.

"If he overplays, it's because he's so aggressive," Schmidt says. "I've never seen him quit. Last year in our final game with the Bears, when we went ahead 20–3, he got the ball on the kickoff with less than four minutes to go and ran down the field trying for a touchdown with the same desire as if it were the opening kickoff." That 28-yard return, which left flattened Lions in its wake, brought a sullen Wrigley Field crowd to its feet in a rare standing ovation. Rare, that is, for last season, when the Bears were 1–13. As Schmidt says, "Butkus has a quality that is instinctive, that all good linebackers have to have. That's the leadership ability that stimulates a team."

God knows the Bears need leadership—though His alter ego, George Halas, apparently doesn't. In the past Butkus has tried to provide leadership by example, and some of those examples proved painful to the objects in the leadership lesson. Johnny Roland, the St. Louis running back, recalls a 1967 game in which Butkus was hobbled by a wrenched knee but played his usual fierce game anyway. "I have a bruise under my lip to this day where he shattered my mask," says Roland. "I was running up instead of low, as I should have been, and he met me head-on—just like somebody he hadn't seen for a while. He actually embraced me, but he also put me down for a time."

Tight End Charlie Sanders of Detroit has equally vivid memories. In the first Lion-Bear game last year Sanders caught a pass and Butkus gave him the old, rib-cracking Bear hug. Then Sanders caught a second pass and Butkus poked his fingers through Charlie's face mask into his eyes. In the course of the afternoon's work the Lions charged Butkus with provoking three fights and Detroit General Manager Russ Thomas called him "an annihilating son of a bitch." Sanders, laughing, took it more coolly. "Dick's just a maladjusted kid," he said.

Still, the ultimate appraisal of a middle linebacker must come from his opposite number, the quarterback. Green Bay's Bart Starr, a man not given to cheap superlatives, has this to say: "Since the day he came into the league Butkus has made the Bear defense what it is. He's the finest example of hustle I've seen—" then Bart frowns, the old Lombardi loyalty surging up—"or one of the finest. Ray Nitschke is the epitome of hustle.

"All middle linebackers are different, of course, and maybe some are a little better pass defenders than Butkus. I can't imagine anyone being any quicker or stronger. Lee Roy Jordan of Dallas is a good one, but Dallas' defense is so well-coordinated that he can go right to a hole and fill. Butkus doesn't need that team coordination to be great. He covers so much ground—you can complete a pass downfield and, son of a gun. he makes the tackle."

Well, son of a gun, quarterbacks sure talk nicer than middle linebackers. That's one of Butkus' major hang-ups—talk. In the public mind the quarterback is to the middle linebacker as the surgeon is to the butcher. Yin and yang, mind and body, human and animal. But—and of course there is a "but" in Butkus—the real man exists in the tension between those opposites. Granted that Butkus is a bruiser (6'3", 245 pounds); granted that his defensive ferocity draws fans to any Bear game nearly as effectively as his superb offensive complement, Gale Sayers; granted that Chicagoans get a kick out of calling him "Buttocks" and "Bupkis" behind his back. The man is something else. Inner-directed, inarticulate, locked into an image he has outgrown and would desperately like to change, Butkus is striving to overcome...what?

The animal image. There was a time when Dick Butkus truly believed he was an animal, and the transmogrification was nearly perfect. Now he is not so sure. In Chicago, where he exercises his territorial imperative to the fullest, Bear fans still think of him as the ultimate in ursine violence. Take the folks at a bar called Chances R on a recent afternoon. Chances R is one of those quasi-Western hangouts on the plastic, northwestern fringes of Chicago, where 19th-century nudes adorn the walls and the patrons are asked to throw peanut shells on the floor to give the place that crackly, Big Shoulders atmosphere. The barkeep is a mountainous Irishman named Larry Mahoney, equally adept at bouncing a drunken house painter or trilling a ballad in his fine tenor.

"Hey, let's play a word game," Mahoney chirps to his assembled parishioners on this particular day. "What do you think of when I say 'Dick Butkus'?"

"Killer," say a young long-haired couple named Bill and Dee, whose motorcycle had just been blown over by a line squall. The wind is still rattling the roof overhead, and the chink of beer glasses is comforting. "Bull," says another patron. Others chime in: "Wild boar." "King Kong." "Mayor Daley." "Mean and nasty." "Elizabeth Taylor." Elizabeth Taylor? "I can see it," says Mahoney. "Butkus has the same kind of ego, the same self-dedication or cruelty or something."

Not far away, at Northwestern University's Dyche Stadium, Dick Butkus is doing a very un-Elizabethan thing. He is filming a breakfast-cereal commercial. A giant among mere advertising mortals, he even towers over the outsized extras hired to simulate real football players. One scene requires him to blitz through a line of extras, who crumble in slow motion. Butkus then charges the cameraman, arms outstretched in true King Kong fashion. He can't do it. Every time the extras fall down, Butkus breaks up. And when that button-nosed, wide-eyed South Side kisser cracks into a smile it looks about 12 years old and fresh out of Mass after Holy Communion. Then he points a finger at the camera and giggles, "Get with it!" Finally, after a dozen takes, Butkus the actor meets Butkus the animal, and he snarls the words. The script girl, a tough Chicago cookie who has been complaining of the heat all day, actually shivers at the line. "Gee," she says with a little thrill in her voice, "he'll scare all those cereal-eating kiddies to death!"

It just so happened that a couple of cereal-eating kiddies were standing on the sidelines when Butkus came in from the take. Mike McHugh, 11, and Mike Rogers, 10, had been planning to sneak into a nearby circus for the day's entertainment when word flashed through their Wilmette neighborhood that a Bear was loose at Dyche Stadium. Since the two young Mikes love the Bears more than anything else in the world (except, perhaps, the Cubs, the Black Hawks, the Bulls and Johnny Lightning cars), they biked over to the stadium. Now they circled Butkus warily, like a couple of Paleolithic hunters on the prod for cave bear. "Hey," snarls Butkus in his meanest voice, "you kids come over here." They do. "Wadya want?" "Your autograph." "Mywhatagraph?"—kidding them and the kids know it, so they get cocky. "You know, your NAME! Like write it down." Butkus takes the proffered pen and drafts the usual message in a neat hand. The kids' eyes bug out: Butkus didn't grab the pen as if it were a dagger, he hadn't scrawled a blotchy X, he is...human!

"It makes me sad sometimes," Butkus said later. He was sitting at a table in the Pump Room, surrounded by the muted tap of solid silverware on bone china, disguised in a well-tailored suit of tropical worsted that made him look no larger, no fiercer than the rest of the entrepreneurs and con men eating in that deluxe, candlelit chow hall. "Nobody thinks I can talk, much less write my name. Why, last year I cut a record of Shakespeare quotes—you know, a parody, like 'Once more unto the bench, dear friends.' The record company said it was too good. Not enough deese, dem and doses. What the hell is this society doing to people? I did what it told me I could do. I wasn't any freak. I didn't have any identity crisis. In the fifth grade I knew what I was going to be: a professional football player. I worked hard at becoming one, just like society says you should. It said you had to be fierce. I was fierce. Tough. I was tough."

Butkus picked daintily at his shrimp salad, parodying in advance his next thoughts. "When I got to college I discovered that you always have to study. Which I did, even though it wasn't easy at Illinois. It hurt, let me be honest about it. But I didn't do too bad." He flashed his 12-year-old's grin at the grammar. "But the main thing was I knew my trade. And it wasn't all that grim. When I got to the Bears, I made it and I made it beyond the Bears. I made it to All-Pro, whatever that means. But I made it. And then what happens? They call me an animal."

Of course, he encouraged it. There is the celebrated incident last August in Miami of Butkus biting a referee in a melee. (He denies it: "If I'd of been dumb enough to bite a referee I'd have bitten his arm off.") Or of Butkus punching out a cop in the Chicago Federal Building last December, when halted on his way to the passport bureau. ("I didn't hit him. Maybe my friend Rick Bertetto did. We'd had a couple of beers and they got snotty. They locked us up for a while but let us out after a few hours. All a mistake. But I keep thinking: what if I'd been an immigrant like my old man, who couldn't talk so good the English. I might still be there.") And, of course, there is the famous–or infamous, if you will–photograph of Butkus with his lips curled (his whole face curled!) in contempt that was taken during a Minnesota game in 1968. That picture hangs in Dick Butkus' basement along with his gilded trophies and the more civilized glossies of him smiling with teammates, coaches, biggies, etc. Perhaps the former is a reminder of the Butkus that his fans demand, or an indication that he is more than that.

A man's home and his homelife reveal far more about his character than his job performance, and Butkus is no exception. He lives in one of those development areas near Chicago Heights–an hour south of the Loop–that are not quite split-level but a few cuts above miniranch. The neighborhood is new; there are still some working onion farms in the vicinity. From his backyard one can see the tan, turbulent wall of smog rising above Gary and Hammond, Ind. A few lightplanes circle in and out of the crud. "That's where Tony Lema went down," Butkus is wont to say, indicating the Hammond airport with a lugubrious wave of the paw.

His house is modest by football-star standards–a tidy yellow-brick, single-story, nondescript he bought for around $50,000 in 1966, his second year with the Bears. In 1968, with his fortunes vastly improved, Butkus expanded the house, adding a workout complex. In it stands Dick's pride and joy: a Universal Gym,$2,400 worth of muscle-building machinery on which he manufactures the strength that makes him the game's best linebacker. "My weakest point is the bench press," Butkus allows during an impromptu tour. "I only lift about 200,and the weights go up to 220. But I don't want to get muscle-bound. I need that mobility." On the military press, which goes up to 200 pounds, Butkus regularly lifts 170 or more–the weight of a minuscule running back. "In competition," he explains, "you can do things that no gym can teach you."

Leg weights, a sit-up machine and many other Charles Atlas adaptations are available on the Universal, and starting in May of every year Butkus begins using them. He works out with two football-playing neighbors, Marty Schottenheimer of the Bills and John Johnson of the Broncos. After a few sit-ups the trio takes off in sweatsuits for a half-mile airplane runway belonging to a neighboring farmer. They run for an hour or two, mixing the action up with competitive sprints and handicapped distance races, then return to the gym for a few friendly leg lifts. "Working out by yourself can be deadly boring," says Butkus, "but with Marty and John it's all a lot of fun. Sometimes, at parties, after we've had a few beers, some of us guys come down here and compete on the weights but I try not to overdo it. This machine is supposed to keep me from injuries, not inflict them."

Back of the gym, past his daughter's toy cookstove, is Butkus' sauna, which he and a few of his pals built. "One of these days," says Dick with a wicked grin, "I'm going to pour a couple of gallons of vodka on the stones and see what happens. Nice for a party."

Butkus has warm relations with his neighbors. His mother lives two doors to the west and the intervening neighbor, a hardhat named Jessam Buck, has given the Butkuses free access across his neat front lawn. (After all, who would start a spite fence-feud with a Butkus?) Dick's own yard is chockablock with kids' toys, swings, bikes and chinning bars. His driveway provides the only clue that something more than a middle-income suburbanite dwells within. In the driveway are parked a Cadillac Coupe de Ville, a Corvette Stingray and a Pontiac station wagon. Dick drives the Caddy and the Stingray; his wife Helen drives the wagon.

If Joe Namath and Dick Butkus, as the optimum men at their opposite positions, represent poles of difference in football character, then their women are important indications of that character. Helen Butkus is no Namath nifty. Born Helen Essenberg of Swedish-American background, she started dating the Lithuanian kid who became the animal that is called Dick Butkus when she was only 14. At that time she was attending Fenger High on Chicago's South Side and Dick was at Chicago Vocational, a few miles away. CVS was—and is to this day—one of those technical schools where the corridors smell of sawed wood and burnt steel from the shops, where the lockers bear two-inch-deep dents from tough kids punching out their frustrations and where you can always find bloodstains from fistfights in the John. Butkus was already marked for greatness: as a hard-running fullback he doubled his ferocity on defense. The kid had his coaches agog. By the end of his high school career he had pro scouts goggling as well. How did he hook up with teeny little Helen? "I don't know," says Dick today, with his little boy half-smile, "she was kinda cute."

Apart from that, Helen is a dedicated *Hausfrau* in the best Midwestern tradition. She worries incessantly about the ineradicable rust spots on the backyard patio, moans mildly with that touching wifely self-martyrdom when she stoops to extirpate a weed from a garden abrim with tuberoses.

"*Oooh*, there's a lot to *dooo*" she sighs, licking a bead of sweat from her dainty upper lip.

There is, indeed. Apart from handling the hearty appetites of her outsized husband, Helen must take care of two children, both cut in Daddy's mold. Daughter Nikki, who just turned 4, is a robust little blonde who could middle lineback for any nursery school (she attends a Montessori school, however, where traditional physical activity is considered "inadequate"). Son Ricky, who celebrates his 3rd birthday this month, rides a tricycle like Custer his cavalry mount. On a recent evening the Butkuses were preparing to go out for dinner and Dick's mother had accepted the baby-sitting assignment. "O.K., kids," piped Helen, "you're going to go over by Grandma's for supper!" Instant deafness. Butkus growled low in his throat, more to himself than the kids. Just as instantly, perfect hearing. The three of them, gigantic Daddy and his two kids, lurched across neighbor Buck's front lawn like a Fearsome Threesome. Helen bit her lower lip as she watched Nikki go. "Oh, golly," she said at last, "Nikki walks just like Dick. I hope she loses that."

Like most pro athletes in the long-seasoned sports, Butkus spends very little time with his family. During the season, even when he is physically present, his head is usually off somewhere else, rewinding cerebral game films and psyching up for next weekend. During the off season there is a semiweekly radio show (yes, Butkus speaks!), dinner appearances, endorsements, meetings with other players (until this season he was Chicago's rep to the Players' Association) and with his coaches (as a defensive co-captain he exercises a weighty leadership function). Understandably, then, Butkus feels guilty about not fulfilling the traditional father role. This summer when Brian Piccolo, the young Bear running back, died of cancer, Butkus felt that guilt all the more. "I kept thinking about what Brian said when he was dying, that maybe football hadn't really been worth it, that it had kept him from being with his wife and kids, and now he wasn't going to be with nobody no more."

Thus motivated, Butkus rented a camper and took off with Helen and the kids for a rolling vacation. "Like the hippies say, it was a bum trip," Dick recalls. "We bit off more than we could chew—2,000 miles in a week, from Ogallala, Neb. through Wyoming and down to Colorado. We were following the ruts in the Oregon Trail part of the way. I kind of liked that—the mountain men, you know, Bridger and Fitzpatrick, they always appealed to me, tough and hard-nosed. But the kids got bored with history." He imitates a child's voice, all whines and tremolos: "Daddy, who cares about a stinky old fort, we wanna go swimming.' So I took 'em down to this lake in the mountains. I'm going down this mountain in this huge camper—I'm shifting into second, into first, I'm braking, I'm scared foofless that we're going to go over the edge. Then we get there and swim. It's colder than a well digger's feet and the rocks cut you. I couldn't wait to get to Denver, where there were people and buildings and TV sets. I tied down all the gear in the camper and, man, we went. Like I say, a bummer."

By contrast to all those chilly mountains and empty plains, dinner tonight is to be in the real world of Dick Butkus. John's Pizzeria in Calumet City, Ill. Wicked old Cal City, the Sodom and Gomorrah of the Lake Michigan steel belt, infamous since the early 1950s for its hookers and pushers and fabulous clip joints. Driving past the onion ranches toward Cal City, Butkus plays rock on the Caddy's stereo. "Don't it always seem to go that you don't know what you got till it's gone? They paved paradise and put up a parking lot...." Cal City has changed. Cozy little discothèques stud the main drag, their freaked-out colored lights casting the shadows of bouffant B girls in miniskirts on the pavements. One of the old-time night clubs—boarded up now—points a telling contrast. The faded facade invites one and all to witness "All Girl Revues—Venus and Her Jungle Beast." Butkus smiles secretly when the sign is pointed out to him. Yeah, the Jungle Beast! All those lower-middle-class high school girl fantasies about being carried off by a lustful gorilla. Helen, too, is smiling.

John's Pizzeria is more than the name implies. A vast, dark, multiroomed restaurant, it hums with nasal Chicago accents and sings with bursts of mellifluous Italian. Butkus inhales the odor of pastas and wines and spicy sausages, his chest expanding to the size of the Goodyear blimp. "Yum, yum," he sighs. John Bacino, son of the owner and top chef, comes up to advise on the goodies. "How's it going to go this year with the Bears, Dick?" "Better," snarls Butkus. "Can't get no worse." The dinner begins to pour in from the kitchen: fragrant orangines, crisp calamari, steamed shrimp, mushrooms the size of kids' hats, chicken, salad, snails. "They get them from the ditches in Hammond," guffaws Dick. Helen won't touch the snails. She sips a Bacardi and drags deep on one of her Kools. Oh, this jungle beast! Butkus eats with the finger-licking, sensuous abandon of that scene in *Tom Jones*, none of that picky stuff he had parodied so well at the Pump Room. Food and the eating of food are big items with Dick Butkus. A couple of guys at the bar request his autograph—"For the kids, you know," and Dick smiles knowingly—then insist on buying a round of beers. Butkus permits it with a resigned shrug. Let them tell all their friends how they were drinking with Butkus, and how the Bears are going to do this year and all the lies sports fans are capable of—no, compelled to tell. "Sometimes it gets tough, going out to dinner," Butkus confides. "Always there are guys wanting to buy you beers. If you won't let them do it, then they want to fight you. I suppose a broken nose from Dick Butkus is some kind of status symbol. Haw, haw."

The Cal City atmosphere, the Italian food, the awed and envious stares of the patrons combined to produce yet another definition of indefinable Dick Butkus. He is a latter-day *condottiere*—a mercenary captain of the sort that led Renaissance Italy's armies through wars that were as much sham as bloodshed. To the *condottiere* cleverness was as important as strength, and this facet of Butkus has never been fully appreciated. Words like "strength," "abandon" and "recklessness" abound in any definition of Butkus' playing style, yet those qualities are guided by a first-rate football intelligence. Though most of the Bears' defensive signals are now called by Coach Jim Dooley, Butkus is perhaps better equipped to do the calling. "I can see it all about to happen," he says. "At the key moment—the instant of the snap—I somehow know, most of the time, just how the flow pattern will develop. It's all there in the backdrop. I stare—I don't know—right *through* the center and the quarterback, right through their eyes. I watch for the keys, and they are very tiny keys, believe me. Tiny little twitches of their shoulders and their heads and their feet and eyes. There's just this split second, before it all starts to move, when you put those keys together and you know—you damned well know—how it's going." Opposing coaches like Minnesota's offensive assistant Jerry Burns realize Butkus' greatness in this seminal defensive role. "He's uncanny on audibles," says Burns. "That helps him considerably on the blitz—Butkus probably blitzes and gambles more effectively than Nobis or Nitschke."

This season Butkus will have the opportunity to broaden his instinctive leadership qualities. As a defensive co-captain (along with Cornerback Bennie McRae), he will be responsible for shoring up the riddled Bear morale. Last year's disastrous season has left the Bears in a growling mood, one which could result in even more disaster if the team's leaders permit it. On the other hand, it could serve as a psychological launch pad for a fine season.

"Leadership has always kind of scared me," Butkus admitted as he mopped up the remains of John Bacino's cooking. "I've always figured that by playing my best and keeping my mouth shut I'd be showing the guys a good example. Ugh, what a cheesy idea: good example. But now I know that it's going to take more than perfect football to make this club move again. I want to try to be more than a superior football player. I'd like to be a real leader." He blushed a shade of delicate pink and then devoured a pear slice left over from dessert. "I don't know, I guess a lot of talking and inspirational stuff goes against my image. The Animal. Maybe it goes against the real me, whoever that is. But I'm going to give it a try."

Helen Butkus stared into the ruins of her meal and said quietly: "He's still growing." It was an incisive insight, perhaps a frightening one to the high school sweetheart who had married the football hero, but it had the ring of truth. The next time they play the Butkus wordgame in Chances R, perhaps someone will answer: "Human being."

OCTOBER 6, 2015

Why Jim Brown Matters

To his football heirs—from Barry Sanders to Adrian Peterson—he's the one player by which their own greatness is measured. To those who played with and against the Cleveland Browns legend, his prowess, intensity and intellect remain awe-inspiring. Fifty years after walking away from the game at his peak, he still towers over the NFL. Yes, he was just that good

BY TIM LAYDEN

LOS ANGELES—The end came suddenly, and from an ocean away. Fifty years ago, in the 1965 season, Cleveland Browns running back Jim Brown led the NFL in rushing with 1,544 yards in a 14-game season, an astonishing 677 yards more than runner-up Gale Sayers, the phenomenal Chicago Bears rookie. Brown had been voted the Associated Press most valuable player for the third time in his nine-year career and had helped lead the defending-champion Browns back to the NFL title game, a 23–12 loss to Vince Lombardi's Packers in mud and sub-freezing temperatures at Green Bay's Lambeau Field. There were other stars in the pre-merger, pre-Super Bowl, 14-team NFL, a professional league that was still in the nascent stages of its climb to multibillion-dollar conglomerate: Colts quarterback John Unitas, Packers running backs Paul Hornung and Jim Taylor and defenders Willie Davis and Herb Adderly, Rams linemen Deacon Jones and Merlin Olsen, Lions pass-rusher Alex Karras and Bears rookies Sayers and Dick Butkus. But Brown towered over the league, a physical and intellectual force like none other in American sports history, at the peak of his powers.

In late November of that year, *Time* magazine had featured "Jimmy" Brown on its cover. The accompanying story was burdened by the awkward, race-tinged prose of the time, including the headline—"Pro Football: Look at Me, Man!"—and a description of Brown as ".... a fire-breathing, chocolate-colored monster..." Beneath all that, however, the story pushed forward an earnest agenda: to establish that Brown was the best football player in the world and quite possibly the best in history. "There is only one player in the game today whose ability on field commands almost universal admiration, and that is Jimmy Brown." In the previous three seasons Brown had rushed for 4,853 yards, averaging 5.64 yards per carry and 115 yards per game. He was 29 years old, punished by a violent game but scarcely diminished. In fact, he was better than ever. He was also finished.

The Browns convened training camp the following July at Hiram College, outside Cleveland, as they had every summer since 1954. They remained a viable threat to Lombardi's budding dynasty, along with the Colts and the Cowboys, a six-year-old expansion franchise with an innovative young coach named Tom Landry. But they were preparing without their star. Brown was in London filming *The Dirty Dozen*, a big-budget (for its time) movie that had been beset by production delays. This was Brown's second film role; he had acted in *Rio Conchos* during the 1964 offseason and received mostly positive reviews when the movie hit theaters in the fall of that year. Brown was also embroiled in a public dispute with team owner Art Modell, who was fining Brown $100 for every day that he did not report to camp.

In retrospect, what happened next could have been foreseen. Yet it was shocking nonetheless. On the night of July 13, eighth-year guard John Wooten, received a phone call in his Hiram dorm from Brown. They were close friends. Wooten heard a strong yet weary voice on the other end of the line. "He wanted to tell me what was going on," says Wooten. "He told me to let the guys in the locker room know that he was going to announce his retirement. He felt he had given his all. He didn't want to go through all this stuff." Brown also made his decision known to coach Blanton Collier and *Cleveland Plain Dealer* columnist Hal Lebovitz, who broke the story in his paper.

On the morning of July 14, 1966, Brown conducted a press conference on the set of *The Dirty Dozen*, wearing military fatigues while sitting in a tall director's chair placed in front of a tank. "My original intention was to try to participate in the 1966 National Football League season," Brown said, reading from a piece of paper. "But due to circumstances, this is impossible."

One day later Brown met with esteemed Sports Illustrated pro football writer Tex Maule on the set of the movie. Their remarkable exchange formed the basis for a single-source story in the July 25, 1966, issue of SI. In it Brown lays out the blueprint for an activist life beyond football, a life that had already begun with his formation of the Negro Industrial Economic Union (again, the language of the times), in which he involved many of his teammates. His movie career and his dispute with Modell accelerated his movement into a life he was already seeking.

Brown told Maule: "I could have played longer. I wanted to play this year, but it was impossible. We're running behind schedule shooting here, for one thing. I want more mental stimulation than I would have playing football. I want to have a hand in the struggle that is taking place in our country, and I have the opportunity to do that now. I might not a year from now."

And later this: "I quit with regret but not sorrow."

In summer training camps around the league that year, players were stunned. "I heard it and I didn't believe it," says Dick LeBeau, at the time a Pro Bowl defensive back with the Lions. "He was much too good and much too young to retire. But I will also say that we weren't sorry to see him go." Ed Khayat, then 31, had come into the league with Jim Brown in 1957 and played against him 18 times in nine seasons with the Eagles and Redskins. He heard about the retirement while working out for one last season with the Boston Patriots of the AFL. "I thought it was impossible that Jim Brown was going to retire," said Khayat. "His play hadn't dropped off at all. I just couldn't imagine it."

Yet the sport moved quickly forward, as it does. The first season without Brown, the Packers defeated the ascendant Cowboys in Dallas to win the NFL title and represent the NFL in the first Super Bowl. The Browns remained an annual contender for nearly a decade after Brown's retirement but famously have not win a title since 1964. Stories surfaced regularly hinting at a comeback, even as late as an absurd cover piece in SI in 1983 with Brown wearing a Raiders jersey. But he never did come back. He finished his career with 12,312 rushing yards in 118 games, a record that wasn't broken until 1984, when Walter Payton went past him in 18 more games and 451 more carries. Brown's career record of 104.3 rushing yards per game remains the 56-game hitting streak of NFL records. (Adrian Peterson, 30, would have to average almost 1,900 yards per season for the next three full seasons to tie Brown's mark; it would take more than 2,500 yards for Peterson to do it in one year.)

And all of this comes with a bold-faced ellipsis. On a summer morning at the Vikings complex in the suburbs southwest of the Twin Cities, Paul Wiggin, 79, sat grading videotape in the office where he works as personnel consultant for the team. Wiggin and Brown came to Cleveland the same year, 1957. "Jim retired two years before I did," said Wiggin. "He could have played 10 years beyond me if he wanted."

At Home

To reach Jim Brown's house in Los Angeles, you drive uphill from the hustle of Sunset Boulevard on perilous, serpentine roadways that sweep past fabulous homes nestled into the hillside bramble, where a person's address alone conveys a certain kind of success. Brown's house is protected by a hulking metal gate—a relatively recent addition to the property—and sits at the bottom of a steep driveway. He lives here with his second wife, Monique, 41, and their two children, son Aris, 13, and daughter Morgan, 12.

Brown comes into the living room wearing Cleveland Browns sweatpants and a black Under Armour T-shirt. He is 79 years old, with graying stubble on his chin and cheeks, yet he retains the physical and emotional presence of his youth. His voice is deep and purposeful, though weakened and slowed by age, with the same hints of his Georgia roots that have always been present. He wants to know what route you drove to get here. You explain: Sunset to Laurel Canyon to Kirkwood, and then, frankly, it was too scary to recall the street names and there was this one time where you had to back down 200 yards to let a garbage truck pass. Brown laughs, a slow, halting series of *Heh...Heh...Hehs*. He does this often, the weary chuckle of a man who has seen and heard everything. "Ooooo," he says. "That's the hard way. When you leave here, just turn right and follow the yellow line down to Sunset." You sense this is a message he has delivered frequently.

Brown's home is a relatively modest two-story bungalow. But out through the tall windows in the living room is a sprawling, wooden deck that surrounds a swimming pool, and beyond the deck is a 270-degree panorama of Los Angeles, far below. On the right day you can see beyond the airport, beyond Long Beach and all the way to Catalina Island. Brown walked into the house in 1966 with his lawyer and a real estate agent, saw the view and bought it on the spot. "Told him, 'I don't even care what else is here besides the view,'" says Brown. "It's a neat place. Served us well. A lot of history. A lot of people have been up here." Muhammad Ali has been in this house. And Elvis. Louis Farrakhan. Huey Newton. Hugh Hefner. Johnnie Cochran. Michael Jackson. Jay Z. Gloria Steinem. Along with hundreds of troubled young men and gang leaders. A lot of people, indeed.

The guest list is a point of pride for Brown, but no more than this: "I came up here in 1966 and lived here since," he says. "I never had to sell my house." As if the world always sought to take away what he had earned.

You are here because Brown, on the 50th anniversary of his final season, and the end of a career unlike any other in the game's history, has consented to an interview about that career. And let's be frank, because each passing year moves us further from that career, so that one day it will be just numbers on a page, unseen by any living soul. But because this is

Jim Brown, the discussion will veer off in many directions, much like the thick, gnarled fingers on Brown's hands, the ones he once used to ward off tacklers. We will get there. But for now, there are the words he spoke to Tex Maule on a movie set in London in that summer of 1966. Words about regret, but no sorrow, and a harsh decision made at a young age.

Brown is sitting at a high glass table with tall chairs, like barstools. "I really wanted to leave on time," he says. "Too many players stay too long. Too many players rely on the game. I retired at the peak of my career. I didn't retire because I was broken down and slow. I retired because it was time to retire and do other things."

You ask him about Art Modell and the $100 daily fines. Brown leans forward. "You want the real story?" he asks. "I had no bargaining power. But the only thing the Browns had over me was that if I wanted to keep playing football, I had to play for the Browns. But they couldn't tell me I had to play football. Art was going to fine me for every day I stayed on the movie set? I said, 'Art what are you talking about? You can't fine me if I don't show up. S---, I'm gone now. You opened the door.'"

Now you ask about the ellipsis. The what-if Jim Brown had played a few more years. Brown doesn't like the question. He doesn't like questions that lead him to answer in a certain way. He likes to frame his own answers into mini-speeches. "My ego is such that I did what I did on the football field," Brown says. "If you like it, cool. If you don't like it, that's all right with me, because I can't do it no more."

The Peers' Perspective

In the summer of 1957, the best graduating (or eligibility-exhausted) college football players in the country gathered for a training camp in advance of the annual College All-Star Game, which pitted those collegians against the defending NFL champions at Soldier Field in Chicago. The concept seems preposterous now, but the game had been a tradition since 1934 and would be played until 1976. Brown had been the sixth player taken in the '57 draft; two running backs were selected ahead of him: Paul Hornung of Notre Dame went first to the Packers, and Jon Arnett of USC went second to the Rams. Wiggin was there as the Browns' sixth-round pick, a 242-pound defensive end. He was anxious to see Brown, and surprised at what he saw.

"He didn't look like what I expected him to be," says Wiggin. "I wondered if maybe [Browns coach] Paul Brown had told Jim to keep things under wraps." (Brown would later write, in his 1964 autobiography with Myron Cope, *Off My Chest*, that he had been frustrated throughout the All-Star camp that coach Curly Lambeau had preferred Arnett to him. "[T]hat night Curly Lambeau made me," Brown wrote.) Wiggin saw a different player in

Browns training camp. “We weren’t even scrimmaging, it was just thud [hitting without tackling to the ground],” says Wiggin. “But with Jim, you could feel the electricity of him going past you. You just knew that son of a gun was special.”

Wiggin remembers that Brown and some of the other African-American players were taunted by Lenny Ford, a 6'4", 245-pound defensive end who was nearing the end of his career and would later be voted into the Pro Football Hall of Fame (and who was also African-American). “Lenny would stand in the middle of the locker room and say, ‘Come on boys, gather ’round. Big Jim Brown here is going to tell you all how he scored six touchdowns against mighty Colgate.’ Jim would just say, ‘Lenny, leave me alone.’”

Brown remembers Ford differently. “Len took me under his wing,” says Brown. “He explained things about the game to me. He was older than me and understood things that I didn’t.”

Brown became an immediate starter at fullback. The position name is a misnomer; into the 1970s most NFL offenses used a split two-back backfield, with the backs positioned on either side of the quarterback or one back directly behind the quarterback. Unlike in modern offenses, both backs carried the ball, and both blocked. Brown rushed for 942 yards as a rookie and then four consecutive seasons in which he averaged 1,380 yards per season (three 12-game seasons and one 14-game season) and 110.4 yards per game.

Brown played at 6'2", 232 pounds, and history has catalogued him as a battering ram who pounded smaller players into submission. He did plenty of that, but Brown was much more. LeBeau was drafted by Cleveland in 1959, spent part of a training camp with the Browns and then was traded to Detroit. “Jim Brown was a combination of speed and power like nobody who has ever played the game,” says LeBeau. “Obviously arm tackles were not going to slow him down, but he was so elusive. If he got into the secondary, he was so good at setting you up and then making you miss. You just didn’t know if you were going to get a big collision or be grabbing at his shoelaces.”

Teammates remember a studious man, physically gifted, but also intellectually engaged. “Back then, the entire offense would watch film together,” says Wooten. “Jim would be right there with the offensive linemen. He would say ‘Guys, listen, I want to be able to hit this one right over here. And I want you to move it right over there.’ And we would block it exactly the way Jim asked. He had a great analytical knowledge.”

Brown also had a historically dominant offensive line with whom to share that knowledge. Paul Brown’s long-time offensive line coach was Frederick K. (Fritz) Heisler, a studious tactician who was among the first teachers of the system that came to be known as zone blocking. In Jim Brown’s early years in Cleveland, Heisler's line included future Hall of Fame tackle Mike McCormack and future Hall of Fame coach Chuck Noll. Paul Brown was fired by Modell after the 1962 season, in part because of a player insurrection led by Jim Brown, who felt that Paul Brown's offense had become predictable. Heisler stayed on under new coach Blanton Collier, and built the offensive line—tackles Dick Schafrath and Monte Clark, guards Wooten and Gene Hickerson and center John Morrow—that formed the foundation of the '64 championship team. "People say Lombardi started 'Run to Daylight,'" says Wooten. "Really it was Fritz Heisler. Go look at Jim's long runs, the 50- and 60-yarders. Run to daylight, just like Lombardi's teams, except it was Jim Brown." In 1963, Brown rushed for 1,863 yards, breaking his own single-season record by 356 yards (albeit in 14 games, rather than 12); the record stood for a decade, until O.J. Simpson rushed for 2,003 yards. Wooten says, "Jim came out of a lot of games early in 1963. I wish we could have kept him in those games. The way we had it going, he would have rushed for 2,500 yards and nobody would ever have broken that record."

Irv Cross, who would later gain fame as one of the first African-American analysts on network television, was an All-Pro cornerback who came into the league in 1961. He remembers facing Brown behind Heisler's wall of linemen. "You would come up to defend the corner, and you cold feel the earth vibrating," says Cross. "And you've got Jim Brown running behind those guys. I remember one play where I came up and Jim is behind John Wooten, and he's got his hand on John's back and he's yelling at him, 'Get him, Woot! Get him, Woot!' Jim had moves like a halfback, and if you caught him, it took several players to get him down."

Cross met Brown at the 1964 Pro Bowl in Los Angeles. "I found a solid, bright man," says Cross. "He cared about the underprivileged in the world. He had a big heart. He also called me Herb. 'Come on, Herb, let's go. Come on, Herb, time for dinner.'"

To a man, Cleveland teammates remember Brown as uncommonly intense. Before games he would sit alone in the locker room, staring at air. "I had never been in the presence of anybody who prepared the way Jim did," says Ernie Green, who was drafted in 1962 to play halfback alongside Brown. "Obviously Jim had the physique and the body to do it all. He could run over people, he could outrun people. But he would spend an awful lot of time visualizing the role he was about to play. And at all times, Jim enjoyed his own space in the world. You got to know him as well as you could, but there was a limit to that."

Before the 1962 season, the Browns acquired quarterback Frank Ryan from the Rams. The new QB was known as Dr. Frank Ryan, because he had earned a doctorate in mathematics from Rice, and he would play seven seasons in Cleveland, including three after Jim Brown's retirement. Ryan threw three touchdown passes to Gary Collins in the 1964 NFL Championship Game, a 27–0 upset of the favored Colts and John Unitas. Brown ran for 114 yards on 27 carries in that game.

Ryan and Brown had a complex relationship. They were not close. Some of that was societal. "It was a different time," says Ryan. "There was not a lot of white-black integration on the team." Some of it was Brown's personality—demanding, perfectionist, self-assured. In November 1964, the Browns' championship season, they trailed Detroit in a game at Municipal Stadium in Cleveland. Paul Brown had used "messenger guards" to shuttle play calls in to Ryan, but when Collier replaced Brown in '63, he allowed Ryan to call his own plays. However, on one third-down call, Collier sent in a play, which called for Brown to sweep around the right side, a very common play in the Cleveland offense. "We ran it, and Jim did not make it," says Ryan. "And Jim was really pissed. He had wanted another play called. I don't remember what play. But as we left the field, Jim jerked me around and yelled at me and well, I was just amazed that Jim would be so angry at me for running what the coach sent in, in a very critical situation."

Ryan also recalled that during practice, if the Browns were executing sloppily on offense, Brown would often stage a protest of his own. "He would just slow down, instead of running full speed," says Ryan. "It was his way of letting everybody know that he didn't like the way things were going."

Yet while Brown and his quarterback were not tight, there was a clear mutual respect. After a season-ending victory at Washington in 1963, Brown and Ryan were invited to the White House to meet with President Lyndon Johnson, who had taken office 24 days earlier, after the assassination of the John F. Kennedy. "We talked about race relations in America," says Ryan. "It was a serious talk. And Jim was the reason I was there."

Two years later, as the Browns were defending their NFL title, they were struggling at a home against the Redskins, three games from the end of the 14-game season. Collier sent backup quarterback Jim Ninowski onto the field to replace Ryan. But Ryan refused to come out and sent Ninowski back to the sideline. "I'm sure Blanton was horrified," says Ryan. "But I was not coming out." The Browns scored two fourth-quarter touchdowns (Ryan passed for one, Brown ran for another) to pull out a 24–16 victory. Traditionally, the players celebrated wins with parties at downtown hotels, but those parties where largely segregated. "That day, I was getting in my car in the parking lot," says Ryan, "And I said to Jim, 'Come on to the party with me.' Usually the black players didn't come to the party. Jim never did. But that night he came to the party. And I think he did it because he admired what I did on the field."

Ryan pauses. "Jim liked to be in control," he says. "But he was a tremendous football player. He was impressive in every possible way, just a superb athlete. We never really warmed up to each other, but I never lost my admiration for him."

Many of the old Browns remember one play better than the rest. On the third Sunday in November of 1965, the Browns played the rising Dallas Cowboys at the Cotton Bowl. With the game tied, 3–3, in the second quarter and the Browns on the Cowboys' three-yard-line, Ryan called 19 Stay, a flip to Brown on the left edge (with "stay" indicating that the back-side guard would not pull). Wooten picks up the narrative: "Jim takes the pitch and when we get out there to the corner, everybody is out there. The end, the tackle, the linebacker, the safety, the corner. Everybody."

Green: "Jim just kept retreating until he's about at the 10-yard line and there are eight guys around him."

Wooten: "Jim just takes off and keeps running until he dives into the end zone. The last couple yards, he's almost crawling, about a foot off the ground."

Wiggin: "That run was beyond human capability. Just the sheer determination to get the ball into the end zone."

Wooten: "I have that play on my phone. Sometimes I just call it up and watch."

The Coach's View

Before the start of a training camp practice, Bill Belichick sits on an equipment truck in the belly of Gillette Stadium, which is silent except for the sound of a forklift operating somewhere in the distance. Belichick first met Jim Brown in 1991, when Belichick was named coach of the Cleveland Browns. But he is a devoted student of football history; as a kid growing up in Annapolis, Md. (where his father was a coach at Navy), Belichick was a Browns fans. "Jim Brown was probably my favorite player," says Belichick. "I loved the guy."

At the start of his tenure with the Browns, Belichick brought Brown back to the franchise and into the meeting room with his running backs. The result was disastrous. "It was embarrassing," says Belichick. "They had never heard of Jim, didn't know who he was. I mean, this was f---ing *Jim Brown*, the greatest football player in history. That was my mistake. After that I made sure to educate the players ahead of time, to explain who Jim was, show them some highlights."

On this day, Belichick is at first hesitant to break down Brown's game. There is apparently no real game film of Brown in existence. The Browns have none. NFL Films has none. CBS, which broadcast NFL games during

Brown's career, was unable to provide game film when asked. There are highlight packages available on the Internet and also one fairly complete reel of the 1965 championship game, skillfully cobbled together from various sources. These highlights comprise most of the Brown canon. The rest is lost to time. "I never coached against Jim," says Belichick. "I've seen the same highlights everybody else has seen, and they are awesome. He was big, he was fast, he was powerful, he had great hands. Everybody knows that. I don't know that I can provide any unique insight."

But of course he can. Belichick possesses one of the best football minds in history. He does not see what everybody sees, even in highlights. You prod him forward. Brown was called a fullback. But was he a fullback? "He was a combination of a fullback and a halfback," says Belichick. "He had great power and leverage, but he was also very elusive in the open field like a halfback. His quickness, straight-out speed and elusiveness were all exceptional. And he was all of 230 pounds. He was bigger than some of the guys blocking for him. I mean, they might have weighed more, pumped up, but Jim's hands, his forearms, his girth. He was bigger."

Brown's place on the evolutionary timeline of the game is a significant factor in his legacy. He did not play the same position that Adrian Peterson plays. "There was no I Formation in the 1960s," says Belichick. "There were two-back sets with the backs lined up flat. Jim was five, maybe five-and-a-half yards behind the quarterback. Now guys are six-and-a-half, seven yards, at least. So Jim had to read things much quicker, but he also got to the hole much quicker.

"The last guy in the league, that I can remember, who lined up that close to the line was [John] Riggins, with the Redskins," says Belichick. "Franco Harris, too." Riggins played from 1971 to '85; Harris from '72 to '84. After that era, running backs lined up deeper, as many do, now. "Guys like Chuck Muncie, Eric Dickerson, O.J. Simpson," says Belichick. "The game shifted to a deeper positioning of the running back."

You ask Belichick for comparisons. Dickerson maybe? He was 6'3", 220 pounds. "Dickerson was more of a straight-line runner," says Belichick. "Not that he didn't have great skills. But Jim moved like a 185-pound runner."

Adrian Peterson (6'2", 218)? "Another guy who is explosive at the line and pulls away," Belichick says, "but Jim had so much short-area quickness. Quick feet, lateral movement. Franco Harris had some of that, but less speed. I'm not saying Franco was slow, but he didn't have Jim's breakaway speed." Historians looking for holes in Brown's legacy often note that he played against much smaller defenders. It's true. But Belichick hammers the point that Brown's lateral quickness, agility and intelligence are evergreen qualities.

During Belichick's tenure in Cleveland, Brown came to counsel the team's running backs, as a sort of adjunct position coach. It was in this role that the same analytical mind that Cleveland teammates had seen three decades earlier presented itself. "He is incredibly perceptive about running the football," says Belichick. "Tremendous understanding of how to beat defenders, how to attack their leverage to give them a two-way go. He has great insight into what a runner sees, and he could explain it in very simple terms. Here is the tackler, here is your leverage point."

More than a half-hour has passed. Belichick has walked from inside the stadium to the practice field, to the applause of Patriots fans ringing the facility. It is clear that he has not only great respect for Brown as a player, but also personal affection. Belichick has visited prisons with Brown and supported his work with at-risk youths. "He's a guy who has a handle on life," says Belichick. "He's worked with the worst of the worst, the baddest of the bad, and he can get them under control. Really an incredible man. I hope people understand that."

One last question: One day earlier you had asked Dick LeBeau this question: If a 22-year-old Jim Brown were drafted into the modern NFL, would that player be effective? "He would be absolutely dominant," says LeBeau. "There are so many more ways to get him the ball in space, and when Jim was in the open field, you had a problem." (Wiggin, who studies athletes for a living, says, "The game evolves. I was a player for my time. Jim Brown was a player for all times.")

The same question to Belichick: *If a 22-year-old Jim Brown...* Belichick interrupts. "Oh my god...."

Descendants

Adrian Peterson trundles out of the Vikings' practice facility locker room and into the sunlight before extending his right hand and crushing yours like a ripe tomato. Before missing all but one game of the 2014 season (under suspension after his arrest on child abuse charges), Peterson was the most obvious modern parallel to Jim Brown: a dominant running back with size, speed and power (putting aside, for a moment, Belichick's more specific evaluation). Brown says so: "Adrian is one of the best that's come along. He has the full physical package and the runner's attitude."

Peterson has never seen Brown in action, so you hand him a tablet loaded with highlights. Peterson takes the tablet, pulls a towel over his head to block the sun's glare and begins watching. Number 32, you tell him. Peterson watches the screen for nearly four minutes, saying nothing. Then he begins talking: "Physical player," he says. "Relentless. Great vision. Great balance. Great effort. Awareness."

Peterson hands you the tablet back and nods. "What do I see?" he says. "Quick feet and great balance. He bounced off defenders, but he also cut around defenders with his quickness. The power is obvious. He drove one guy back about five yards and just kept going. I mean, yeah, man, he was one incredible running back."

When Peterson was growing up in Texas, he looked up to Barry Sanders, Emmitt Smith, Terrell Davis. "And Eddie George," says Peterson, "because I was a tall back, and he was tall. But my dad would talk about Jim Brown, so I heard the name." In 2008, after Peterson won his first rushing title with 1,716 yards, *The Sporting News* arranged for Brown to "interview" Peterson at Brown's home in those Hollywood Hills. "Beautiful view, man," says Peterson. "And around Jim, I stayed pretty quiet for a while. He's a straight shooter, scholarly guy. Cares about his people. Without a doubt, there's a presence when you are around him."

Peterson doesn't know the whole story, how Brown retired at age 29 after nine seasons. (Peterson is 30, in his ninth season, although he played just that one game a year ago). And how Brown had rushed for those 4,853 yards in his final three seasons, more than Peterson has gained in any three consecutive seasons. "Wooooo, fifteen hundred in his last season and then he retired?" says Peterson. "I mean obviously he didn't let football consume him. But if he played four or five more years? His records. I guess that's the scary thing, there's always that open space to wonder about if he kept playing."

You tell Peterson what Belichick said about Brown's elusiveness and small-area foot quickness being more effective than his. Peterson picks up the tablet and watches a little more. He hands the tablet back and laughs. "I think," he says, "I would have to agree with that."

Barry Sanders' career is the one that most closely parallels Brown's. The Lions great rushed for more than 5,000 yards in his last three seasons and retired abruptly at the top of his game after 10 years in the league. Sanders has known Brown for many years, visited his L.A. home and played golf with him; Sanders' father, William, was a fan of Cleveland and Jim Brown ("He would wear a Cleveland Browns jacket to my Detroit Lions games," says Sanders), and Barry introduced the two men before William Sanders' death in 2012. He is an unqualified fan.

"Jim was a dominant specimen," says Sanders. "He was physically strong but also just a beautiful runner. He had quickness, he had vision for finding open space, but he could also run you over. When you talk about the best players ever, who would you put ahead of him? He was dominant. I know I wasn't dominant. Not like Jim. Jerry Rice, maybe? Lawrence Taylor was dominant. I can't think of anybody I would put ahead of him."

Sanders has a unique perspective on the what-if, having left the game just 1,457 yards short of Payton's career rushing record, since broken by Emmitt Smith. "It's fine to consider what Jim would have done," says Sanders. "There are times when I think about what it was like out there. I don't know if that translates into, 'I wish I played longer.' I played the right amount of time. I think that's true with Jim, too."

Back Home

You began with an apology of sorts to Brown. He played professional football for nine years and has lived a full, vibrant (and frequently controversial) half century since. Nine years versus 50. Yet you came to talk about football. Brown knew this, and through his wife, he agreed to the meeting. "It's your interview," says Brown. "So the topic is up to you." But in truth the topic is never up to you. The topic is always up to Brown. "I want my points to be my points," he says. "I want my voice to be my voice." (Brown's life is not unexamined: He wrote autobiographies in 1964 and 1989; journalist Mike Freeman wrote an unauthorized biography in 2007; Spike Lee made a feature-length documentary in 2002.)

Yet the voice wants something understood. "God gave me a combination of skills," says Brown. "I was 232 pounds, six-feet-two. I had enough strength to be uniquely physical. And there are times when the game depends on that physicality. We called those 'attitude' plays. And that's where you go at a man to get one yard and you want to tear him up. But did I want to hit people? Of course not. My job as a running back was to get as much yardage as I could get, and if I could do that without touching a single defensive player, it would not mean a doggone thing to me. It was never my job to see how many guys I could hit. That was Jim Taylor's job, or somebody else. Heh...heh...heh. For me, it was daylight first."

And this: "I studied the game." Like his teammates said. Like Belichick said. "I studied my opponents, and I studied other running backs. I had an ego, but I didn't have so much talent that it kept me from respecting other people. There was a guy named Don Bosseler [a fullback who played for Washington from 1957 to '64]. He would throw himself into the air from the 1-yard line. I tried it a couple times and was not successful. Heh...heh... heh. So I studied the films, and I saw that he was not just jumping. He was studying the linemen and then making a decision whether to jump or not jump. I learned from Bosseler. You have to study everything."

On the one hand, Brown makes clear that he was ready to leave football. "I had a full dose," he says. Yet as he sees the game from further away, he views it more affectionately. "I have a greater appreciation for it," he says. "It gave me an opportunity to express myself on a personal level. As a black man in America, there were certain disadvantages to my existence. Football gave me certain other advantages. It has been a major part of my existence."

Still, he will not be judged. "I did the best I could, and I played hard," he says. "I don't care if some person says I was the best this or best that. I like the respect that I get when I move among other players. I do like that."

There was a time when Brown could be counted on to denigrate the modern NFL, allowing that button to be pushed and supplying a brief homily on running backs who too often ran out of bounds (Franco Harris was on receiving end of many such rebukes) or made too much money. He doesn't go there quite so often nowadays, expressing great admiration for Peterson and respect for Jamaal Charles, whom he admits to not having seen often enough. He attended the memorial service for Junior Seau in 2012, helping connect generations. If he moves and speaks just a little more slowly at 79, his thoughts remain lucid and sharp. He occasionally forgets a name, but to a layman there is little obvious evidence of the cognitive damage that afflicts so many former players. Perhaps nine years was long enough, indeed.

The NFL remains mired in a crisis on domestic violence. Five times in Brown's life he has been accused of violence against women, though none of those charges were proved in court. Most recently, in 1999, he was charged with vandalism and making a terrorist threat after smashing the windows of Monique's car during an argument. (The terrorist threat charge came because Monique told a 911 operator that Jim had threatened to kill her, a charge she later recanted.) At the time, Brown was 63 and Monique was 25; they had known each for four years and been married for two. The couple went public together and fought the charges in a series of media appearances. Jim was found guilty on the vandalism charge, and rather than accept any plea bargain he served six months in prison.

Monique says now, "We had an argument, and Jim damaged his own property. There has never been any domestic violence in our home. He has talked to our son. It is not something that Jim would ever tolerate." She says that Jim has "settled into a wonderful family life." (Thought she rejects the verb mellowed.) Aris, an eighth-grader, loves to play lacrosse, the game at which some think Jim was the greatest player in history. They play catch in the driveway behind the house.

When you ask Brown how he would counsel young players on how to treat women, there is a pause. Then the laugh. "I know what you're trying to get at," he says. "There is no excuse for violence . There is never a justification for anyone to impose themselves on someone else. And it will always be incorrect when it comes to a man and a woman, regardless of what might have happened. You need to be man enough to take the blow. That is always the best way. Do not put your hands on a woman."

At the end, you ask him to watch himself. Brown agrees. You open your laptop's screen and begin streaming highlights that must have seen hundreds of times, but perhaps not in a long time. As the plays unfold, Brown goes silent, offering only occasional comments. He smiles, almost perceptibly.

In one sequence he outruns a Lions defensive back and compliments the opponent.

In another, he spins away from a Washington defender, only to be drilled in the back by another. "Lucky I didn't get hurt there," says Brown, stroking the whiskers on his chin.

He scores easily against the hated Giants. "Walked right in," says Brown. "Good blocking."

After 15 minutes, the videos are exhausted. Outside the windows and far to the west, the sun is falling toward the Pacific. Another guest has arrived in the Brown household. "Thank you for showing that to me," says Brown. "It's funny. I keep seeing things I could have done better. Things I could have done differently. That's the way it is with football." One last laugh. Heh... heh...heh. "That's the way it is with life, too."

NOVEMBER 13, 2006

The Gospel According to Ray

Ray Lewis has a story to tell, of persecution and redemption, of fathers and sons, of pain caused and pain endured. The trials he's suffered—and Lord knows there have been many—are all part of a master plan

BY S.L. PRICE

The sinner is breaking a sweat now. He's been telling his story for just over a minute, just enough time to start feeling it all again, and the reliving always brings rage. Called him liar, monster, abuser of women? Yes, the world did that. Called him killer? Yes, the world did, and does it still: He saw the poster in Cleveland in September, back of the end zone, with the drawing of a knife and the words asking how Ray Lewis can still be free. But here? Tonight? No. Or as he sometimes lets slip, "*Hell*, naw!" He's got his people, a bobbing, loving, understanding sea of 2,000 black faces before him. He's got his pastor, Jamal-Harrison Bryant, standing behind him, saying, "Talk, Ray, talk." Tonight, indeed, Lewis has the Holy Spirit settling on him like never before. He grips the microphone in both hands, crouches ever so slightly, as if girding himself for the collision to come.

"God has done something in my life—and not just for me to see it," Lewis says softly. Then his eyes flash, and he starts shouting, pointing. "God has done something in my life for ev-ery *hat-er*, ev-ery *enemy*...."

A noise—"whoooaaa!"—rises out of the rows at the Empowerment Temple in northwest Baltimore, like the roar of an ocean wave gathering itself to crest.

"*...every person who said I wouldn't walk or ever play again!*"

Applause, shouting, the wave full-faced and beginning to crash. Oh, he's got 'em now. Not that they didn't come here on this Tuesday night in late September—some dressed in Sunday-best suits and dresses, some in Sunday-best R. LEWIS Ravens jerseys—primed to adore him anyway. After all, Lewis was the molten core of the defense that anchored Baltimore's Super Bowl XXXV championship in January 2001, and this season, with him recovered from hamstring surgery, the 6–2 Ravens are again a threat to win the AFC. Still, he's not here to talk football. They're not here to hear it. Tonight is about redemption. Tonight is about loving the sinner and hating the sin. Tonight is about Ray Lewis, once accused of double homicide, the father of six kids by four women, living the word and spreading it through TV cameras dollying around the stage.

"See, I had to face, face-to-face, my four-year-old child, who couldn't understand why his father was in shackles," Lewis is saying. "I had to face that I couldn't touch my mother for the first time in my life. And God asked me a question. I was in jail 15 days, and He asked me, *How long are you gonna cry?*"

He goes on to say how men have to treat their women like "queens," sweet music to the ladies whooping at his words. But the 31-year-old Lewis, stalking about in an ash-gray three-piece and a thick-knot tie the color of clear sky, is going after bigger game tonight. For when you ask him, and often when you don't, Lewis will tell you these days that he's "anointed," that he enjoys "favor," that he is a "king" charged with fostering a national ministry on the order of Martin Luther King Jr. and that, once football is done, his mix of piety and street cred and that spectacularly nasty, Court TV–chronicled fall will drag even the most hardened hearts to the light. Indeed, Lewis's revamped faith, like the man himself, is a raw, loud, electric thing, a muscular mix of the sacred and the profane. Every game day, just before another 60 minutes' worth of NFL hype and violence, Lewis will dip his fingers in consecrated oil, seek out a half dozen of his fellow defenders and trace a cross on each of their foreheads.

And he doesn't limit his touch to teammates. "You are blessed," Lewis told San Diego Chargers linebacker Shawne Merriman on the phone the night before the two teams met in October. "Limit yourself with how many women you see. And strap up!" It's a constant refrain to any young player who crosses his path. "You know how foolish I was?" Lewis says. "One thing Ray's going to tell you: Don't you sleep with no woman without a condom."

A few other things Ray will tell you are that off the field he's not a vicious man and never hurt anyone, much less the two men who were stabbed to death outside Atlanta's Cobalt Lounge on Jan. 31, 2000; that he regrets the mistakes he made that night; that the resulting trial was a blessing because it made him change. It's a compelling narrative, and Lewis tries hard to make it stick. "Life is so *great*," he will often begin a thought. When Lewis saw that poster at Cleveland Browns Stadium he strode along the sideline reciting the Lord's Prayer. Lewis says he's all about love, but when he talks about the Fulton County prosecutor, the former Atlanta mayor, the people who tried to send him to jail? Then he goes all Old Testament, his love full of loud and righteous fury.

"The battle is: Am I O.K.?" Lewis is telling the crowd. "Even though I was persecuted, crucified.... *Am I O.K.?* Let me give you a quick read-back on me, Church. When I walk into another stadium, 52 other players walk in there with me, plus coaches—and all [the fans] do to them is boo." He pauses, then grins. "Now, when *Ray Lewis* walks out there..." he says, but the whole room cuts in laughing, ready for the roundhouse to come. "Church? I'm going to tell you something about God, now.... When Mr. Lewis walks out, child, I hear everything from 'Murderer,' I hear everything from 'N———,' I hear everything from 'You shouldn't be playing football!' And when I break it all down, I know they're talking about yesterday!"

Now they're all in it together. Lewis starts bellowing, the crowd loses all control, clapping, stomping. He's going for a big finish: voice cracking, face wet, the words coming fast. Ray Lewis is feeling so justified that he's like a runaway train. And for all his spiritual growth these past few years, for all he will tell you about his new walk, it's clear now that Lewis retains every bit of swagger, menace, that palpable promise of violence that made him one of football's greatest defensive players. He's not about to let this testimony end in a haze of peace or love. No, this is payback, a bit of that Miami Hurricanes in-your-face, a holy f-- you to the world that tried to shut him away.

"Church: Every time I step on the football field, He's prepared a table for me in the presence of my enemy!" Lewis says, and now he's jeering. "And every time they think they want to say something to me? Every time they think they want to boo me? They have to pay—to come see me."

And it's over. Bryant steps toward him, reaches for the microphone, but Lewis is too far gone. He flings the mike down, and it hits the stage with a reverberating thunk. God's linebacker stalks away, certain he's feeling nothing but grace.

A week later, on Oct. 2, Lewis is sitting at a table in the lunchroom at the Ravens' practice facility in Owings Mills, Md. "Then I watch TV," he is saying about the aftermath of his trial six years ago, "and I hear [one victim's] younger brother say, 'Oh, Ray Lewis is going to get his one day. Just like he killed my brother, he going to die.' This is on TV, a 13-year-old child. All because of what y'all wanted to report that was dead-ass wrong! So the rest of my life I don't know if somebody's going to walk up to me and put a pistol to my head. For the rest of my life."

You could say he's paranoid, except that after District Attorney Paul Howard dropped the murder charges against him for the deaths of two men from Akron, Jacinth Baker and Richard Lollar, Lewis testified against the remaining defendants, his former friends Reginald Oakley and Joseph Sweeting. Both men were acquitted in June 2000, and that fall Sweeting released a rap song lambasting Lewis as a snitch, reportedly with such lyrics as Oakley should have stabbed ya, and If I knew what I know now, it'd have been three bodies. In February 2005 the FBI investigated death threats e-mailed to Lewis's charitable foundation.

When the Ravens go on the road, Lewis still draws increased security at hotels and stadiums, and his attitude from moment to moment ranges from devil-may-care bravado to perspective-warping fear. An hour after the subject of Atlanta has passed and the conversation has long shifted to children and faith, Lewis abruptly points to a TV hanging over the table. "Look," he says. Reports from Pennsylvania Dutch country flash on the screen, the crawl detailing the shooting of five Amish schoolgirls. "Right there: 'Murders were revenge for a 20-year-old incident.'" He nods, eyes full of meaning. "See?"

But he moves on because, well, what choice is there? One by one, a dozen teammates stop to assure Lewis they'll be at his barbecue restaurant for the weekly get-together later that night—one more sign that Lewis, the face of the franchise, is back as its heart too. Last year, sidelined for the final 10 games with the torn hamstring and unhappy with Ravens management, he had been a distracting, isolated figure, his misery confirmed when he publicly ripped the team's defensive schemes before the April draft. Taken together it felt like the beginning of a bad-taste end to Lewis's Baltimore career; the team even briefly scrapped their game-day player introductions, always capped by Lewis's signature gyrations.

Then, during the Ravens' 4–0 start, Lewis reasserted control of the locker room, of M&T Bank Stadium and of the intros: His dance has returned. He again leads the team in tackles, quieting questions about age and health. "Ray strikes fear in a lot of people—even when you're on his team," said Baltimore defensive end Trevor Pryce, an off-season acquisition, after the Ravens' loss to the Carolina Panthers on Oct. 15. "He hit me in the face today, friendly fire, and I was like, 'Oh, my Lord.' I can't imagine getting 20 of those a game as a running back. When you see him as an opponent, the city of Baltimore and this team built him up for so long that you expect, I'm Ray Lewis, I'm on billboards. There's none of that. From the first day I got here, he started preaching, 'We need to win. We, we, we.'"

Such a one-year turnaround was small change for Lewis, a lock Hall of Famer who has spent six years disproving F. Scott Fitzgerald's lament that there are no second acts in American lives. Fitzgerald, of course, wrote in a time before talk-show mea culpas and high-speed news cycles made almost anyone famous and any deed forgivable. But even by today's standards, the second act of Lewis's public life has been a marvel of image rehabilitation. Murder suspect one night after the Super Bowl in 2000 and Most Valuable Player of the Super Bowl the following year, he once seemed the embodiment of the Entitled Athlete, the culmination of a thuggish era that featured O.J. Simpson, Latrell Sprewell and Rae Carruth. When the Ravens won it all, Lewis got no trip to Disneyland, no spot on the Wheaties box, but he was still the best player in the NFL—and for the image-obsessed league, a dancing, jawing, unrepentant nightmare.

Yet since then, Lewis's charity efforts—his annual donation of Thanksgiving meals to 400 Baltimore families, his purchase of Christmas gifts for 100 needy kids, his providing of school supplies to 1,200 city students—have helped make him Baltimore's most-beloved public figure. Lewis's replica jerseys fill the 70,000-seat stadium; his face is indeed plastered all over the city, as once-wary corporations such as EA Sports and Reebok and KBank use his name to sell product. Even the league that fined him $250,000 for his role in the Atlanta incident surrendered; in recent years he has appeared in ads for NFL Equipment and worked as an NFL Network analyst. The cynical will say Lewis bought his way back into favor, but it's not as easy as it sounds: Neither O.J. nor former Green Bay Packers tight end Mark Chmura nor any other recently scandalized athlete has come close to Lewis's recovery.

"The question was what direction was he going to take?" says Ravens general manager Ozzie Newsome. "Some athletes, if they get out of a situation like he did, say, 'You know what? I got a free pass to just do it again.' Others learn from the lesson, and it makes them a better person. He jumped on the [right] track in a hurry."

Much of that can be attributed to the power of Lewis's personality: as big as his 6'1", 250-pound body and, when it's on, just as winning. His outsized energy and openness inspire devotion even from those seemingly hurt by him. "He's an extraordinary man," says Ravens coach Brian Billick, after an off-season in which Lewis pointedly and publicly declined to give Billick a vote of confidence. "The most naturally dynamic leader I've ever been around."

"Ray has a huge heart and will help anybody in need if he's able," says Tatyana McCall, who met Lewis at Miami and has three sons with him. "I would be remiss if I didn't say I was proud to be the mother of his kids. It's not always easy, but I am very proud."

In March, Cheri Blauwet, a Paralympian, traveled with Lewis to Ethiopia on behalf of the Vietnam Veterans of America Foundation to help in the creation of a sports program for land mine victims. Lewis was there for two weeks and plans to return after this season; he's donated $67,500 for the expansion of a rehabilitation center for amputees and pledged a similar amount for the next phase of construction. Blauwet's friends and family had warned her of Lewis's reputation: This is a man who, even before Atlanta, had been investigated three times for assaults on women, though no charges were ever brought. "He pretty much turned that reputation on its head," says Blauwet, a wheelchair marathoner. "He was incredibly gentle, introspective. Every time a child would pass within his field of vision, there would be a comment or an act that was very genuine, and he treated the people working with him that way. I got numerous lifts up stairs and onto airplanes. He would say, 'Hey, babe, let me give you a lift.'"

Hall of Fame linebacker Mike Singletary had been retired for a decade when he met Lewis in 2003. Renowned for his singular on-field intensity, Singletary had been convinced he'd never again feel that passion. But during his first week as Ravens linebackers coach, he was standing in the end zone in practice when it came time for a goal line stand. The defense came alive. Lewis started screaming, "You ain't getting nothin'! You ain't!" and a stunned Singletary found himself thanking God, tears streaming beneath his sunglasses. "I was seeing everything I missed," says Singletary, now assistant head coach of the San Francisco 49ers. "Only a few guys play the game with their hearts and their souls. A lot of guys don't know what you mean by that. You don't know it until you hear it, and then you see it and you go, *There it is.*"

Yet it's that passion—the obvious relish Lewis takes in football's brutal essence—that makes it easy for those who only see him on TV to believe him guilty of murder. Early in the morning of Jan. 31, 2000, Lewis and a group of acquaintances, including Oakley and Sweeting, exchanged words outside the Cobalt Lounge with another group that included Baker and Lollar. Within minutes Baker and Lollar had been stabbed to death. Lewis's panicked group piled into his stretch limousine and sped off, gunfire blowing out one of the tires. Lewis told everyone in the car to shut up about what they'd seen, and during his initial interviews with police he gave false information. The limo driver at first told police he saw Lewis strike one of the victims, then recanted. Lewis maintains that he saw no one being stabbed and had acted only as a peacemaker.

Sunseria Smith was in Hawaii, on the phone with her son, when the police came to the house where Lewis was staying. She heard her son yell, "What are you doing?" and then, "Mama, I didn't do nothing!" before the phone dropped. When she visited Lewis at the Fulton County detention center for the first time she put her hand on the glass separating them and said, "Is there any blood on your hands?" Lewis told her he had nothing to do with the crimes. "And I said, 'That's all I need to know,'" Smith says.

The prosecution's case against Lewis fell apart quickly, and the murder charges were dropped. Lewis pleaded guilty to one count of misdemeanor obstruction of justice, was sentenced to a year's probation and testified in the case against Oakley and Sweeting. As he walked down the courthouse steps in June 2000, Ray turned to Sunseria and said, "Mama, you have a changed man." In '04 Lewis settled civil suits with members of both victims' families for roughly $2 million. He addressed the families during mediation for the settlement, at once expressing sorrow and raging over his certainty that he'd been prosecuted solely because he was rich. Still, some family members will never be soothed by the settlement or Lewis's perceived transformation. "I hope he can actively feel what it means to have a loved one taken away, the way my nephew was," says Lollar's aunt, Thomasaina Threatt.

"The saddest thing?" Lewis says now. "Take me out of that equation, you got two young dead black kids on the street. The second sad part is, because of the court system and the prosecutor's lies, I got two families hating me for something I didn't have a hand in, and the people who killed their children are free. The people who killed their children could be having dinner with them and they'd never know. Because all they know is the big name, Ray Lewis."

Hero to villain, good to bad, is a very quick walk in America. The reverse is much more difficult; the fall is always easier to believe than the redemption, if only because nobody wants to be played for a sucker. Yet suddenly Cindy Lollar-Owens is willing to try. She helped raise Richard Lollar in Akron and for six years has been a persistent voice blaming Lewis for the deaths of her nephew and Baker. In 2001 she stood outside the stadium in Tampa where Lewis would win his Super Bowl MVP award, holding a photo collage of her nephew. More than once when Baltimore played in Cleveland she passed out fliers there demanding justice.

But last month, after restating that belief in a phone interview, she called back. “This is my conscience,” she said. “I’ve been praying on it, and I’m saying I believe [Lewis] was totally set up. I didn’t want to say nothing; I was worried about how my family would feel. Come to realize, I’ve got to live with myself.”

Lollar-Owens says that before her father died of cancer in 2002, he told her she had to speak about her change of heart. It has taken her four years. She has talked to Lewis only once, by phone after the 2001 Super Bowl. She says he called to tell her he was sorry for her loss. “There was something in his voice,” she says. “I just felt he was innocent.”

Ray Lewis knows what his problem is. He’ll tell you up front about his faults, about how he was wrong for years in the way he allowed “broke people” to get close enough to jeopardize his career and his reputation, and how he “would walk around and might not treat a woman the right way.” But to him those are symptoms of a larger malfunction. It’s now conventional wisdom to decry the prevalence of single-mother households in black society, the lack of strong father figures for young males. Lewis offers himself up as Exhibit A. “I had no one at home to confirm, help, release, whatever,” he says. “I’ve got six kids? I’ve never had a conversation with a man about a woman—ever. I’ve never had a man sit down and say, ‘Son, let me tell you about women.’”

When Ray Lewis was born to the 16-year-old Sunseria on May 15, 1975, his father, Elbert Ray Jackson, set a tone that would endure for three decades: He wasn’t around. It was left to Ray Lewis, a friend of Sunseria’s, to sign the documents and give the newborn his name. Jackson moved in and out of their lives in Lakeland, Fla., with some regularity, then all but drifted away when Lewis was six. Occasionally Jackson would call to say he was coming to see little Ray, “but he always would lie,” Lewis says. “My mother would say, ‘Your daddy’s coming to get you,’ and there were days when I would pack my bag, go outside and just sit there. Sun goes down, my mama comes to grab me, and I would be boo-hoo crying, and she’d say, ‘It’s gonna be all right.’ That was my whole life: It’s gonna be all right, it’s gonna be *all right*. So as I’m getting older, I’m like, When is it going to be all right? Great mother, but you can’t teach me how to be a man. And I’m screaming inside, Can somebody please *help* me?”

Ray eventually was the oldest of five brothers and sisters, the man in charge. As a teenager he would braid his sisters’ hair, take his little brother Keon Lattimore—now a junior running back at Maryland—to day care, go to school, hit practice, do push-ups until he passed out next to his bed. Lewis became a football and wrestling star at Kathleen High, like his father before him; everyone remarked on how he resembled Ray Jackson. His father's coach, Brian Bain, once gave Lewis a program detailing Jackson's wrestling marks. "I posted it on my wall, and every night I'd see it," Lewis says. "Every one of those records? I shattered them, and every time, I shattered them with pain. It was like, Yeah! It's over! His name is out of there! That was my push: to erase everything about him."

When Ray was in high school, Sunseria showed him a letter stating that Jackson had legally changed his son's name to Ray Jackson. Lewis ignored it. "I will never walk in his name," Lewis said then. "Ever."

The absence of a father figure—a "lack of," Lewis simply calls it—has been an ongoing crisis that he has been speaking about from the moment he broke into prominence as a Miami freshman in 1993. SI's attempts to contact Jackson were unsuccessful, but Sunseria, McCall and Ernest Joe, Lewis's high school football coach, all confirm that Jackson was absent from Lewis's youth. Yet Lewis's fixation has only intensified with time and what everyone around him insists is a true spiritual growth. Christianity explains itself through stories, and now that Lewis is witnessing, now that he's looking at himself as a feather buffeted by forces far greater than man, he has no choice but to comb through it all again and attempt to understand himself in a new context. All the bad events? His daddy? The trial? Mere tests and hurdles and setbacks he was meant to endure to get him to today. Never mind that Lewis may not know all the facts of his parents' relationship. "He was a child," McCall warns. "Whatever transpired between his parents, all he knows are the stories."

On the football field, Lewis was undersized and unstoppable. He had 17 tackles in his first start at Miami and declared his intention to be the greatest Hurricane ever. Off the field, he seemed incapable of creating anything less than a Category 5 impact. He met McCall when she was a freshman at Miami in the fall of 1994. While she was carrying their first son, Ray III, the two got into a shouting match that prompted Lewis's first run-in with the law; a resident assistant said she saw Lewis push McCall, strike her in the face and put his hands on her neck. McCall didn't press charges. If anything, she says now, she was the aggressive one in the incident. A year later Lewis stepped into an argument between McCall and Kimberlie Arnold, a former girlfriend of Lewis's. Arnold told campus police that Lewis shook her shoulder and scratched her, but again no charges were brought; in 2000 she told *The* (Baltimore) *Sun* that "he's not a violent or abusive person, not to me he wasn't."

Yet violence has shadowed Lewis at nearly every step in his life. While he was away at college, a dozen close friends and relatives from Lakeland died, one trying to rob a bank. Each time Lewis went home it seemed he was attending a funeral. Then in April 1996, UM linebacker Marlin Barnes and a female friend were bludgeoned to death by the woman's ex-boyfriend in the apartment Lewis and Barnes shared; Barnes was buried the day Baltimore drafted Lewis. More than a decade later Lewis still cries at the mention of his friend's name. Barnes wasn't just the one workout partner who could keep up with Lewis; he also pushed him, told him he was unique, even predicted his trouble. "Man," Lewis remembers Barnes telling him, "everybody ain't going to like you." Barnes filled the void left by Lewis's father; he organized his clothes with care, so Lewis did, too. He shaved off his body hair, convinced that it would give him that extra 10th of a second, so Lewis did, too. When Barnes died, Lewis felt he'd been thrown back out on that stoop, waiting for a face that would never come. He punched a hole in a wall and thought, *Now you're gone too?*

After signing with the Ravens, Lewis tried to reconnect with his father, gave him $5,000. "He burned me," Lewis says. "Blew the money, left my life again." Every once in a while Jackson would surface, and everyone would remark on how alike the two men looked. Lewis thought he could understand himself if he could understand the dead ringer in the room. But over and over he would end up saying, "Dad? Can you just come around and don't ask for nothing? Teach me something."

In 1997 Lewis and McCall went to court to establish child-support arrangements. By then she was expecting her second child by Lewis; the court mandated payments of $3,800 a month. The following year he was ordered to pay $2,700 a month, plus back payments of $29,700, to a Baltimore-area woman with whom he had daughter. The process left him drained, and he told his mother that maybe he'd just wait to know his kids when they were older. Smith would have none of it. According to McCall, Lewis has since made great efforts to spend time with his children (three live in Baltimore, three with McCall in Florida). He calls them daily, has movie dates with his two daughters on Fridays, sometimes brings all six kids to stay at his house on the weekends of home games. "That's the beauty: I give them what I never had," Lewis says. But he's only half right. Like his dad, he doesn't live with their mothers, doesn't see his children every night.

His world has always been one of extremes—quotes, emotions, troubles, triumphs—and people's reactions follow suit. Lewis's history and his raw views, about "devious women" or how a black man in America is "still a n——— in a lot of peoples' eyes," will only reinforce the perception of those who call him a thug. But plenty of people also sit on the other end of the spectrum, ready, like Singletary, to put their names on the line and speak about "the pureness of his heart."

When Singletary took over as Ravens linebackers coach in 2003, Lewis was playing at a level few had ever seen, with a young man's fire, a veteran's knowledge and a once-in-a-generation hunger. But the first time they spoke, Lewis begged for instruction—and not only in football. They set up regular meetings, and the two went heart-to-heart for the next two years, discussing faith, family, "disciplines and desires and what a man is supposed to be," Lewis says. Whatever Singletary said, Lewis soaked up; once he suggested Lewis play more on the balls of his feet, and in the next practice Lewis collapsed because his calves were cramping. He'd been trying to play on tiptoes.

After the 2004 season Singletary left for San Francisco, and Lewis got that feeling again: what he needed, walking out the door. But Lewis was also pushing 30, and maybe some lessons had sunk in. Bryant, his pastor, sensed Lewis learning something new and necessary: "If I'm a king, I am responsible to the kingdom I've created around me," Bryant says. "He has found that he had to father himself."

Last spring, after a long silence, Lewis says he heard from Ray Jackson again. His father called from Tampa to say he'd been put out by a girlfriend and hospitalized. Against his better judgment Lewis rushed from his home in Boca Raton, intent on moving his father in at last. He sent a car to pick up Jackson; they were to meet at Lewis's grandmother's house in Lakeland. But when Lewis arrived, Jackson wasn't there. He stewed for a few hours, then got a call: His father wasn't coming.

On the long ride home, Lewis tried to grab hold of himself and say, Toughen up! But it was no use. He cried the whole way, shaking, empty again, with familiar words rolling through his head: *That's the last straw. I'm done.*

Lord knows, it hasn't been an easy path. But who said it should be? Lewis studies the story of David, who slew Goliath and became a king and had woman trouble too. He studies Job and all the trials God put him through. What was 2000, after all, but the work of the same master hand? From jail to a Super Bowl stage, with millions watching so he could become more famous, wield a greater voice than ever? Ray Lewis knows people will respond to him; he'll show you, with just a flick of his hands, how he can get 70,000 strangers to scream for him.

So now, Lewis can feel it happening all over again. People had written him off after last year, marked him down as fading. Lewis was furious at the criticism. Billick and Newsome characterize Lewis's off-season sniping as a continuation of contract haggles from a year earlier; before the 2005 season he had sought to renegotiate his seven-year, $50 million contract, signed in 2002. People were calling for Lewis to be traded after he demanded the team beef up its defensive line, called him a malcontent for questioning the team's commitment. "Persecutions" is the word Lewis uses to describe the affair, at once paranoid and proselytizing: They're out to get him, *and* it's part of God's plan.

Yet the next thing you know Baltimore spent its first-round draft pick on defensive tackle Haloti Ngata. Then Lewis became the central factor in bringing quarterback Steve McNair to the Ravens. Give me the pieces, Lewis told team owner Steve Bisciotti last February. Give me a real chance at another Super Bowl, or let me go.

"What do y'all want me to do, seriously?" Lewis says of his critics. "The thing you've praised me for—being a courageous leader—is the same thing y'all trying to crucify me for now. I'm doing what you want, to say, 'Dammit, I'm not going to put up with this!' and suddenly [the team] said, 'Ray wanted to talk about money.' I never played this game for money, but now I do?"

Yes, there's that word again: *crucify*. It's no slip. Lewis won't go so far as to call himself the Second Coming, but he's close to believing himself a prophet of sorts, and if martyrdom is the price, so be it. "God has *me* to do what people are afraid to do: tell the truth," he says. "Yes, racism does exist. Hatred exists every day. I'm not afraid. The worst thing that could happen to me—and I don't see it as the worst—is to be killed and go to heaven."

Delusional? Maybe. There are many who won't take kindly to Ray Lewis, of all people, telling them how to live. After Baltimore's season-opening win at Tampa Bay this season, three of Lewis's sons were standing outside the Ravens' locker room, their dad's name and number on their backs. A woman walked up to their mother and, speaking just above their heads, hissed, "I can't believe you let your kids wear that murderer's jersey."

Five weeks later in Baltimore, it's different. The Ravens have lost a seesaw spectacle with Carolina that left McNair with a concussion. The plan looks shaky for the moment; McNair has struggled, the running game is a mess. Still, Lewis led the defense in tackles again, and now he's in his family suite high above the empty stands. His kids are there, four boys and two girls squirming about his legs. "Let me see your abs!" Lewis commands two of the boys. They lift their jerseys, and he laughs and says, "You got to do your push-ups and sit-ups."

The kids spill into the hall, Lewis bellowing, "Who knows my birthday?"

"May 25th...no, 15th," says one. "1975!" blurts another.

"Grab your brothers' and sisters' hands now."

The group stops at the elevator, Lewis's mother and sisters and friends bringing up the rear. A Baltimore police officer sidles up; a few hundred fans line the barriers outside, waiting. "Do you want us to walk you out there?" the cop asks Lewis.

He thinks, then says, “No, there’ll be lots of people.”

On the ground floor Lewis stands inside the main doors of the stadium, gathering the kids around him again. The crowd outside sees him through the glass, and you can hear his name in imploring tones, over and over, the pleas already starting for a signature, a photo. “Come on,” he says and pushes; the doors fly open. His head is down. Sinner hits the late afternoon air, plunging forward to greet his flock.

AUGUST 9, 2004

Master and Commander

With football principles learned under his dad, a coach at Navy, brainy Bill Belichick has turned New England into the NFL's mightiest vessel

BY PETER KING

"Would you like to see Bill's room?"

The kindly voice belongs to Jeannette Belichick, a petite 82-year-old who is standing in the living room of her Annapolis, Md., home. Back when she taught Spanish at Hiram (Ohio) College, Jeannette spoke four languages fluently and understood seven, but now, as she says with a smile and a twinkle, "The only language I speak is football."It's a short walk to the onetime bedroom of Steve and Jeannette Belichick's only child, now 52 and coach of the two-time Super Bowl champion New England Patriots. The twin beds are made pristinely, as though awaiting military inspection. Two maritime paintings done by amateur painter Steve hang on the walls. A high school graduation photo of Bill sits on the dresser. The bookshelf is crammed with volumes from his days at Annapolis High. *A Separate Peace*, by John Knowles. *Future Shock*, by Alvin Toffler. *The Case of the Screaming Woman*, a Perry Mason mystery by Erle Stanley Gardner. There's The Gettysburg Civil War Battle Game and a signed football from the 1963 Navy team and four trophies from Bill's childhood athletic triumphs. "That room hasn't changed in 40 years," Bill says when asked about it later.

The room is, to be frank, a little barren. "It's not a big deal," Jeannette says. "That's the way we live."

The contents of the room provide a window into the mind of Bill Belichick. They tell us that the hottest coach in the NFL is well-educated and uncluttered in his thinking. Through a roller-coaster coaching ride that has included a trying stint with the Cleveland Browns in the 1990s and a Captain Queeg-like performance in walking away from the New York Jets 24 hours after being promoted to head coach in January 2000, Belichick has in many respects remained unaltered. "I don't think he's changed from his Cleveland days," says good friend Jim Brown, the Hall of Fame running back, who remains close to the Browns' organization. "He's acquired some life experiences, but he's exactly the same man I knew 10 years ago."

As a coach, however, Belichick has continually educated himself, never allowing himself or his team to become too predictable. Less than a month after the Patriots beat the Carolina Panthers to claim their second Lombardi Trophy last February, he flew to Baton Rouge and spent two days drawing up schemes with his former defensive coordinator in Cleveland, LSU coach Nick Saban. For the second straight year he traveled to the Florida Keys to pick the brain of fellow two-time Super Bowl winner Jimmy Johnson. During a vacation on Nantucket before training camp, he listened to audiotapes of a book by retired Navy captain D. Michael Abrashoff called *It's Your Ship: Management Techniques from the Best Damn Ship in the Navy*. He also found time for one of the Harry Potter tomes. Hey, even a guy as intense as Belichick has to have fun once in a while.

"Frank took the hawk to its perch in the garage, set the burglar alarm, and locked the door. He had just sat down at the table for lunch when Joe appeared, carrying a volume of the encyclopedia."

—FRANKLIN W. DIXON, *THE HOODED HAWK MYSTERY*

Even at age nine, Bill Belichick had football on the brain. He was devoted to his father, a longtime assistant coach and scout at Navy. Son joined Dad whenever he could. If Steve had to drive to the Baltimore airport to pick up films on that week's opponent, Bill rode with him. Once home, Bill not only watched the films but also saw how his father diagrammed plays. When Bill was nine or 10, he tagged along to the weekly Monday-night meeting, at which players were given the scouting report for the next game.

"He'd sit in the back of the room, maybe for 90 minutes a session," says Steve, now 85. "I never had to say a word to him about his behavior. He'd stare at the front of the room and not say a word."

When Bill was 10 or 11, the assistant in charge of the offensive game plan, Ernie Jorge, sent him an envelope every Thursday night. BILL'S READY LIST was written on the envelope, and inside was the game plan for the week, including all the plays. Before he was a teenager Bill knew terminology, formations, schemes. He also knew bona fide football stars from the time he spent at Midshipmen practices. When he was seven, Navy's biggest standout was running back Joe Bellino, the 1960 Heisman Trophy winner. "That was his first hero," Steve Belichick says. "Joe was the hero of a lot of kids in America then, and Bill was his friend."

To this day Bellino, now an auto-auction executive in the Boston area, remembers playing catch on the practice field with Bill. "Imagine what Bill must have absorbed," says Bellino. "He'd sit in the back of the room listening to his father give the scouting report. He's a six-, seven-, eight-year-old youngster hanging out at the Naval Academy. Midshipmen in uniform, parades, the brass, the visiting presidents, the football team with two Heisman winners [Bellino and 1963 recipient Roger Staubach]. And he saw his father's work ethic. He saw everyone in that room soak up what his dad was telling us, believing if we did what he said, we could beat anybody."

As he got older and the Staubach era began, Belichick was able to do more. If Staubach wanted to work after practice on a pass he knew he'd be using that week, Belichick often served as his receiver. "Say Roger would be working on a sprint-out, throwing to the sideline," recalls Belichick. "I'd go to the spot on the sideline and practice the throw. Not a few. I'm talking 20, 30 of them. People ask me now why I do things a certain way. Look at the way I grew up. I grew up thinking, This is the way it's supposed to be."

Meanwhile at home, he and Jeannette read books to each other. Bill lived for the Hardy Boys. Sometimes, while his mom was getting dinner ready, he would sit in the kitchen and read a chapter aloud. Mother and son might trade off at bedtime, Jeannette reading a chapter, then Bill. In high school, the reading with Mom didn't stop. *A Clockwork Orange* one month, *The Godfather* the next.

Bill got a taste of the real world when Annapolis High was integrated before his freshman year, in 1966. It was also then that he began playing for the second influential football coach in his life, Al Laramore. "There was no individuality on his team, other than the number you wore," says Belichick, who worked his way up to first-string center as a senior. "I learned a lot about the team concept and about toughness from him. We used to have one bucket of water at practice. Everyone drank from it. If he didn't like the way we were practicing, he'd walk to the bucket, kick it over and say, 'You guys ain't gettin' a water break today.'"

"Change is avalanching upon our heads, and most people are grotesquely unprepared to cope with it."

—ALVIN TOFFLER, *FUTURE SHOCK*

Actually, Belichick was better at lacrosse than he was at football. But what he did best was organize. After a year at Phillips Academy in Andover, Mass., he enrolled at Wesleyan University in Middletown, Conn. Turned off by the poor facilities at Wesleyan, Belichick got permission from the Naval Academy athletic director for the Cardinals to hold lacrosse spring training on the Navy practice fields, and during consecutive spring breaks the team practiced in Annapolis. The players bunked at the Belichicks'.

When he graduated with a bachelor's degree in economics in the spring of 1975, Belichick wasn't sure what he wanted to do. He thought working in virtually any capacity for the coaching staff of a college or professional team would be his best way to build his résumé for a full-time graduate assistant's job in college football, which sounded like fun to him. So he wrote letters to 250 coaches. The Baltimore Colts hired him as a special assistant. He made $25 a week, and he hitched a ride to and from work with head coach Ted Marchibroda. Belichick's duties included telling players who were about to be released that the coach wanted to see them in his office. On NFL teams that individual is known as the Turk, but Belichick inherited another nickname: Bad News Bill.

The pro game grew on him. From Baltimore he moved on to assistant jobs with the Detroit Lions and the Denver Broncos, and then for 12 years with the New York Giants, first as the special teams coach, then linebackers coach, then defensive coordinator. He worked under Bill Parcells for the last eight years, six as coordinator. "Bill gave me a lot of latitude to do my job," Belichick says. "There was probably never a week where he wouldn't adjust something in the defensive game plan, but he had a lot of respect for the coaches' doing their jobs." Because Parcells was a domineering presence with a strong defensive reputation, it took a while for Belichick to be seen by NFL owners as his own man. But Browns owner Art Modell hired him after the Giants won their second Super Bowl, in January 1991.

From the beginning in Cleveland, Belichick was tougher and more demanding of the players than any of his recent predecessors. With reporters he was notoriously uncommunicative. His monosyllabic answers became so legendary ("Sitting through his press conferences was like putting a sharp pencil into your eye," says Tony Grossi, who covered the team for *The Plain Dealer* in Cleveland) that when Patriots owner Robert Kraft was thinking of hiring Belichick in 2000, an executive from one NFL team sent him a tape of one of the coach's media sessions and said, "Are you serious about hiring this guy?"

In the middle of the 1993 season Belichick decided that quarterback Bernie Kosar had become ineffective on the field and, with his complaints about what he thought was an unimaginative offense, a distraction off it. Backup Vinny Testaverde was hurt, but that didn't stop Belichick from releasing Kosar. The Browns, 5–3 at the time, lost six of their last eight games. "We've kissed and made up," Kosar said recently. "We were both type A personalities who had different ideas about how we should be doing things. Now, as you can see, the man can coach."

Unlike many of the Cleveland players, Browns coaches loved working for Belichick. Every Monday after a win over an AFC Central opponent, he would have his secretary cash a check from his personal account, and $200 in cash would be left on the desk of every assistant. Before the coaching staff headed off on vacation every June, he would distribute the proceeds from his TV and radio shows to his assistants—maybe $12,000 a man—and take nothing for himself. "Bill remembered what it was like to be an assistant coach," says his former line coach Kirk Ferentz, now the head coach at Iowa. "He gave everyone a second Christmas. You think that doesn't make you loyal?" One time Belichick left a $100 bill in the car ashtray of low-level scout Scott Pioli. When Pioli protested that he didn't need the money, Belichick replied, "Shut up and take it. I've been where you've been."

Before the staff split for vacation one summer, Ferentz remembers, Belichick gave each assistant a book to read. One got *The Winner Within*, by Pat Riley. One got a book on the history of the Browns. One got *Educating Dexter*, about the drug addiction of former All-Pro defensive end Dexter Manley. Ferentz got *One More July*, by George Plimpton, about former Alabama and Green Bay Packers center Bill Curry. Belichick thought Ferentz could benefit from learning about Bear Bryant and Vince Lombardi. "Bill wanted us to read the books, then give reports on what we learned that could help the staff," Ferentz says. "He was always doing things like that."

"That's the thing about Bill," says former Browns player personnel director Mike Lombardi, now an Oakland Raiders executive. "He was always 'in search of.' When the salary cap and free agency were coming into the league, I told him I thought we should go see Jerry West, because he'd done such a great job managing the Lakers. We met [West] in Chicago at [the NBA] summer camp for draftees, and we spent three hours talking." West's advice: Develop your own players so you can manage salaries, and don't buy into the one-player-at-any-cost mentality.

That was tough when you worked for Modell. "Around the office," says one Browns staffer, "we used to say our organizational philosophy was, 'Ready, fire, aim.'" In the spring of 1995, following an 11–5 season and a playoff win over Parcells's Patriots, Modell signed troubled but talented free-agent wideout Andre Rison to a five-year, $17 million deal. Rison lasted one season. Following a chaotic 5–11 season in '95—the one during which Modell announced he was moving the franchise to Baltimore—Belichick was fired.

"I didn't walk away from there saying I did a bad job," says Belichick, who was 36–44 in five seasons. "Not at all. We took a bad team, made it pretty good, made the playoffs, had a bad year in the most off-the-charts negative situation maybe in football history, got fired. It just wasn't a good mix between Art and me."

No one except those closest to him realizes it, but it was because of his experience with Modell that Belichick walked away from the Jets' job. Belichick knew he might get only one more chance to be an NFL head coach, and he didn't want that to be under the thumb of an owner he didn't know (the Jets were up for sale), with a club president he viewed as a know-nothing (Steve Gutman) and, to a much lesser degree, a director of football operations he felt he had outgrown (Parcells). If he was going to be a head coach again, he would do it on his terms.

"Each small victory improves the odds that you will triumph at the moment of truth."

—PAT RILEY, *THE WINNER WITHIN*

Then he joined New England 23 days after bailing on the Jets, Belichick had two important things going for him. He had an owner, Kraft, who was committed to letting him make all the football decisions. And in Pioli he brought along a personnel man who had his full support. On the day Belichick took the job, the Patriots were $10 million over the salary cap, so in 2000 he made his first order of business eliminating the surplus. That season the Patriots finished 5–11. "It was a rude awakening," says Kraft. "We paid so many guys, and we were still losing. We had to shut off the financial spigot."

Kraft saw a slightly different Belichick than the one he'd known in 1996 as a Pats assistant. "He used to be a junior Parcells," Kraft says. "He walked around saying things like, 'This team's worse than I thought,' or, 'We can't win with this.' I told him to cut it out. Who needs that? Talk to me about what we can do to make it better. And he did."

Belichick and Pioli studied more than 200 free agents in the early months of 2001. They signed 17 bit players who made the Patriots the next season for a piddling combined signing-bonus charge of $2.7 million. One was Mike Vrabel, miscast as a special-teamer and a backup linebacker with the Pittsburgh Steelers. Belichick thought the speedy and athletic Vrabel could fill two roles—dropping into coverage from defensive end or linebacker and playing as a nickel pass rusher.

"Until the Patriots called me, I thought seriously of going to law school, because my career with Pittsburgh wasn't working out," says Vrabel. "I didn't think anyone would find a way to use me. But I was amazed how much Bill knew about me. One day he came up to me and said, 'Remember in that Miami preseason game last year, how you played the power block? That's how we want to do it here.' In situational football, which is basically what the NFL is today, he's got to be the best mind out there." Against the St. Louis Rams in Super Bowl XXXVI, Vrabel pressured Kurt Warner into an interception that cornerback Ty Law returned for a touchdown. In Super Bowl XXXVIII, Vrabel had two sacks against the Panthers and, in a classic display of Belichick ingenuity, caught a fourth-quarter touchdown pass from Tom Brady.

Having studied the game for so long, and having understood it with such clarity since age 12, Belichick has the confidence to try anything that makes sense to him. He is always open to suggestions from his assistant coaches. Before the Super Bowl he was concerned about the power running of Carolina's Stephen Davis, so defensive coordinator Romeo Crennel suggested disguising a scheme that got backup linemen Jarvis Green and Ty Warren more involved. Davis carried 13 times for 49 yards.

The first time New England faced quarterback Drew Bledsoe after trading him to the Buffalo Bills in 2002, the Patriots surprised the Bills by not blitzing. Seven or eight times in the game, New England used a defense that had no linemen, four linebackers standing at or near the line and seven defensive backs. The Pats won 38–7. Against the Indianapolis Colts in the AFC Championship Game last January, New England told its players to be extremely physical with the Colts' wide receivers. On eight to 10 plays the Pats flopped Law and safety Rodney Harrison in their coverage of Marvin Harrison. The idea was to encourage Peyton Manning to throw short to Marvin Harrison, which would allow the defense to clobber the All-Pro wideout. If Manning elected to throw deep, Law would be there with blanket coverage. The four interceptions thrown by Manning, three of them by Law, told the story of the game. "There was a lot we hadn't seen," says Indianapolis coach Tony Dungy. "But that's the thing about Bill. He's not afraid to take risks."

Adds former Giants quarterback and current CBS analyst Phil Simms, "Bill changes all the time. To continue to win, you've got to."

That's why Belichick was in Baton Rouge last February. Even though his defense allowed the fewest points per game in the league last season (14.9) and held opponents to the fewest yards per pass attempt (5.23), Belichick wasn't about to stand pat. "He had just won the Super Bowl, for crying out loud, but here he was," says Saban. "We went at it for two days."

One new scheme Belichick came away with was a way to make his Cover 4 look like Cover 2. In Cover 4, a quartet of defensive backs spreads out across the deep secondary, each taking a quarter of the field. In Cover 2, two deep safeties are responsible for half the field. A quarterback has maybe three seconds from the time he takes the snap to the time he releases the ball. If he's expecting two deep safeties, he'd be pretty comfortable throwing an 18-yard out, assuming the receiver can beat his corner to the sideline. If while the quarterback drops, Cover 2 morphs into Cover 4, the intermediate and deep areas suddenly get more crowded. A panicked quarterback might not recognize the change until it is too late.

At a minicamp in June, Brady went against Belichick's new scheme for the first time. "I was sure it was Cover 2, then all of a sudden I'm seeing Cover 4," Brady says. "The more I don't understand what I'm seeing, the longer it takes me to get into my read progression. The later I throw, the better the chances are for an incompletion or interception."

Belichick knows, however, that sustaining success in today's NFL requires more than just devising defensive wrinkles. When he met with Johnson this year, the topic was how to keep a championship team together. "Don't think I'm going to give you a solution you'll be happy with," Johnson told him. "You've won two of the last three Super Bowls, and the problem with that is that everyone in the organization thinks they're a bigger reason than they are for your winning." Johnson's advice: Quietly put incentives into the contracts of players you want to keep, don't redo any contract until the last season of the deal and figure out who you can win without.

"Jimmy's really the only guy in this era who's lived it, who's dealt with what we're dealing with, and more," Belichick says. "Who else am I gonna talk to?"

"You must adapt to your opportunities and weaknesses. You can use a variety of approaches and still have a consistent result."

—SUN TZU, *THE ART OF WAR*

Befittingly, Belichick has a library full of books in his brick house in a leafy Boston suburb. While examining the titles one day this summer, a visitor came across a thin, worn paperback.

"*The Art of War*," the visitor said, looking at the translation of a 2,500-year-old treatise on the Chinese principles of warfare. "Wow. You read that?"

"Yeah," Belichick replied, getting a look on his face not unlike the one he wears when a play goes wrong. "I got something out of it. But, you know, 'Don't move your troops when the ground is muddy'? I mean...."

He's not saying he's any smarter than Sun Tzu. He just knows that he's got a pretty good brain, and he's willing to use it. Just as Jeannette and Steve Belichick taught their boy to do.

JUNE 27, 2016

The Refrigerator's Stubborn Spiral

At 53, the Fridge is doing what he wants to do, even if it causes pain and divisiveness in his large family, as members watch the former Bears star slowly implode and are at a loss to help him

BY RICK TELANDER

We can start with this: Everybody loves the Fridge.

William Perry could have been called the Car or the Shed or the Washing Machine or even the Water Heater. But he wasn't. The Refrigerator it was—Fridge, for short—ever since his days as a 300-plus-pound All-America nosetackle at Clemson. Because it fit. Nicknamed for that most wonderful of American kitchen appliances—the one with the good stuff inside that keeps us alive and happy, and sometimes fat—Fridge in his heyday was as well-liked and cheer-inducing as that leftover piece of apple pie, wrapped in cellophane, just behind the mayonnaise and cold chicken.

"If you didn't like Fridge," says Mike Ditka, his former NFL coach in Chicago, "you didn't like anybody."

When the world champion Bears started to pull in endorsements and celebrity gigs following Super Bowl XX, in 1986, and Perry, just a rookie, hauled in more than anyone—more even than Walter Payton or Jim McMahon or even Da Capitalistic Coach himself—"it would have been easy for us to resent him," says Dan Hampton, Perry's defensive linemate. "But we loved Fridge."

There was a role—convivial southern goofball—that the swollen, gap-toothed Perry played in that magical 1985 season, and he played it well. Some of it was artifice, from mythology and expectation and the media's need for simplicity. Fat equals jolly, you know. But much of it was Perry, for real. He was as easygoing as you would expect given his Deep South roots, in Aiken, S.C. He did have 11 siblings; seven brothers and four sisters. He did love to fish in ponds. He had, indeed, seen his front tooth shot out by a cousin's BB gun as a lad. He had drunk a couple cases of beer after one college game. He could eat like a shark, guzzle like a horse, take off like a rabbit, jump like a lion. Yes, at 6'2"-and-change he could dunk a basketball. I saw him do it. My guess is that he weighed 330 at the time; maybe 340. We were at the Multiplex Fitness Club in suburban Deerfield, Ill., a couple of years after his rookie season, playing afternoon pickup ball. The rim survived.

His fame started when Ditka put him in to block for Payton and then to tote the rock himself against the defending champion 49ers in Week 6 of that rookie year. San Francisco's coach, Bill Walsh, had used 275-pound guard Guy McIntyre in the backfield the previous season, in an NFC championship game victory over Chicago, and Ditka remembered. A feisty, vindictive competitor, Da Coach had no problem with payback. Give me big? I'll give you immense. Plus, as Ditka always says: It was fun.

But Fridge's notoriety really exploded, like a grenade in a tomato patch, when he lined up and ran for a touchdown on Oct. 21, 1985, in a Monday night game against the Packers. Much of America was watching as he became the heaviest man in NFL history to score a touchdown off a set play. All the overweight, Barcaloungered, chip-dipping, vicariously living fans across the country were mesmerized and thrilled. *Hot damn!* This was entertainment.

Back then, you have to remember, 308 pounds (and that was the lightest he ever weighed as a pro) was a crazy-big deal, like something from a tent show. Fridge was the "best use of fat since the invention of bacon," one sportswriter wrote.

Now there are hundreds of players in the NFL Fridge's size or larger. Many high school teams have one or two. Looking back at the video from when Fridge went on *Late Night with David Letterman* in November 1985, it is stunning how slim he actually appears compared to what we're used to seeing on the football field these days. Humor was maintained that night on *Letterman* with some gags about eating, and when Fridge saw 43-inch, 36-pound teenage actor Emmanuel Lewis (of TV's *Webster*) in the green room, he told a reporter, "Man, last time I was that small was when I was born."

So who could dislike this fellow? As long as he wasn't played for a complete yokel or freak, he could get along with anybody. And as long as you weren't lined up opposite him, trying to stop him—like, say, 220-pound Packers linebacker George Cumby, who drew that assignment on one play that fateful Monday night and got plastered like a mayfly on a truck grill—then he posed no danger to anyone or anything.

As Fridge, 53, says now, "I'm not doing anything bad. That's not in me, not in my family—we weren't raised that way. I do things in a correct way, a respectful way."

But not, alas, in a healthy way. And not—if we're thinking of life as a brief moment to be tended to with diligence and care—in a proper way. Fridge drinks. Too much. That he drinks *at all*, really, is a problem. He has physical and mental issues that demand sobriety. ("I'm sure he's got traces of CTE," says younger brother Michael Dean, himself a former NFL defensive lineman.) In 2011, just 11 years after he flashed his famous imperfect smile for the cheery cover of SPORTS ILLUSTRATED's first Where Are They Now? issue, Fridge declared publicly that he is an alcoholic. He has been to rehab. He's been told by doctors to stop drinking. He's been told by family members.

None of it matters. He's got drinking buddies. Alcohol's his special pal. He's back in slow, sleepy Aiken and, by God, he's doing what he wants to do. Even if it causes pain and divisiveness in his large family, as members watch him slowly implode and are at a loss to help him.

"I'm home and I'm happy," Fridge says. "I ain't got no plans. I'm just gonna relax and take my time."

So the love and support he receives from others is dead-ended by his stubbornness. Perry can barely walk, and only then with a walker. He's at least 150 pounds overweight—around 430, even 450, according to friends and family. He doesn't work with physical therapists, or wear the compression socks or orthopedic shoes that he should. His hearing is terrible but he won't wear his hearing aids, so he ends up virtually reading lips unless you are close to him and speaking loudly.

He has four children and he doesn't see them much, or at least not as often as one would expect. Both of his ex-wives are out of the picture. He lives alone in a retirement facility.

What does one do? Let him be? He has diabetes and the residual effects of a nasty thing called Guillain-Barré syndrome, which hit him in 2008. Tellingly, one of the concerns with the mosquito-borne Zika virus, plaguing pre-Olympic Brazil and threatening to spread to the rest of the world, is that researchers believe it can cause not only birth defects but also Guillain-Barré syndrome, which creates neurological problems that can leave victims paralyzed and sometimes on life support. Its effects can diminish or last forever.

Fridge was nailed by it, possibly because of a severe dental infection, and at one point in 2009 he was near death. He couldn't move and was wasting away in bed, dehydrated beyond recognition, without any family near. Willie, one of his older brothers, says that when he found Fridge, he looked like a gaunt war camp victim, down to 190 pounds. Look at Perry now and you might guess that his skeleton alone weighs 190 pounds.

Oh, and the millions of dollars that Perry made over his 10-year NFL career are long gone too. So is his Super Bowl ring—at size 25, believed to be the largest ever made—auctioned off a year ago for $200,000, without Fridge getting anything for it.

It's all a mess, it seems, from health to finances. And sadly, in a sense, the people suffering the most from Fridge's demise are his children (three girls and a boy) and family members, who all claim to want to help him, but who are too busy fighting amongst themselves to actually accomplish any change. Michael Dean, a six-time Pro Bowl defensive tackle who lives in Charlotte, was named by a judge as guardian and conservator of Fridge's affairs when the big man was first incapacitated, in 2008. But Perry's son, William II, told a Chicago TV reporter last year that he has doubts about Michael Dean's stewardship and legal control. "It's a bad situation," he said. "Hopefully we can get guardianship over [my dad] and go forward, and get him removed so he can do the right thing and be independent."

Willie is more desperate than that. "Jealousy," he says, is why Michael Dean keeps Fridge under his power. "When William was messed up, it made sense, but not now." Willie claims that Michael Dean, who lives 150 miles away from Fridge, is only giving his brother the "minimum care" that he needs; he suggests that Fridge doesn't see the necessary doctors or attend certain autograph and celebrity outings where he could make much-needed money. This Michael Dean finds hilarious; he says that he was the one who nursed Fridge back to health in 2009, that his sister Patsy is now in Aiken taking care of their brother and that William's own stubbornness explains his missing appointments. He also claims that Willie wants to pry guardianship away so he can use Fridge himself as "his cash cow."

If this makes no sense, so be it. The Perry family is tight but torn, with age difference, gender and competitiveness all leading to a big, interwoven, fractious ball of domestic dysphoria. Willie claims that Michael Dean profits off Fridge's minimal income (from social security and from his NFL pension; public records show Perry with total equity of $35,245 and net income of $13,921 for 2015) so that it's financially worthwhile to keep Fridge down, pointing to an annual $1,250 "caretaker/conservator" fee in his records.

But Michael Dean flat out denies any improprieties; any money, he says, goes toward accounting and bookkeeping. "I'm getting rich off Fridge?!," he says, incredulous. "I don't want anything to do with the mess! He still owes a couple hundred thousand to the IRS. Everything you put in place, he fights. I'm out of options. I can't babysit him for the next 20 years. I've tried to get rid of the guardianship and conservatorship for the last three or four years. I'd give it up to anybody—*except Willie*. Anybody but him."

Fridge is in his office—that is, he's in his white Hummer H2, parked in the driveway of a ramshackle house on Ridgewood Lane in Aiken. It's 6 p.m., early April, 72° outside, and 10 or more people hang around the SUV as if it's a tiki hut on a beach. Fridge is tipping back a beer and appears to be a tad inebriated, louder than usual, more demonstrative.

Hanging by the driver's window is a hefty guy in a white T-shirt, smoking a menthol cigarette, drinking vodka from a plastic cup. His name is Darrell Epps. Both Willie and Fridge's sometimes manager—a mysterious woman from Aiken who goes by Jaye, whose email begins Perrymediamgt and who occasionally finds him paying gigs—feel that Epps is the worst enabler around. What she wants to tell all these friends is: "You're sitting there watching him die!" Willie says simply of Darrell, "He's William's leech." Again, fingers point across the divide like daggers. Epps says that Jaye is the real fraud in all of this; "a b----!" Michael Dean, meanwhile, paints Jaye and Willie as trying to make money off it all, "trying to drain [Fridge]."

Despite all the tumult, this is pretty much what Fridge does every day now: hang out with people who lack apparent jobs or places to be, shoot the breeze and drink. He's got his own vodka cup. Maybe it's not that much different from what high-class retirees do at the 19th hole of country clubs, calling it socializing rather than wasting away. The thing is, Fridge can't move from his driver's seat. His car reeks of urine because he sometimes can't control his bladder, sometimes doesn't care. And there's not a medical journal on diabetes or the central nervous system anywhere that recommends alcohol consumption of this frequency for good health.

"I'm his best friend," says Epps, cordially pouring a little vodka for a visitor. "Listen to me. *I'm his best friend!*"

I remember the good old days back in Lake Forest, Ill., when the Bears practiced at the original Halas Hall on the east side of town and the Ditka-led circus was the wildest, craziest thing ever to hit the NFL. Before the 1985 Bears went on to outscore their foes 91–10 in the playoffs, before the regular season was even over, half the team filmed an arrogant rap video called *The Super Bowl Shuffle*. Their coach got a DUI on the way home from one game.

Their star QB mooned a New Orleans news helicopter on the eve of the Big Game.

And that's not even mentioning the amazing Fridge, who was penalized in one game for attempting to throw Payton over the goal line. Fridge would sometimes walk over to my house, a block from the training facility, just to see if I wanted to play basketball. Once he sat in my kitchen and watched, mesmerized, as Manute Bol, his physical opposite, played hoops on TV. Who would have guessed that a decade and a half later Perry would box the 7'7" Dinka Dunker in as absurd a Las Vegas fight as has ever been seen? "What a great visual image this is!" said ringside announcer Chris Rose that night, not long before Fridge—so fat that he looked like a truck tire inflated 10 times past its limit—almost collapsed from exhaustion and lost a unanimous decision to the human pencil.

Back in the mid-1980s, Perry was a naïf. Maybe he still is, though the world has taken its toll on his innocence. He has lost several Aiken houses, one of which went into receivership and is starting to rot, another of which—a semimansion with a palm tree in the huge front yard and big football cutouts in the surrounding metal fence—is occupied by his first wife, Sherry. Perry has been diagnosed with mild cognitive impairment, perhaps from the Guillain-Barré, perhaps from headbanging. "Nah," he says when I ask him about football-related brain trauma. "I didn't get concussions. I gave 'em." Funny line. Maybe only half-true.

The thing about Fridge is that early on he was a rare physical talent, not simply lard. He was a very good swimmer, a former lifeguard at the park pool just a couple hundred yards from his childhood home. His short-burst running speed was shocking, his basketball jumper deadly, his raw strength unworldly. "On the D-line, all of us—me, Richard Dent, Mike Hartenstine, Steve McMichael—could power clean 370 pounds," says Hampton. "But Fridge just did it like he was picking up a cat. We called it goofy strength."

"He was a different individual when I had him, at 308 pounds," says Ditka. "He was a hell of an athlete, with a great attitude. Most of it now has to do with alcohol. You think you're invincible, nothing can hurt you.... I know. I've been through it."

But the William Perry I see here in the spring dusk, in his car, in this driveway, doesn't look invincible in the least. He simply looks like a man trying very hard not to think about anything at all.

The following night we meet at an Applebee's. That the actual intersection of Whiskey Road and Easy Street is nearby tells you something about this town that is by parts pretty and decrepit, with Civil War memorials, gas costing $1.37 9/10 and a place that's still referred to as the Aiken Colored Cemetery. Nearby, off Willow Run Road, there's a weedy field where a black fellow named Harry McFadden, an acquaintance of Willie Perry's, was reportedly lynched in 1978.

Fridge comes in with Epps, placing his walker next to the table. He doesn't eat much, just nine wings. "Not like the old days," he says. But he has four double Jack Daniels and Cokes, and once he has hobbled back to his car he asks Epps to go back and get him some pecan pie and a brownie to go.

A couple of months before this I had visited Fridge at Northwestern Memorial Hospital in downtown Chicago. He had come to town for a 30-year reunion event celebrating Super Bowl XX, with his brother Willie and Jaye escorting him. But after being roundly cheered at halftime of a Bears-Lions game at Soldier Field he'd become ill with a leg infection related to his diabetes. He told me he could no longer feel from the shin down and that his hands were numb, too.

That night there was talk that he might need to have a foot amputated if things didn't improve. Lying in his bed with a hospital gown on, catheter in place, Fridge didn't frown or complain. He'll never say he's hurting. Former Bears trainer Brian McCaskey remembers when Perry came to the sideline during a game, held his forearm out and said, "What do you think?" "It was bent down and up," recalls McCaskey, amazed, "broken all the way through."

The doctor comes in. He says that for some reason Perry has been taking pills he wasn't prescribed; meanwhile, he's *not* taking the ones he *should* be. Willie and Jaye think this shows, again, how little Michael Dean is caring for his brother. They think it might be damn close to poisoning him. Which Michael Dean finds bewildering; guardian though he is, he points out that Patsy is the one who now oversees William's medicine intake.

But when it comes down to it, shouldn't a grown man take care of himself? Especially one who in 2014 was declared by a doctor, cognitive issues and all, to be capable of managing his own affairs and no longer in need of a guardian?

"When I'm ready, I'll take [Michael Dean] back to court and I'll get my guardianship back," Fridge says. But he's done nothing. And it's likely he never will. He's slip-sliding away. He seems tired of any struggle whatsoever.

"Talent can be a curse," says Hampton. "At 14, Fridge was the biggest thing in Carolina. Everybody expected him to play football. It's almost like he was a reluctant participant. He didn't have to sell out to be the best, and now he doesn't have to care."

Ditka, whose Gridiron Greats charity has helped pay for some of Perry's debts, finds it all heart-wrenching. "It's a great life wasted," he says. "There's no reason it has to happen. A bad deal? *No, he got a great deal!* In life you gotta help yourself. It's tragic. I think he's given up. And the question in my mind is, Why?"

The air is clear and fresh at 1 p.m. on a Wednesday in Aiken; it's 78°, bright sun. The Masters will start soon in nearby Augusta, Ga., and flowers will start opening from south to north, like popcorn seeds cooking in a pan.

Fridge is in his car, parked under a shade tree near some men playing checkers. Two months from now he'll be hospitalized briefly for what Willie describes as a ministroke, his second in a short period. Michael Dean will deny that either ever occurred. But for now the big man is at ease, drinking beer from his cooler, his buddy Epps nearby, smoking and drinking, wiping away sweat with a white towel draped over his shoulder. We're barely two blocks from where Fridge was raised, and that seems relevant.

"I'm home," he says. "And I'm happy. I can't say everything is peachy keen, but I'm still enjoying life. I love Chicago, but there's no place like home."

The acrid stench from his car interplays with the fragrance of apple blossoms drifting in the breeze. He's making a stand right here. A declaration.

"I'm my own man," he says, seemingly tired of people trying to improve him. "It's simple. I ain't never trying to be famous. I never, ever try to be extravaganza. I'm just a plain old country boy!"

As if that explains it all. Or anything, really.

FAN-TASTIC

FEBRUARY 5, 2001

Good Vibrations

The boards were buzzing at the Electric Football Super Bowl in Canton, Ohio

BY JEFF PEARLMAN

"We're dealing with a lot of freaks here," says Steve Feit, an account executive with Silverman Media&Marketing Group, which represents Miggle Toys. Have truer words ever been spoken? Feit is standing in the middle of the NFL Films Theater at the Pro Football Hall of Fame in Canton, Ohio, watching... well...what is he watching? There are men—big, big men—cooing over tiny figurines, talking to them, caressing them, begging them for one fantastic moment. "Just do it for us, Jimmy!" one man bellows. "Do it! Do it! Do it!"

Uhhh....

Jimmy is Jim Brown. Were the real Jim Brown present, slamming into defensive tackles and pummeling cornerbacks, perhaps it would seem normal to scream, "Just do it for us, Jimmy! Do it! Do it! Do it!" This Jimmy, however, is an inch-high figure buzzing about on a piece of vibrating green metal. He has a plastic head and no eyes. His owner is wearing brown Zubaz pants. "You have to understand," says Feit, smiling. "Many of the people here—they take this very, very seriously."

Translation: The people here are nuts. How else to describe most of the 2,000 spectators and participants at the seventh annual Official Electric Football Super Bowl & Convention, held on Jan. 20 and 21? There was Paul Bartels (a.k.a. Raiderman), a 26-year-old architectural draftsman from York, Pa., who enjoys painting his face silver and black, swinging a thick plastic sword and showing off his handcrafted collection of Oakland and

Los Angeles Raiders figurines, from Jim Otto to Bo Jackson. There was Lynn Schmidt (a.k.a. Weird Wolf), a 40-year-old website designer who arrived in red-and-yellow Kansas City Chiefs face paint, red Chiefs shoulder pads, a red Chiefs bandanna, red Chiefs sunglasses and a red Chiefs Bobby Bell jersey.

One guy who seemed almost normal was Ron Bell, a 32-year-old assistant district attorney from New Orleans, who turned out to be the world's best Electric Football player. As the other competitors paraded loudly through the hallowed hall in oversized Junior Seau jerseys, faded Eric Metcalf T-shirts, Oilers hats and Jets hats, Steelers hats and Seahawks hats, the conservatively dressed Bell coolly, calmly demonstrated the magic that one year earlier had made him an out-of-the-blue sensation. In the 2000 Super Bowl, played in Washington, D.C., Bell shocked the world (well, 78 guys in a room) by guiding his little Miami Dolphins to the title. This year, with a last-minute 30–24 victory over David Redmond's Atlanta Falcons, Bell repeated.

Like most of his Electric Football brethren, Bell discovered the game as a youth. Back in the early and mid-1970s, when Twister was the rage and play stations were backyard swing sets, every American boy had—or at least recognized—an Electric Football table. The idea was simple, fun and sort of inane: Line 11 little plastic men on one side, 11 little plastic men on the other side, turn the power on to make the table vibrate and the players move, and see what happens. "It wasn't a complex game, but it was fun for kids and dads to play together," says Bartels, whose Raiders lost to Bell's Dolphins in this year's AFC championship. "Now there's no more family time. Both parents work, and everyone comes home dog-tired. So the kid plays a video game by himself instead."

In the 1960s four companies made Electric Football games. By 1991, after the bankruptcy of Superior Toys, there were none. Since Miggle began producing the game board and pieces in '93, there has been something of a revival. The Electric Football elite, like that of Dungeons & Dragons or Magic: The Gathering, is a tight community of mostly single men (note: Electric Football tournaments are not good spots to meet the honeys) who communicate through Internet chat rooms. Secrets—how to make the players move faster, ways to illegally widen the base of each player—are the hot topics. Fashion is not.

Watching Electric Football is, 99% of the time, *Meet Joe Black* dull. The switch is flicked, the little men vibrate. If a receiver happens to get open, the switch is flicked off, everything stops, and a tiny quarterback figurine chucks an even tinier foam football. If the football hits the receiver, the pass is complete. The switch is flicked on again and—*yawn*—everything moves. Still, the Dolphins-Falcons Super Bowl had its moments. Miggle spared no expense. Two young women sang the national anthem. There was a coin toss. Tom Rubin, an Ohio high school football official for 20 years, wore his black and white stripes and refereed the event, whistle blasts and all. Two men provided commentary over a loudspeaker. On their path to the title game Redmond, an Atlanta-based postal employee, and Bell took drastically different approaches. Redmond is a defensive specialist, jamming receivers at the line and forcing short screens to the running backs. The pass-happy Bell, as Ira Silverman, president of Silverman Media&Marketing noted, "makes Joe Montana look like a bum."

For most of the title game, spectators wandered to and fro, peeking at the board and checking the display tables, then grabbing overpriced hot dogs. As soon as the fourth quarter began, however, things got serious. Ninety-eight people surrounded the tiny field, some standing on plastic chairs, little kids on their fathers' shoulders. With 7:25 remaining, Redmond's Tony Martin figurine did the impossible. For the second time he returned a kickoff 100 yards, a Super Bowl record that gave the Falcons a 24–22 lead.

As Martin buzzed up the field, it was as if Redmond had him on a string. A Dolphin approached from the right, Martin zigged left. A Dolphin approached from the left, Martin zigged right. A hole opened and—*zoom!*—Martin burst through. "Tony can flat-out play!" noted Ken Allen, the color commentator. "He's a player!"

He's plastic. On the next possession Bell guaranteed himself a place in the Electric Football Hall of Fame—if there ever is one. On first and 10 from his own 45, Bell flicked a short pass to a wide-open Mercury Morris, who flew all the way to Atlanta's eight-yard line before, inexplicably, turning a hard right and going out-of-bounds. With seven seconds left Bell connected again with Morris for the game-winning touchdown. "Yes!" he said, turning to Jim Bell, his proud father. "We did it! We did it!"

As the final whistle sounded, Bell and Redmond shook hands, then hugged. Both men were emotionally and physically spent. "My team had a lot of experienced guys, a lot of guys who have been through the battles with me before," said Bell, holding the gold championship trophy. "I looked my players in the eyes, and I knew they would come through."

The champion smiled. He was kidding—I think.

DECEMBER 25, 2000

The Mile High Club

Denver's South Stands are the second home to a close-knit gang of diehards bonded for life by their passion for the Broncos

BY LEIGH MONTVILLE

Hey, how ya doin'? You got a ticket for that seat? Let me check it out. Sure enough, you're in the right place. Section DD. Third row. Seat 18. South Stands. You must have bought one of Victor Marquez's tickets. Am I right? I heard his granddaughter wasn't feeling well, a cold or something, so you got her seat. Welcome to Mile High Stadium.

I know you're new here, so let me tell you that you're in for a different kind of day, a day...Well, how should I describe it? You're joining a family, my friend. You're joining a football family. A Denver Broncos football family. So settle in. And try to keep warm.

This is watching sports the way it used to be. You've probably gone to games in other stadiums, maybe even sat in somebody's luxury box and been wined, dined and maybe caught a T-shirt shot into the air from a backpack cannon by a group of management troglodytes. Oh, yeah, and you probably watched a little bit of the game too. Well, this isn't like that.

You're going back in time here. This is Boston Garden and Franklin Field in Philadelphia and the old Yankee Stadium with the old New York football Giants. This is bedrock sports. We watch the *game* here. Watch it? Man, we *inhale* it.

There used to be a guy, Billy—sat right near here, two rows down—who used to get mad when people going up the stairs stopped to watch what was happening on the field, blocking everybody's view. Billy doesn't come much anymore, not since the divorce, but he would tell those people to sit the hell down. The people would say something back, and then, wow, it would start. We watch the game here. Yes, we do.

We're fans the way fans used to be. Nobody's here on a corporate account, getting a tax write-off for the money he spends. This is money from the cookie jar, from the Christmas club account or something. I know $25 for a ticket doesn't sound like much, but 10 games times $25 is $250. If you buy two tickets, that's $500, and if you bring a family of four, that's a grand. You throw in parking and some dogs and maybe a few adult beverages, and it adds up. It's all worth it, though. We're paying to follow our hearts.

Look around you. Look at all the Broncos stuff. Everybody's wearing something. Look at those two big guys two rows back, the Oletski brothers, in their Romanowski jerseys. That's their sister, Carrie, in the Griese shirt. And her friend Harold in the Easy Ed McCaffrey shirt. Everybody is here for the Broncos. Here for the game. Here for the win. We want the Broncos to rip some hearts out. So take your seat...

Yeah, that's your seat, that little 16-inch-deep stretch of wood covered by that bleached-out skin of orange fiberglass. Yeah, it's a little small for the modern backside, especially when everybody's wearing a ski parka against the cold, but scrunch up. Everybody does. Scrunch up and lean back against the knees of the guy behind you—that's O.K., it's John Soper Sr., a good guy—and kind of get your breathing in sync with the rest of the folks in the row and enjoy. You're in the group now. Let me tell you about it.

The South Stands have room for 8,096 backsides, and 8,096 backsides have filled those spaces for 33 years. All these seats are for season tickets, most of them owned by the same people for most of that time. Anywhere you go in the South Stands, you'll be sitting in the middle of a bunch of people who know one another, three-row and four-row societies, each one bleeding into the next. If you're a stranger, you stand out like a kicker's clean jersey, like Jason Elam in the fourth quarter on a rainy, muddy afternoon.

Kathryn Harding, that tiny woman, looks like a retired schoolteacher, three rows back? She did work for the Boulder Valley school district, in the cafeteria. She says she has to call people if she can't make it to a game because they'll worry about her, think she's dead. She's 77. She's been a season-ticket holder since 1967.

Victor Marquez—the guy whose seat you're in—is 80. He grew up two blocks from here. He remembers when this was a garbage dump. Then Bears Stadium, a Triple A ballpark, was built in 1948, and it was enlarged to create Mile High when the Broncos were formed in 1960. Victor's had his tickets since '67 too. He says he would have had them earlier, but there was no need. That was when the Broncos had those vertical stripes on their stockings and played in the old AFL. They were terrible, but for five bucks you could buy a ticket and sit just about anywhere. When the AFL merged with the NFL and tickets became a hot item, he and his brother, Jo-Jo, the one who sparred with Willie Pep and Sandy Saddler, decided they liked the South Stands best of all, so that's where they went.

The Oletski brothers? The big guys? They're second generation. Their dad, Ben, bought season tickets just about the same time Victor and Kathryn did. At first Ben went to the games with his brother, but Ben's wife, Marilyn, started pestering him about taking her to the games. Ben finally said he would. But on the day of the game, there was a terrific snowstorm. Marilyn bundled up and grabbed a shovel and headed toward the door.

"What do you think you're doing?" Ben said. "Three feet of snow are out there."

"I'm going to shovel out," Marilyn replied, "so we can go to the game."

"My father looked at her," Greg Oletski, the brother with the shaved head, says. "He said, 'O.K., I'll take you to the game. But the first time you start pissing and moaning, we're coming home, and you're never going to another game.' They went to every game for the next 27 years."

When they were kids, Greg, now 37, and his brother, Ray, 40, would sit at home and listen to the games on radio. They were Broncos fans too. They had pennants of all the NFL teams on their bedroom wall and rearranged them each week according to the standings in each division.

Ben bought a third ticket and started taking Ray when he was 12. When Greg turned 12, he and Ray alternated games. A year later Carrie, their sister, was added to the rotation. Eventually more tickets became available, and all the kids went to every game. Eventually Ben and Marilyn stopped going. Eventually Ray and Greg each got married and brought other people. Carrie invited Harold Lif to go to the games with her. "He wasn't my boyfriend or anything, just a friend," Carrie says. "I wanted someone to go with because my brothers were married. Now both my brothers are divorced, but I'm still going to the games with Harold."

The Sopers (those are John Sr.'s knees in your back, remember) are second and third generation. John Sr.'s father, Frank, also bought tickets early in Broncos history. Frank was a character. "He was a big man," John Sr., 60, says. "Pleasant, but tough. A real type A. The one thing he hated was people walking in front of him on the way out of the parking lot after games, so he just drove over 'em, hit 'em. We'd leave the game, and he had this big car, and people would be pounding on the side after he hit 'em—the car was all banged up, all these dents on the side—and he'd keep going."

"My first memory of a Broncos game, I must have been about seven, was of my grandfather driving out of that parking lot," Soper's son John Jr. says. "He just hit some guy. Bam! The guy punched the side of the car with a full fist. Bam! My grandfather kept driving."

Now John Sr. brings his sons to the games. John Jr., 36, lives in Salt Lake City, where he is a district manager for Payless Shoe Source. He starts driving on a Friday night or Saturday morning, a minimum of eight hours on the road, sometimes with his wife and two kids, sometimes alone, then drives back after the game on Sunday. Tom, John Sr.'s other son, is a doctor in suburban Sterling. He comes to the games when he can, but he has to miss them when he is on call. That is when Dan Gabbron, John Sr.'s grandson, gets the ticket. That's Dan in the fatigues.

"Everybody knows everybody else in our section," John Jr. says. "It's nice. Sometimes you don't see these people anywhere else except at the games. But when the next season starts, you pick right up."

For a long time, Victor Marquez would go to the games with his wife, Pat, and son Mike, both of whom suffered from muscular dystrophy. Victor always parked in a handicapped space right near the stadium—for years he would have to get in line at some city office and stay there overnight before the season to sign up for that spot—but the walk to the seats was still filled with peril for Pat and Mike. Soper Sr. noticed this while driving through the lot on Sundays, and he started a ritual. Every week he would arrive with his two sons and have them escort Pat and Mike to their seats.

"We did this for a few years," Soper Sr. says. "It wasn't any big deal. Then one summer, about 27 years ago, I had trouble with my garage-door opener. I called a place, the V&A Door Company, to have it fixed, and who shows up? Victor. I never knew that was his business. It turned out, he lived in Westminster, not too far from us. We got to talking, and he said, 'Hey, I have a van. Parking is tough. Why don't you and your boys come to the games with me? I have a lot of room.' So we did."

Pat died in 1991 and Mike, now 44, is too frail to go to the games anymore, but the arrangement remains in effect. The Sopers arrive at Victor's house on the morning of the game, and Victor—80 years old, remember—still takes the wheel. "He's sort of like Mr. Magoo," John Jr. says. "He's this little guy, sitting up there in this big van, talking away, looking everywhere as cars jam on their brakes. It's hilarious."

"Put it this way," John Sr. says. "At an amusement park you would have to pay five bucks for the ride that Victor gives us."

So this is the basic group. Get comfortable. Relax. Victor now sits with members of his family, and Kathryn, whose husband died in 1996, sits with her daughter, or a friend. Greg Oletski, who this year took custody of his 12-year-old son, Zach, sometimes gets an extra ticket, but this is the core group in Section DD. There are other people, on the edges, to know about. Like Eric Hayes, who isn't here because his mother-in-law is getting married today, and that group of 10 metro Denver firemen on the other side of the aisle, the ones who get into a jam every now and then. There are characters to know from Section DD history, like Leroy, the big guy who now has a job moving the chains down on the field, and the heavyset woman who used to dress up as the Bronco Bunny (she stopped coming after her husband died)...but this is the basic group.

You will probably notice that this group doesn't do a lot of drinking, not anymore. Victor used to bring a bunch of stuff in the van for a pregame tailgate, even though he doesn't drink, but he stopped a few years ago. A friend, a policeman, got him nervous about even carrying open liquor bottles in the van. Greg will fill up a couple of plastic squirt bottles with "whatever I can find around the house, usually peppermint schnapps," and he'll have a celebratory shot after each Broncos touchdown—not field goals, never—with his brother and sister and Harold, but that's it.

The one betting ritual also involves the Oletskis. Greg collects two bucks at the start of each game from whoever wants to play. (Are you in?) Sometimes the pot is $10, sometimes it's as much as $30. The money is passed from left to right, then back again, from one person to the next after every point—even an extra point—scored during the game. The person holding the money at the end of the game gets the pot.

Football, however, is the really big thing. Not so much football as the Broncos. "I'm not a football fan," John Soper Sr. says. "I'm a Broncos fan. I want to see them win."

"It's different now with the Rockies, the Nuggets and the Avalanche in town," Victor says. "For such a long time, the Broncos were the only thing we had."

These are people who have been around for the team's entire bumper-car ride. Victor remembers when practices were on a dirt field outside the stadium, when he and his friends could walk up to the players during a break and start talking with them. Soper Sr., an electrician, remembers when the team practiced across the street from his union's headquarters at 56th and Union. You could just look through the fence, except on the weeks of big games against the Oakland Raiders or somebody, when canvas was hung to foil inquisitive eyes. Greg Oletski remembers his first live game, Broncos against the Baltimore Colts in the early '70s. His mother took him to the Colorado School of Mines the day before the game to watch the Colts practice. He collected autographs from Johnny Unitas, Bubba Smith, a bunch of people. He then went to Mile High the next day and joined the crowd rooting to have Unitas's head knocked off.

The long stretch of lean years for the Broncos gave way to years of frustration—so close, all the way to Super Bowl in 1990, then disappointment—which ended with back-to-back championships, in 1997 and '98. Floyd Little gave way to Randy Gradishar, who gave way to John Elway, who gave way to Romo and Terrell Davis and Easy Ed. They were characters in a drama more than people in real life, knights sent out to save the reputation of the city. "I don't know any of the players," Greg Oletski says. "They all live south of the city now, in the rich neighborhoods. I never go down that way. I yell to Romanowski on the field, 'Hey, Romo,' and sometimes he waves back. But I don't know him. I don't know any of them.

"Wait, I do know one, kind of," Oletski says. "We had a family reunion this summer. This cousin showed up; she was beautiful. I hadn't seen her for about 21 years. I asked my aunt how closely related this girl was to me, you know, to see if I had a chance. My aunt said, 'Forget about it. She's going out with Brian Griese.'"

The passion is more for the team than for the individual players. When Kathryn's late husband, who most of the time preferred fishing or playing cribbage to sitting through a football game, refinished their basement, he looked at her and said, "O.K., I'll give you one wall." She turned the wall into a Broncos shrine, covered with team pictures and autographs and posters and pennants. For years Soper Sr. has flown a Broncos flag in front of his house during the season. John Jr. has carried on the tradition at his own house, even when he lived in Houston for three years. Ray Oletski, facility manager at the Arvada Covenant Church, teaches Sunday school there. On game days he teaches in his Broncos gear. "The kids know it's a game day," he says. "We get into their minds early."

There is some history out here too. Did anyone tell you? The South Stands are one of the main reasons the Broncos even exist. The stands were built in the late '50s for baseball. Branch Rickey was going to start another major league, the Continental Baseball League, and Denver wanted to be a part of it. The rub was that each franchise had to have a park that seated more than 25,000 fans. The stands were added to fulfill that requirement. But the CBL never got off the ground, and the city still had the stands and was still paying for them when this goofy new football league, the AFL, was looking for teams. That was a way to pay for the stands.

The cool thing about being here—you probably noticed—is that all of us are practically sitting on top of the Broncos' locker room. Coach Mike Shanahan's words are pretty much going through the ceiling and into the soles of our feet, good vibes, and you can see the players, close-up, coming on and off the field. The visiting team's locker room used to be at the other end of the South Stands, underneath Section BB, and that used to be a bit of a problem. People would throw whatever was available, especially snow, at the visiting players.

That's changed, probably for the good. The visiting teams come out of the north end now, underneath that green canopy, but this still is known as the place where the true spirit lives. Joe Ellis, the vice president of business operations for the Broncos, says that every week he notices the difference between the South Stands and the rest of the stadium. Parking is terrible at Mile High, so by kickoff the stadium is still only 75% full. Except in the South Stands, where everyone is in his or her seat. The end of the game? Same thing. During a blowout half the stadium will be empty, but the South Stands will be full.

You get a different view here, the end zone view, but as Soper Sr. says, "You can watch the game from this angle best, see the holes open in the line." You might miss some things when the ball is at the far end of the field, but you know what? Every quarter, they switch everything around. You have to pay attention—no replays for us because the big board is behind the South Stands, but that's all right. See it once, replay it in your mind. Catch the highlights at home.

You're here with people who care. That's what matters. You want to shout? You shout. Ray Oletski says the greatest relief he has in life is standing up here and bellowing like the big bear he is. Nobody says a thing. The frustrations just come out. You want to be tough? Be tough. Victor says he never has had a fight, but his late brother, the one who sparred with Willie Pep and Sandy Saddler, had more than a few. His brother loved the Broncos. "Somebody'd say something bad about the Broncos?" Victor says. "Jo-Jo would coldcock him."

Here's how much these people care. On Nov. 27, 1994, coming back from the rest room, Kathryn was knocked down from behind by two kids who were running. She broke her hip, wound up in St. Anthony's Central Hospital. "I went to a football game," she says, "and didn't get home until three weeks later." Those two kids gave an old woman a lot of misery. You know what she says was the silver lining? That it happened at the final home game. She was back in her seat for the first exhibition game the next season.

O.K., now the bad part: You're a little late. When the playoffs are done this season, Mile High is done. As you came through the gate, did you notice that giant concrete and steel spaceship right behind the South Stands? You had to see it, right? That's the future. That's where the Broncos are going to play the 2001 season, and that's where all of us are going to be. I hate to say it, but nothing is going to be the same.

Oh, they're going to try. There will be a South Stands, and everyone has signed up, requesting the same seats. John Soper Sr. even made a list of the seat numbers and names and gave it to the Broncos' ticket department. He's been assured that every effort will be made to fulfill all requests, and I'm sure the Broncos will give it a shot. But you know what? It won't work.

As we speak, there's talk about keeping the name Mile High for the new stadium, rather than accept some big advertising money, but that'll last until the cost overruns start arriving. This will be an Alltel, Intel, Do-tell, some kind of dotcom stadium like the rest. Wait and see.

There will be two giant scoreboards to bring you every slo-mo, stop-action replay and to sell you green beans or something during all those TV timeouts. There will be luxury boxes decorated better than most people's homes. (Soper Sr. is working, right now, as an electrician in the new stadium. He wired Broncos owner Pat Bowlen's box the other day.) There will be glitz and glamour, the showbiz approach that makes the game—*the game*—simply a part of the overall attraction.

In the new South Stands everyone will have an actual seat with an actual back and actual armrests and an actual cupholder. There will be actual room to cross your legs, lean back and enjoy. The up-to-date shopping plaza, with its up-to-date food courts and souvenir stands and interactive exhibits, will be outside the gates. The prices also will be up to date. Each ticket in the South Stands will cost $50 instead of $25.

"What will happen?" the Broncos' Ellis says. "I don't know. It's safe to say that as ticket prices have gone up in all sports, the fan base has changed. Will that happen in the South Stands? Probably, to a degree."

Kathryn Harding wonders what effect the new prices will have on a retired woman with a fixed income. Victor Marquez sees a rise in prices everywhere. Hot dogs will be more expensive. Soft drinks will be more expensive. Parking will be more expensive. And once a new fan base is established, Victor's ticket, which will be $50 to start, will cost more and more in coming years. Greg Oletski wonders how many games his son will be able to see, because "there aren't enough chores for him to do, not enough dog poop to pick up in the backyard to work off $50 a week."

The sad fact is that everything will be different. There will be some good parts—maybe you won't go home with your parka smelling of someone's spilled beer, and maybe you won't get hit in the head anymore by a snowball thrown by an idiot in the back of the section, and maybe a full seat and cupholder aren't entirely bad ideas—but there will be a change in the atmosphere. The new South Stands will be the suburbs. The old South Stands are the city. Tenements. The closeness will be gone. The need to connect, to meet your neighbor, greet you neighbor, to get to know him so well you eventually trade Christmas presents, will be gone.

Settle back, my friend, but not too far back. Enjoy. This is the way it used to be.

FEBRUARY 9, 2022

Sofi Stadium Went Up—and Then Everything Changed

Crushing traffic, soaring rents and residents forced out. The home of Super Bowl LVI brought prosperity to Inglewood, but at what cost?

BY JOHN GONZALEZ

It's a sleepy Sunday morning in Inglewood, save for the never-ending parade of planes zooming overhead on final approach to nearby Los Angeles International Airport. But as the afternoon nears, the early-hour hush gives way to the usual crush of out-of-town visitors rumbling in.

"Oh s---. It's crazy as hell," Yolanda Johnson says. She's standing outside her house on Arbor Vitae Street in mid-December doing what a lot of residents here do: waving a handmade cardboard sign stamped with PARKING as football fans slowly inch past her driveway on their way to SoFi Stadium for today's game between the Chargers and Giants. She won't tell me how much she charges to let strangers leave their cars at her house, but other residents say the going rate for the regular season is somewhere south of $100—which is a bargain compared with the outrageous prices parking spots are going for ahead of the Super Bowl. (There are Inglewood residents who told me they think they can cram five cars into their backyard for the big game—at $1,000 per car—and they live roughly a mile and a half from SoFi.)

Making some money on the side is a small consolation, though. Sometimes, just to get out of their driveway, Johnson's husband has to stand in the street and stop traffic so she can back the car out. And if she has to run errands or work on a Sunday, things get dicey. Her job is about 15 minutes from her house—on a normal day. A couple of weeks ago, she had to work on a Sunday and it took her an hour to get home. Later today, she's going shopping. She plans to stop by her sister's house in Chino Hills and just wait there for a few hours until the game is long over and the fans are long gone.

"It wasn't as busy as this, at all," Johnson says about what the neighborhood was like before SoFi opened. "We have The Forum over there, but it wasn't as busy as it is now, especially on the weekends. It's real hectic—traffic and all that. Loud. Loud, loud, loud. People coming and going."

Not far from Johnson, one of her neighbors leans halfway out of his front door. He's a big guy with messy hair and no shirt on, with a moderate belly that greets everyone as he shouts instructions. His name is Josh. He wants to make sure that a couple of fans who just parked on the street outside his place don't get their car towed by the city. Like Johnson, Josh says it's like this every weekend. He lives on Buckthorn Street. But barely a go-route away, just a few blocks east as it crosses Prairie Avenue, Buckthorn turns into Touchdown Drive, one of the many generically named conduits that funnel 70,000 football fans into SoFi Stadium each weekend to watch the Rams or Chargers. For Super Bowl LVI, the stadium will increase its capacity to 100,000, effectively doubling Inglewood's population and bringing an even-bigger-than-usual circus to town.

The Bengals and hometown Rams will be most fans' focus that day, but the stadium itself is a can't-miss attraction. Literally. The view from Josh's house is dominated by SoFi—a massive and beautiful (if incongruous) piece of architecture that looks like an alien edifice dreamed up for a *Star Trek* movie and then plunked down in Inglewood. The stadium is located next to the famed Forum, previously home to the Showtime Lakers, on land once occupied by Hollywood Park Racetrack. Unlike most major stadiums and arenas, SoFi was privately financed. Rams owner Stan Kroenke spared no expense, spending six years and at least $5 billion on the project—in a recent City Council meeting, the mayor of Inglewood pegged the price at $5.8 billion—making it the biggest football stadium ever created and the most expensive in the U.S., if not the world. Everything about the 3.1 million–square-foot facility is supersized—including the art collection, commissioned from 40 California artists to include "300 original pieces of work, 200 photographs, two hand-painted murals and 15,000 square feet of graphics." As Cowboys owner Jerry Jones put it when asked about the stadium, "it's iconic."

Super Bowl LVI, the first NFL championship in L.A. in 29 years, is merely the kickoff to a long list of mega-events coming to Inglewood. Kenny Chesney will play the stadium in July. So will the Red Hot Chili Peppers. The college football national championship and WrestleMania 39 will be held there in 2023. In '28, SoFi will host the opening and closing ceremonies, as well as soccer and archery, for the Summer Olympics. Big events for the big stadium are seemingly endless from here on out. And that's without considering upcoming affairs at the Los Angeles Clippers' new home, the $1.8 billion Intuit Dome, set to open next door in '24.

Not everyone is excited about all that activity. Members of the community have been raising questions and concerns since SoFi opened—about the increased traffic and noise, the influx of people into their neighborhood, the impact on local businesses and, perhaps most worryingly, the soaring home prices and rising rents that have already forced some residents out of town and threaten to push out many more.

In short, some of the people I spoke with in Inglewood are worried about Inglewood. It's an incredible stadium. One of a kind. But as more than one resident asked, would you want to live next to it?

For his part, Inglewood Mayor James Butts is aware that some members of the community are uneasy with the fancy new addition to the neighborhood. But he's also fine with the trade-offs that were made to bring SoFi to his city. He calls having the NFL in Inglewood "a statement" and describes what's going on in his town as "a resurrection."

"I couldn't be happier," Butts says. To underline that point, the city paid for a promotion in the *Los Angeles Times* ahead of the Super Bowl hyping Inglewood's renaissance. "When you think about it, there's only three mega-cities in this country that have had the number of events and teams that we have in nine square miles and that's San Francisco, New York and Los Angeles. But what took them a generation we did in less than seven years."

Butts tells me he has this saying: "The only thing that's changed in Inglewood is everything. Everything has changed here."

On that point, everyone agrees.

Aside from Kroenke, no one was more instrumental in bringing SoFi to Inglewood than Butts. (The Rams declined to make Kroenke available for this story.) Inglewood is one of 88 incorporated cities in Los Angeles County, with a population of about 108,000 people, more than 90% of whom are Black, Hispanic or Latino according to the latest census data. For years, Inglewood, which runs up against LAX and the 405 freeway to the west, was one of the most affordable communities in notoriously expensive L.A. It is also one of the poorest. Between 2015 and '19, the median household income was $54,400, compared to $68,044 for L.A. County as a whole. When the Rams started looking for a place to build a new stadium and relocate from St. Louis to Los Angeles, Inglewood officials immediately put up their hands. The land already existed, and the town had a history of catering to sports teams. It seemed like a happy union. (The Chargers contributed a $200 million loan from the NFL toward the construction costs and chip in revenue generated from suits and seat licenses. In return, they pay $1 a year as tenants.)

The partnership between Inglewood and the Rams is just beginning. SoFi is part of a 298-acre multiuse development that calls for the construction of retail shops, restaurants, office space, a hotel and residential housing.

To hear Butts tell it, bringing SoFi to his city is an unqualified win and an economic success story. When he was elected in January 2011, one of his first efforts was to revitalize The Forum. Back then, he says Inglewood's "bond rating was triple-B-minus at the time, which is one step above junk. We had $10 million in the bank. And we had an $18 million structural deficit." He feared that by September or October of that year, "we would have been bankrupt." Butts thought the surest way to avoid all that was to "make your city a destination." With SoFi—and soon enough Intuit—he figures Inglewood has done just that.

But a destination for who? That's what Miguel Alvarado, the pastor of Iglesia Hispana Central, has been wondering. He's been at the church since 2004. It's in a small, nondescript building sandwiched between a motel and a pest control company on Prairie Avenue, directly across the street from SoFi Stadium. On the December morning when we meet, he's standing in the parking lot out back greeting his parishioners as they arrive, decked out in his Sunday best: dark suit and tie; crisp, white shirt.

Alvarado's church has two services each Sunday: one at 10 a.m., the other at 6 p.m. Before SoFi Stadium was built, he says the traffic wasn't too bad by L.A. standards. (If I might translate for the good pastor, that means it was still a special kind of hell.) Now, though, stadium traffic causes issues for both services. In the morning you have fans coming in for the standard 1 p.m. PT kickoff, and in the late afternoon you have fans leaving. As a result, Alvarado says, some of his flock no longer come to church because "they don't want to deal with the traffic."

"The traffic is the issue here," Alvarado says. "And not only the traffic, but the people, too. Because people who never live here, they're coming in. Another thing is, they're pulling people out from the neighborhood because the rent, the houses, is very expensive now."

Just this morning, in fact, Alvarado says a member of his church told him he was moving his family to Lancaster, a city slightly larger than

Inglewood that's about two hours north. He told Alvarado they couldn't afford Inglewood anymore.

"It's more expensive," Alvarado says. "It's going up. Everything is going up."

Alvarado says he's concerned about the neighborhood and what will happen to people who have lived there for years. He has reason to worry. In January 2016, the NFL announced the Rams were moving to L.A. and that the Chargers would have the option to join them. In the first quarter of that year, the median sale price on a home in Inglewood was $345,000, according to PropertyShark.com. As of the last quarter of '21, the median sale price had ballooned to $655,000—an increase of 90%. (Home prices have lately swelled nationwide, but not to the same extent: By comparison, over the same period, prices in Los Angeles proper increased by 60%.) Butts sees that as a good thing. He calls it "huge" and trumpets families that now have "generational wealth to pass on to their children." Indeed, for home owners it's been a boon. But according to the latest census data, only 35.8% of the city's housing units were owner-occupied. Put another way, most people in Inglewood rent.

Not surprisingly, rent prices have also increased over the last five years. According to Zumper, which tracks rent data, the average price for a one-bedroom apartment in Inglewood in January 2016 was $1,100. As of January 2022, the average had spiked to $1,750—an increase of 59%. (Over the same period, Los Angeles's rent increased by 17%.) Inglewood has a 3% rent-control cap in place to prevent price gouging, but various loopholes have nevertheless provided the wiggle room for some landlords to charge more money. Still, Butts touts the rent cap as "the lowest in the state of California" and points out that Inglewood has some of the cheapest rents in the South Bay area of Los Angeles—much lower than far pricier beachfront communities like Manhattan Beach, Hermosa, Redondo and Palos Verdes.

"So what is it that you would have of us?" Butts asks when I mention the rising housing costs. "I've heard this said before. But the alternative is to be crime-ridden, to have no job-generating businesses in town. To have no drive-through traffic that spends money where the taxes stay with the residents. And then, you know what? Then you'll have very, very cheap [rent]. But you'll have a very undesirable city to live in."

Rather than equivocating or obfuscating as some politicians are wont to do, Butts takes every opportunity during our conversation to voice his unwavering support for SoFi. His enthusiasm for the project has sometimes created PR problems. During a recent City Council meeting, the mayor admonished some constituents for suggesting the Rams should pay for a proposed people mover that would connect to the nearby Crenshaw Metro line as a make-good to the neighborhood, scolding them that "This is our responsibility. It's not enough to say 'Oh, somebody else should pay for it.' That's not what mature adults do." Following a different City Council session—as these things go, Inglewood's civic gatherings are can't-miss—Butts was apparently caught on an open mic telling an activist to "go choke yourself" after she was critical of the Clippers' use of public land to hold a press conference. (Butts has claimed he has no recollection of saying it. The video of the meeting on the city website has been edited to end before the statement occurred, though activists have posted what they say is the original footage, where the statement can be clearly heard.)

While all that might not be great political optics for the mayor, Derek Steele understands where Butts is coming from, even if he doesn't necessarily agree. Steele has lived in Inglewood since 2008. He's an activist for Uplift Inglewood, an organization created in '15 that aims to provide a voice for residents during a time of rapid change in the city. Steele credits the mayor for engaging with his constituents about what that change should look like, and he says that while "the convo has its contentious parts, all parties have the community's best interests at heart." He stresses that. He loves Inglewood. He stresses that, too. But Steele says it all got real for him when his daughter started losing friends at school. "It's like, well, why did they have to move? Oh, yeah. The rent went up a thousand dollars," Steele tells me. He says stories like that hurt his heart. When it comes to rent, Steele insists that for people in Inglewood, "it's not about cheap. It is about affordability. Because when you're talking about affordability, you're looking at what people can actually afford to spend."

The tipping point between what residents can and can't afford—something that's impacting renters nationwide—is what troubles him and others in Inglewood most. Estefany Castaneda has lived in Inglewood and Lennox (an unincorporated part of L.A. County neighboring Inglewood) her whole life. So has most of her family. The 25-year-old community organizer is part of the Lennox-Inglewood Tenants Union, which bills itself as "a grassroots community organization dedicated to fighting for the rights of renters." Castaneda says she feels "a mixture of frustration and disappointment" over the housing shortages and rising costs. She agonizes over "a large population of folks that are a paycheck away, a hundred-dollar increase away from having to move because the cost of living continues to go up."

It's part of why the stakes here are so high. If Inglewood represents one of the few affordable communities in L.A. County, that doesn't leave many options for lower-income residents as housing costs spike. Like Alvarado's parishioner, some people might move farther away to places where they could potentially get more for their money and lower their cost of living. But in some circumstances, that also means increasing the time they spend commuting to work. And then what?

"The other side of what [Butts is] saying is, if Inglewood is the most affordable place to actually live in the South Bay," Steele says, "then when people are displaced from here, where are they going?"

If the economic impact report commissioned by the Los Angeles Super Bowl Host Committee is to be believed, they shouldn't have to go anywhere. The report was conducted by a company called Micronomics, an economic research and consulting firm with offices in L.A. and Long Beach. Unsurprisingly, it predicts the Super Bowl will greatly benefit Inglewood.

Based on the report's "most likely" estimates, it projects the city will "realize up to $52 million in economic activity and generate close to $2 million in tax revenue that stays in Inglewood from Super Bowl LVI alone." The report went so far as to say those gains are associated with "an increase of up to 800 annual jobs." The study further outlines philanthropic efforts around the Super Bowl that include planting 56 trees at an Inglewood park, a separate program that will "identify and support" 26 businesses in Inglewood owned by people of color, women, LGBTQ+ people and veterans, and a "festival-style event" in Inglewood that will feature "fun activities for kids to both get them moving and introduce them to community service activities," as well as "various other youth actions/programs in and around Inglewood." In all, it paints a glowing picture of a boom town that will thrive thanks to hosting the big game and having SoFi Stadium in town. (In preparation for the event, the *Los Angeles Times* reports, the city has cleared homeless encampments near the stadium.)

"This is the same old, same old that advocates for stadiums and for large events like Super Bowls and the Olympics have been saying for 20 and 30 years," says Rick Eckstein, a professor of sociology and criminology at Villanova and coauthor of the book *Public Dollars, Private Stadiums*. Looking through the Super Bowl report, he says he sees the usual dubious methodology. "They come out with these documents, we like to call them advocacy studies—a colleague of mine calls them fantasy documents—and they're basically just a wish list and pie in the sky.

"Even though there's this real consensus among social scientists that these things do not bear economic fruit in the long run, the stadiums keep getting built and people keep justifying it with these economic arguments and folks in the media keep parroting it."

Micronomics did not return multiple requests from Sports Illustrated for comment.

Eckstein also takes umbrage with the framing of SoFi and the Intuit Dome, as well as other stadiums and arenas, as privately financed. He says that conveniently ignores the public money involved in preparing the site, infrastructure such as sewers and electricity, and game-day public safety, which is usually paid for by communities rather than teams.

Andrew Zimbalist, a professor of economics at Smith College, offers many of the same overarching takeaways. He's written several articles and books about the impact that stadiums and large events have on communities. He says, "Stadiums and arenas do not support higher per capita income, and they do not support employment." Which doesn't mean stadiums don't change matters for area residents. Zimbalist believes they do, just in ways that aren't necessarily as rosy as they're portrayed.

In the case of Inglewood, he says the neighborhood is obviously gentrifying. As a result, he thinks home owners "might benefit a little bit because they can sell their land at a higher price, if it's not taken by eminent domain." The problem, he contends, is that most people in Inglewood rent and "get shafted." That includes retail renters—business owners who don't own their buildings and might get priced out of the neighborhood as higher-end shops and chains move in.

"You put all this together," Zimbalist says, "and it's very dubious."

Butts pushes back on all of this—especially the complaints from his constituents about traffic. When he sees cars streaming into his city, he doesn't see inconvenience, he sees exactly what's written about in those reports: economic impact. At a City Council meeting in December, Butts cited an environmental impact report that said Inglewood has "plenty of capacity on your roadways" and added, "We want to have the least impact for our residents as possible. We want Inglewood to be the most desirable location possible for people to come to because they know they can get in and out."

The mayor maintains congestion is nothing new for Inglewood, anyway. He says that during the 1970s, '80s and '90s, when The Forum was hosting several games a week and the racetrack was doing daily business, the area was every bit as busy as it is now. And where football games are mostly held on Thursday, Sunday or Monday, Butts says, "It was all week long before."

That might be true, but there's a big difference between 20,000 people for a basketball game and 70,000 people for a football game. (The difference is 50,000. I did the math.) Not to mention, with The Forum still holding events and the Clippers opening up shop in 2024, it will soon be all week long again.

When I raise all this with Butts, he is as undeterred as ever. He says residents "learn that if there's an event" they don't use certain streets, including Century, Manchester and Prairie, which sounds to me like a lot of main thoroughfares to avoid, but which the mayor dismisses as "common sense." To Butts, the choice between less traffic and what traffic represents—"prosperity for the city, thousands of jobs for the residents, paved streets, [redoing] our water system," which he says is 60 years old, "[trimming] your trees"—is no choice at all. If that means "you take alternative routes to come home," the mayor is cool with that swap.

"So that's my answer to that," Butts says. "I mean, no situation is ideal. But I'll tell you what, there are a lot of cities that would want to be in our situation. I'll tell you that as a fact."

If it's merely a matter of being aggravated by the traffic, Butts makes the trade-off sound worthwhile. The problem, as Eckstein sees it, goes well beyond inconvenience. He calls Barclays Center in Brooklyn "the poster child" for how arenas impact urban areas. Eckstein says the community was pitched on "all the promises that there's going to be all this stuff going on and all the people who've been living on Flatbush [Avenue] for years are going to be riding that gravy train." Instead, he says, the local hardware and grocery stores are gone because they were priced out of the neighborhood and replaced with "posh restaurants popping up." Eckstein imagines the same sorts of developments will unfold in Inglewood. And if residents are inconvenienced by the stadium, Eckstein thinks "it almost doesn't matter" to the people who made building it possible. He points to where stadiums are located as a key point: predominantly middle-class and working-class neighborhoods where communities might not have the political or economic power to push back. So if residents are inconvenienced on game day, Eckstein says, that's "better than inconveniencing people who could actually maybe do something about it."

"They build it in places like Inglewood," Eckstein concludes. "They're not going to build it in Beverly Hills, put it that way."

Sandra Estrada is the co-owner of Blessed Tropical Jamaican Cuisine, a small restaurant in a tiny strip mall across the street from SoFi Stadium. It's been there for 13 years. She was worried that the pandemic would hurt their business, but she says "we did real good" during it. She thought once SoFi started admitting fans for the 2021 season it would make things even better.

"Everyone saying, 'The stadium is coming and you guys gonna do good.' But we not doing good with the stadium," Estrada says. We're standing outside her shop. She's in a white T-shirt with her hair pulled back, and she has a couple of customers inside, but not nearly as many as she'd like. "The business went down really, really bad."

Before SoFi came along, Estrada tells me she used to sell about 140 oxtails on Sunday. That's her big day and their most popular dish. Most weeks she says they'd sell out by 7. Customers would come in, and she'd have to tell them the food was already gone. It was a huge chunk of their business—about $5,000 for Sunday alone. Now she says she's "praying" to see customers come in and she feels lucky if they sell 80 oxtails on a Sunday. The week before we talked, they sold only 60.

Part of the problem is parking. The owner of the building rents out the lot on game day to fans. Blessed Jamaican has only a couple of spots on Sundays as a result—and it's hard to get into the lot in the first place when there's a game. That's another issue. There are movable barriers set up on Sunday dividing the street outside her restaurant so that cars traveling west on Arbor Vitae can't make a left into the lot to buy her food.

"I don't know if it's just because people can't go in and out or what, or because of the traffic, I don't really know," Estrada says. "It's just not good. My business is not good."

When I relay Estrada's story to the mayor, he says he's "very sorry" that her business was better before SoFi opened but adds that "businesses operate under the system of capitalism we have in this country." He tells me "it's a little difficult to understand" how Estrada's shop is suffering when "so many businesses benefit from the additional traffic." He mentions that the Sizzler at the corner of Prairie and Manchester ran out of steak for the first time since he's lived in the city, and he's been there since 1972. He says another local haunt, Dulan's, at the corner of Manchester and LaBrea, is "doing record business." A Rams spokesperson also mentioned Dulan's as one of the local restaurants that the team has a relationship with (Dulan's catered events during the stadium construction), along with several others like Three Weavers Brewery, Woody's BBQ and Sweet Red Peach, which I'm told is a particular favorite of team president Kevin Demoff. Leading up to the game against the 49ers in January, the Rams and Pepsi purchased meals for fans at The Serving Spoon. And for Juneteenth in 2020 and 2021, the Rams worked with area businesses to provide special promotions and giveaways to residents.

"So I don't know how to respond to one individual situation," Butts continues. "But I would tell you this: You have more opportunity if you sell things, if tens of thousands of cars come down your street than if none come down."

The mayor's underlying point, as ever, is that SoFi is a net positive for Inglewood. And here he ticks off the many benefits as he sees them, including the stadium development agreement that called for a local hire goal of 35%. "So," Butts tells me, "3,000 people a day worked on SoFi Stadium, and 1,200 of them on the average were Inglewood residents. We had a hard-to-hire provision, so that people that have been convicted of felonies could not be automatically excluded from employment. So we had over a hundred people that had served their debt to society that made between $60 and $90 an hour, working with the iron workers and the electrical union."

Beyond that, Butts says Inglewood is finally financially stable. In addition to all the tree-trimming and water-system-fixing and library-upgrading the city can now afford, he says they've "paved and resurfaced more miles of roadway and more linear feet of sidewalk in the last seven years than the prior 40 years combined." And in the process of all those improvements, the mayor boasts that Inglewood has attracted the LA Philharmonic youth orchestra program—which he proudly notes is "firmly settled 50 yards from City Hall"—and the Girl Scouts of Greater Los Angeles, who moved from nearby Marina del Rey. NFL Network, previously based in Culver City, also built a new headquarters next to the stadium, and YouTube has a 6,000-seat performing arts theater adjacent to SoFi. And the city started a youth tennis program for lower-income kids. All of which are possible, he argues, because SoFi pressed the reset button on the city.

An NFL spokesman also touts the league's community-based initiatives, including a sports content lab at Inglewood High School, beautification efforts in the city, helping local small business owners with physical upgrades, Thanksgiving canned food drives, turkey giveaways and holiday gifts for the community, as well as a music education program for the neighborhood designed to foster local talent.

Butts is clearly pleased with the partnership between Inglewood and SoFi, but the way the stadium construction was approved in the first place suggests he and City Council weren't completely confident that residents would have approved the build. Butts and the City Council used a loophole in state election law to avoid putting the stadium up for a vote. Instead, they gathered 22,000 signatures from registered voters, which gave Butts and the City Council the authority to vote it up or down. They approved it unanimously.

Butts later told *USA Today* that Inglewood "avoided the circus of an election," and a SoFi Stadium spokesperson says those 22,000 signatures mean "the community was overwhelming in their support." Butts also tells me it was "smart" for him and City Council to go that route because they had to be "decisive" and act fast to outmaneuver competitors in downtown L.A. and Carson that were also bidding for the stadium. When I ask how residents should feel about not having a vote in the matter, he answers with a question of his own.

"Was it legal, John?" Butts asks. "You said it was an 'end-around.' Was it legal?"

I concede that it was.

"O.K.," Butts replies. "So it was within the law."

The fact remains that Butts and the City Council ultimately got what they wanted. Steele admits that he thinks all the new activity in Inglewood is "a net positive"—provided that the community that was here before the stadium was built can remain in Inglewood and reap the benefits moving forward. That's something he worries about. Steele went to SoFi for the Steelers-Chargers game in late November and had a great time. If other people in Inglewood have the opportunity for similar experiences, he's all for it.

"But," Steele says, "if it's a situation on the other side where they're getting displaced from it, they didn't even have a say in it, rents are being raised in ways that they can't even take on and nobody's doing anything about it, those things are not good, not only just for those adults in the space, but also the youth, because what does the future hold for them?"

That's a fair question. But the answer, when and if it's knowable, is also incidental at this point. The deed is already done. SoFi isn't going anywhere, and neither is Intuit. For better or worse, it's all part of the new Inglewood now. Besides, it's not like the City Council or the mayor are offering apologies or second-guessing the situation. When I ask Butts whether he'd change anything about how everything has gone down, he's unequivocal.

"I'm sorry," he replies. "I can't think of a thing that we would have done differently."

FEBRUARY 2, 2015

Every Sunday Is Super Bowl Sunday

Snake drafts and keeper leagues, rinky-dink payouts and dime-store trophies—that's all so yesterday. The way fantasy sports are increasingly being played, each new morning brings a new chance to cash in. *Big-time*

BY ALBERT CHEN

High noon at the Cosmo in Vegas, and the eight cinema-scale TVs wrapped around the room flicker like the video screens in Times Square. The bros lounging on the couches down beverages at a tailgater's pace, the sharks hold court at the bar, a Playboy bunny—it's never explained how she got the invite—sashays through the glittery, chandelier-lit ballroom. Men cheer and groan and clamor on about stacks, fades, FPPGs, Odell Beckham Jr.'s insane ROI and how any knucklehead who doesn't have Derek Anderson in his lineup—the best QB value play of the day—may as well hit the Bellagio tables next door because he's screwed, absolutely screwed. Occasional roaring eruptions drown out the game broadcast that's blaring over the speakers; in one pocket of the room a 45-yard Mason Crosby field goal is celebrated as if it's the first moon landing. Projected on a JumboTron-sized screen, refreshed every few seconds, come the live scoring and standings: The Super Bowl of daily fantasy sports (DFS) is in full swing, and the lineups to beat belong to Wanker14 and 3rd_and_Schlong.

"I was up all night," says the pro known as KillaB2482, his eyes fixed on the screen showing Giants-Redskins. (He's rolling with a Giants stack of

Beckham and Eli Manning.) "I did the most research I've ever done." KillaB began playing daily fantasy sports six years ago, back when it was a niche hobby like taxidermy or genealogy. But over the last year, DFS—a faster, more addictive, potentially more lucrative iteration of traditional fantasy games—has experienced a boom that's bringing cash and new players to the industry in unprecedented numbers, as well as providing gainful employment to the sports-obsessed fan with a mathematical cast of mind. A pro like KillaB can pocket tens of thousands of dollars on a given day. Or, just as easily, lose it. A week earlier KillaB (Brett Hartfiel, 32, of Minneapolis, a top-five-ranked DFS player) lost $120,000. Every Sunday, though, is a new opportunity for a big score, and here he is, mid-December, in a room of 75 qualifiers—a testosterone-charged brew of pros, wannabe pros and amateurs, many of whom, until just a few months ago, were unaware that this world existed—at the FanDuel Fantasy Football Championship (FFFC). Each player gets one lineup, one shot at a share of the $10 million purse, with the winner's take at $2 million.

Another eruption: an Aaron Rodgers pick in Buffalo, where the big upset of Week 15 is brewing. The crowd cheers and groans, and the conversation at the bar turns to the rumor that professional bettor Billy Walters, godfather of Vegas sports gambling, put $5 million on the Bills a few days ago and single-handedly swung the Buffalo–Green Bay line from 6½ to 4. "When I heard that, I faded the Ravens and bought the Bills' D," says a thirtysomething holding a plate stacked with glistening slabs of prime rib. His Johnny Manziel jersey and pants that resemble pajama bottoms seem perfectly appropriate for this daylong bacchanalia of fantasy sports. "It's my birthday, but if I win the $2 million, I'll send Billy a gift."

Believe it or not, the fantasy sports universe continues to expand. There were 40.5 million fantasy players across all sports in 2014, a figure that's more than doubled over the last seven years. But the industry is changing: Fantasy sports of the traditional variety—draft a team, then manage your lineup through the slog of a full regular season—have become an old man's game. The generation of fans that became fantasy-obsessed with the rise of the Internet in the late 1990s, the dudes who fell in love with live snake drafts and five-hour auctions and the day-to-day micromanaging of a single team over a full season—all for the reward of bragging rights, a cheesy trophy, maybe a few hundred bucks—are now in their 40s. Their teenage children, meanwhile, live in a world of 140-character quips, six-second videos and instant gratification; theirs is a generation for which the idea of playing one game over several months seems as thrilling as Parcheesi.

"This is going to be *the* thing," says emcee Bob Harris, who's standing at a table in the Cosmo ballroom, his eyes darting among 10 early games, the tweets on his smartphone and the iPad he's using to track today's live scoring. "I've been playing fantasy football since 1983," adds the bald, bantering fantasy sports pundit, a sort of James Carville for the DFS world. "I'm in 26 leagues now. I've seen the evolution of fantasy. I see all the weaknesses that piss people off. Daily fantasy fixes it all. It's not just a fad. It's the future."

The rules for DFS—for NFL games, as well as NBA, NHL, MLB, MMA, NASCAR, college basketball and football, golf and soccer—are simple: Every real-life athlete is assigned a salary, and every lineup is subjected to a salary cap. Once you've assembled a lineup, you win or lose based on the performances of your players that day. You cash out the next morning, then start all over again. Participants compete in head-to-head cash games for anywhere from $1 to $5,000 or in tournaments, where only a top percentage of finishers win money but take higher payouts—up to $1 million off a single entry on an NFL regular-season Sunday.

"If the NFL is looking for its [most ardent] audience, this is where they find it," says Harris. "There's not a more passionate group." The DFS demographic is young (the median age is 15 years younger than that of the traditional player), male (more than 90%), mobile (over 70% play on their phones) and college-educated with disposable income. Four years ago 12 finalists squeezed into a Las Vegas hotel suite for the inaugural FFFC, and "the winner ran around the room pumping his fist after winning $25,000," says Cal Spears (aka Braskey), a finals qualifier in 2010 and '14. "Now $25,000 is an afterthought." Last year's FFFC, with a $3 million prize pool, was a watershed moment in the evolution of DFS from time-sucking diversion to viable profession. Pros (many of them transplants from the poker world) make up a small subset of the DFS player pool, but with their high volume of entries, they provide DFS companies with a large portion of their revenues. Given today's rising prize pools, pros can now routinely compete in high-stakes weekly tournaments and win up to $1 million—what players call "life-changing money."

"There's never been a bigger change in our industry than what's happened with daily fantasy," says Paul Charchian, president of the Fantasy Sports Trade Association. "We've had more investment in the fantasy industry over the last year than we've had in the entire history of the industry."

FanDuel, the industry leader in DFS with more than one million paying players, a market share of 75% and $57 million in total revenue in 2014, raised $70 million in venture capital last year; DraftKings, which entered the space in '12 and represents FanDuel's biggest competition, raised $41 million. Rival sites are cropping up like weeds (Sports Illustrated owns the DFS provider FanNation), but FanDuel and DraftKings make up 95% of the market and have such loyal followings that it may be too late for even a media behemoth to become a serious player without acquiring either of the mainstays. That lead was built with an all-out advertising assault (the two have spent upwards of $70 million combined on marketing) and shrewd alliances with teams and leagues, each deal a further validation and endorsement of a fledgling sector.

Last year MLB announced a sponsorship deal with DraftKings and the creation of "official mini fantasy games" like the ones for the NFL, in which players set a daily lineup. (MLB's version is free; prizes include tickets and memorabilia.) DraftKings has since added partnerships with the NHL, three NBA teams and the Patriots, marking the first involvement of an NFL team. And FanDuel recently struck deals with the Redskins, Jets, seven NBA teams and, in the most significant industry accord to date, a four-year partnership with the NBA itself, including an equity stake in the fantasy company. "For those of us that have been in the industry since the beginning, this was the tipping point," says Dan Back, the lead analyst at RotoGrinders, which offers DFS players oceans of statistically driven analysis. "The NBA is saying, Not only do we support daily fantasy games, but we believe in it so much that we want a piece of the endgame."

On the eve of the FFFC, a 33-year-old personal fitness trainer from Pasadena named Scott Hanson sat awake in his hotel room with his wife, Danielle, fast asleep while he scanned a color-coded spreadsheet on his laptop. At 3:30 a.m. he was assessing the return on investment (ROI) of Bengals rookie running back Jeremy Hill.

Until September, Hanson was like most Americans: He'd never heard of daily fantasy. He and Danielle saw a FanDuel commercial during an NFL game ("Hey, you're pretty good at that; why don't you try it out and make some money for us?" Danielle suggested to him), and the following week Scott deposited $15 into a tournament. He finished out of the money. He tried again the week after and failed again. But in Week 5 he turned a single $5 entry into a first-place finish among 57,000 lineups and won $15,000.

Having tasted success, Hanson began treating his new hobby as a second job. He built a system to identify undervalued players based on their salary, past performance (as measured by fantasy points per game, FPPG) and projected output. He began listening to RotoGrinders podcasts in his spare time. He started investing $1,000 every week into multiple lineups on various sites, and by finishing first at a qualifying tournament in Week 8 ("the week Ben Roethlisberger went off"), he won a seat at the Vegas finals.

"You learn pretty quickly that if you're good at it, yeah, you can make quite a bit of money," Hanson says.

Some dismiss daily fantasy as nothing more than a dice game, but that analogy doesn't hold up. DFS is strategic, and it can be unforgiving to the casual participant who chooses players based on emotion, media narratives and hometown favoritism. Often that participant is facing analytically inclined opponents who rely on game theory and probability to calculate their likelihood of winning from an assortment of variables: injuries, coaching tendencies, weather. Smart risk-taking and attentiveness are rewarded. And advantage can be gained by tracking updates from beat reporters, who are the first to know if a player had bad sushi the night before, leading to the promotion of a rookie no one has heard of.

Johnny Manziel's being named midweek as the Browns' starting quarterback is the big news leading up to the Week 15 Sunday games that play out at the FFFC. Player salaries are established at the beginning of the week. By rule, no calibrations are made to reflect injuries or late-breaking news; as a result, many of the pros view Johnny Football, who's priced like a backup, as a value pick compared with, say, Andrew Luck or Aaron Rodgers at premium dollars. Earlier in the week, while he was scavenging the Web, Hanson had come across a far less obvious lead, a story in which Bengals offensive coordinator Hue Jackson told reporters that he might use one feature back instead of his typical committee of rushers against the Browns. Taking this as a tacit endorsement of Hill, Hanson decided to roll with the rising star.

The decision pays off, big: Hill scores two first-half touchdowns in Cleveland, and Escot4 (Hanson), the only player with Hill in his lineup, rockets to the top of the standings during the day's early games. Meanwhile, it takes about two ugly incompletions for everyone to see that this will be a very long day for Manziel and the pros who believed in his upside.

Later, with the second slate of games in full swing, KillaB is the only remaining pro with a shot at big money (Beckham is having a monster outing against Washington), but it's Escot4 in the lead, with Beez1973 breathing down his neck. "I had eight weeks to prepare for this, and it's great to see the hard work pay off," says Beez, a self-employed utilities trader from outside Toronto. "I'm analytical, a total stats guy. In my profession, you hit a big utility, you make a ton of money." It's early, but for the moment he's in second place, his name slotted next to the $1 million second-place prize. "You've got to remember, it's all about value. You've got to stay focused," he says with great conviction, though, admittedly, it's not exactly clear if he's talking energy futures or undervalued tight ends.

You might expect to find a group of sports-obsessed brogrammers behind the fantasy world's party of the year, but the five founders of FanDuel are entrepreneurs from the United Kingdom, a mix of consultants and academics who got bitten by the startup bug. "We weren't sports fans—not even soccer," jokes FanDuel's marketing director, Lesley Eccles, about herself and her husband, Nigel, the company's CEO. Seven years ago Lesley urged Nigel to leave his job at McKinsey and pursue his entrepreneurial dreams, and the Eccleses teamed with three business acquaintances to launch a website that offered news-prediction games. The site, Hubdub, attracted nearly 100,000 users, but a small problem remained: It didn't make money. Looking to pivot into a more profitable venture, the team considered the sports-prediction business. At Hubdub they'd found that even though politics and celebrity gossip were their more heavily promoted verticals, sports was always their most popular. They studied American fantasy sports and were amazed to see the industry was losing its younger demographic. For such a robust industry, there was a surprising "lack of disruption and innovation that we thought needed to be addressed," says Tom Griffiths, now FanDuel's chief product officer.

The FanDuel group was not the first to imagine fantasy games that compressed the traditional seasonlong model into a single day, but it was the first dedicated startup to pump significant resources into developing a daily fantasy site. The company's light-bulb moment, according to Griffiths, came during a marketing session with a "gruff gentleman from the Bronx" who had been shown FanDuel's simple interface listing players and their salaries. "He said it looked like something his 12-year-old nephew would do," says Griffiths, "and I was like, *Damn, another one who doesn't like it.* Then we asked him if he would pay $5 to play this game if he could win some money. He said, 'Well, that's an entirely different question.'" The group found that people were more than happy to pay to enhance their sports consumption experience. "People see the cash that people are winning [on FanDuel] and they say, 'These are gamblers; these guys are out to find a loophole,'" says Griffiths. "But it's really not that at all. It's simple: They play because it makes watching games more exciting."

While DraftKings holds strong ties to the poker industry (it sponsors the World Poker Tour), it's clear that FanDuel wants to distance itself from gambling, having recently capped daily deposits at $10,000. Instead, it's focused on attracting casual fans who don't mind losing, say, $25 for the entertainment value—fans who will ultimately determine whether the industry reaches a mass market. That goal remains a considerable challenge: Still only one out of every 40 traditional fantasy players participates in DFS. There also remain lingering legal questions, compelling

FanDuel to carefully toe the line: They issue 1099s to players who win more than $600 and exclude residents of five states from cash games because of local legislation. (Washington, for example, prohibits all Internet gaming.) Some also believe that daily fantasy benefits from the ban on legal sports betting outside of Nevada, and that if that ban is ever lifted, daily fantasy will face a downturn.

"We're still in the early days of a relatively new sector, with a lot of variables yet in play," says Adam Krejcik, an industry analyst with Eilers Research. "It's obvious that fantasy is a cultural phenomenon, but whether *daily* fantasy can penetrate is the million-dollar question. You could argue that it has the upside to almost become a media of its own—a disruptive consumer-technology industry that changes how we watch and consume sports."

The upside is higher than anyone imagined just a year ago. Eilers now estimates that the number of active daily players could reach seven million by 2020, with participants spending as much as $17 billion per year. While participation in daily NFL games is highest, the bigger growth opportunities lie in the NBA and the NHL, leagues without strong traditional fantasy games and with younger fan demographics. Even MLB, with its older-skewing audience, is a potential gold mine, given its 162-game season. "Daily is going to continue to grow, but I'd be surprised if, in the next few years, it overtakes seasonlong fantasy football, which has a huge social component where you have husbands and wives and coworkers playing," says Back. "But in basketball and baseball, I'd be surprised if it *didn't* overtake [seasonlong games]."

For the home offices of the NBA and MLB, the appeal of DFS is clear: more eyeballs, plus an opportunity to reach younger fans and close the gap with the NFL. "What's been perhaps most eye-opening," says Griffiths, "is that 15% of our users have never played fantasy of *any* kind; daily fantasy is bringing in a new audience. We always talk about the 40 million [total] fantasy players as the market opportunity—but we can go outside of that, to the 200 million sports fans just in North America."

The mainstreaming of fantasy sports is FanDuel's focus. Ultimately, the company (whose staff has doubled to 120 in the past six months) sees itself at the center of an ecosystem of fans, advertisers, broadcasters and teams, all helping to create a "virtuous circle," providing a product that, in making the games we watch more interactive and more exciting, makes everyone happier. They envision giving fans the ultimate second-screen experience from their couch and at live games. "ESPN changed sports consumption by giving local news a national platform," says Matt King, FanDuel's CFO. "I think you can analogize us to that—this generation's ESPN—in the sense that we have tailored a product that allows people to consume sports [the way] they want to today, which is different than the way they've always consumed sports. If we can do our job, we will make the market far bigger than everyone thought it would be."

"Any donkey can win a tournament," says KillaB. "There's a ton of variance in the short run, particularly in a one-day tournament. But like any skill, in the long run the cream will always rise to the top."

At the Cosmo, the final slate of afternoon games is coming to a close, and it's becoming clear that KillaB will finish out of the big money—blame Jamaal Charles's dud of an afternoon—though he'll still end up pocketing $40,000 for his 23rd-place finish, the best showing among the pros. There's a hint of disappointment in his voice, but overall 2014 was a very good year for KillaB. "For a long time I was a poker player that enjoyed playing daily fantasy [on the side]," he says, "but next year I'm thinking of doing only the World Series of Poker. I've done well enough to make [DFS] a full-time job." As proof, he says he's in the process of hiring two workers who are ready to leave behind six-figure jobs to work as analysts.

A final eruption in the ballroom: ear-numbing, beer-fueled chants of *DE-LANE-EE! DE-LANE-EE!* All eyes are on the Titans-Jets game, as the most meaningless Week 15 matchup has become the most meaningful of the FFFC. Tennessee's Delanie Walker, it turns out, was a popular pick at tight end and, after the refs have added two seconds to the clock in this dreadful game between 2–11 teams, Walker picks up 33 junk-time yards on a lateral as time expires. With that lone play, one contestant jumps from eighth to third place—a $400,000 difference. "This is so ridiculous," says Tirella12, the head of IT at a nonprofit in Boston who made an extra $10,000 on the Walker catch. "People ask me if this is luck, and I say, 'Well, I spend 30 to 40 hours on it a week.... But yeah, sometimes it's luck.'"

First place, however, has long been decided: As the Jets celebrate reaching 3–11, Scott Hanson stands on the stage holding a $2 million prop check, thanks largely to Hill's breakout game for Cincy. FanDuel has its Madison Avenue moment: *Personal trainer turns $5 into $2,000,000 with fantasy games. You can too!*

Soon, perhaps, it will be upon us, the day when fans everywhere follow sporting events with one eye on their smartphone as they root for their team—not the local team they grew up idolizing or the one they hand-picked in August, but the one they drafted two minutes before kickoff. It was easy to visualize that kind of future after a day at the Cosmo, especially if you'd just won the largest prize in fantasy sports history. Just a few days after his big score, Hanson was already talking like a seasoned pro as he explained his strategy, going forward, of putting "$35,000 as a baseline, and whatever I make on top of that, I'd cash out 80% and add to my bankroll." One week after the FFFC, Hanson submitted $10,000 worth of NFL lineups to FanDuel.

"I have a goal of making at least $200,000 in the next calendar year," he said. "Stay-at-home dads do this for a living. I could see that as a possibility for me down the road. That sounds like living the dream, doesn't it?"

BETWEEN THE LINES

OCTOBER 25, 1999

A Matter of Life and Sudden Death

The 1982 playoff between the Chargers and Dolphins wasn't just a football game and wasn't a war, exactly, but it did change a few people's lives

BY RICK REILLY

One player sat slumped on a metal bench under a cold shower, too exhausted to take off his blood-caked uniform. Four were sprawled on the floor, IVs dripping into their arms. One of them tried to answer a reporter's questions, but no words would come out of his parched, chalky mouth. And that was the winning locker room.

On Jan. 2, 1982, a sticky, soaked-shirt South Florida night, the Miami Dolphins and the San Diego Chargers played a magnificent, horrible, gripping, preposterous NFL playoff game. For four hours and five minutes, 90 men took themselves to the limit of human endurance. They cramped. They staggered. They wilted. Then they played on, until it was no longer a game but a test of will. "People remember all kinds of details from that game," says San Diego tight end Kellen Winslow, "but they can't remember who won, because it wasn't about who won or who lost." It was about effort and failure and heroics. Each team's quarterback threw for more than 400 yards. Combined the two teams lost four fumbles and missed three easy field goals. They also scored 79 points and gained 1,036 yards. Miami coach Don Shula called it "a great game, maybe the greatest ever." San Diego coach

Don Coryell said, "There has never been a game like this." Years later Miami fans voted it the greatest game in franchise history. And their team *lost.*

For his first 24 years Rolf Benirschke may not have had the perfect life, but it was at least in the class photo.

Handsome. Gorgeous smile. Son of an internationally acclaimed pathologist. Honor student. Stud of the UC Davis soccer team. Star kicker on the school's football team. Beloved San Diego Chargers kicker—by 1979, he was on course to set the career NFL record for field goal accuracy. Wheel of Fortune host. Spokesman for the San Diego Zoo, best zoo in the country. It was all blue skies and tables by the window. Looking back, maybe he should have seen trouble coming.

It all started with bananas.

Squalls had just blown through Miami, and the weather report called for nasty heat with humidity to match by game time, so Coryell ordered his players to eat bananas to ward off cramps. Lots and lots of bananas.

Problem was, it was New Year's Day in Miami Beach, and except for those being worn by the Carmen Miranda impersonators, bananas were a little hard to come by. Chargers' business manager Pat Curran had to go from hotel to hotel rounding them up at one dollar apiece. Not everybody got enough. "I think I had a couple beers instead," says San Diego quarterback Dan Fouts.

The Dolphins were three-point favorites, what with their Killer B's defense and their home field advantage—the dingy, rickety Orange Bowl, where Fouts remembers fans "blowing their nose on you as you walked out of the tunnel." Fouts was the brilliant, belligerent boss of the turbo-charged Chargers offense that knocked pro football on its ear. But the team had started that '81 season 6–5, and was routinely dismissed as a bunch of underachievers. Even Winslow, who led the league in catches for the second straight year, was hearing catcalls. "They call me the sissy, the San Diego chicken," he said the week before the game. "I'm the tight end who won't block. They say I need a heart transplant...that our whole team has no heart. But I know what I can do."

All of which set the game up as a barn burner: the unstoppable San Diego O versus the immovable Miami D, the two highest-ranked kickers in the AFC—Miami's Uwe von Schamann and San Diego's Benirschke.

On San Diego's opening drive Benirschke hit a 32-yard field goal, which figured. The guy hadn't missed a road kick on grass all year. Then San Diego wideout Wes Chandler returned a short punt for a touchdown to make it 10–0. Benirschke wedged the ensuing kickoff high into the wind, and when it hit the ground, it bounced backward into Chargers hands. That set up a one-yard touchdown run by bespectacled halfback Chuck Muncie. Three plays later the Dolphins' wunderkind 23-year-old quarterback, David Woodley, fired a beauty straight into the arms of Chargers free safety Glen Edwards, who ran the interception back far enough to set up another easy score—24-zip. And how's your Sunday going?

"I wanted to dig a hole and crawl in it," says Miami tight end Joe Rose.

Across the sideline the Chargers' veteran receiver, Charlie Joiner, had his head in his hands. "What's wrong?" Winslow asked.

"Man, you just don't do this to a Don Shula team," Joiner moaned.

"He's gonna pull Woodley, put in [backup veteran Don] Strock, start throwing the ball, and we're gonna be here all damn day."

Joiner was wrong. Strock kept them there all night.

The year he nearly died, Benirschke was perfect. He opened the 1979 season with four-for-four field goals in four games, then spent the rest of the season in area hospitals. He had what the doctors originally thought was a demon intestinal virus that they eventually identified as ulcerative colitis. Basically, it was eating up his intestines, microscopic bite by bite.

Two surgeries, 78 units of blood and 60 lost pounds later, Benirschke wasn't dead, but he was a reasonable facsimile. "After the second surgery," he recalls, "I knew that if I had another, I wouldn't make it."

Three days later the doctors told him he needed a third operation.

Everything changed the instant Don Strock and his mod-squad haircut and double-hinged arm strode on the field three minutes into the second quarter. "You could just sense the difference," says Chargers linebacker Linden King. "Strock had a real presence out there." Calling his own plays, with nothing to lose, Strock drove the Dolphins to a quick field goal, then a touchdown.

The Chargers' O, meanwhile, was suddenly getting battered. The Killer B's strategy was to turn Winslow into a complicated collection of lumps, so on every pass play the defensive end would take a lick at him, linebacker A.J. Duhe would say a quick hello with his forearm, and then one of the defensive backs would take a shot at him. Early in the second quarter Duhe opened up a cut in Winslow's lip that needed three stitches.

Winslow had been a one-man outpatient clinic coming into the game: bruised left shoulder, strained rotator cuff in his right, sore neck from trying to compensate for both. It was so bad that Sid Brooks, the Chargers' equipment guy, had to help him put on his shoulder pads before the game. Brooks would get good at it—Winslow went through three pairs that night.

Ahead 24–10 with just 36 seconds left in the half, Benirschke attempted a 55-yarder that was plenty long, but right. His first miss since November. With good field position off the miss, Strock came back sizzling. In three plays he took Miami to its 40-yard line with six seconds left in the half—too far out for a field goal. Just for fun, Miami called timeout and tried to dream something up. "What about the hook-and-ladder?" said Shula. Interesting idea. Dumb idea, but interesting. The Dolphins hadn't tried that play all year, possibly because it hadn't worked once in practice all year.

So they tried it. Strock hit wideout Duriel Harris on a 15-yard curl on the right wing. Nothing fancy. In fact the pass was underthrown, so Harris had to dive to catch it. Every Chargers defensive back on that side rushed to finish Harris off...except that when they got there, Harris was missing one thing: the ball. He'd lateraled to running back Tony Nathan while falling down. Nathan had come straight out of the backfield, cut right and tucked Harris's lateral under his arm without breaking stride. It was the alltime sucker play. "I never saw him," says San Diego corner Willie Buchanon.

Neither did Harris, but buried under the pile of duped Chargers, he could hear a roar. When he finally sat up, he saw Nathan in the end zone, lonely as an IRS auditor, holding the ball over his head. Touchdown. The lead was suddenly just seven.

The Chargers' sideline froze in shock. "It was a beautiful, beautiful play," remembers Coryell. "Perfectly executed."

Said Fouts, to no one in particular: "Aw, f---! Here we go again." Then he went into the locker room and set new records for swearing, punctuated by a heaved helmet that nearly decapitated Chandler.

Not that anybody could hear Fouts ranting. The schoolyard flea-flicker had so inflamed the Orange Bowl crowd that Shula could not deliver his halftime speech in the Dolphins' locker room because of the din. "I've never heard anything like it," says Strock. "It was like we were still on the field. It was *that* loud. We were in the locker room, what—10, 15 minutes?—and it never stopped!"

It would get only louder.

Benirschke never had that third operation. While looking at a pre-op X-ray, doctors noticed that the abscess in his abdomen had disappeared. They couldn't figure it out. Benirschke's father couldn't figure it out. Benirschke, now a devout Christian, calls it a miracle.

Still, the stud college hero was down to 123 pounds and the approximate shape of a rake, and was going to have to learn to live with two tubes coming out of his abdomen for his ostomy pouch. Kick again? He was hoping just to walk again.

He asked the Chargers' conditioning coach, Phil Tyne, to help him get back some strength. Tyne started him on weights—a dumbbell bar with nothing on it. Benirschke couldn't even lift that.

Still he made his way back. By 1980 he not only was a spokesman for sufferers of ulcerative colitis (von Schamann eventually became both a sufferer and a spokesman) and the 120,000 Americans who have ostomy surgery each year, but was also back playing football.

He showed his "bags" to his teammates one day in the shower. It was a little awkward, explaining it all, until special teams captain Hank Bauer finally said, "Hey, Rolf, do you have shoes to match?"

When the second half started, the Orange Bowl fans were still roaring, and Strock was still firing, throwing another touchdown to Rose on the Dolphins' first possession. The game was now tied at 24 and starting to look like the ultimate no-heart loss for a no-heart team. Except to Winslow. "No," he said to himself on the sideline. "No. We are *not* going to be the team that blew a 24–0 lead in the playoffs."

A whole bunch of Chargers must've felt the same way because this is when the game *really* got good. "Never in my life," says Eric Sievers, the second San Diego tight end, "have I been in a game like that, when nobody took a single play off."

Back came the Chargers. Winslow took a 25-yard touchdown pass from Fouts to give them the lead again, 31–24. Returning to the bench, Winslow started to cramp—first in his thighs, then in his calves. "And I *ate* my bananas," Winslow says.

Back came the Dolphins. Strock hit reserve tight end Bruce Hardy for a 50-yard touchdown. Now the noise in the Orange Bowl sounded like a DC-11. "It made my ears pop," recalls Ric McDonald, the Chargers' overworked trainer that day. "It would be at this incredibly loud level and then it would go *up* about 10 decibels. Guys were coming up to me and screaming, 'My ears are popping!' You could stand two feet from a guy and not hear him."

Maybe that's why a Fouts pass was picked off by Lyle Blackwood, who lateraled to Gerald Small, who ran it to the San Diego 15 to set up another easy touchdown run by Nathan and a 38–31 Miami lead less than a minute into the fourth quarter.

That score seemed to kill the Chargers. They tried to put together a drive on their next possession but had to punt after seven plays, and Strock, starting on his own 20-yard line, led a brutal, clock-munching drive that put the Dolphins on the San Diego 21 with five minutes to play. A three-pointer by von Schamann, the AFC leader in field goal percentage, would ice it. “We thought they were dead,” Rose told NFL Films. “It was like, C'mon, throw in the towel! It's hot, we're tired. Let us win the game.”

On first down, Nathan ran right for a short gain. On second down and seven, Andra Franklin took a safe handoff and plunged up the middle, where he got tortillaed by Gary (Big Hands) Johnson, and the ball was ripped out of his grip by San Diego's 280-pound lineman Louie Kelcher. Safety Pete Shaw fell on it. San Diego lived.

San Diego, the city, however, had no idea. Right around then a storm there caused a huge power outage. It was as if half a million people were simultaneously stabbed in the knee. All over town, in the wind and rain, fans huddled in their cars listening to the game on the radio. One caller to a TV station threatened to shoot the president of San Diego Gas and Electric if the game didn't come back on. This was the *playoffs*.

Back came the Chargers. Fouts connected with Joiner for 14 yards, Chandler for 6, Joiner for 5 and then 15 more, Winslow for 7 and Chandler for 19. “It seemed so easy,” says Fouts. “There was just no pass rush from Miami. They were gassed.”

Winslow was really cramping now—his thigh, his calves and now his lower back. If you ever get your choice of cramps, do not pick the lower back. A cramp there means you can't stand and you can't bend over either. “Kind of like paralysis,” Winslow remembers. Each time Winslow was helped to the bench by teammates, the San Diego trainers surrounded him like a NASCAR pit crew: one working on his calves, another stretching his shoulder, a third massaging his back, a fourth trying to pour fluids into his mouth through his face mask. Somehow, Winslow got up each time and got back into the game.

First-and-goal from the nine. Fouts dropped back, scrambled and lobbed one toward the corner of the end zone to Winslow, who jumped for it but couldn't get high enough. Fouts had cursed his overthrow the instant he released it, but then something strange happened. James Brooks, the Chargers' sensational rookie running back, had the ball and the grin and the tying touchdown. On his own initiative Brooks had run the back line of the end zone—behind Winslow—just in case.

“That was one of the alltime brilliant heads-up plays I've ever seen,” Fouts says. “In all the hundreds of times we'd run that play, I'd never thrown to anybody back there.”

When Benirschke added the pressurized extra point, the game was tied at 38. Fifty-eight seconds left. For the first time in more than two hours, the Orange Bowl crowd was silent.

Just when Benirschke figured he had his problems licked, his insides attacked him again. During the 1981 season, the small section of colon the doctors hadn't removed in the previous two surgeries began sloughing blood. More tests. More hospitals. More surgery. More impressions of a rake. And yet he built himself back up—again. He didn't miss a single game that year. "You discover within yourself a greater courage," he says, "a greater perseverance than you ever knew you had."

It would turn out to be a handy trait.

Fouts is still ticked off that Coryell had Benirschke squib the ensuing kickoff. The Dolphins took over at their 40, 52 seconds on the clock. Strock's first pass was nearly intercepted by Edwards. His second pass was intercepted, by Buchanon, who fumbled it right back. First-and-10, 34 seconds left, Strock hit Nathan for 17, then running back Tommy Vigorito picked up six yards, to the San Diego 26. Miami let the clock run down; Shula called timeout with four seconds to go, and von Schamann ran out to kick a 43-yard field goal that would bring this game to an unforgettable end. It was as good as over—von Schamann had already won three games this season with last-second kicks. Winslow, who was slumped on the bench trying to hold down some liquids, ran back onto the field to try to block the kick. He was on the "desperation" team. Never in his career had he blocked one, and now he could hardly stand, much less leap, but he went in anyway. Why not? It was the last play of the season. "Get me some penetration, guys," Winslow yelled to Kelcher and Johnson, "so I can have a chance at the block."

They did. The snap was a little high, but Strock's hold was good. Winslow summoned everything that was left in him, heaved his 6'6" body as high as it would go and blocked von Schamann's kick with the pinkie finger on his right hand. "To get as high as he did after all he'd been through?" Fouts says. "Amazing."

When Winslow hit the ground, he got history's first all-body cramp. He lay on the field, spasming from his calves to his neck. He was carried off again. He would return again.

Overtime.

Benirschke is a humble man who has spent half his life raising cash for critters and blood for people, but he seems to have "trouble" on his speed dial. He nearly lost his wife, Mary, in childbirth after she'd spent the last five months of her pregnancy in bed. He nearly lost his newborn daughter, Kari, that same day—the nurses woke him up in the hospital at 4 a.m. so he could say goodbye to her. Somehow she survived. She has cerebral palsy, but she's alive and she's happy.

He and Mary adopted a second daughter, Christina, in 1995 and were beside themselves with joy. Eight days later, the biological mother rang their doorbell and took Christina away.

He flew to Russia to bring home an orphan, only to be told he also had to take the boy's brother, who had a cleft lip, refused to eat, was malnourished and infected with scabies. Benirschke was given no health reports. He couldn't reach his wife. He ran out of time. He brought home two orphans.

"We never ask, 'Why us?'" Benirschke says. "We just try to build our patience and resolve as deep as they'll go."

He'd need more.

The idea of overtime on this thick, broiled night was about as appetizing to the players as a bowl of hot soup. Still, the marathon ran on. "You hear coaches say, 'Leave everything on the field,'" says Miami lineman Ed Newman, now a judge. "Well, that actually happened that day. Both teams. We really did give it all we had. Everything."

Even Benirschke was exhausted. Not physically, *mentally*. All game he'd been stretching, running, kicking—always averting his eyes from his teammates. He was the one apart, the one man on the team with the clean jersey, getting himself ready for the moment he knew was coming: when all the gazelles and gorillas would leave the field and ask him to finish what they could not.

San Diego won the flip, took the kickoff and cut through Miami. In five minutes they were at the Miami eight-yard line, second down. Coryell called for Benirschke to kick a 27-yarder. On the sideline, San Diego's Shaw started pulling the tape off his wrists. Rolf just doesn't miss from there, he thought. No lie. Benirschke hadn't missed from inside the 30 all year, and two of those kicks had given the team last-second wins. Come to think of it, Benirschke had kicked a 28-yarder to beat Miami in the Orange Bowl in overtime last season.

But a field goal unit is not one man, it's 11, and some of the sapped men on San Diego's field goal team were getting water and didn't hear the coach's call. They were late getting onto the field and didn't even make the huddle. "Eddie," Benirschke called to his holder, Ed Luther, "We're not set!"

"We're O.K.," Luther said. "Just kick it."

Benirschke prepared for the snap, but his rhythm was off. The ball was snapped, Luther put it down, and Benirschke hooked his kick just left of the goalpost.

Benirschke was nearly sick with regret. "I knew I'd never get a second chance," he remembers. "I thought, How long will I have to live with this?"

That miss was, strangely, a blow to *both* teams. The players were now on a death march. Men in both huddles leaned on one another for support. "Guys would refuse to come out of the game just so they didn't have to run all the way to the sideline," says Sievers. Whatever side of the huddle receivers happened to be on was the side they lined up on, formations be damned.

Neither offense was able to sustain a drive, and the two clubs staggered through what seemed to be a pointless, hopeless, endless dance. There was a punt, a lost San Diego fumble, two more punts. "I remember Kellen had his eyes closed in the huddle, mouth hanging open," Sievers says. "He looked like a slow-motion picture of a boxer—his mouthpiece falling out, saliva dripping from his lip."

Shula was hot that his players were helping Winslow up after a play only to see him beat them with another great catch. (He had 13 in all, for 166 yards.) "Let him get up by himself!" Shula kept yelling.

At one point in this blast furnace of noise and sweat and exhaustion, Winslow was blocking Miami cornerback Gerald Small. When the play ended, both men tried to get off the field for the punt, but they couldn't move. They just leaned on each other for a few seconds, too tired to get out of each other's way. They shoot horses, don't they? "I'd never come that close to death before," Winslow says.

Finally, nine minutes into overtime, Miami made one last Jell-O-legged breakaway. Strock hit wideout Jimmy Cefalo for a big gain, and von Schamann set up for a 34-yarder to win it. Across the field Benirschke looked like a man about to get fitted for a lifetime of goathood. He knelt on the sideline, "waiting for the inevitable," he says. "It was like watching your own execution. Only in slow motion."

"I wanted to get the kick up right away," said von Schamann later, thinking of Winslow's block earlier. He tried too hard. His shoe scuffed the painted green dirt and the ball went straight into the right arm of defensive end Leroy Jones. It was the only NFL field goal attempt Jones ever blocked.

Three times Strock had prepared to ride off into the sunset at the end of the movie—and three times his horse had broken a leg.

In 1998, 19 years after his last surgery, Benirschke took a standard physical for a life insurance policy. Doctors said his blood showed elevated levels of liver enzymes. This time, Benirschke had hepatitis C, which causes an inflammation of the liver that can lead to cancer and, often, death. Doctors told him that one of those 78 units of blood he received during his surgery in 1979 had probably been infected with the hepatitis virus.

Benirschke dug in. Again. As he'd done with the ulcerative colitis, he decided to make himself an expert on hepatitis C. There were days he wished he hadn't.

Back came the Chargers. "You find something deep down inside you," says Winslow, "and you push on." Almost robotically Fouts drove his team again. He hit Brooks and Chandler and Chandler again, and then Joiner for 39 yards, down to the Miami 10.

Fate, in a forgiving mood, presented Benirschke with a second chance. Guard Doug Wilkerson approached Benirschke on the sideline. "You know that giraffe at your zoo?" he asked.

"Yeah?" said Benirschke, warily.

"Well, if you miss this, I'm gonna go down there and cut its throat."

The giraffe lived. This time San Diego's field goal unit was ready and the rhythm was fine. Benirschke says he didn't even have butterflies. The snap was sweet, and the kick perfect. Wasn't it? "There was just this silence," Benirschke remembers. The linemen for both teams were still lying on the ground. Nobody was celebrating. Benirschke turned to Luther and said, "Didn't it go through?"

"Yes!" Luther said, and Benirschke was mobbed by his teammates. "Hold on! Hold on!" Benirschke yelled. Not every hero has to watch out for his ostomy pouch.

San Diego 41, Miami 38. Sudden death.

At the bottom of the pile Winslow felt a spoonful of joy and a truckful of pain. As players from both teams struggled to their feet, a Miami player gave Winslow a hand up. Winslow took three or four wobbly steps, then fell, wracked by spasms. Sievers and tackle Billy Shields helped Winslow up and carried him off, a moment recorded in the famous Al Messerschmidt photograph.

At the line of scrimmage, the massive Kelcher and 270-pound Chargers guard Ed White hadn't moved. The photographers and the reporters and Winslow were long gone, and still they lay there. "Louie, you know we're gonna have to get up and walk," White groaned. "They don't carry fat guys off the field."

Both locker rooms looked like field hospitals. Miami's Newman wept. Wilkerson was so overheated, he sat under a shower fully clothed. Despite the IV in his arm, White had no color and couldn't connect his brain to his mouth. "I really thought Ed was gonna go," says McDonald, the trainer. "I'm not kidding. I thought we might lose him."

Winslow's body temperature was up to 105°, and he'd lost 13 pounds. Pretty much everything on the sissy had stopped working—except his heart.

Kelcher, hair matted with sweat, blood caked on his hands, needed someone to cut the socks off his feet. He could not stand. An hour later, he said, "I feel like I just rode a horse from Texas to California."

Said White, "I feel like the horse."

Reporters mobbed Benirschke, who had scored the first and last points in this epic game. Is this your biggest thrill? they asked him. "Yes," he said with a little smile. "In a football game."

No player on either team would ever take himself that far or that high again. There would be more misery: San Diego went to Cincinnati the next week and lost the coldest playoff game in NFL history—a -59° windchill. There would be payback: Miami beat San Diego in the playoffs the next year. There would be sorrow: Miami linebacker Larry Gordon would die the next year jogging; Muncie would be arrested for cocaine trafficking; Woodley would have a liver transplant. And there would be honor: Shula, Coryell, Fouts, Joiner and Winslow all were inducted into the Hall of Fame. But there would never be another game like the one they played that night.

"People come up to me sometimes and say, 'Too bad you never went to the big one,'" says Fouts. "And I say, Really? Well, do you remember who played in Super Bowl XIV? And they'll say, No. Super Bowl XXII? And they'll go, No. How about our playoff game with Miami in 1982? And they all go, Oh, yeeeah!"

Winslow retired six years later at 30 with a bum knee and an aura of glory that just won't fade. "Not a day goes by that somebody doesn't bring up that game," he says. "It's wonderful and it's humbling to be remembered for something people see as so heroic."

A motivational speaker now, Winslow has two enduring memories from that day. One is his permanently sore shoulder. The other is a shoebox filled with pictures of kids named after him. Winslow's count was up to 129, until the author showed him a picture of his son, and made it an even 130.

Reach for a can of beer in Benirschke's fridge these days and what you will mostly find are the needles he uses to inject the drugs he hopes will save his life. "There's a chance I'll die," he says, "but we're not focusing on that." Instead, he's a spokesman on hepatitis C. Five million Americans have it, he'll tell you, but only 250,000 are being treated for it. Some people think there's a reason God gave Benirschke all these diseases. Who would handle them better?

Doctors say the virus is undetectable in his system, but he'll be tested again in six months because 65% of those who get rid of it get it back. He may need a liver transplant.

Whatever happens, Benirschke is ready for it. His wife, Mary, says, "People don't realize what you can go through."

Funny, isn't it, how much of Rolf Benirschke's life has been like that game? Up, down, joy, woe, win, lose and start all over again? Would it be asking too much for him to get one more second chance?

DECEMBER 7, 2021

One for the Ages

To cap a year in which he led the Buccaneers to a Super Bowl and turned 44, Tom Brady was named SPORTS ILLUSTRATED'S Sportsperson of the Year for the second time

BY L. JON WERTHEIM

Age is just a number. But that number is on the move, and longevity is on its way to running up the score. According to the United Nations, in 1990 there were 95,000 people on the planet who made it to 100. Today there are more than 500,000 centenarians, and, by 2100, it's projected there will be more than 25 million. In 1980, around 382 million people were 60 and older. By 2050, that number will exceed 2 *billion*. There are some gerontologists who believe the first person to live to age 150 has already been born. Others ask: Are we so sure there are age limitations on human life?

What are fun facts and dinner-party conversation starters for us are foundational to the School of Aging Studies at the University of South Florida. It's the largest—and, appropriately, one of the oldest—school of its kind in the country. Its mission statement cites a commitment to "understanding the biological, psychological, social and public policy aspects of aging." But talk to faculty casually and it's clear that one of the core principles of the curriculum is this: to teach life hacks that help human beings get older with grace.

Located as it is in Tampa—the U.S. metro area with the densest concentration of senior citizens—the school has always had plenty of subject matter and data points nearby. But now, the campus is also within a golf-cart drive of the archetype for aging gracefully. Want to conduct a field study to see what longevity looks like in practice (not to mention in games)? Well, Tom Brady lives and works just a few miles away.

For all his manifold football gifts, Brady's true superpower is his ability to take time, stretch it out like the resistance bands he uses and then double it back. For the 44-year-old, time is a construct, measurable by ways other than revolutions around the sun.

"I'd say there are parts of me that are 55, and I think there's parts of me that are 25," says Brady. "What parts? I think I'm wise beyond my years. I think I've had a lot of life experience packed into 44 years. When I go through the tunnel and onto the field? Probably mid-30s—and I've got to work really hard to feel good. It's a demolition derby every Sunday. I feel 25 when I'm in the locker room with the guys. Which is probably why I still do it."

He explains this theory of time on a warm Tuesday in November. He's seated inside a Tampa yacht club—he's *not* a member, he's quick to point out—that looks out over Hillsborough Bay and is convenient to Brady's home. He has risen early this morning (of course). Walking with energy and purpose he enters the main dining room carrying a water bottle the size of a fire extinguisher. He is wearing designer sweats and a big, warm smile that makes his teeth look like a row of white iPod Nanos—kids, ask your parents—aligned perfectly inside his square jaw.

Back to time: How the hell is he still doing this, volunteering for those weekly car crashes for months and months, well into his 40s? It's complicated. "It's not like I wake up every day, like, *Hey, man, it's another sunny day!*" says Brady. "No, it's like, *All right, let's grind and move on.*" Then he quickly adds, "There's still joy. The competition's fun and, uh, you know, I'm still pretty good at it, too."

There's also the specter of the alternative: "I imagine not playing. And I imagine watching football on Sundays going, *These guys suck. I could do way better than that.* And then still knowing in my heart that I actually could still do it. If I stopped, I think I'd have to find something else that I'm pretty good at. And I don't think that, you know, I'm going to be able to jump into something that has the same amount of excitement."

So long as that's the case, so long as he can continue finding fulfillment, Brady will play on, thanks. He's fond of a phrase that suggests continuity, one that befits someone so committed to hydration: Why not keep drinking?

If, in the manner of Brady's career, we want to extend that analogy: It's not just that he is still drinking; he is chugging. And there's no indication he's near the bottom of the glass. He is at an age when even the finest of his peers are beyond their prime. Roger Federer (40), Serena Williams (40),

Albert Pujols (41), Tiger Woods (45). Titans all, but not acclaimed for their athletic achievements in 2021.

Then there is Brady. *Still pretty good at it* warrants a 15-yard penalty for flagrant understatement. He continues to discharge his duties with his customary, clinical excellence. He still throws with precision and maneuvers deftly in the pocket. Maybe more than ever, he maintains command of himself, and by extension his team, projecting comfort, evincing poise when it matters most. And he is still winning.

Brady started the year by piloting his new team, the Tampa Bay Buccaneers, to five straight wins, one to end the 2020 regular season and four in the playoffs. The culmination came on Feb. 7, when Brady started his 10th Super Bowl. He walked away with his seventh ring and was named Super Bowl MVP for the fifth time, leaving his heel print on yet another NFL season.

Early in the offseason Brady flew to Los Angeles and "cleaned up" (his phrase) his left knee. In this season, his 22nd, he has turned in some of the most brilliant shifts of his career. Brady leads the league in touchdown passes (34), the unprecedented 600th of his career coming in October, and the Bucs lead the league in scoring (31.4 points per game). His team is 9–3, and Brady is among the favorites to be named MVP. And he has already, officially, taken this honor: Tom Brady is the 2021 SPORTS ILLUSTRATED Sportsperson of the Year.

Brady, this year, is the recipient of the 68th annual SOTY. He also—mind the gap—won the honor in its 52nd year. That was for his excellence in 2005, a time when cars ran only on gasoline, squarely in the flip-phone era. How long ago was this? In the SI article celebrating Brady there is a reference to his posing once while holding a goat. And it's describing a bizarre photo shoot—not nodding to the GOAT, the honorific that now, of course, accompanies most mentions of Brady.

Titled "The Ultimate Teammate," the story praises Brady for his work ethic ("You can see his innate ability to carry the logic of practice to the conclusion of a game") and his commitment to incremental improvement ("the grinding work of constructing football excellence that pays off in the public performance"). Brady, then in his 20s, speaks cautiously but describes his passion for football: "I love it so. Just running out there in front of 70,000 people." Also, his sheepishness about standing out: "I don't need to be the showstopper, the entertainer. I'd much rather people assume I'm one of the guys."

Here, in 2021, Brady's coach, Bruce Arians, takes inventory of his quarterback, reeling off a string of superlatives but landing on a familiar turn of phrase: "He is the ultimate team player." To a man, the Buccaneers describe Brady being "down to earth."

Brady is, you might say, committed to the role. His organizing football principles are largely unchanged. Same for his leadership traits and his character. And yet in other ways Brady is a much different man than that 28-year-old bachelor. Handed the cover from 2005, he smiles. "I *think* I recognize that person," he says. "But there's so much more to me now."

He is the best-ever practitioner of the most important position in his sport—perhaps in all sports. But let's be clear: This award is not for lifetime achievement but based on Brady's body of work over the last 12 months. This is not an aging athlete admirably hanging on. This is an athlete who may never have performed better.

It happened not even two years ago and already it carries a historic ring, cemented into those hinge-point New England moments, deserving of its own shorthand, right up there with "Revere Rides Through Town," "Tea Dumped in Harbor" and "Sox Exorcise Curse." And, for that matter, from fall of 2001: "Backup QB Brady Thrown Into Fray."

On March 16, 2020, as COVID-19 was just ramping up in the U.S., Brady drove to the home of Patriots owner Robert Kraft to make official what he had decided privately months before. As Brady recalled to Howard Stern, "I was crying. I'm a very emotional person." After 20 unbroken years with New England, "Brady to Become Free Agent."

Brady didn't arrive at the decision easily. He knew well that this stay-or-go athlete dilemma tends to yield mixed results. The player with whom he always will be bracketed, Peyton Manning, left Indianapolis for Denver, won a Super Bowl and never played another NFL down. That was nearly six years ago. The day Brady won his first Super Bowl, in 2002, Michael Jordan was playing, unmemorably, for the Washington Wizards. And Brady still winces when he recalls when, as a teenage 49ers fan in San Mateo, Calif., he learned that his idol, Joe Montana, was decamping late in his career to Kansas City.

Two days after Brady met with Kraft, Arians sat in his home with Bucs general manager Jason Licht. For months they had been running point on a recruiting mission they called Operation Shoeless Joe Jackson. (*Field of Dreams* . . . get it?) That afternoon Brady called Arians, who passed the phone to Licht, who recalls that when Brady began the conversation, "Hey, babe," it was safe to assume the Buccaneers had their man. "It was a phone call, and it was during COVID," says Licht. "But it was one of the biggest moments in franchise history."

First came the yuks. Brady was going to Florida, because . . . Florida. Where else do well-preserved Northeasterners go when it's time to throttle back? Then came the cynicism. Brady was availing himself either of the state's lack of personal income tax or the congenial weather or the Buccaneers' soft expectations. Here was a franchise that, pre-Brady, had an all-time winning percentage of .386 (267–424–1), the worst of any major men's U.S. pro team.

Brady, though, is nothing if not a pragmatist. Tampa was a market with low-intensity lighting, and still a short flight away from his son Jack, who lives in New York City. Brady is also a football pragmatist. He saw a team with a loaded defense, exceptional skill-position players and sturdy offensive line. He also saw the opportunity for an invigorating culture change. Arians, 69, was born within six months of Bill Belichick but cuts a different figure—enjoying, as he does, laughter, self-deprecation, motorcycle rides and a reputation as perhaps the least autocratic coach in the NFL.

But that was only the start. Brady laughs as he plays the compare-and-contrast game: "different conference, different division, different coaches, different offense, different terminology, different players, different drive to the stadium." Determined that the divorce remains amicable, Brady gently reroutes conversation about the Pats. But this he will say: "Our team here, I think there are more voices. And it's fine. There's different ways to be successful."

With Brady, the Bucs started out 7–5. In New England this might have marked a crisis. ("Belichick always had a saying," Brady recalls. "When you win, your quality of life is better for everybody.") In Tampa it did not. The COVID-19-constricted season was supposed to be one of transition for the Bucs; in 2021, they would really be a cohesive unit. But then Tampa Bay didn't lose another game the rest of the season.

Before Super Bowl LV, Brady recognized a sort of power imbalance. He had played in more big games than the rest of his teammates, combined. So he sent a blizzard of texts to them. Some were sent individually, some to a group. Some contained motivational saws (*process over perfection*); some were concrete instructions about schemes or observations that Brady had picked up while watching film of their opponent, the Chiefs.

Licht recalls that hours before the game he took time to try to savor the moment, to drink it all in, as his quarterback might put it. One season earlier Tampa Bay was 7–9 with an offense piloted by Jameis Winston; now, with Tom Friggin' Brady under center, the Bucs were in the Super Bowl. The game was at Raymond James Stadium (even if cardboard cutouts filled two-thirds of the seats); no other host team had ever played in a Super Bowl.

Brady noticed Licht, walked over, sat down beside him on the bench, smiled his smile and said simply but firmly, "Jason, it's going to be a great day." And it was.

Ask Brady about a singular moment from the game and he strokes the light stubble on his chin, trying to come up with something specific. The defense played well; the opponent did not. Brady was at his Brady-est; his best plays didn't stand out in the way they do for other star quarterbacks, but the ball always got where it had to be with virtually no mistakes. Unflustered and unhurried, he completed 21 of 29 and connected with his old buddy, tight end Rob Gronkowski, for two of his three touchdowns.

Tampa Bay, a three-point underdog, prevailed, 31–9. In the weeks before the game, Brady strenuously—and probably wisely—avoided the obvious story line, the one that traced back to New England. Arians did not. "Tom is playing for his teammates right now," Arians told SI in January. "I think personally, too, he's making a statement. You know? It wasn't all Coach Belichick."

Brady recalled the postgame scene after the Patriots won Super Bowl XLIX in 2015: "We had beaten Seattle and we flew home to Boston, and I came home to a house that was flooding. I mean, literally, I had a broken pipe and I had a waterfall coming down. And that night you thank God. It's so glorious the night after a Super Bowl. [But] the reality? I got to fix this leak in my house."

In a sense it was a healthy reminder that the real world happens, even to Super Bowl MVPs, so it's important to savor the moments before the pipes burst. Now it comes to him: The highlight of that night, of Super Bowl LV, was when he brought his family—his wife, model Gisele Bündchen; their kids, Ben, 12, and Vivian, 9; and Jack, 14, Brady's son with actor Bridget Moynahan—onto the field to celebrate.

That Brady was—and is—a winning football player makes for something other than a news flash, especially for the men who recruited him to Florida. Even so, both Arians and Licht marvel at the full force of the Brady Aura.

Arians tells the story of watching Brady lead an early informal workout with tight end O.J. Howard and wide receiver Scotty Miller. Arians had recently told both players about the need to pump their arms on their routes. When they didn't, Brady also noticed and pointed it out to his two teammates.

Says Arians, "They look at me [when I tell them] and go, *Oh, O.K.* And when Tom tells them they go, *O.K., Tom!* And they do it." Arians then cackles, thinking of other messages he would let Brady communicate to players on his behalf. "He tells 'em to do it, and they listen!" (Pause for a thought exercise: Imagine Brady's previous coach joking about delegating some of his duties to the charismatic quarterback.)

Brady may have, like the rest of us, binged *The Last Dance*—"That's my era!"—but his leadership style is at striking odds with that of the basketball GOAT. Michael Jordan demanded that his teammates match his intensity and humiliated those who couldn't handle his lacerating edges. Brady is all soft power. Teammates should feel seen and heard. Gaps in accomplishments and fame—and commitment levels—among players must be bridged. Experience is something to be shared.

Licht laughs when Brady introduces himself warmly to rookies and new teammates by saying, "I'm Tom Brady." *No s---, you're Tom Brady*. But the message is clear, as is the effect. "Tom is known as the greatest player of all time, and I get the sense they were expecting him to come in and want preferential treatment and have an ego—which would be well deserved," says Licht. "But he just wants to be one of the guys. He wants to earn their respect. And they think, *I don't want to let this guy down*. We all think that."

Early on Brady issued a request to his new center, Ryan Jensen. Could he apply baby powder to his backside to keep the football free of sweat? Jensen complied, then walked around the field trailed by chalky plumes, as if he were announcing the new pope. Before it could be a source of embarrassment or teasing in the locker room, Brady spoke to teammates to make sure it was taken as instructional: These are precisely the kind of small sacrifices and adjustments you make when you are fully committed to winning.

More than ever Brady is surrounded by teammates who entered the league with more fanfare. Mike Evans, his favorite downfield target, was the seventh pick in 2014. Tampa Bay's top running back, Leonard Fournette, went fourth in '17. Even Brady's backup, Blaine Gabbert, was the 10th choice in '11. Two decades after he left Michigan, Brady's modest draft slot of—all together now—199, still galvanizes him. "He had to work for everything," says Arians, "and he just never, *never* lets himself forget that."

But the coach noticed something else: Brady has taken a source of personal motivation and alchemized it into something to benefit his teammates. What was once about—to use the tired trope—*proving the doubters wrong* has evolved into, *Guys, if I can go from good to great, you sure as hell can, too.*

It's hard to exaggerate just how statistically outlying Brady's longevity is. The NFL's next-oldest player is Rams offensive tackle Andrew Whitworth, who will be 40 on Dec. 12. Brady is closer in age to Dan Marino, who played his last game in 1999, than he is to Chiefs quarterback Patrick Mahomes.

Nearly half the NFL's coaches—13 of 32—are younger than he is. (Though Brady's own coach, pointedly, is the league's third-oldest.)

Keep going? Brady is older than 59 members of Congress. On that fateful day in 2000, when 198 other players were summoned into the NFL workplace ahead of Brady? Bill Clinton was president. There have been six presidential elections since. Remember, too: Brady's longevity-to-the-point-of-absurdity is coming in pro football, a sport in which careers are notoriously nasty, brutish and short. And there hasn't been any sign of falloff.

That's not just the eye test; advanced statistics bear it out too. Arians's offense attacks deeper than most—*no risk it, no biscuit* being the operative phrase. In 2020, Brady's air yards per intended pass, a measure of how far downfield a quarterback throws on average, jumped to 9.3 yards, a 22% increase from his last season in New England. Yet, despite the higher degree of difficulty, his completion rate also rose, from 60.8% to 65.7%.

He's doing it at a time when defenders have become freakish in their own right. From 2000 to '03, Brady's first four seasons in the league, 10 defensive linemen clocked in under 4.7 seconds in the 40-yard dash at the NFL's scouting combine. Over the past four years, 41 have done so. That has led to an emphasis in athleticism among the new class of quarterbacks. Indeed, according to Next Gen Stats tracking data, through Week 12 of the 2021 season only Steelers vet Ben Roethlisberger was covering less ground per play (7.2 yards) than Brady (8.0).

Retirement has its appeal—golf, time with the family, business opportunities—but it is outstripped by the lure of continuing to work. And so it is that Al Michaels, 77, the voice of NBC's *Sunday Night Football*, has consulted with and confided in Brady. Their pregame broadcast production meetings, once filled with football shop talk, now veer toward weightier topics and shared experiences. Says Michaels, "When I see Tom, I think, *Damn, you can go at that level no matter what you're doing*, and I feel like I can. It's just a cool thing, the kind of symmetry."

Michaels isn't alone in finding inspiration in Brady's longevity. UFC fighters, European soccer players, pro golfers, athletes of a certain maturity—they all try to see some version of themselves in Brady and come seeking his counsel and inspiration. Comb social media and you'll find teachers crediting Brady with their decision to get back in the classroom, pilots referencing him when they decided to stave off retirement.

Even though serving as a standard-bearer for manipulating time only adds to his pressures, Brady welcomes the opportunity. "If people want what I want, then I'm there to help them," Brady says. "If they don't? All right, let them do their own thing. No problem. But if you come to me and you say, 'Hey, how can I have a career like yours?' I'd be very happy to help anybody."

At the same time Brady readily admits that he holds no secrets; he, too, looks to others. His wife. His parents. Towering athletes—Montana, Jordan, Steve Young—who came before him. But he also turns to a sort of council of elders, who've lived well and lived long. Ageless Tom Brady might work alongside teammates half his age, but he often socializes with men twice as old, many of them successful entrepreneurs or titans of industry. They neither want nor need a selfie or comp tickets or the nimbus of Brady's celebrity. These friendships come without the whiff of transaction.

The tribal elder in this circle might be Sam Reeves. Armed with a wealth of stories he tells in a slow Southern drawl, Reeves made his fortune as a cotton merchant. He recently gave up bodysurfing but still plays 150 rounds of golf a year. He's 87, but he puts his functional age in the early 60s. "I'm not really paying attention to the chronological," he says.

Reeves recalls meeting Brady while playing golf at Pebble Beach "maybe 20 years ago," and the two have been close friends ever since. "I didn't know much about him," says Reeves, "but he was so gracious." Through Reeves, Brady has met various other wise men, including Jimmy Dunne, 65, vice chairman and senior managing principal of Piper Sandler investment bank.

When Brady is in the company of these wise men, decades older, he spends a lot of time listening. "Learning from those people is really important to me," says Brady. "I don't think you can go through life and be fixed. I was listening to someone the other day, and they said, 'The words *I don't know* are the most powerful words because they're limitless. It's limitless potential.' And as soon as you think you know something, you're fixed."

Reeves has given great thought to what makes Brady special and has come up with three bullet points:

• *He makes people feel valued.* "That could mean really listening—he's an extraordinary listener—to someone he's meeting for the first time."

• *He thrives on excellence, for himself and those around him.* "He wants you to have what he has. He wants people to be the best they can—but he'll help you get there."

• *He is a person of joy.* "Pain is inevitable—certainly in football—but misery is optional, and Tom does not accept misery. Tom runs the opposite way. He runs to joy."

Then Reeves absently adds a fourth. "Tom keeps his routines, but he is open to adventures." And . . . wait . . . catch that? It sounds like a throwaway line, but *aha*. That, as much as anything, might unlock the secret to Brady's—and, for that matter, our—longevity.

Yes, Tom keeps his routines, so much so that his fanatical habits figure prominently in the mythology. His sleep schedule and his infrared pajamas. His training and his plyometrics. We know about his hydration and his electrolyte intake. Lord knows we know about his diet and nutrition. He dares to eat a peach . . . and avocado ice cream. (There is a sports-media edict that says Brady cannot be discussed without a reference to avocado ice cream.) But he dares not ingest carbs, nightshades, dairy, white sugar or white flour.

Ross Andel, director of the School of Aging Studies at USF, notes that routines and good habits are essential for optimal aging. A Bucs fan, Andel sees Brady and his defiance of time and is unsurprised. "His ability to stay disciplined is second to none," says Andel. "Other people look for a quick fix or go to extremes. He doesn't mind hard work. He holds onto his schedule. There's such a resilience."

Yet when discussing keys to graceful aging, Andel also references an opposite, even contradictory, instinct: a willingness to adapt—"I never want to be fixed" . . . "he is open to adventures"—to stimulate new parts of the brain and pleasure centers. In short, to evolve.

Andel points to a German study in which volunteers were taught to juggle. As the subjects picked up a new skill, brain imaging revealed changes in gray matter. As the subjects became capable jugglers and the skill was no longer novel, the gray matter reverted to its levels before the study. "The brain had nothing to adapt to, so it put the neurons elsewhere," says Andel. "It's the stimulation, the change of environment that challenges the brain and redistributes our bodily resources." That, says Andel, encapsulates Brady. "He's unbelievably adaptable."

So credit Brady for his rigidity. But his relentless success owes just as much to the opposite trait, his flexibility. Does he contradict himself? Very well then, he contradicts himself. He is large. He contains multitudes. Moving to a different franchise in a different state with a different corporate culture? That example of his adaptability is just one of many.

Brady might, rightly, be depicted as the exponent of clean living. But there he was in February, giving new zest to the phrase *drunken fling* as he hurled the Lombardi Trophy Frisbee-like from one boat to another during Tampa Bay's Super Bowl celebration. He then put to rest any questions about his sobriety with the unforgettable tweet, "Noting to see her . . . just litTle avoCado tequila."

Brady is an unapologetic capitalist. His NFL salary of $25 million is dwarfed by his various businesses and investments, from the TB12 health and wellness brand he co-founded with Alex Guerrero to his clothing line

BRADY, to his 199 Productions content studio, to his stake and promotion of a cryptocurrency firm. His NFT company, Autograph, is widely considered an industry leader in digital collectibles. He's arrowing toward billionaire status, if not there already. And he's not simply slapping his name on products. He is poring over balance sheets and Zooming into board meetings, glimpsing his post-NFL life while still playing.

On the other hand, Brady doesn't always show fidelity to the market. His NFL salary, which does not consign him to eating ramen, still ranks ninth in average annual value among QBs. "He's never wanted to be the highest-paid quarterback," says Arians, "because [doing so] would mean not getting maybe two other good players."

As much as Brady values health, he mourns the rule changes that diminish the physical risk of football. "The game I played 20 years ago is very different from the game now, in the sense that it's more of a skills competition than it is physical football," he says. "It's like being in the boxing ring and saying, 'Don't hit your opponent because you might hurt him.' Look, we're both able to protect ourselves. I'm looking at you. You're looking at me. Let's go."

Brady made those remarks recently on *Let's Go*, the podcast he hosts with former receiver Larry Fitzgerald and sportscaster Jim Gray each week. And this might represent the most striking example of Brady's adaptability. For most of his career he was willfully, even strategically, unknowable. Not surly or standoffish, but you might say that long before COVID-19, Brady wore a mask. As he put it this summer on HBO's *The Shop*: "What I say versus what I think are two totally different things. I would say 90% of what I say is probably not what I'm thinking."

Whatever the case, lately we're hearing from Brady more often than ever before. There he is on late-night couches. There he is in a self-effacing Subway commercial. And calling into Howard Stern. The podcast medium suits him especially well—not just his own, but others ("What did [I] major in? F------ football, man," Brady said on actor Dax Shepard's *Armchair Expert*). He's also jacked up his activity on social media, often hilariously. After a tweet surfaced comparing the TB12 Method with Terry Bradshaw's "TB 12 beers a day methods," @TomBrady issued the A-plus retweet last month, "Tomato, tomahto."

Brady accepts the premise that lately he has put himself out there. "I'm rediscovering my voice," he says, "and I'm having fun with it." The obvious correlation: Brady feels he is able to reveal himself and have this fun now that he is liberated from his coach in New England and from the tight organizational controls. He doesn't deny that.

But there's another correlation. His age. "I think there's more comfort just as an older guy, too. My give-a-s--- levels are probably a lot less. I'm kind of like, *O.K., what's it gonna be like in 10 years?* I'm *really* not going to give a s--- then."

It is, of course, irresistible to hear Brady talk about his future and not indulge in speculation about how many more times the odometer can turn over. Licht has already stoked fires (and social media accounts) when he predicted Brady would play until age 50. He doubles down with SI: "I don't see any signs of decline whatsoever."

Brady predicts that the source of his decline—whenever that may be—will be spiritual, not physical: "Regressing would be a very difficult thing for me to see. As soon as I see myself regress, I'll be like, *I'm out.* I don't really want to see myself get bad. So it's just a constant pursuit of trying not to be bad."

Trying not to be bad? Really?

"I think if anything, the most challenging part is the emotional aspect of football for me," Brady says. "When we lose, it's depressing. When we win, it's a relief. It's not like the joy, the happiness—it's a relief. Because when we win, sometimes just winning isn't good enough for you, because you expect perfection, and when you expect perfection and it's less than perfect, you feel like there's a down part to that."

Then again, this drive, this internal combustion engine, is what keeps Brady playing at this exalted level. Winning a seventh Super Bowl doesn't dull his ambition for an eighth. Throwing a pass into a window the size of a playing card only increases his desire to deliver another one.

"It's like hitting the perfect 7-iron," he says. "You go, 'How was that?' And I go, 'That was pretty great! I want to do it again!' You just constantly keep chasing it."

It was recently put to Brady: Is there anything specific he has yet to achieve in his unrivaled career? His first answer: not really. But he did note that, in all his years and for all that success, he has never won a game on a last-second Hail Mary.

The temptation is to tell Brady that he's completed football's ultimate Hail Mary. The backup at Michigan whose 40-yard dash time could be clocked with a sundial going from the sixth round to the GOAT pasture, with seven Super Bowl rings? Whose excellence remains unabated at 44? Except that a Hail Mary implies a level of luck. The Legend of Brady is predicated on anything but fluke or chance. It's deliberate and smart and rational.

So here is a man—and a sportsperson—for all of time. And for this time. And as aging does its thing, as mitochondria begin to deteriorate, as the mortal coil unwinds, Tom Brady comes bearing lessons for us all about contorting and distorting time, if not stopping it altogether. Balance routine with new adventure. Even more than anatomy, it's attitude and character that shape destiny. Head off into the sun, not the sunset.

And if we hydrate and eat right, so much the better.

NOVEMBER 19, 2018

Yes, This Is the Face of the Future

With all due respect to Patrick Mahomes, Tyreek Hill and Travis Kelce, the 9–1 Chiefs—and the whole NFL, really—owe a debt of gratitude to the offensive innovations of a forward- (and backward-) looking 60-year-old: Andy Reid

BY JENNY VRENTAS

For the entire 2017 season there was one play that Andy Reid's Chiefs practiced every Friday. That's the day for goal line work, and the goal line is where this play was designed to shine, taking advantage of the defense's confusion to carve out a window of open space in a compact area.

Before the snap, one receiver sprinted across the formation. Then he did it again. Then, comically, a *third* time. Each time he passed behind the quarterback, who was under center, the receiver faked as if he was taking a handoff—but this play was not intended for him. Instead, after the motion man's third trip across the field, the QB would take the snap and dump off a little pass to a running back in the flat, in the opposite direction.

Coaches still joke that Tyreek Hill logged at least 10 miles on these motions alone. But for all the practice reps, Hill's hard work never paid off. The Chiefs never ran the play in a game. It stayed on the call sheet, unused.

Flash forward to August 2018. Matt Nagy was standing on the opposite sideline. A Kansas City assistant of five years, and the coordinator who'd overseen all of Hill's back-and-forth-and-back-agains, Nagy was now the Bears' head coach, and as he faced off in the preseason against his old mentor, Reid, he saw an opportunity. Midway through the fourth quarter, on a third-and-three with his team up 24–13, Nagy dialed it up: Garrett Johnson, a Chicago rookie, streaked across the formation one, two, three times, and amid all the misdirection, quarterback Tyler Bray tossed the ball to fullback Michael Burton for a 10-yard gain.

Coaches on both sidelines fought back smirks. Nagy had done it: He'd finally called Lollipop.

This was a single first down in a game that meant next to nothing, but Lollipop represented something bigger: Regardless of who actually called the play, here was Andy Reid reimagining how offense is played in the NFL. He was connecting the present to the future.

Really, it was a simple play, made confusing for the defense by a ridiculous presnap motion. And it had been lifted from the college ranks. (Specifically: the presnap chaos practiced in 2017 by LSU offensive coordinator Matt Canada.) Both the play's name and the formation, Weezy Right, were a nod to Louisiana-born rapper Lil Wayne. The first time the Chiefs installed Lollipop, quality control coaches queued up that chart-topping 2008 Weezy track in the meeting room. The music might not have been Reid's style, but, as is his way, he embraced it.

To watch Kansas City's offense in 2018 is to participate in a sort of shell game, striving to keep track of movements as objects are deftly rearranged in front of you. Reid's Chiefs send someone in presnap motion more often than they don't. And through Week 8 they'd sent three or more players in motion 15 times, more than any other team in the league. Their two most dangerous pass catchers, Hill and tight end Travis Kelce, dart all over the formation, creating for quarterback Patrick Mahomes endless possibilities for where to go with the football.

This—is this where the present meets the future? It's a time warp from three yards and a cloud of dust, but, shrugs Reid, "I don't know if I'm on the forefront of anything." The stats suggest he's being coy. The 9–1 Chiefs are scoring at a clip—4.4 touchdowns per game—matched by only two other teams in the modern era, across 16 games: Peyton Manning's 2013 Broncos and Tom Brady's '07 Patriots. By the midpoint of this season, Mahomes had tossed 26 TDs; only two other NFL QBs have ever topped 25 in the first half of a season, and we've already mentioned their hallowed names here.

So where did this all *come* from? NFL coaches tend to be late adopters of schematic trends—in part because pro talent levels are so even, unlike in college, where overmatched desperation spurs innovation; and in part because NFL coaching leashes are the shortest, which discourages risk-taking. But 13 years ago Reid saw the need to adapt—to bend his ways and borrow from others—in order to succeed. This was in February 2005, and Reid's Eagles were playing the Patriots in Super Bowl XXXIX. Philadelphia spent the two weeks before that game preparing to pass-protect against New England's 3-4 front—but then Bill Belichick's team came out with four down linemen. Two defensive players plugged the A gaps all night and Reid's QB, Donovan McNabb, taking almost all of his snaps under center, was something of a sitting duck. The Eagles, and a battered McNabb, lost 24–21. Now fast-forward to today: Mahomes takes 80% of his snaps out of the shotgun.

The West Coast system has been the foundation of Reid's offense ever since he began his NFL coaching career as an assistant on Mike Holmgren's Packers staff in the early 1990s. But as Reid transitioned later from McNabb to Michael Vick, the most talented dual-threat QB of his time, the coach recognized the possibilities of adding to that base the spread concepts he saw trickling up through the high school and college ranks—formations and motions that stretch the field horizontally, creating more permutations to befuddle a defense.

Reid had learned an important lesson about the power of space back in 1986, when he was the O-line coach at Northern Arizona under coordinator Brad Childress. The Lumberjacks' freshman QB back then, Greg Wyatt, was struggling against the blitz, so NAU moved to a spread look, reasoning that if the defense had to cover five players across the field, some heat would be lifted off the QB. And that it did. The Lumberjacks went 7–4, their first winning season in seven years, and when Wyatt finished the year with I-AA freshman records for attempts and completions, it cemented another lesson: Do what works for your QB.

Reid's vision, though, didn't *really* blossom until he came to Kansas City in 2013. Back in Philly he had control of the Eagles' personnel, but he didn't want that burden with the Chiefs; he preferred to spend his time ironing out every nuance of the offense rather than searching for a player to replace someone who'd gotten injured on Sunday. And so down the hill from Arrowhead Stadium he set up an R&D unit for offensive football, scouring film and tinkering with new play designs. He hired Childress as a spread-game analyst (Childress would sort the Pro Football Focus database for every NFL play run out of an empty formation, looking for anything worth pilfering) and Chris Ault, the former Nevada coach, to coach K.C. in the pistol offense he popularized with Colin Kaepernick, replete with options and misdirections.

Reid would later tell his successor in Philadelphia, Chip Kelly (now at UCLA), that Kelly was the one who opened up the NFL's offensive imagination—but, concurrently, that's exactly what Reid and his staff were doing in Kansas City. A month after Reid joined the Chiefs, he traded for 49ers quarterback Alex Smith; then he dug back into Smith's college tape from Utah, where Smith ran Urban Meyer's spread-option offense before Tim Tebow ever did, including the zone-read plays that would be the precursor to run-pass options (or RPOs). Nagy remembers walking into Reid's office on Monday mornings and watching the whiteboard fill up with ideas, inspiring the nickname "A Beautiful Mind."

Then, on opening night in 2017, Reid's Chiefs roughed up the defending Super Bowl–champion Patriots with an offense that looked like nothing the league had ever seen.

Kareem Hunt scurried up the right hash marks en route to a 78-yard touchdown catch, and NFL defenses still haven't quite caught up. This was the play that flipped that game against New England two Septembers ago, when Kansas City scored the most points (42) and gained the most yards (537) ever against a Bill Belichick–coached team. The Chiefs had flooded the short (right) side of the field with four players. Tyreek Hill ran from left to right on a fly-sweep motion, pulling down the deep defender, and three other Chiefs sprinted downfield on vertical routes: Travis Kelce went on the diagonal, and receiver Albert Wilson sprinted up the sideline while Hunt arced out of the backfield. That left Patriots defensive end Cassius Marsh to try in vain to peel off the line of scrimmage and chase Hunt up the seam. In the end, it all worked exactly as the Chiefs staff had seen it play out before... *on North Dakota State's film.*

Kansas City wasn't planning on drafting a QB in 2016, but Reid and his offensive staff always study and grade the top prospects at that position each year anyway. That's when they saw a young quarterback named Carson Wentz hit this play again and again for big gains against the likes of Northern Illinois and Weber State. Yup, Reid says unapologetically, "we were studying Carson and kind of snuck that one [from them]." (The Bison called this play He-Man because the H-back worked into the seam up the field; the Chiefs call it All-Go Special Halfback Seam.)

Such is the football circle of life: The Patriots used a variation of this play the following week for a 24-yard completion to James White in a win against the Saints. As did the Rams, a few weeks later, on a 53-yard Todd Gurley TD against the Cowboys. And when Drew Brees broke the NFL's all-time passing yards record in Week 5 this season with a 62-yard touchdown, he did it on a similar concept: A player moves horizontally to draw down the secondary, while three vertical routes develop downfield.

It's not just coaches like Nagy, Belichick, Sean McVay (in L.A.) and Sean Payton (New Orleans) who check the Chiefs' film each week to see what Reid is up to. When a reporter prefaced a question in the lead-up to the Nov. 4 Browns-Chiefs game by guessing that Baker Mayfield hadn't found much time to watch K.C.'s offense on film, the Cleveland QB jumped in: "Oh, I *have* been able to," he said. "It's a thing of art."

As a young assistant in Green Bay, Reid would often bring new ideas to his fellow coaches. Alas, they were loyal to the gospel of the West Coast offense, a rhythm-based passing system in which a QB takes snaps under center and works through progressions. (Reid once persuaded Holmgren to let Brett Favre try the shotgun, but that experiment ended after one snap went flying over Favre's head in a Saturday walk-through). When Reid pushed a new idea, "Holmgren's pat answer, and [then Packers assistant] Jon Gruden's pat answer," reports Childress, "was, 'Yeah, that looks like a good play—but you know what? I don't *know* that play. When you get your own offense, you go ahead and feel free to put that in.'" But, Childress says, "that's not Andy."

Today a big part of the job for K.C. quarterbacks coach Mike Kafka and for passing-game analyst Joe Bleymaier is to scour the college ranks for plays their coach might consider. And Reid doesn't care who or where these plays come from. The offensive principle to which he is most loyal is simple: He'll do anything for a first down.

The 2016 Chiefs traveled in November to play the Panthers in Charlotte, and after checking into their hotel on Saturday afternoon, several coaches caught a glimpse of a game between unranked Pitt and No. 3 Clemson. As they watched, it was more than just the unfolding upset that caught their eyes—they were sucked in by the misdirection tactics discombobulating Clemson's defense. That was the first time they noticed Canada, who back then was Pitt's OC.

"The plays in our playbook could be from any year, anywhere," says receiver Chris Conley. "They just seamlessly come together. There's this conglomeration of good plays [Reid] has accumulated over time. *That's* what makes up this offense."

It's not far-fetched to say that Reid has spent much of the last decade preparing for Mahomes's arrival. The marriage of QB and coach is such a perfect union, bubbling in offensive fertility, that Washington State coach Mike Leach, himself well-versed in the art of scoring points, muses, "There's times you wonder if [their pairing] should even be legal."

For Reid, 2018 is just the next step in a progression he's been working at for some time now. "We looked at some of the college stuff, we got it growing and incorporated it into what we do," he says plainly, modestly. "And then Patrick came in, and you just keep growing."

Even that's an oversimplification. For years NFL coaches have groused about the glaring holes that exist in the games of players coming from college spread offenses. But, especially when it comes to QBs, Reid's perception was different. He focused on what Mahomes gained from throwing the ball 1,349 times in Texas Tech's Air Raid system rather than on the fact that the QB rarely took snaps under center. Coaches could teach him that. And while much of what the Chiefs run today was already in place before they drafted Mahomes at No. 10 in 2017—QB and coach have shared a few laughs over the fact that some people think they're running a straight Texas Tech Air Raid—Mahomes does say he got Reid to install two of his favorite college plays: one concept K.C. has run a few times to Kelce, and another that Reid has yet to unveil.

As the Chiefs have continued to build their offense around principles familiar to their players from the college ranks, it has been easier to put them in positions to thrive. Hill is a perfect jet-sweep runner. Hunt can zip down the field on the seam route. Kelce and Hill are among the most moved-around players in the league at their respective positions, lining up tight, out wide, in the slot and in the backfield. Collectively these tasks are the underpinnings of the spread systems these chess-piece players learned at Oklahoma State (Hill), Toledo (Hunt) and Cincinnati (Kelce).

"It's a neat transition we are in right now with these offenses," says Nagy, who today is teaching his own young quarterback, Mitchell Trubisky, the system he had a hand in developing with Reid. "Everything comes full circle—and before you know it, down the road, I'm sure teams will be running the wishbone again."

Perhaps it's not so surprising that Reid—at 60 the NFL's fourth-oldest coach—is at the front of the current offensive revolution when you consider it this way: What we're seeing on the field today is the product of many different eras. The Chiefs' playbook even includes one scheme from a 1970s veer offense. It's a pitch trap, a bit of a tricky concept in which the quarterback fakes a pitch to the back on one side while a guard pulls to execute a trap block in that direction. Everyone flows one way, but then the QB whirls around to face the opposite direction and gives the ball to the *other* back on an inside handoff. Reid learned that one at John Marshall High in Los Angeles, where he played on the offensive line. His fellow Chiefs coaches laughed when he first installed the play, but Reid always knows when to call it, and they say it always works.

"I said this at the beginning of the year and people looked at me askew," says K.C.'s right tackle, Mitchell Schwartz, "but a lot of what we do, the roots are in the '60s and '70s and '80s. The game was more constricted back then, so you had to find ways to create good matchups. Now you add the space to it, and...."

Schwartz trails off here, but we'll finish his sentence for him: *And you get what we're seeing on the field now—the future of NFL offenses.*

AFTER THE WHISTLE

OCTOBER 4, 1993

'We're Going to Beat This Thing'

Boomer Esiason, the rejuvenated quarterback of the New York Jets, is confronting a new opponent—a disease that has invaded his family

BY GARY SMITH

There was quiet in the New York Jets' locker room, the quiet of men awaiting violence. A few players stared at their playbooks. Some talked to God. Some wrapped earphones around their heads and waited for the music to take them away.

They took turns walking into a side room, emerging with thick white crusts of tape around their arms and knees and ankles in preparation for all the collisions and twists. Their quarterback, Boomer Esiason, needed the tape for something else. He carried it to his locker, unzipped his black shoulder bag and pulled out a photograph of a 2½ year-old boy with a blue cap tugged over his blond hair. Boomer taped the picture of his son to the back of his locker and sat on his stool.

In earlier years he often spent this hour remembering insults from the media, opponents or fans, working himself into the state of mind he needed to stand calmly at the heart of the violence. Now all that seemed almost silly. Now he stared at the photograph and thought of how sweetly this boy lay upon the sloped board twice each day, how willingly he let his loved ones beat on his back and chest and sides to dislodge from his lungs the mucus that could kill him. And the feeling seemed to surge up inside the quarterback. They could beat on him today all they wanted. But no one could touch him.

There was silence on the Jets' practice field, the silence of men trapped inside helmets and pads in the third week of two-a-day practices under a killing sun. They looked over to the long row of pine trees that lined the field. There he was again, the old man with the black shoes and white socks, sitting alone in his lawn chair among the pinecones. The old man with the St. John's Redmen cap pulled down to his sunglasses, little leather tool holder hooked on his belt, pack of Tareytons tucked inside his sleeve.

Every practice he sat there. At the end of the morning session he drove 40 minutes to his home in East Islip, Long Island, and then climbed right back into his truck two hours later and drove 40 minutes back for the afternoon workout. "The man in the lawn chair," some called the 70-year-old man. Many players had no idea he was the quarterback's dad. Boomer looked over to the shade and gave a little wave.

Somehow life had washed Boomer back to the place where he had grown up, where he had been hurt and healed. The little boy whose mother had died of lymphoma, who had looked over to see his dad on the sidelines every year, every practice, every game...was now the adult, the father of a little boy with cystic fibrosis, the object of whispers that his arm was dead, looking over and seeing his dad, every day, once again.

He never said a word, the old man, about who you have to be for your children, how much of your life you have to give away. He never had to say it. He just sat there each practice under the pine trees. The man in the lawn chair.

"God, Cheryl," Boomer said to his wife. "You wouldn't believe how many times I thought about G Man today." That was what he always called his son, Gunnar. It was a Sunday night 2½ weeks ago, hours after the Jets had shocked the Dolphins in Miami, 24–14, and Cheryl had come to meet Boomer at the airport in New York. He stared out at the traffic, euphoric and woozy at once, and shook his head. "The whole day, G Man was right there with me."

Right there in the photograph in his locker. Right there on the field in Joe Robbie Stadium when the temperature hit 100° and all the water in Boomer's body was running in rivulets down his back and legs, and the Dolphin defensive line was driving its helmets into his ribs. Right there, most of all, when dehydration overcame Boomer on the flight home, when he blanched and vomited and watched two intravenous needles going into his arm. How could he not think of G Man and that day last May in the hospital when the boy was vomiting mucus, lying wan and pale with the IV in his arm and the oxygen tube up his nose, unaware that the doctor had just told his parents that their son had cystic fibrosis?

On first hearing the diagnosis, Boomer had decided to retire from football and to always be with the boy. But now he was off at war again, and somehow it was the boy, instead, who was always with him. After his first three games as a Jet, Boomer was 68 for 94, for 909 yards and five touchdowns, leading the National Football League in completion percentage and average gain per completion, posting the same kind of glaring numbers that had made him the league's MVP in 1988. Every pass he completed was a spiral hurled into the future, a message his son would read one day: NEVER GIVE UP! Every touchdown he threw meant another microphone to speak into and tell the world about the disease that afflicts 55,000 people, another chance to explain about the mutated gene that causes so much thick mucus to clog the lung walls that they become a haven for infection, limiting the average CF patient to a life of 29 years and killing three people every day. "I am going to be the biggest enemy that this disease has ever had," Boomer said. "We're going to beat this thing. I know beyond a shadow of a doubt that we're going to beat it."

Funny. Everything about Boomer was *Boomer*, his voice, his size, his shocking white hair, his life. He had more friends—not the artificial, slap-your-back kind of friends, but real friends—than any man on earth. He had a three-year contract with the Jets worth $2.7 million a year, a string of commercial deals on the side, a weekly radio show, a fleet of big vehicles and big, big TVs.... But his real name was Norman, the same as the man sitting quietly in the lawn chair under the pines. Now that Boomer had a little son in trouble, now that Boomer was back home on Long Island, driving the same streets as he had long ago, walking into the same stores, bumping into the same people, he had this feeling...almost as if he might turn the next corner and see himself as a boy. And the question that kept going through his mind was, God, how did my dad ever do it?

Norman—that was who Boomer had to find inside himself now. The man who had kept ack-acking away at Messerschmitts while his buddies bled puddles around his ankles in the Battle of the Bulge, and who never told a soul about it when he came home. The man who had taken charge when one of Boomer's friends was struck dead by a car and when cancer took Boomer's mom.

Norman never laid eyes on another female after Irene died; forget it, what was the point? Tall woman, big voice, long rippling blonde hair, runner-up (*that* was a rip-off) in the Miss Lake Ronkonkoma beauty pageant back in the '50s. Before Norman knew it, she had him by the hand each Saturday night, first on the dance floor at the cafes and bars, those long poodle skirts she loved to wear pluming as they jitterbugged. Or he would look up and see her bouncing onto the stage to join the five-piece combo, one hand flying across the organ keys, the other across the piano, pounding out a Sam Cooke or Chuck Berry song. "Run, children, run!" Irene would shout when the heels of her children and nieces and nephews clickety-clacked across the brick patio behind the Esiasons' home. "I *love* that sound!" She would scoop up the little boy whose nickname came from the kicks he had delivered inside her belly, beam at him like the sun and ask everyone the same question: "Isn't he special?"

And then one day when Irene and Norman were sledding in the Poconos, she said her neck hurt. Six months later she was dead, and Norman Esiason was a 44-year-old man alone with two teenage daughters and a six-year-old son. A few years later Norman's own dad, Henning—slowly wasting away from emphysema—would move in with them too.

No one ever saw Norman cry, not even at Irene's funeral. No one saw the little boy cry, either. All they noticed was that he never, never wanted to be alone. At night Boomer would appear at the foot of his oldest sister's bed, his blanket stuffed under his arm. "Can I sleep here, Robin?" he would ask. It wasn't until six months after his mother's death, when Fawnie, the family dog, went berserk in the basement and died of a stroke, that some of the grief spilled out of Boomer. "How come?" he sobbed. "How come everybody's leaving me?"

The girls were just about old enough to fend for themselves, thank god, because Norman didn't quite know what a man could do to help a pair of grieving teenage girls. For the boy, though, he knew *exactly*. The boy became Norman's life. The old man woke up each morning at 4:45, then burrowed through the dark on the hour-and-10-minute train commute to his job as a safety engineer for Continental Insurance in Manhattan. Up onto the steel girders 40 floors high, across the collarbones of skyscrapers, to check the welding...down into the tunnels when construction crews were about to blast within inches of a gas line, making sure every safety precaution was being taken on the big jobs his company insured. "You don't build on rock, Norman," the underwriters would protest when he tried to persuade them to insure the mammoth apartment complexes going up on the Palisades in New Jersey. "You do build on rock," he would argue. "You cement all the fissures, you build fences to catch the falling pieces, you stay on 'em like a hawk, and you build on rock." *He* knew. He was rock. He could easily have been talking about himself and his motherless children.

Home he would race, finishing his paperwork on the train back to East Islip, yanking off his tie and changing into sneakers in the car to go watch his boy play baseball, basketball, football. "I've never seen a father like him," says Sal Ciampi, Boomer's high school football and baseball coach. "Never interfered, never complained, never missed a day."

Home to play catch with Boomer, or to pick him up, turn around and take that hour-and-10-minute train ride back to the city to Madison Square Garden or Shea Stadium to catch a game. Or home to turn on the TV and radio to simultaneously watch the New York Rangers and listen to the New York Mets, the old man sprawled on the couch, the boy lying right on top of his chest, then both of them erupting—Norman in a way he could never let himself do in public—when a Ranger *scoooooored*! or a Met hit one *outahere*! or a Giant broke free at the 30...he's at the 20...*the 10...touchdowwwn, New York!*

Imagine Grandpa Henning each time the TV room exploded. Imagine the bewilderment of the old glassblower, his lungs giving way from all the dust he had inhaled working beside the blast furnace in Philadelphia. Henning had refused to sign Norman's scholarship offer to play football at Georgetown University. Henning had refused to attend a single game during Norman's years as a three-sport athlete at Olney High in Philly. Every night the family ate dinner at six; nearly every night Norman would be late because of practice and trudge to his room, waiting with a hollow gut for his mother to sneak him dinner. Henning wasn't a bad guy. He was just off the boat from a little town in Norway. He just didn't understand.

But Norman was *not* going to raise his son that way. This was Scandinavian rebellion: slow...patient...noiseless...relentless. Picture this: Boomer is 11 or 12. Boomer's already a real piece of work. Boomer calls up Commack Arena, home of the local minor league ice hockey team, the Long Island Ducks, and rents the place so he and his buddies can play hockey. Only it's not available until 2 a.m., and it's a school night, and the parents of the other nine kids Boomer has involved in the scheme are furious, and the kids are a couple of tens shy of the money they need to rent the arena, and Boomer's old man has to be up for work at 4:45 a.m. So what does Norman do? Antes up the rest of the cash, drives the kids to the arena, watches them run around like a bunch of lunatics for an hour—Boomer never had a clue how to skate. Yes, Norman was resolute. Norman was Norwegian winter.

Funny, but he never once clobbered Boomer, no matter how many times the kid tried to climb over the glass and *join* the fights at Ranger games. No matter how long Boomer grew that shocking white hair, no matter how much swagger and how little patience he had, how many number-7 decals he plastered on the windows and bumpers of his candy-red convertible Olds in case someone out there didn't realize it belonged to the QB at East Islip High...no matter how *opposite* to Norman he grew. All the old man ever had to do was lift his right fist and growl, "Which do you want: the convincer"—then his left fist—"or the convincer's helper?" Norman, back then, was 6'2", 280. But more than anything, Boomer just hated to let the old man down.

There was such dignity in the old man, especially under stress. Boomer could never forget the day in ninth grade when Norman was coaching Boomer's Senior League baseball team and the boys were playing pepper before a game, and one of Boomer's teammates darted across the road to retrieve a ball. All at once there was a screech of rubber, a boy dead in the road and a man a mile from a telephone. A man surrounded by 15 kids, half of them hysterical with grief, the other half, including Boomer, threatening to take off the head of the woman driver. Norman sent someone to find a phone, covered the body with a blanket from his car, herded his team away from the woman and went from boy to boy, putting his arm around each one's shoulders and saying over and over, "Remember the good moments in his life.... Don't look over there, that's not him.... Remember the good times."

From a distance, people looking at Boomer saw a tall kid with ice-white hair and too little self-doubt. He walked out of the locker room after a high school basketball game one Friday evening and found all four tires on his candy-red convertible slashed. But up close you couldn't miss the sensitivity to hurt and fear, the understanding of what lurked just behind the manicured hedges and aluminum siding, the thin peel of Long Island suburbia. Boomer was the kid who beat up the bullies.

He became the quarterback—of his block, of his friends as well as of his teams. A quarterback, unlike those who played the other positions in life, could always make sure there was a plan, a group, a movement. A quarterback could always make sure the silent house he came home to at 3:30 p.m. would be hopping by four. The Esiasons' house became headquarters, the place for Boomer's boys to plot and sleep over and wake up to the old man's jelly crepes. Even on summer vacation trips, Boomer made sure he took three or four friends along. "Between his father, his sisters, all his aunts and uncles and grandparents and friends, he was surrounded by this bottomless pit of love," says his old friend Michael Dooley.

And then Boomer got a scholarship to the University of Maryland, said goodbye to his father, left the love pit. Suddenly he was a seventh-stringer in a strange land, flunking half his classes, watching all his dorm mates go home on weekends to get their laundry done and dinner cooked by Mom. Suddenly there was silence. He was about to quit school and go home. He was sure he would leave after that night when 25 upperclassmen on his team cornered him, tied him up, dumped him in an elevator alone and pushed the button, echoes of their laughter following him up and down the shaft.

But just when he was about to give up, he would look over during practice to the sideline. Arthritic left knee stiff from the five-hour drive, there would be the man in the lawn chair.

Boomer set 17 records at the University of Maryland, was a consensus All-America his senior year, became the Cincinnati Bengals' starting quarterback his second season. His life gathered momentum, grew wider each year. Boomer loved *big*...but he preferred *gigantic*. Jacked-up monster trucks with tinted windows. TV screens that took up a quarter of a wall, orbited by slightly smaller screens in case anybody dropped by with a hankering to watch four games simultaneously. An 8,000-square-foot house with four beers on tap at the bar, an electronic board flashing up-to-the-minute scores from the NFL, NBA, NHL and major leagues, a swimming pool Cheryl laughingly called a "polar bear pit," and a basketball court.

It was all for sharing, not for lording over. Boomer's friends became like family; his family kept growing larger. Every home game, 15 to 30 of them would fly in to Cincinnati and camp at Boomer's. On New Year's Eve and the Fourth of July, 60 or 70 people would respond to his call—friends from Long Island, from the University of Maryland, from Cincinnati. You would walk in Boomer's door and be handed a party bag containing a T-shirt that said HOTEL ESIASON, FOURTH OF JULY, MOTHER OF ALL PARTIES, inscribed sunglasses and a plastic drink container. You would see the refrigerator shellacked with a couple of dozen stick-on notes giving flight numbers and arrival times so Boomer could arrange rides from the airport for his guests, and a sign-up list so you could volunteer to prepare meals in shifts of 10. You would play killer pickup basketball, darts and Ping-Pong, then go in buses Boomer had chartered to a riverboat or a restaurant he had rented for the night with a live band. Or perhaps eat in, a pig roast by his backyard pool, and then everyone would end up sprawled on beds, pull-out couches and sleeping bags, some farmed out to next-door neighbors.

"Let's keep it simple this year, honey," Cheryl, the woman he had met at Maryland and married, would say. "That's no fun," Boomer would reply, thumbing through his monster Rolodex. Somehow, no matter how last-minute the plan, Boomer always pulled it off. And Cheryl, a wry, philosophical sort who loved to sit back and observe the human pageant that Boomer emceed, would shrug, grin and go with it.

There was such zest and innocence to it, you couldn't get in its way. Boomer was a boat pulling an ever-widening wake—one of those rare people who fused all the phases of his life, who grew big without devouring the small. Sitting at your table, the one Boomer assigned you at the restaurant he had rented, might be Boomer's Pro Bowl guard and his wife, Boomer's cleaning lady and her husband, Boomer's high school coach and his wife, and the guys who sold him his satellite dish and did his kitchen cabinets. Some of them started having babies, and that made it even better. "It's a lunatic asylum," Boomer would say. "I love it. It's *life*." The doorbell would ring a half dozen times, neighbors' kids asking, as if he were eight years old, "Can Boomer come out and play?" Likely as not, he would.

Boomer babies—sure, why not four or five? For years Boomer had this snapshot in his mind, a gaggle of little blondes in pigtails following him everywhere, adoring everything he did, the way most women seemed to. A boy...well, he never talked about that. A duty came with that. Nobody knew that like Norman Esiason's son.

He went to the airport in Cincinnati one Sunday afternoon in 1987, before they had any children, to pick up Cheryl. The NFL was on strike that autumn, and Boomer, quarterback to the bone, had stepped out front to lead his teammates against management. He and 30 others had sat in front of a bus that team officials had arranged for replacement players to use; he had lent money to players buckling under the financial strain of going without paychecks; and that very Sunday, an hour before the first "scab" game, he had stood and begged for calm between a mob of strike-supporting Kentucky coal miners and a mob of antistrike fans who wanted at each others' throats. Boomer had become the lightning rod for criticism in one of the most antiunion cities in America.

As he drove to the airport, his head still throbbing from the confrontation outside Riverfront Stadium, he flicked on the radio. The host of the local sports talk show was "breaking" a story that Boomer had ordered the Bengals' wives, in deference to the strike, to boycott the fund-raising fashion show they had organized to benefit Cincinnati's Children's Hospital. Radio callers were in a frenzy. The story was untrue. Few athletes anywhere gave as much time to charities as Boomer did—in a public way, raising $700,000 for the Arthritis Foundation and the Caring Program for Children, and in a private way, making frequent visits to kids with leukemia and cystic fibrosis at Children's Hospital.

"Turn it off," Boomer told Cheryl as they headed home from the airport. "You don't want to hear this."

"Leave it on," she said.

A male caller was on the air. "You know what I hope?" the man said. "I hope the Esiasons have a child that has something wrong with it someday and Children's Hospital turns them away."

Cheryl and Boomer looked at each other, the air sucked out of them. "That's unspeakable," said Cheryl. "My god, that's...."

Boomer went from the villain of Cincinnati in '87 to its hero in '88—life happens that way in movies and sports. He led the AFC in passer ratings and touchdown passes in '88 and '89, was voted to his second and third Pro Bowls, whipped the Bengals to the '89 Super Bowl, appeared in his underwear for a Hanes ad, played Goldilocks in a Diet Coke commercial and made a zillion appearances for corporations and charities. He had such presence on the field, such command and camaraderie in his voice, you felt as easy in his huddle as you did in his house. Hell, the Bengals decided, who even needed a huddle? Let Boomer organize everything, just like one of his Fourth of July reunions—last second, seat of his pants, hut, hut, hut! Hadn't Boomer always felt best amid a swirl?

Cheryl got pregnant. The moment Boomer found out it was a boy, pictures of his own past, warm and wonderful black and whites, began to flash in his mind. If he could have called an 800 number that day and ordered tickets for all the hockey, basketball, baseball and football games he planned to take his son to, he would have. But Cheryl was determined: This baby would *not* get swept up in the public whirl of her husband's life. "Baby Sub Rosa," she called the child in her womb. It was a Latin term for everything Boomer was not: private, confidential, secret.

After Gunnar came home from the hospital in April 1991, Boomer would lie on the rug holding the baby on his chest. A remarkable thing was happening. Boomer sometimes lay there for hours, just staring in wonder at the boy. He fell asleep like that. "It was the first time," says Cheryl, "that I ever saw Boomer stay still."

Gunnar kept getting sick. Earaches. Three-week colds. Pneumonia. Diarrhea. Barely ate. Asthma, the doctors said. God, it was almost scary how similar Gunnar's problems were to those of the little girl with cystic fibrosis, Sarah, with whom Boomer had fallen in love at Children's Hospital...how alike in look and smell and sound they were, how even Gunnar's personality was that same achingly sweet, accepting personality that all those CF kids Boomer had hugged seemed to have. Asthma, the doctors said. Asthma.

Something was happening, meanwhile, to Boomer's no-huddle, no-prisoners offense. Some blamed the deterioration of his offensive line. Some blamed the Bengal defense, which had grown so porous that Boomer always seemed to be digging himself out of a hole. Some blamed Boomer's left arm. Sometimes Boomer wanted so badly to make a football game do what he wished it to do, he tried to take what wasn't his, what wasn't there. In his last 41 starts for the Bengals, he threw 53 interceptions.

The fourth game last season was at home against Minnesota. Gunnar had never been to a game, but he was six months shy of his second birthday, and, for a change, he wasn't sick. It wouldn't be quite the same as when Boomer was a boy, sitting knee-to-knee in the stands with Dad. But the snapshot in Boomer's mind was, in many ways, even more magical: little boy watching Dad evade the Viking rush; Dad cranking up and hurling the 50-yard bomb...*he's at the 20...the 10*...the crowd going berserk.

The crowd went berserk. The ferocity of the boos that day, the insults, the filth....Boomer threw four interceptions; the Bengals lost 42–7. In the third quarter he stepped away from his teammates on the sidelines and turned to the crowd, searching for his wife and child, frantically waving: *Go home, go home!* Cheryl wouldn't budge.

He stood half bent in the shower afterward, looking as if he were about to cry. For the first time in his life, he couldn't go back to the crowd of friends awaiting him at home. He drove in circles that night and talked to Cheryl about quitting. His snapshot of a father and a boy and a ball game had been ruined.

The Bengals benched him with four games left in the season. Gunnar couldn't sleep, couldn't eat, could barely breathe. Some nights at 4 a.m. Boomer would drive in loops around Riverfront Stadium with his son in the car, trying to get Gunnar to drop off to sleep, numb to what was happening inside those concrete walls and ramps on Sundays, just scared about his boy. A test for cystic fibrosis six months earlier had come back negative, so Boomer and Cheryl kept giving Gunnar cough suppressants, unaware that mucus was the enemy, that the boy needed to cough to *live*.

The trade came on March 17, 1993. Few teams lusted for Boomer Esiason anymore. The Jets got him for a third-round draft pick in '93 and a conditional second-round selection in '94 that hinges on Boomer's performance. "He hung up the phone after he found out," recalls his business assistant, Tami Amaker, "and he let out this whoop. He shouted, 'Tami, I'm going *home*, I'm going *home*!' The way he said that word, *home*...he said it like Dorothy in *The Wizard of Oz*."

They called him off the field during the Jets' minicamp in May. Cheryl was at Children's Hospital in Cincinnati. Gunnar had pneumonia, again. The doctors were retesting him for cystic fibrosis.

Boomer rushed back to Cincinnati. The doctor walked into the hospital room with the test results. The boy had it: The disease that clogs the lungs with bacteria-trapping phlegm, leaving parents to wonder which invisible particle in the air might be the end of their child. The disease that shuts off the work of the pancreas, making it impossible for the body to absorb most foods unless enzyme pills are ingested before each meal. The disease that often makes males sterile.

Boomer asked the physician to leave. He and Cheryl looked at each other, the air rushing out of the room, the thought in both of their minds the same. The radio caller that day six years ago...nothing to do with this, of course not, but...god, the sickness of it all. They walked over to the crib, stared down at the sleeping two-year-old with the tubes in his arm and his nose, the child to whom they had passed the mutated gene without ever dreaming they both were carriers. They cried. "We're sorry, Gunnar," they both kept telling the sleeping boy. "We love you. We'll always be here for you. We're sorry, we're sorry."

Then they looked at each other again. Everything would have to change now. All the film study, practice sessions, football games, appearances, commercials, interviews, reunions, laughs—the life Boomer had filled with people and plans and had kept spinning, faster and faster, ever since his mother had died—it would have to end. All the time and energy it took to be Boomer would have to go to the little boy. Wasn't that the legacy of the man in the lawn chair? "I'm going to retire," Boomer told Cheryl.

He drove past Riverfront Stadium on the way from the hospital to their home in Villa Hills, Ky. He still couldn't believe it—his body, a Pro Bowl quarterback's body, had betrayed him, betrayed his son. A sad song was playing on the radio. He kept looking at the stadium. It just didn't feel right, turning inward to fight this war, becoming smaller.

He snapped off the sad song. "No," he decided. "I'm not going to quit. They won't listen to me if I quit or have a bad year. I'm going to have a great year. I'm going to go on a crusade. They'll listen to me if I have a great year. They'll *have* to listen. They'll *have* to."

On a Friday night, 41 hours before Boomer Esiason's first regular-season game as the Jet quarterback, there were 30 people and five pieces of furniture in his new house in suburban Long Island. Little kids scrambling up and down stairs still sticky with polyurethane, laughing and screaming. Buddies searching for a corkscrew for the wine. Wives tearing open cardboard boxes, searching for pillowcases and sheets. Bare-chested construction workers painting rooms, sticking tiles to the kitchen wall, carrying beds and mattresses to the upstairs bedrooms. From room to room walked Boomer, hair askew, belt unbuckled, playbook under his arm, looking futilely for a toilet with a seat. "Isn't this great?" he said. "I love it."

He could ask his friends to stay home if they or their children had colds. He could eliminate dust and plants and animals from his home. But not people.

At 9 p.m. he pulled out the sloped board covered with black vinyl. He pulled Gunnar away from his train set, away from the swirl. "Ready for P.T., G Man?" he boomed.

"Ready for P.T., Daddy," said Gunnar. His voice rasped. That was the only clue. He grinned and thumped his father on the back—if he had to be pounded for 20 minutes twice every day, two sessions of physical therapy, so did everyone else in the world.

First Gunnar sat on the bed for 15 minutes wearing a mask, inhaling a mixture of two vaporized drugs designed to open the breathing passages. Then Boomer laid him on the board—feet up, head angled down—cupped his hand and began to beat on Gunnar's back. "Wooooo," went Gunnar. "A-wooooooooo."

"Where are we, G-Man?"

"Big Appaw."

"Who does Daddy play for?"

"Jets...a-wooooo."

"What position does Daddy play?"

"Cowbark."

"What do you think of the Bengals?"

"Bengals stink."

"Thumbs-up, by Jove?"

"Thumbs-up, by Jove."

"All right, G Man. Now cough. That's it. Cough."

"It's over, Daddy."

"Not yet, G Man. Big cough this time. Now turn over."

"It's over, Daddy...it's over."

On that Sunday, Boomer completed 29 of 40 pass attempts for 371 yards and two touchdowns in his first game of the season, a 26–20 loss to the Denver Broncos. There were 68,130 people in Giants Stadium, 70 of them in the Boomer Esiason party. Norman sat on the 40.

"I'm sick and tired of losing," Boomer said in the locker room afterward. He was pulling his son's photograph off the locker wall, balling up the tape that had framed it, tucking it back into his bag for the next game. "No one in this locker room should sleep tonight. No one."

He drove home, his mind churning as always. Next Sunday, the Dolphins, at Miami. Two days later the press conference to announce the NFL Properties–sponsored fund-raising campaign to fight cystic fibrosis, then the *Good Morning America* show with Gunnar on his lap, followed by Regis and Kathie Lee. Goodbye, Baby Sub Rosa. Hello, CF Poster Child. Anything the Cystic Fibrosis Foundation needed, anything Boomer could possibly do, he was going to.

But all the cameras and microphones would go away if the Jets didn't start winning, Boomer knew, and all the radio talk-show listeners would start gnashing their teeth. The clock was ticking, and there were still millions of people who didn't know that scientists were closing in on the cure, that they had pinpointed the gene on the seventh chromosome that caused the disease and had even found a way to manufacture a healthy gene, but until they found a way to get the healthy genes everywhere they needed to go, children by the thousands would continue to die.

He walked into his house. He kissed Sydney, his one-year-old daughter, who has tested negative for the disease. He picked up Gunnar. He sat in the reclining chair in front of the six-foot TV screen, turned on the Sunday night football game and laid the little boy on his chest to watch with him.

The game ended. They both yawned. Boomer carried the boy past the kids' room. He laid the boy in his own bed, snuggled against him and fell asleep.

JULY 12, 2004

A Life After Wide Right

Thirteen years after missing a Super Bowl–winning field goal, the ex-Bill views his worst moment as a step in the right direction

BY KARL TARO GREENFELD

This stocky man, in brown, rubber-soled shoes, gray Dockers and a tan polo shirt, walking across the narrow street from his car, the white Chevy Prism with the cracked windshield, he is a failure. An abject, wretched failure. And yet he is, incontrovertibly, a winner, a success. He stands there in his wraparound sunglasses and breathes the wet spring air and talks to you about interest rates and square footage and backyard park adjacencies and finished basements in this northern Virginia suburb. Houses. Condominiums. A nice parcel out by Centreville. In Chantilly. Mortgage rates are low. Now is the time to buy. He speaks in a quiet, slow, gravelly voice. Thoughtful. You lean in to hear him. His steady monotone wins out over your urge to interrupt.

He finishes talking and looks away, at the waving poplar trees and the unweeded grass, the minimall in the distance and the Mobil station where kids are filling up their bike tires with air. You look at him and you know you know him. He hands you his card. This is an upscale area, he explains, comfortable, a bit pricey perhaps, but great for families. A strong sense of community. The card says SCOTT NORWOOD, REALTOR, and it is red, white and blue. He looks at you to see if you recognize the name. He lives with this, a combination of burden and opportunity. A salesman needs any edge he can get, and he knows that merely being recognized as a former NFL kicker can help win over the husbands but rarely the wives. The wives must be reminded that this is the guy who blew that kick, who, you know, lost that Super Bowl for the Buffalo Bills; then there is understanding and sympathy. And that could help cajole a couple into bidding on a split-level colonial at the end of a cul-de-sac.

But he never asks for the pity. He has known anger and disappointment. Has felt responsible for a city's stifled aspirations. But he will not accept pity.

We are a fickle nation, quick to dismiss failure and embrace success. Prove yourself a champion, and we will love you forever, overlooking murder raps and drug busts and spousal abuse. But fall short on the field, and we may never forgive, no matter how you conduct yourself away from the game. So consider how it would feel to live as the answer to a trivia question, the punch line to a joke, a synonym for misses and muffs and screwups, or, perhaps even more humiliating, the MacGuffin in a Vincent Gallo movie (*Buffalo '66*). That is the burden Scott Norwood has borne since Super Bowl XXV. And you know what? He has not only survived, but he has also thrived—and not as some lovable loser, a Throneberry or Uecker who uses his haplessness as a huckster's tool.

The measure of a man should no more be his worst moments than it should be the color of his skin or the cut of his suit. It is how we deal with those moments that make us who we are, and that is the most American measure of success: to fail once, to pick yourself up and try again. We are a nation of losers made good, descendants of those who settled here in search of a second chance. To fail is not American, it is *human*. But it *is* American to overcome that failure.

It took years for Scott Norwood to get here. To walk down this sidewalk and point to this house and say that it will go in the mid-4s. To raise his three children who have his blue eyes and his beautiful wife's blonde locks and to take up his position as man of the house. This man, in his journey, has transformed himself from taciturn failure to stolid hero. It is a small sort of heroism, quotidian, really—the heroism of failing at something and still persevering. Of missing a field goal wide right in the most televised sporting event in the country, and then having to get up the next morning and continue to live your life. We've all known moments of failure, of blowing an exam, of being fired, spurned, disgraced, yet these moments are seldom public. How do you go on when every time you walk into a liquor store or a gas station, there is someone pointing at you, reminding you of your worst moment? You see, this is also a particular kind of American heroism—the simple, quiet heroism of continuing to be a dad and a husband despite knowing, deeply, that life can be a bitch.

The path to Scott Norwood's failure, and the redemptive success of overcoming that setback, begins at Thomas Jefferson High in Alexandria, Va., where a stocky, 5'10", 17-year-old sweeper is heading back to the locker room after soccer practice. The football coach, Mike Weaver, stops him and says, "Hey, son, I hear you can really kick the ball."

Scott is a quiet boy, the discomfort of adolescence reinforcing his taciturn nature so that when he speaks it is as surprising as a voice coming from a statue. "I'm O.K., sir."

"We need a kicker, son," says Coach Weaver, "Why don't you come out for the team this season?"

Scott nods. He's been a standout soccer player since he was old enough to tie his shoes and would make the All-Metropolitan team twice at Thomas Jefferson. But such is the straightforwardness of his world view that he has never thought about applying his skill at kicking a ball to another sport.

At dinner that night at the Norwoods' house in Annandale, his father, Del, who will later be inducted into the Virginia High School Hall of Fame as a baseball coach, listens as Scott recounts his conversation with Weaver. A Maine native and the coach at Washington-Lee High School in Arlington, Va., Del pitched in the minor leagues and was invited to camp with the Boston Red Sox, but never made it to the majors. Yet as much as he once dreamed of the big leagues, he now enjoys playing with and coaching his three children in baseball and soccer. Scott's older brother, Steve, is a pitcher and outfielder for the University of Virginia who will later be drafted by the Milwaukee Brewers. His younger sister, Sandra, is a standout in field hockey, basketball and soccer. Del had been a little disappointed that Scott, when he reached high school, had chosen soccer over baseball. But the nature of Del's commitment to his children was that he would have supported Scott if he had chosen ballet. So when Scott mentions the possibility of kicking for the football team, Del asks him if this is something he wants to do.

"You know, Dad," Scott says, swallowing a bite of chicken-fried steak, "I think I do."

Del nods and tells Scott that he will be happy to help out any way he can. That summer the father and son spend every morning at Thomas Jefferson, teeing it up and catching kickoffs. The two begin the process of charting the accuracy of Scott's field goals and the distance of his kickoffs. They don't talk much about their progress, but there is a sense that things are going well. Scott, because of his soccer background, has an intuitive feel for how to approach the ball. Del's books tell him that Scott should take three steps back and two to the left, but Scott just sort of backs up at an angle and sets up, arms swinging, and then makes the smooth run up to the ball followed by the stiff sound of the stuffing being knocked out of the Wilson, which travels 45 yards through the uprights.

"It just felt good," Scott recalls. "I was comfortable with it pretty quickly." He goes out for the football team, and the coach, of course, is grateful to have a real kicker instead of a backup quarterback who kicks because he doesn't get to play as much as he would like. For Scott—shy, reserved—the position offers an assured place in the universe. There is a simplicity to this role that appeals to him: He scores points. By increments of one and three he becomes the leading scorer on the team, in the county and, finally, in the region. The steadiness of the accretion is pleasing, like interest accumulating in a bank account, and by the time he makes the winning field goal in a game against archrival Annandale High, college scouts who have come to see other players are making notes about this kicker.

Every off-season, Scott comes home to Annandale. After every year at James Madison University, where he earns a football scholarship. And then, after he graduates with a degree in business in 1982, and Del and Scott blanket the NFL with videotape, and after he signs with the Atlanta Falcons—and is cut. After an upstart league called the USFL is formed and he wins a job with the Birmingham Stallions and kicks 25 field goals in '83. After he tears some cartilage in his knee in his second season with the Stallions and is released. After successes and after failures, he comes back to work out with his father at the same old high school field. They never speak of what it feels like to be cut by an NFL team. Or how it feels to drive from Atlanta back to Fairfax County in the light-blue Riviera and move back in with your folks. Or what it is like to be a guy a few years out of college still practicing field goals with your dad. They never talk about how life isn't fair, or how, no matter what happens, you keep showing up. Del will occasionally express displeasure with the Falcons for cutting his son, or with the NFL or USFL for not appreciating what a good kicker they passed up. And then Del and Scott will jog down the field to retrieve the half-dozen balls and stuff them into the sack and drag them back upfield and set 'em up again, five yards deeper. And when Scott's knee heels, they don't talk about how excited they are when the Bills invite him to camp. He is one of 10 kickers they're bringing in. That doesn't matter, Del tells him. You just keep showing up.

The weather in Buffalo drives other kickers mad, but it suits Norwood. The wind, the cold, the rain, the spartan practice facilities. But Norwood has been through worse. He's been cut, injured and overlooked, and compared with that, kicking in rain or a harsh wind blowing from the north is almost a pleasant diversion. He's comfortable with the elements, and from his career as a soccer player he knows how to control the ball in inclement weather, to keep it down in the wind, to improvise. The other kickers are cut, one by one, and finally Scott shows up and looks around the locker room one morning and he's the last kicker left.

Before you belittle the placekicker or make light of him as an athlete, ask yourself: Are you among the 28 best in the world at anything? Scott Norwood is in that exclusive club. In 1988, his fourth season with the Bills, he makes the Pro Bowl. In '89 he becomes the alltime leading scorer in Bills history, taking the record from O.J. Simpson. "I felt like I fit in to that team," Norwood recalls. "That's one of the special things about sports, the camaraderie." His teammates treat him not as a kicker but as a fellow football player. "Everybody looks at kickers as being a little sissy to a certain point," says quarterback Jim Kelly. "But Scott was one of us. He had that mean face, that linebacker face. I loved that guy."

The Bills are winning games, the division title and playoff games. Coach Marv Levy and general manager Bill Polian have assembled a remarkable group of football players, starting with Kelly, Thurman Thomas, Andre Reed, Bruce Smith and Cornelius Bennett and extending all the way to Norwood. He meets Kim Burch, a salesgirl in domestics at a J.C. Penney in Buffalo. She sells him bedding. She smiles. She is slender, strawberry blonde and beautiful. They are married three years later.

And still, Scott comes home, every off-season, though now he's driving a black Ford Bronco that he gets from a dealer in Virginia in exchange for a few ads and personal appearances. Do you know how good that feels, to get something just because you are you? A pro football player, a Pro Bowler, and you make six figures a year? You're on a winning team? You've married a beautiful woman?

Of course you don't. Very few of us do. But it feels like this: You are in the flow of life, not trying to wrestle it down or beat it into submission or twist it and forge it and shape it, but you are instead riding along and each bend or turn reveals a pleasant surprise. And still, Scott keeps coming home, to kick with his dad. Some of the commuters returning from Washington along Annandale Avenue point to the kicker on the grass and the older man holding the ball and say, See that guy? He's the kicker for the Buffalo Bills. And Scott could never imagine a time when that recognition, the same recognition that wins you free automobiles, could make it hard for you to leave your own house.

As the ball goes wide right, the instant it is passing the upright, before the official has even signaled, Kim is in the stands thinking, Oh, this is going to be tough for Scott. She has come to Tampa to watch the game with Del, Sandra and Scott's aunt and uncle, and all of them at that instant think some version of that same thought. Kim winds her way down the stands and into the tunnel and then around the stadium to the players' entrance, this petite bobbed blonde in a white sweater, slacks and pumps, darting between cursing Bills fans and elated New York Giants fans, wending through dense clusters of elation and despair as palpable as parade floats. She desperately wants to be there for Scott, to hold him and tell him that it will be O.K., that it was just a kick, that it's just a game, all things he knows, but in the aftermath of the biggest miss in Super Bowl history it might be easy for him to lose perspective.

She waits near the players' entrance—the wives are not allowed into the locker room—and she waits and she waits.

In the Buffalo locker room there is a mixture of anger, disbelief and confusion. The emotional rush of that last drive, in which Kelly took the Bills down to the 30-yard line with eight seconds left, was such that even after Norwood's miss it's hard for the players to absorb what has happened. Some of the Bills are still milling around near the coach or standing near the entrance, as if this is some sort of second halftime and the team will soon be going on to play a third half. Levy tells his team that he has never been more proud of any group of men, and that he could not have asked for anything more from his team—well-intentioned banalities that can't begin to heal the hurt. Then he surveys his team and watches as Reed begins to pull off his jersey and Kelly wipes his face with a towel. Levy wants to talk to his kicker. He finds Norwood and walks over to sit down with him on the wooden bench in front of his locker, between him and wide receiver Steve Tasker.

"I didn't know what to say to him," says Levy. "I was searching for words to buck him up, but I knew how he felt. We engineered that drive to get him in field goal range. It was a 47-yard kick off natural grass. Fewer than 50% of those are made. He had been such a great kicker for us over the years, and he won a few games for us with his leg, but you don't think about things like that at a time like that."

As Levy is trying to console his kicker, linebacker Darryl Talley and cornerback Nate Odomes approach Norwood and explain that if they had made a crucial tackle in the third quarter on a third-and-13 pass play, then the Bills would have never been in the position where they needed to make that kick. Then Reed comes over and says that if he had hung on to a few key passes in the second quarter, then the Bills could have put the Giants away. Teammate after teammate visits with Norwood and reinforces the message that this was a team loss. Fellow special teams player Tasker, who watches all this from his locker next to Norwood, recalls, "None of the players on that team blamed him. They knew you could take back any one play and the game might have been different."

Then the reporters are let into the locker room. They've rarely bothered to speak with Norwood. But today, of course, he is trapped in the incandescent TV lights and on the business end of three dozen microphones. His special teams coach, Bruce DeHaven, stands by him as he answers every single question from every single reporter. He will stay in the locker room a full hour after most of his teammates have gone. *How does it feel, Scott? Were you nervous? Did you feel like you hit it good? What are you going to do now? What do your teammates think? How does it feel to miss that kick and lose the Super Bowl?*

DeHaven asks him every few minutes, "Have you had enough? Do you want me to get rid of these guys?" And Scott shakes his head and replies, "I think I owe it to the fans to answer some questions."

Sports psychologists will tell you that openness is the first step to healing from this sort of loss. They use words like *process* and *grieving* and *cleansing*, but Scott just sees it as his duty. His father would simply call it showing up.

"The biggest thing about that kick," says Norwood, "was not how it impacted me, but how it let the team down. But I had prepared as well as I could. I had done the best I could. I could look at myself in the mirror."

In the 1998 film *Buffalo '66*, a placekicker named Scott Wood misses the field goal that costs Buffalo the Super Bowl. Billy, the character played by Vincent Gallo, loses a $10,000 bet on the game and comes to view the kicker as the cause of all his frustrations and shortcomings. He goes looking for the kicker, intending to murder him. In the movie the kicker in retirement becomes the owner of Scott Wood's Solid Gold Sexotic Dancers—a shirtless, sequined, bow-tie-wearing fat man who offers up naked women as a palliative for Buffalo residents devastated by his missed field goal.

Norwood was offered what he calls a "large sum" of money to play himself in *Buffalo '66*. He turned it down and says he has never seen the movie. "I think if he saw that film, he would be hurt by it," says Gallo, a Buffalo native. "I love Scott Norwood, but I used the kicker character because Scott became symbolic of all of Buffalo's problems." While there is no doubt that Buffalo fans suffered with Norwood after his kick, Buffalo is one of the few cities where Scott is remembered for the totality of his career and the great character he showed both before and after that Super Bowl. When he returned to Buffalo after the game and appeared at a post–Super Bowl rally, 25,000 fans showed up and cheered for Norwood almost as loudly as they did for Levy and Kelly, chanting, "We love Scott!" The fans understood, perhaps subconsciously, that Norwood's failure could become either an albatross or an opportunity, just as their city's rust-belt decline had prompted them to find hidden depths of character and strength.

"Scott Norwood is one of my three or four favorite Buffalo Bills," says Gallo, "because of what he went through." Buffalo has not won a major sports championship since 1965, the third-longest such streak of futility for any city that has at least two major sports franchises. (Only San Diego [1963] and Cleveland ['64] have suffered longer.) As Buffalo would return to three more Super Bowls in the greatest run of NFL title-game appearances since the Browns of the '50s and then get blown out each time, Norwood's wide right would take on even greater significance. It became clear those few feet between the ball and the right upright were as close as those Bills would ever get to a Super Bowl championship. "Look, a lot of things happened out there," says Scott. "A lot of other players didn't make plays, but that doesn't excuse me. I'm a player and I'm paid to perform, and I failed in that instance."

After the 1991 season the Bills sign a promising new kicker, Steve Christie of the Tampa Bay Buccaneers, and waive the 31-year-old Norwood. If he was not associated with that missed field goal, Scott believes, he would get a call from another team looking for a kicker. But the phone never rings. He no longer bothers to show up at the Washington-Lee High School field to practice his placekicks.

The first years out of football are the hardest. He refuses to discuss the Super Bowl with reporters, and when he returns to Fairfax County, he becomes almost a recluse, carefully avoiding the media. "An experience like that has to be a blow to his ego," says Kim, "and then he's out of football and he has to find his place. It was very hard for him to talk about it." Scott retreats into his family, moving into a house with Kim in Clifton, Va., near his parents. He goes hunting with Del and Steve, the three of them heading out to Kmart before every deer season, buying ammunition and camping equipment, new boots and camouflage vests before setting out for Long Island, off the coast of Maine, where Del has hunted since he was a boy. They seldom shoot at anything, the three of them, instead taking long walks through the wilderness. Del doesn't really like the act of killing deer, but the ritual of pitching tents, setting up camp, making a fire and spending time with his boys in the woods keeps him coming back season after season. The laconic talk around the fire is reassuring to Scott, the crackle of burning wood and the chirping of crickets an aural reminder that life still has meaning and purpose and fine moments.

Scott seeks to put his business degree to work selling insurance, mortgages, annuities and trusts. It's hard work, especially the cold-calling, having to dial his way through a list of phone numbers every day and say, "Hi, I'm Scott Norwood, and I have a great opportunity today for you to take care of your family." It takes weeks and months of cajoling to get a prospective policy buyer or annuity purchaser to write that check. For the first time in his life, he finds that just showing up isn't enough.

Everywhere they go, to movie theaters, to doctor's offices, to restaurants, Scott knows what everyone is thinking: *He's the guy who missed.* "I would try to talk to him about other things," Steve says, "but you just knew it was on his mind."

"I saw him working through it," says Sandra. "He would come and tell me, 'This is real tough for me, but I'll get through it.' And we would all tell him, 'Scott, it's football. There are other things out there in life.'"

Scott wants children, suspects that he may find some distraction in the richness of family life, but there, too, he is disappointed as he and Kim struggle to conceive. "They had some problems having kids," explains Steve. "Who knows; maybe that was related to all that stress?" There are moments when, after returning home from work, he confides to his wife that he doesn't understand why he has been put on this particular path. Why should this have happened to him? And Kim stops him right there and says, "Look, life is full of so many different moments—yes, that was awful what happened—but you were an All-Pro. If someone said, 'We'll take back that kick, but you also have to lose everything you accomplished in football,' would you do it? No way. So you take the good with the bad, only our bad is just really, really bad."

But the good is so very, very good. Twins, Carly and Connor, are born in 1995, and then Corey is born in '96. Still, this healing is a gradual process. The missed kick appears in his consciousness at odd times, and suddenly, in the middle of a phone conversation, *wide right* will replay itself, and every time it is a sickening moment. Then, over a few seasons—but he no longer calls them seasons; they're years now—thanks to the continued good health of his children and the love of his wife and family, he begins to understand that without that failure, that defeat, he might not have everything he now has. It is an obvious truth but one that comes to him with a most unlikely feeling: gratitude.

"I like the people we've become," he tells his wife at one point, not smugly, but in wonder. How can you measure the health and happiness of three beautiful children against a field goal? Three kids versus three points? "If everything always worked out for you, then you don't have that sense of appreciation," Norwood says. "You can always think you understand what it means to have things not work out, but until you live it, you don't really know."

Scott dusts off his Pro Bowl jersey and has it framed, along with a complete set of his football cards, over the big screen RCA in his wood-paneled den. There's a leather sofa and two chairs, and a desk with a computer where sometimes, in the evening, after he and Kim have gotten the kids bathed and into bed, he will sit and listen to the house settle and consider his future. Everyone seems to be buying, selling, moving. There's a real estate boom afoot, every baby boomer in America seems to be in escrow, making a bid, securing a second mortgage, adding on, remodeling, and he thinks maybe that's for him. He likes the implied optimism of offering people a stake, rather than the pessimism of selling insurance or annuities. Through a friend, a Bills fan, he hears about an opening and then, just like that, he leaves his career in financial planning in 2002 and joins Re/Max, the real estate brokerage.

Stolid and squinty-eyed, he makes an unlikely real estate agent. You arrive at an open house, you don't expect the kicker who missed in the Super Bowl. But years have passed, and now those who don't remember or who never knew outnumber those who do, and even for those who recall the missed kick, it is no longer a source of embarrassment or disappointment but rather a curiosity, like finding an old letter from a girl you once liked but thought you'd completely forgotten. In this housing market, though, in this era of low interest rates and buoyant real estate prices, there is room for even a taciturn, thoughtful broker in his little Chevy Prism. He's not a great financial success, but he has a feeling that things are about to turn around. A few more listings, another handful of referrals. Every day potential buyers are calling him, and he takes them out in the Prism and shows them properties, a few listings south of Clifton, a new development out in Chantilly. And when he talks about life, he nods and leans forward a little, because he is now looking ahead, not back.

Del stands by him, recognizing that his son is finally getting over the missed kick, but he never mentions it, that's not his way. He takes the grandchildren to Orioles and Redskins games, begins to teach and coach them the way he taught and coached his own children. And he can take pride in the man his son is today, a fellow who keeps showing up. It is a tribute to the closeness of the family that all three siblings, Sandra, Steve and Scott, settle within 20 miles of the Annandale home in which they grew up and where Del and his wife Anne still live. Del, at 74, drives himself to ball games, and on a humid July night arrives early at Camden Yards to watch the Orioles take batting practice. After the game, as he's cruising home on the beltway, heading south into the suburban incandescence of Fairfax

County, his black Maxima rear-ends a tow truck, stopped in the fast lane without hazard or brake lights. Del dies on impact.

Scott gets the call from Steve the next morning. He gets dressed and heads to his mom's house in Annandale. "That's a lot harder than any missed kick," Scott says. "You realize what matters pretty quickly."

Norwood lines up for the kick with just a few seconds left. The rest of the team is gathered on the sidelines, holding hands, panting, exhausted. The gray-haired coach kneels down, watching with squinted eyes. The kicker stands in place for a moment, at an angle to the ball, and then charges, putting cleated foot to the ball and sending it soaring over the defense.

The Boomerangs have managed to salvage a tie, and Carly Norwood, who takes many of her team's free kicks, runs off the field as dad, assistant coach Scott Norwood, scratches his chin and worries that he didn't evenly divide the playing time. It's hard keeping the nine-year-old soccer players shuttling on and off the field, and often he'll forget to remove a girl who has been in for a while. Parents can usually be counted on to complain if their daughters have been out for too long, but sometimes even they lose track. The scarlet-uniformed Boomerangs gather around for their "two-four-six-eight, who do we appreciate" chant, and then Scott and Kim and the rest of the parents join hands in a tunnel as the girls run through. Several other children join in and run through after the team, and there is some discussion among the players about whether the tunnel is actually more fun than the game.

A few yards away from the sidelines, Connor and Corey are playing in the shade of a crab tree, the purple blossoms taking flight from the boughs in the spring air and wafting across the field to where Scott and the rest of the parents are gathering cones and coolers. These are the games that represent, somehow, American sport at its best. Of course we are a million miles from the sleek arenas and enormo-domes of big-time professional sports, but this Southeastern Youth Soccer league game is part of a cultural continuum connected to those playoff games and Super Bowls, and no one knows both ends of that spectrum better than Scott Norwood. And he will tell you that these sweet afternoons coaching kids or playing pickup soccer are the soul of our athletic obsession, the part that all of us can and do share. And as Corey runs up to Scott and tells him that some kid named Hunter just hit him—"Then don't play with Hunter anymore," is Scott's answer—he thinks about what he had to endure just to get here, with all the rest of us, coaching our kids on a Saturday afternoon.

American sports, Scott will tell you, will break your heart. But they will also, in their most basic form, nurture your soul. He thinks about Del, and about showing up. That's how you really win in life. Not by kicking Super Bowl–winning field goals or covering yourself in glory, but by showing up. And as you look at this life, at Carly sipping from a juice box as Kim braids her hair and Connor and Cory climbing all over Scott as he walks in his steady gait toward the family's Plymouth Voyager, you think, *I know this guy. He's sort of like me.*

The children draw pictures. Crude, stick-figure football players in navy-blue-and-white jerseys and Crayola crimson helmets—the kids find it difficult to render the Bills' charging buffalo logo—in field goal formation. The holder kneeling down. The kicker following through. And in these revisionist drawings by Carly, Connor or Corey Norwood, the kick is never wide right. It is always straight down the middle. It is always good. They represent a portal into one possible alternate universe. A *Mr. Destiny* retake in which the goat becomes the hero, the failure a success.

The pictures are a jumping-off point for a thousand what-might-have-been conversations, thoughts and musings on how the life of the Norwoods could have been different if Scott had made that kick in Super Bowl XXV. Kim sits the kids down and says to them, "It's all right that your father missed that kick. Your dad went out there and did his best—and sometimes, even when you do your best, things don't work out. And you know what?" She looks at each of them.

Three expectant faces gaze back.

She smiles. "That can be O.K., too."

DECEMBER 11, 2017

The Kap Effect

Yes, the QB took a stand by kneeling. But just as important: he pledged $1 million to the issues that drove him to protest. A close examination of how Kaepernick has given that money away—and to whom—reveals a blueprint for real social change

BY GREG BISHOP AND BEN BASKIN

Kevin Livingston was driving home with his daughter when he received a random call one Saturday morning last April: Colin Kaepernick has something for you. How far away are you?

Livingston runs a charity, 100 Suits for 100 Men, that provides business attire for job seekers who have recently been released from jail or suffered hardship, and after he dropped off his daughter, he raced to the Queens parole office, where he keeps a desk. Kaepernick was waiting for him in his SUV, where he'd been sitting for almost an hour. The QB stepped out wearing lime-green sneakers and a black T-shirt emblazoned with a panther, lugging two overstuffed cardboard boxes toward a glass door marked STAFF ONLY. He opened a box, pulled out a gray, custom-made three-piece suit, draped a striped tie over the jacket and posed for a few cellphone pics, flashing a smile. One of those photos became an Instagram post, and that post went viral.

The visit marked a rare public sighting for a man defined by contradictions: a quarterback, just four years removed from a Super Bowl appearance, who can't land an NFL roster spot. An activist who has rarely spoken publicly. An athlete who ranks among the most divisive and socially conscious figures in sports. Anyone who wondered what Kaepernick had been up to caught a glimpse that day, but little more. No one saw what happened next.

Of the dozens of suits Kaepernick delivered—some new, some his own—the one in the photo wound up with 26-year-old Mario Lloyde, who had been living month-to-month with his girlfriend in a cramped Baltimore apartment, unable to get more than a temporary gig as a file clerk at a hospital or a cashier at a bookstore. "I was trying to get into real estate," he says, "but I had to dress the part."

The first time Lloyde put on that suit, he says he "felt like Superman." A month later he walked into the offices of Vision Realty Management, where—he swears this to be true—the first thing his interviewer said was, "Well, you already completed step one: You look nice."

Lloyde got the gig, became a full-time clerk and is now studying to become a licensed broker. He also found that suit life suits him well. He has bought nine more ensembles—but nothing that tops the first. "When I put on [that original]," he says, "I feel like I'm representing on behalf of Colin Kaepernick."

That's how Kaepernick, 30, speaks these days: through this kind of work, and then through those he touches. He's the most prominent athlete activist in decades and is close to fulfilling his pledge to donate $1 million to dozens of charities. Much has been made about his choice not to comment on the legions of NFL players protesting during the national anthem—a movement he began last year, kneeling to draw attention to issues like police brutality and racial inequality—or to challenge President Donald Trump's portrayal of his kneeling as unpatriotic. Instead he stays up late, on his laptop, Googling charitable organizations.

Kaepernick declined to comment for this story. But the key information—what, specifically, his donations go toward—is readily available on his website. And yet an odd notion festers, in part because Kaepernick has not addressed one question, the answer to which is both simple and incredibly complex: What, exactly, are you doing to fight for the causes to which you have drawn so much attention?

Much more than one might think.

On Oct. 5, Kaepernick pulled up to DREAM, an East Harlem charter school, where officials whisked him through a back door. He wore a black T-shirt that read I KNOW MY RIGHTS as he strolled through halls decorated with relevant questions painted in red and white: WHAT STORY DO YOUR ACTIONS TELL? WHO ARE YOU GOING TO IMPACT TODAY?

In the front row of the auditorium 14-year-old Kassim Samassi says he sat "hyperventilating" in anticipation. A month earlier he and his ninth-grade classmates had been assigned to read Ta-Nehisi Coates's *Between the World and Me*, an exploration of the nation's racial history, and they had found similarities between Coates's message and Kaepernick's protest. "As a person of color, when you see inequality and police brutality [against minorities], you feel like you don't belong in this world," Kassim says. "And Kaepernick is standing up for all of us."

DREAM's ninth-graders are divided into houses—not unlike Hogwarts, except that here each house is named after an influential American minority. Kassim belongs to the Toni Morrison House, but he foresees a day when there may be one named after Kaepernick as well.

The quarterback's relationship with DREAM began before he ever knelt or pledged a penny. His girlfriend of two years, Nessa Diab, has spoken in the past with the school's female students about self-esteem and body image, and for several years has emceed their Diamond Ball fund-raiser. Kaepernick made a quiet guest appearance at that event in 2015, during a 49ers bye week.

Even with that existing relationship, the QB kept a typically high level of involvement this fall, taking multiple phone calls with the foundation's development group before granting them $25,000 and earmarking much of the money toward college- and career-readiness programs. And in November, 54 DREAM students visited SUNY-Albany, marking the first trip to a college for most of them. Included in that group: Kassim, who wants to attend Stanford and become a software engineer.

The man who enabled those aspirations showed up in Harlem that Thursday in October, flanked only by Diab—no camera crew, no publicist. More than 100 students lined the school's gym in folding chairs as Kaepernick spoke for 45 minutes, mostly answering questions. How does it feel to be at the origin of controversy? What are the specific reasons you decided to protest?

Kaepernick's answers focused on the importance of 1) being "just in unjust places" and 2) confronting "ignorance not with ignorance, but with education." Toward the end, one student asked, Why is it important for you to stand up for a greater cause, even though you lost your fame and fortune?

Here Kaepernick selected two kids from the audience and brought them up front. "If you," he said to one of them, "saw him," he pointed to the other, "sucker punch someone, and I offered you $20 not to tell anyone, what are you going to do?"

Kaepernick answered his own question. "No matter what I have to sacrifice," he told the students, "if you see wrong in the world, you must say that it is wrong."

Rupa Marya grew up in a 49ers household, but she was never a football fan. For years she waited for prominent athletes to use their platform to address the issues she's devoted her career to fighting—police violence and racism. Then Kaepernick came along. Last August, Marya, 42, wrote a letter to the QB, praising his bravery. She invited him to meet with her fellow volunteers at the Do No Harm Coalition, a San Francisco–based group of 300-plus public health and medical professionals who, rightfully, treat racism and violence as public health emergencies. Forty doctors signed the letter, which ended, "We would like to welcome you into our ranks as a healer."

Marya's still not sure whether Kaepernick saw that note, which she blasted across social media. But a few months later he pledged $50,000 to DNH's Mni Wiconi Health Clinic Partnership, a free clinic being built on the Standing Rock reservation in the Dakotas.

The Lakota Dakota people suffer from a host of ailments at strikingly high rates—from diabetes to depression—and while the main Mni Wiconi clinic will sit on a permanent site, there are remote areas across the 8,000-square-mile reservation that lack resources. Kaepernick focused his support on the creation of a mobile health clinic that will make weekly rounds and deliver medications.

At first glance that donation might seem misaligned with issues like police brutality and racial inequality, but Marya sees the connection. The Lakota Dakota people were one of the fiercest resisters of westward expansion, which she calls the first act of white supremacy in America, and they've faced long-lasting consequences. Today the youth attempted-suicide rate among Oglala Lakota, one of seven Lakota subtribes, is more than seven times the national average.

Kaepernick's Mni Wiconi donation speaks both to the specific nature and the wide breadth of his support. Between October 2016 and December '17 he doled out 31 grants and $900,000 (with $100,000 to be distributed by year's end). He has chosen organizations in big cities (New York, L.A., Chicago) and small ones (Fayetteville, N.C.; Lithonia, Ga.), and he stood behind causes that ranged from police reform to climate change to the need for organic ingredients in community cooking workshops.

In January, Nancy Northup, CEO of the Center for Reproductive Rights, received $25,000 to help finance her outfit's emergency litigation fund, which was created after Donald Trump won the presidency on an anti-abortion platform. (CRR's litigation team, for example, would fight to ensure Planned Parenthood funding.) Northup was initially surprised by that donation—then she, too, saw the connection. "What he's really taking a stance for," she says, "is human rights and equality and fairness and making sure that everybody gets a shot."

Cat Collins, in his role as an informal adviser, helps Kaepernick connect with his charitable partners, and last May he emailed the Arizona office of the American Friends Service Committee, a 100-year-old Quaker organization that advocates for ending mass incarceration. When program director Caroline Isaacs got that email, she reacted as many do when they hear from a stranger with a simple question: If Colin Kaepernick gave you $25,000, what would you do with it? She thought it was a prank. This, roughly, is Step 1 for every Kaepernick donation: the random reach-out.

After that email exchange Isaacs skipped into her office in Tucson. "Colin Kaepernick might be interested in funding us!" she breathlessly told her colleagues. Next she would have to lay out exactly how they'd use the money. Step 2. (Some groups are asked to submit short bullet-pointed proposals; many recount Collins saying, "Keep it simple—and, for the love of God, no PowerPoints!")

Collins and Isaacs lobbed ideas back and forth. He asked if the AFSC needed a van; it didn't. She wanted to film promotional videos; Kaepernick's team felt that was too much like marketing. Eventually they focused on the AFSC's program called Reframing Justice, run by Grace Gamez, which aims to give voice to the formerly incarcerated and ease their transition back into society. Perfect, Collins said.

A week or two later Isaacs's cellphone lit up with text messages. "Holy s---," one read, "we got the Kap money!" Her colleagues had found out on Twitter. Step 3. "It's like we won the lottery," Isaacs says.

Step 4: Spend the money. Gamez decided to hire Glenn Martin, the founder of JustLeadershipUSA, which is trying to cut the U.S. prison population in half by 2030. Martin runs expensive seminars where he trains former inmates (and other volunteers) to assist current convicts in transitioning out of prison. Gamez hopes to bring Martin to Arizona next spring for a session in front of as many as 100 AFSC employees and volunteers. If not for Kaepernick's money, Gamez says, she likely could have sent just one person to the same seminar.

Step 5: Impact. In 2010, Joe Watson was sentenced to 12 years in prison following a string of robberies. Inside, he wrote articles for *Prison Legal News*, and in that work he came across the AFSC. When he was granted early release this year, he volunteered for the outfit, eventually becoming a contracted staff member, and now he'll attend Martin's training session, paid for by Kaepernick.

When Watson recently praised Kaepernick on Facebook, an old prison buddy who'd also served in the U.S. Army commented. "Why do you support him? What does he do for his community?"

"Well, funny you should ask ..." Watson began.

As Kaepernick knelt during the anthem throughout the 2016 season, Adam Jackson, the CEO of a grassroots Baltimore-based think tank, tweeted, "Noble ... Just hope [he] invests money in black people."

Jackson thought back to that post when Collins called in April. He, too, wondered at first if he was being punked. Instead, Jackson submitted a short proposal, then opened the mail one day and there it was: a $25,000 check.

Jackson's subsequent experience embodies the methodology behind Kaepernick's pledges. Leaders of a Beautiful Struggle, Jackson's seven-year-old organization, advocates on behalf of black Baltimoreans. In this case Kaepernick and Jackson decided to apply the donation to LBS's youth development programs, which train high school students in advocacy and activism. "In the black community," Jackson says, "we don't have enough voices that are of and from here to speak for ourselves in terms of [policy making]."

Kaepernick's work, he argues, is fundamentally different from typical celebrity philanthropy, starting with Kaepernick's view of donations as investments, not just charity. Crucial, too, are the targets (mostly minority-led, grassroots organizations based in communities impacted by the issues he supports) and the intent (resources, infrastructure, trainees who become trainers) of his contributions. What the QB's not doing: feeding large corporate entities (say, March of Dimes) who Jackson says "are basically hustling off suffering poor people and black folks."

Beyond the cash influx, Jackson points out, Kaepernick's backing can serve as affirmation of the work done by a smaller organization, like his, which makes it easier to obtain further donations, then invest in more infrastructure and so on.

If all athletes took such a specific, targeted approach to their charitable endeavors, Jackson says, they could affect immediate structural change in their communities. "They all tweet, they talk, they wear T-shirts—and that's cool," he says. "But that's cultural. And cultural change can go but so far.

"The purpose of protest is to change the environment that gives everyone else permission not to care about these issues. If there were 100 Colin Kaepernicks—or 2,000!—then you'd be talking about a real social movement.

"Just kneeling," he says, "is a cop-out."

Barbara Fuller isn't interested enough in football (or politics) to have noticed when Kaepernick announced on March 1 that he was opting out of his contract with the 49ers. Besides, Fuller had spent the majority of her 86 years across the Bay, near the Oakland Coliseum, as the matriarch of a family steeped in Raiders fandom. The news that caught her attention came two weeks later, when President Trump announced his Skinny Budget proposal. That plan (which, ultimately, never made it past the House) called for the elimination of the $3 billion Community Development Block Grant program, a financial feeder for programs such as Meals on Wheels, which delivers food to at-risk seniors. Such organizations, Trump's budget director noted, "sound good but don't show results."

Tell that to Fuller, a retired special education teacher of 46 years who eats more healthily and on a regular schedule through the program, which keeps her food costs down, helping her afford her house in an otherwise unaffordable neighborhood. "I felt angry," she says. "I worked until I was 74, and now that I'm old enough to qualify, the program is going to end?"

There was no TV interview, no ribbon-cutting when, one week later, Kaepernick donated $50,000 to Meals on Wheels. Just a bank transfer. While Kaepernick's charitable aims are not overtly political, they have been colored and driven by the current presidency. In this case his donation was a direct response to the announcement by the President, who one day earlier had stomped deeper into the Kaepernick fray, giddily telling a Louisville rally that the QB hadn't yet found a team because NFL owners "don't want to get a nasty tweet from Donald Trump."

The next afternoon Mary Gregory, the director of development for SOS Meals on Wheels in Oakland, was out delivering food with the city's mayor when she received an unexpected phone call. The organization had seen an uptick in volunteers following the White House announcement, but not an influx in cash—and now her superiors were telling her that Kaepernick wanted his $50,000 earmarked for Oakland residents. Like Fuller.

Kaepernick's money would go toward everything from raw ingredients to packaging to fuel for delivery trucks. And while others could continue to ignore the work he was doing, that was no longer the case for Gregory. She sees hypocrisy in NFL teams and fan bases that want players to appear charitable—visiting sick children in hospitals, for instance, or cutting ribbons at community center openings—but not actually jump into the fray themselves, especially on thornier issues. Kaepernick's work directly impacts the Barbara Fullers of the East Bay. SOS Meals on Wheels had introduced her to vegetables she'd never heard of; she even came to love couscous. Weren't those direct results?

Says Fuller, "I'm praying for Colin Kaepernick."

Clinton Allen loved football. Two of his uncles played in the NFL, and he grew up obsessing over the Cowboys, working into conversation the names of long-ago stars like (Bullet) Bob Hayes and Drew Pearson. Outside of his team he admired Jim Brown and, in boxing, Muhammad Ali, athletes who stood for racial equality decades before Kaepernick ever knelt.

But in March 2013, when Allen was 25, he was shot and killed by a Dallas police officer. The details of that night remain disputed—the possible presence of drugs in Allen's system, the seemingly high number of gunshots fired—but the incident followed a familiar pattern: an altercation, two drastically different versions of events, another young black man dead ... and no indictment.

When Kaepernick first took a knee, he clearly (and later frequently) noted the reason for his protest: to draw attention to police brutality and the need for reform. That act meant even more to Collette Flanagan, Allen's mother, than did the $25,000 he donated to Mothers Against Police Brutality, the organization she started in her son's honor. It has pained her to see Trump and other detractors misrepresent the quarterback's initial intentions, to see the meaning of his kneeling shift beneath him. Kaepernick's protest was never about the military or the flag, as the President has suggested. It was always about injustice, specifically young black men being killed. Men like her son.

As the 2017 season unfolded and Jerry Jones, the owner of Allen's favorite team, demanded that Cowboys players stand for the anthem, Flanagan noticed how police brutality no longer seemed like part of the conversation. When players and owners across the league locked arms on the weekend of Sept. 24, it felt, she says, like a sanitized, gentrified version of Kaepernick's original protest. The impact was less powerful for that very palatability.

"I don't think Colin has lost focus," she says. "Everyone else has, so they can get comfortable. I hear all these crazy things, like 'He was [kneeling] for attention.' Who in the world would want that kind of attention? That's like saying I wanted to be in this club of mothers whose sons were killed."

Kaepernick has gone out of his way to maximize the impact of his philanthropy in a manner that garners minimal attention. He has mostly avoided large organizations. He has empowered those in need, providing them with the infrastructure and the means to build on that momentum. He has stood with those who fight against all varieties of injustice.

Only a scant few of those people who have benefited from Kaepernick's donations have ever met him. Mostly he speaks with the money he gives and the approach he takes to giving. While legions of people argue about his kneeling and whether that disrespects the military, Kaepernick has focused on the issues he originally fought for, using his own money even while remaining unemployed.

Colin Kaepernick may never again play football, but as he has fulfilled his pledge he has said nothing and he has said everything, all at once.

MAY 9, 2017

'I Feel Lost. I Feel Like a Child.'

Nick Buoniconti was the heart of the 1972 Dolphins' perfect defense and a leader in raising awareness about spinal injuries after his son was paralyzed. Now the game appears to be taking its toll on him, and he's being pulled in every direction by doctors and family who disagree about what to do next

BY S.L. PRICE

"Teddy!" Nick Buoniconti yells across the lobby of The Inn at Spanish Bay, near Pebble Beach, Calif.

It is a November Sunday in 2016, past twilight. The Hall of Fame linebacker, 75 but only slightly bent, is sitting with his wife, Lynn. The fresh faces behind the front desk don't know Buoniconti; it has been 44 years since he co-captained the Dolphins to three straight Super Bowl seasons, including the league's only undefeated campaign, in 1972. He's not alone: Two dozen greats from the '70s, '80s and '90s are here, wandering through the lobby toward the ballroom for the 26th annual Legends Invitational dinner.

In the next few hours a roster of venerables—Paul Warfield, Jan Stenerud, Jim Hart—will each utter a small shock at being remembered at all. This will at first seem odd, but it makes sense once they speak of how they missed out on free agency, or spent years fighting the league for better pensions, or are scrambling now to hack through the thicket of the NFL's $1 billion concussion lawsuit settlement.

"Teddy!" Buoniconti yells again, and over comes Ted Hendricks, 69, along with his longtime partner, Linda Babl. Hendricks, the 6'7" linebacker, played 15 years in the NFL, partied epically and never missed a game. Nick and Lynn stand. "How are you doing, Teddy?" Lynn asks.

"Good," says Ted, grinning. At that, Buoniconti unleashes a deep sigh, one so operatic that at first it seems involuntary; but later, after spending hours with him, one comes to know it as his fallback signal of dismay and, quite often, a looming explosion. Linda's head pivots.

"How've *you* been?" she says.

Buoniconti doesn't explain that he can't figure out how to knot a tie or towel his back. He doesn't speak of his increasingly useless left hand, the increasingly frequent trips to the emergency room or how, just a few days earlier, he hurtled backward down a staircase and sprayed blood all over the hardwood, screaming afterward at Lynn, "I should just kill myself! It doesn't matter!"

"You know," Buoniconti says.

And he's right. Like most everyone who's close to a former NFL player, Linda is living some variation of the same story. They've all seen the big-budget concussion movie and the news clips; they've read about the deaths of Junior Seau and Dave Duerson; they're comparing notes on Facebook about the damage caused by repeated head trauma. They study their men. They accompany them to brain studies and name-drop superstar CTE researchers.

"We went to see Dr. [Julian] Bailes last month," Linda says. "He's really impressive, as far as one-to-one."

Buoniconti releases another sigh.

It's so random. Hendricks has only minor memory lapses. Some of Buoniconti's Dolphins teammates, meanwhile, are crumbling. Quarterback Earl Morrall, the supersub so key to the Perfect Season, died at 79, in 2014, with Stage 4 CTE. Running back Jim Kiick, 70, lived in squalor until he was institutionalized last summer with dementia/early onset Alzheimer's. Bill Stanfill, a defensive end who long suffered from dementia, died in November at 69.

"Everybody's searching," Buoniconti says. "Some go to North Carolina, some to BU, some to UCLA. And it's all related. That's why it's so unnecessary, what the NFL is putting players through, making us document the neurological deficiencies. Not everybody can afford to go through that. And they say they'll pay for it—but do you know what that's like, actually getting the money?"

Ted and Linda leave for the ballroom. Nick and Lynn sit. Hall of Fame Vikings defensive end Chris Doleman stops by. He talks about how even the most familiar routines have become confounding, how he wakes up in his own bed wondering, Am I in a hotel? "And I'm 55," he says.

"At 55, I was very normal," Buoniconti says. "I'm not normal anymore."

This is hard, at times, to believe. Everyone tells Nick he looks "great." Indeed, he'll soon get up before a packed room and emcee the night's program, tick off the names of every cohost, sponsor and speaker, tell war stories. But few saw Buoniconti teeter as he walked off the stage, perhaps because of the atrophy to his right frontal cortex. Fewer noticed Nick motioning for Lynn as he bolted from the room, perhaps because of his neurodegenerative dementia, or the yet-unspoken opinion that his condition could actually be corticobasal syndrome, complicated by an atypical Parkinsonian syndrome or CTE or Alzheimer's. He had to pee. And Lynn had to stand by to unbutton and unzip him and ensure that he'd emerge from the men's room dry and unexposed.

And no one here saw him before all that, when Buoniconti stood up in the lobby and headed toward the ballroom. "I feel lost," he said. "I feel like a child."

It's forever easy to think Miami's top industry, after tourism, boils down to the cliché of political chicanery, petty vanities and believe-it-or-not news stories (FLORIDA MAN ARRESTED WITH ALLIGATOR IN HIS BACKPACK) that continue to make Carl Hiaasen and Dave Barry very rich. Few fly into MIA expecting gravitas. Yet, of course, serious work goes on here. After a helmet-first tackle in 1985 made a quadriplegic of Buoniconti's son Marc, a linebacker at The Citadel, Nick teamed up with University of Miami neurosurgeon Barth Green to cofound the Miami Project to Cure Paralysis, leveraging every angle of his celebrity to raise $2 million in year one. By '90 the Project was well on its way to becoming the world's largest center for spinal cord-injury and paralysis research, one of South Florida's few civic anchors.

Much of that was due to Nick's backstory. The Dolphins' 1972 and '73 titles command unique reverence as the fractured region's first. And Marc's paralysis, widely covered in the media, lent Nick's fame horrific depth; he became an unwilling model for life after the cheering stops and was accorded universal respect, even awe, for enduring what seemed an unending penance.

For though Marc became the Miami Project's face, it was Nick who provided the indefatigable fuel for a money engine—the Buoniconti Fund—that has now raised more than $450 million, pays the salaries of 300 scientists and staff, and provides hope and comfort to thousands. Year after year, it was always Nick recruiting doctors, cajoling athletes to attend the

Project's annual New York City gala, making call after call on a mission that, on a personal level at least, seemed doomed.

"I would trade this [Super Bowl] ring in, and all my individual accomplishments, if one thing could happen in my lifetime," Nick said to conclude his Pro Football Hall of Fame induction speech, in 2001. "My son Marc dreams that he walks. And as a father, I would like nothing more than to walk by his side."

The ironic tragedy—that the very game which made Nick's name also destroyed his son—became South Florida lore: how his first wife, Terry (Marc's mother), pleaded with Marc's older brother, Nick III, to cut short his career at Duke rather than risk facing another devastating blow. How, consumed by guilt, Nick once threatened to wrench off his Perfect Season ring and never wear it again. When Terry divorced Nick in 1997 after 35 years together, the news went notably uncovered; no one, it seemed, had the stomach for what seemed the last casualty of Marc's collision, even if Nick didn't publicly indulge any narrative connecting the events or guilt. "I never blamed myself," Buoniconti told me when we first met in 2009, ring still on his hand. "I never blamed football."

No, Nick saw Marc's fate as a lightning-bolt rarity, a freak event. Conceding the irony of his family's relationship with the game is one thing—"Our greatest joy and greatest sadness, *right*"—but condemning football as inherently destructive was always something else. Wasn't he himself proof otherwise?

Few longtime players emerged from the NFL fray more spectacularly intact. After retirement in 1976, Buoniconti went on to hit a pinnacle in three more careers: attorney and agent for 30 pro athletes; millionaire president of U.S. Tobacco; cohost for 23 years on HBO's *Inside the NFL*. In 2009, when I met him to write a Sports Illustrated piece on Marc, Nick was humming along with number 4, the Miami Project. He was 68, looked 15 years younger, played golf daily; he and Lynn lived in a $1.98 million home in Coral Gables. He sat on the terrace of his nearby country club, dynamic and bluntly eloquent. People kept stopping to say hello.

The family liked the story, but I didn't speak to Nick again. Then, last October, he left a phone message. Nick, his words slightly halting, asked me to call him back and recited his number. "O.K.," he said. "Goodbye."

Then came a long pause. You could hear him turn away from the phone. Finally Buoniconti asked, "How do you hang up, Lynn?"

Her voice, quavering, rose in disbelief. "How do you *hang up*?" Lynn called from the background.

"Yeah."

Then the line went dead.

Was there ever a more American life? Was there ever more reason for a man to be happy? Nick Buoniconti, born in 1940 the grandson of Italian immigrants, was raised in Springfield, Mass., by loving parents, surrounded by countless relatives, enveloped in the scent of fresh bread. He came of age in a U.S. rising to world dominance and lived out its favorite narrative: Forever underestimated, time and again he proved all doubters wrong.

But Buoniconti wasn't light of heart. Even at his warmest he possessed a hard, judgmental eye, wary of depending on anyone. Maybe that came from being a baker's boy, ambitious in a home with no money for college. Or maybe it went deeper; his mother, Patsy, was a Mercolino, the Neapolitan family line streaked with a dark certitude: *Life is out to get you.* And wasn't it? Nick nearly drowned at two, fell out of a moving car at three and survived scarlet fever at eight. At 12, when the school year ended, he worked the tobacco fields in draining heat for $6 a day.

Sure, for a six-year altar boy, the pride of the nuns at Cathedral High, Buoniconti's ascension to play football at Notre Dame in 1958 seemed the apex of Catholic dreams. But disillusion came fast. An all-state outfielder, Nick loved baseball like his dad, Big Nick, who'd pitched semipro all over New England. Notre Dame lured young Nick with the promise that he could play baseball, too. But upon arrival, Buoniconti found he was there for football, period. "Notre Dame lied to me," he says.

No wonder that, compared to headhunting peers like Dick Butkus, Buoniconti always came off as strictly business. Buoniconti was the only player to survive telling Dolphins coach Don Shula, in front of the team, to "shut the f--- up." Shula bristled, but he respected it: Buoniconti was rushing to a teammate's defense. He didn't do anything for effect. He couldn't afford to. This was an All-America who, after Irish coach Joe Kuharich dubbed him too small to play pro ball, had been humiliatingly ignored by the NFL and passed over in the first 12 rounds of the upstart AFL's draft.

Buoniconti, at 215 pounds, played guard and linebacker during one of Notre Dame's worst eras and seemed a Fighting Irish epitome—pious, macho, consumed by football. But he wasn't. Irked freshman year by his boring quarterback roommate, Buoniconti kicked him out and moved in with newfound pal Richie Catenacci, a 5'4" civilian. Told by the dean of men, a priest, that he was breaking Notre Dame's long tradition of housing athletes together, Nick dug in. "The rule is stupid," he said.

As a pro, opponents sniffed at Buoniconti's size, compared him to a fire hydrant, even if he led the Patriots in tackles and interceptions during his seven seasons there. Nick didn't care. "When Butkus hits you, you fall the way *he* wants," he said. "When I hit you, you fall the way *you* want. But you still fall."

Such satisfactions went only so far. He married his high school sweetheart, Terry Salamano, his rookie year, and it quickly became clear that his $15,000 salary was never going to be enough. In 1963, Terry had Gina, the first of three quick babies, and Nick enrolled at Boston's Suffolk Law School, racing to courses at night, briefing cases on road trips, studying while teammates partied. He finished in four years. "I didn't care for football," he says. "I was tired of it."

Buoniconti didn't know it then, but such is the secret of all good negotiators: He could walk away. He had just signed a lease to open a law office in Chestnut Hill when the Patriots traded him to the hapless Dolphins before the 1969 season. Miami owner Joe Robbie was a famous skinflint; Nick, acting as his own agent, demanded double his pay, guaranteed. "We don't give guaranteed contracts," Robbie said. Buoniconti sent his retirement papers to the NFL. Robbie tried holding firm, but—even with the law practice stalled and his only alternative a $10,000 job at the U.S. attorney's office—Nick wouldn't budge. "It really didn't matter to me if I retired," Buoniconti says. "I didn't care."

Robbie folded. Buoniconti was named the Dolphins' MVP his first season and, after Shula took over, again when they improved from three to 10 wins in 1970. In '71, with Buoniconti the hub of the defense, Miami surrendered just 12.4 points a game and blanked the defending champ Colts in the AFC title game. By then the assault on Buoniconti's body and brain was well under way. He says he was knocked unconscious four or five times over his 14-year career, the worst during the Cowboys' 24–3 rout of Miami in Super Bowl VI that postseason. Buoniconti smashed into a player in the third quarter and blacked out—but stayed on his feet and on the field until game's end. "I was gone," he says. "I don't remember playing."

The subsequent Perfect Season, 17–0 in 1972, remains the team's monument, but in '73 the Dolphins allowed even fewer points, just five touchdown passes all season, and Buoniconti set a team record with 162 tackles. Of those, 91 came unassisted, and over time it would become clear which flank he favored. Buoniconti's right wrist, knee and ankle would become arthritic; his right hip would need to be replaced; range of motion in his right shoulder was limited. Buoniconti has estimated that over his 14-year pro career (not to mention 13 more years in boyhood, high school and college football), he has absorbed some 520,000 hits to the head. That MRIs in 2015 and '16 would reveal brain shrinkage—surfacing first in the right frontal and temporal regions—seemed almost logical.

At the time Buoniconti noticed none of it. When he said goodbye for good, at 36, he was certain he'd gotten out clean.

"My last game, at the end I got on my hands and knees and kissed the ground and thanked God that I'd never gotten seriously hurt," Buoniconti says. "Fourteen-year career? I could've been maimed."

Instead, he looked great. Wavy hair just starting to gray, hawkish nose: From the neck up Nick looked like Michelangelo's David, done slinging rocks and ready to be anointed king. He radiated authority, though that on-field ferocity needed softening, first in the courtroom and later as the agent for Yankees shortstop Bucky Dent, Expos outfielder Andre Dawson and others.

Loaded with leverage after Dent's epic playoff home run over the Red Sox in 1978, Buoniconti nearly laughed when New York owner George Steinbrenner threatened to trade Dent the following winter. "Go ahead!" Buoniconti told him.

Steinbrenner stonewalled through the 1979 season, and Dent walked out of Yankee Stadium after the final game certain his time in the Bronx was over. Buoniconti, unfazed, mused to reporters about the team's hardships, told the Yankees' GM that Dent was signing with the Angels and booked their flight to L.A. Steinbrenner signed Dent to a five-year extension. "Good luck with your prenup, honey," Steinbrenner later told Lynn, when Nick introduced her as his fiancée at a New York benefit. "That's the meanest guy I ever negotiated with."

Buoniconti's plate, meanwhile, was piling up high. People kept tapping him for leadership, for connections to his old buddies from his days in Boston and the AFL, guys like congressmen Jack Kemp and Tip O'Neill. In 1982 the Dade County Democratic party named Nick chairman; he quickly organized a $250-a-plate dinner, induced the governor to come and raised $80,000.

At the same time, his long association with U.S. Tobacco, the nation's largest purveyor of smokeless products, was beginning to pay off. UST's president, Louis Bantle, first asked Buoniconti and some other Dolphins to mingle at a client cocktail party in the early 1970s. Then he hired Nick for legal work. In '83, Nick was named executive VP in charge of legal and federal affairs and public relations. Sales had spiked fivefold over the previous decade, but clouds loomed. In '88, the U.S. surgeon general declared nicotine goods such as chewing tobacco to be as addictive as heroin.

But even as Buoniconti lobbied for the tobacco industry, his image as an athlete—and a perfect one, at that—prevailed. Indeed, he proved so valuable a spokesman that in 1985, Bantle made him UST's president and COO. The one-time tobacco picker—who had never smoked or dipped himself—became the industry's most famous, and ardent, defender.

In one typical interview that fall, Buoniconti railed against "anti-tobacco forces" and touted scientists who, he said, maintained "there's absolutely nothing wrong with your product." He went on: "We'll survive. We were the first packaged good in the U.S. We helped fund the Revolutionary War!"

It wasn't the last time Buoniconti's mind, shrewd and curious, would dodge a discomfiting truth. He liked to believe the world came at a man head-on, laid out choices and left him free to choose. *Use tobacco or don't. Play football or don't.* It's not in Buoniconti to admit the sheer weirdness of the fact that in 1985 he became a human fulcrum—at once seller and sufferer, perpetrator and victim—of public health crises involving *two* titanic American pastimes. "I'm not getting into that, O.K.?" he yells. "One has nothing to do with the other!"

The first blow came in the summer when Big Nick, a lifetime smoker, died at 75 of lung cancer, just as his son was taking over UST. Asked if he ever felt conflicted, considering tobacco's now-confirmed harmful effects, Nick says, "In my mind, we never marketed it to kids. It was a good job. I enjoyed it."

The second blow came 12 days after he invoked the American Revolution in the press. Nick and Terry were at the New Jersey spread of his old roomie, Catenacci. It was a perfect Saturday, the kind where you can't help but think, *Yes, we made it*: 72°, sitting in the gazebo, sipping champagne. Nick asked Catenacci's nephew to check the football scores; both games featuring his linebacker sons—Marc at The Citadel, Nick III at Duke—had been going for an hour. The phone rang. It was Bantle. Marc had been hurt; no one knew how bad. Bantle gave Nick a number to call. He dialed thinking, *Shoulder, maybe a knee....* A doctor answered. His first words were, "Mr. Buoniconti, your son dislocated his neck and he's going to be paralyzed for the rest of his life."

Nick fell to his knees. Richie reached down to grab him, but for the first time in their 27-year friendship, Nick looked lost. "How am I going to tell his mother?" he begged. But he did it; he went outside and blasted a hole in Terry's world. She'll never forget that day, how beautiful it was, Nick's face coming closer, his mouth saying that Marc would never walk again. She'll never forget, too, how a day later, outside of intensive care, she found her husband sitting on the floor, tears streaming, saying, "God is punishing me, God is punishing me."

And right then, amid a mother's worst nightmare and a scuttling fear, Terry had this one moment of clarity. She leaned over to her husband. "God doesn't work that way," she said.

Once Marc was stabilized and placed into Barth Green's care in October 1985, Nick moved fast. He landed a $100,000 pledge from UST and within a month organized a fund-raiser at a Dolphins game that raised another $300,000. The Miami Project was under way. "Nick is extraordinary," Green says. "I've taken care of thousands of patients with brain and spinal-cord injuries and paralysis, but I've never had a person stay so committed so long. Everybody's gung ho for a year or two, then they disappear."

Some believe the accident changed Nick. How could it not? Before, he was ensconced at UST headquarters in Greenwich, Conn., hardly a presence as Marc smoked pot, vandalized cars and homes, and bombed grades. Before, he'd see someone in a wheelchair, think *Too bad* and keep walking. Marc's paralysis humbled Nick, grounded him in a way that fame and fortune never could. His focus shifted south, to Miami and Marc and the Project and home—"to the degree that he got fired from UST," Green says. "The CEO said, 'We need a full-time president. Otherwise....' And that's when Nick left."

The fact that UST health insurance would continue to cover most of Marc's estimated $500,000 in annual expenses made the move easier. And hustling for the Miami Project filled the void of attention and purpose felt by many retired athletes. But Nick also found himself more tolerant. A squeamish Nick held Marc during each of Marc's ensuing health scares. In 2014, when a near-fatal respiratory infection had his son saying, for the first time, "Just let it end," Nick spent eight hours a day, for six weeks, by Marc's side.

"Every day in the hospital—and he hates hospitals—he sat with me," Marc says. Then, after a deep breath, he adds, "And with my *mom*!"

Such emphasis assumes a knowledge of how tough that might be. In the fall of '95 the 54-year-old Nick met Lynn Weiss at a Manhattan bar. *Monday Night Football* was on TV; she was 12 years his junior and vivacious. "The smartest person I've ever met," Nick says. He was entranced; Lynn wasn't. But soon they were an item.

Nick and Terry, together since Cathedral High, were still married. She was furious when she found out about Lynn. At least once Buoniconti wondered, to Catenacci, why they couldn't carry on. A mistress—*goumad*—wasn't unheard of in some Italian households. "There's a side of Nick that wants to have it all, and a side that recognizes you can't," says Catenacci. "I said, 'The world has changed, and you can't have a wife and a *goumad* anymore. You know Terry's not going to put up with that. You know the right thing—do it.' And he did."

That may sound like the morality of a man cornered, but Buoniconti resists glib pigeonholing. A former Democratic leader once horrified by cannabis, he supports Donald Trump and now entertains using medical marijuana. Appalled by the racist welcome doled out to black players before the 1965 AFL All-Star Game in New Orleans, Buoniconti boycotted the game.

After decades of dating women, in the early '90s Catenacci fell in love with a man, but he didn't tell Nick. Years passed. Finally Buoniconti confronted his old roommate. "So when are you going to tell me?"

"What do you want to know?" Catenacci asked.

"Does he love you? Because you know I love you, and I would never want anybody to hurt you."

Lynn's first real scare came with Nick behind the wheel. This was in 2013. During a drive in Fort Lauderdale, all the stimuli absorbed without thinking—lights, pedestrians, directions, radio—came confusingly alive for Nick. A simple turn across oncoming traffic became a mess, and his car jumped a curb. But he was also 72, had been forgetting things: a phone number here, a social commitment there. Lynn chalked it up to age. Then he started falling. Yet even to his doctors, it was hard to see anything out of the ordinary.

Because unlike Mike Webster or Duerson or Seau, who suffered dramatic depression in their 30s and 40s and were dead at 50, Buoniconti's brain trouble only surfaced in his early 70s, when even non-football-playing brains present signs of shrinkage and decay. And even then, he was still speaking and flying and golfing; a February 2014 MRI at the University of Miami attributed the "mild asymmetric volume loss" in Nick's right anterior temporal lobe—and his balance and memory issues—as "compatible with age-appropriate involutional changes."

But then food became an obsession. Dinner with friends would start off well—wine flowing, fun couple—then they'd notice Nick hadn't spoken for a bit. He spent long minutes staring at his plate. Lynn tried alerting his children, but they didn't see Nick daily. Besides, he'd always been a handful. *That's just Dad: Intense, likes to be waited on.*

His handwriting slowed and became spidery. On a freezing day he came home distressed from the gym; he couldn't figure out how to put on his coat. By then his falling had become commonplace. He'd drop like a sack of cement, face-first, and bleed plenty but feel no pain; by the end of 2014 he was averaging nearly one serious spill a month. And with each fall he got angrier, resenting his body—the instrument that gave him everything—for betraying him.

Doctors at the University of Miami seemed less alarmed, recommending close observation. A December 2014 exam noted that Buoniconti "does seem to be altered in his mental status," but attributed that to, among other things, a recent fever. Lynn felt otherwise. In January '15 she arranged a summit meeting.

Lynn, Nick and Gina recall that the medical staff in the meeting seemed settled on the idea that Buoniconti's balance and mental issues were typical markers of aging, probably compounded by his football history. Green insists that he and the rest of the UM doctors were hardly that casual, that they told the family "that Nick had a post-traumatic syndrome," Green says, "that some of the things that were happening to him were definitely related to his multiple head injuries, but he also had other stuff going on and it wasn't classical for anything—for Alzheimer's or Parkinson's."

At one point Marc speculated that by harping on Nick's difficulties, Lynn was creating a "self-fulfilling prophecy"—and only making matters worse. Finally, Gina cut in. "No: You have to listen to Lynn," she said. "She *lives* with him."

A subsequent round of tests found that though Buoniconti did not "meet criteria for dementia or mild cognitive impairment," he had mild decrements; another brain MRI that same month, however, again revealed only "age-appropriate involutional changes." But if the medical picture was foggy, other proof seemed clear. On April 13, 2015, an ambulance rushed Buoniconti to the ER after he gashed his nose and eye in another fall. A month later Lynn filmed Nick's tortuous, nearly two-minute process of figuring out how to put on a T-shirt and ball cap. And both were losing patience with Buoniconti's colleagues at the Miami Project.

"I felt let down, that they didn't understand what I'm going through—or they didn't seem interested in finding out," Buoniconti says.

In fact, Green says, the UM team had long been concerned by Buoniconti's "cascade of sequelae"—physical and mental symptoms—and suspected CTE and its precipitating brain-clogging protein, tau, as one possible cause. But "all of us were in denial," Green says. "And once we saw what was going on, we faced a dilemma: Are we going to tell him, 'Nick, you're going downhill'—when there's really no treatment? Or should we say, 'Nick, you look great and you're doing well and I wouldn't worry about this'?

"So we decided we weren't going to shove it down his throat unless we have something that could stop this cascade of neurological events and reverse it. As his symptoms grew, we tried to reinforce the positive—the fact he still was a kick-ass guy, he could get in front of these people and empty their pockets of millions of dollars to help research, and he could play in a golf tournament.

"Lynn was never ignored. She loves Nick a lot, but in her zealousness to get help for him, she's constantly—publicly and in private—telling him that he's going to hell. So: different philosophy. We didn't think that was the way to go. I don't think it does any damn good to tell him, 'Your whole brain is going to be full of tau. You're dying and you're just going to keep getting worse.' What did that accomplish? That's not the way I fly, and it's not because I'm stupid. It's not because I don't love him. It's just a different strategy."

At the same time, Green did recommend the testing regimen that led University of Miami doctors to a more specific diagnosis. In the spring of 2015, the head of UM's Neuropsychology Department, Bonnie Levin, became the first to cite CTE as a possible cause of Buoniconti's mental decline. Another UM neurologist, Carlos Singer, declared in a May '15 summary that Buoniconti's symptoms were most compatible with senile dementia, Alzheimer's disease, CTE and frontotemporal dementia.

A definitive CTE diagnosis is possible only by autopsy, but experimental testing regimes have increasingly showed evidence of CTE in small samples of living patients. In May 2015, at Lynn's suggestion, Singer referred Buoniconti for an experimental PET scan at the Feinstein Institute in Manhasset, N.Y., on Long Island. But Nick was tired of the prodding. They flew to their Long Island home, and summer and fall passed with him refusing to go. Lynn issued a winter ultimatum: *Do the scans or I'm not going back to Miami.* Now he knew how Robbie and Steinbrenner felt.

Though they did not measure specifically for tau, the two Feinstein scans indicated damage that went beyond "involutional"—consistent with Parkinsonian syndrome and CTE. The Feinstein neurologist, Andrew Feigin, confirmed to Nick that atrophy had set in on the right side of his brain and believed it was due to abnormal amounts of tau. He said the protein would soon spread to the left side, and that it could never be reversed. "It was like a car accident," Lynn says. "The point of impact."

The couple stopped at a diner on the way home. Nick said "yeah" when she asked if he understood, and then they sat there crying.

It felt like a death sentence. There was no word, no possible treatment, offering any hope. And Buoniconti wasn't a glass-half-full guy to begin with. Even when his life had seemed a testament to optimism, his disposition had folks calling him Negative Nick. Now, with neither work nor golf to distract him, Buoniconti's lifelong terror of dying had room to run. The Mercolino darkness kicked in hard.

"He's frustrated and depressed," Marc said in November. "He's lost in his own physical disability, and there's no break from it. He's sitting at his house; he has no outlets. He falls down, and that conversation only exacerbates it. That's his life, man—a vicious cycle."

Marc calls it "heartbreaking" to watch his rock crumble, but he didn't doubt the reason. For decades he had pushed back against those who cited his paralysis as Exhibit A in the case against the game, celebrating it as a vehicle for character building and teamwork. No more.

"If someone asked if their child should play contact football, I could not in good conscience recommend it," Marc says. "I don't think it's safe. It's pretty evident that something significant is happening to the brain as far as disrupted development over time. I cannot recommend football for, really, anybody. I was 50-50 on this already but, then, watching my dad—that sealed it."

Though he knows this admission cements the Buonicontis as the first family of football tragedy, Marc won't play the victim. Early predictions had him living 20 years, tops, as a quadriplegic, and he's survived at least four near-death scares in the 31 years since. He calls his existence "gravy." And in his 32nd year inside a lifeless body, something has changed; for the first time, father and son's roles have reversed. Now Marc's the one urging Nick to stop with the self-pity. There's always someone worse off than you.

Says Marc, "I've told him, 'You've got to get your s--- together. Look at me. My life sucks, but I make the best of it.' And he's like, 'I know, I know.' But it hasn't changed his approach to life."

Though he knows Lynn's lot is thankless—"God bless her for taking care of him; my dad's a pain in the ass"—Marc still wonders if her focus on Nick's deficits makes them worse. Nick and Lynn scoff at this; it remains a touchy issue. But drained of family drama, Marc's theory on positive reinforcement seems less a potshot than one more desperate response to an epidemic without cure. *Everybody's searching.*

And the fact is, one reason Nick decided to make public his decline was to mine some good from it. No ailing ex-player, after all, has had more resources—a blue-ribbon health care plan, money for the travel and costs of experimental tests that insurance won't cover, instant access to an innovative and grateful medical staff, a partner with patience enough to research studies and sift medical files and schedule appointments—with which to navigate his condition. Yet even he is a confused mess.

"So if I'm having this problem and Lynn is hovering over me making sure things get done, can you imagine someone in the same situation who *can't* figure it out?" Nick asks. "I feel for these guys. They have no direction. It's not fair that you make the league all this money, and they don't care about you anymore. You think they care about a player who no longer can contribute to their financial success? Come on."

The NFL, the Players Association and the Hall of Fame Players Foundation do have various outreach programs for former players; NFL Player Care, set up in 2007, has provided more than $12 million to 980 former players in financial need and contributed $6.6 million to medical research studies. (In late April, Nick hired three medical aides for round-the-clock assistance, tapping into the NFL and NFLPA's jointly run 88 Plan, which provides up to $118,000 per year for in-home care.) In '10 the NFL added a neurological care program to evaluate and treat "possible" conditions for vested retirees. But the outreach for all of the above has hardly been ideal, and the $1 billion concussion settlement has added a huge new layer of bureaucracy—and resentment.

Few of the estimated 20,000 players covered by the settlement would seem better equipped to understand its legal issues and jargon than Buoniconti. The older the former player, the less likely that diseases such as Alzheimer's, ALS or dementia can be attributed solely to football; CTE remains undiagnosable in the living. That means that virtually all those who played before 1993, when NFL free agency took effect, will again miss out on the big money. For example: Nick's dementia diagnosis, combined with his age and 14-year career, make him eligible for a settlement of just $132,000.

He doesn't need that money to finance his evaluations and treatments, but others of his era do. "The NFL should be volunteering to pay for this," Buoniconti screamed abruptly in a UCLA examination room last November. "I'm so f------ pissed off at them!

"We're the players who built the game but have been forgotten. The settlement is a joke; the way it was structured is a joke. They are waiting for us to die. They're going to play the clock out until everybody dies."

So Buoniconti has one last fight on his hands. It's not simple. It's not clear, like his mission to cure paralysis. No, this battle lies within, between warring impulses. There are days he wants to know exactly what's wrong with his brain, if only because naming an enemy gives you a better chance of defeating it. And there are days when he doesn't. What difference will it make? He's not looking to end football. The game was his steel mill, his coal mine—a way out.

"I didn't have any idea the price would be this debilitating," Buoniconti says. "Had I known, would I have played? There was no other way for me to get a college education. Football kept rewarding me—I can't deny that. But I'm paying the price." He shrugs, grins. "Everybody pays the piper."

He's hardly so resigned day to day. His temper ignites over the smallest frustrations—a ringing phone, bed blankets, a hand proffered to help him stand. In January 2016 he was diagnosed with prostate cancer and Lynn with breast cancer, and the treatment has been draining. Just before the family gathered for the annual Miami Project gala in New York City last

September, Nick tumbled over a chair and gashed up his forehead and nose again.

"When you marry your best friend and now he's not your best friend anymore because there's someone else in there, it's very difficult," Lynn says. "He looks like the person I married. But he really isn't there."

The night Buoniconti was to emcee the gala in New York, an HBO makeup artist slathered pancake on the fresh gashes on his face. A *New York Times* videographer tried interviewing him, but his mind derailed 46 seconds in. "I'm not ready for this," Nick said, wandering abruptly off camera. It took 20 minutes of sitting alone in the Waldorf ballroom before Lynn could calm him down.

Still, it was to placate Lynn, as much as anything, that Buoniconti agreed to ride from Pebble Beach to Westwood last November for a preliminary workup at UCLA's groundbreaking BrainSPORT Program. But that set off another roller coaster. First, a lift: Initial exams there seemed to rule out Alzheimer's disease and CTE. Then, six weeks later, a drop: Buoniconti's UCLA MRI revealed significant atrophy in his frontal lobes, and the resulting diagnosis of corticobasal syndrome was what Green had been wrestling with all along. Not only is CBS a catchall that could indicate Alzheimer's and CTE, but it's often paired with corticobasal degeneration, a disease with a sharply defined prognosis. With no treatment or cure, "we didn't want to pin that diagnosis on Nick because he could Google it," Green says, "and see that the average life expectancy is six or seven years."

The UCLA team thus recommended a cerebrospinal tap and an experimental PET scan to test for Alzheimer's-type amyloid and the tau prominent in CTE. Nick wanted nothing to do with either. For months Lynn pushed, and he dug in. She wanted confirmation of what they were facing; he wanted only reversal.

Then, in early February, the thinnest straw presented itself: One of Nick's brothers emailed about a news story in which Joe Namath controversially claimed marked brain improvement following 120 sessions of breathing pure oxygen in a hyperbaric chamber. Despite being claustrophobic, Nick lunged for it. He called Namath, who described a complete cure. He called Green, who was skeptical. Four University of Miami doctors weighed in, calling the procedure—which is highly effective for wound care—"relatively safe" but utterly unproven to render long-term brain improvement. Nick didn't care. He stopped physical therapy and insisted instead on going to UM Hospital for a 140-minute, five-day-a-week experimental course of inhaling pure oxygen at high pressure in what looks like a giant transparent tanning bed.

At first he came home exhausted but "mentally brighter," says Magaly Rodriguez, the UM surgeon in charge of Nick's hyperbaric course. "By the end of the first week I was very encouraged. He was lighter on his feet, more focused, sharper."

But on March 11, Buoniconti fell again while walking his dog, cutting and bruising his head, hand and elbow and requiring five stitches in one leg. His temper flared again, and the dizzy spells hit; he began to dread going inside the chamber. All signs of progress faded. On the night of March 26, Rodriguez was at home. She watched the movie *Concussion*, again, and prayed for Nick Buoniconti.

"We have to find a way to stop the progression of this ailment," she says. "I remember watching him as a child, growing up [in Miami]. It's a labor of love."

The next morning Buoniconti phoned four times to say that he would meet me at the chamber at 10:30 a.m. "Did I already call you?" he said after the third. After having viewed his stagnant results and rising anxiety, Rodriguez decided that after 25 sessions, it was time to hit pause. She recommended Buoniconti undergo a new round of cognitive tests. He was relieved, really, but still sighed: another dead end.

Waiting for Nick's car outside the hospital, the Miami Project—the building that holds Buoniconti's monument—loomed tall and white across the street. Later, at a nearby Starbucks, Lynn mulled a rushed retrofit of their bathroom, the mechanics of arranging 24-hour in-home care. Nick ate cheese and crackers and said his dizziness had passed. At one point he stood, one of the great names of a generation, and asked for help slipping his phone into his front-left pocket. The table went quiet, and he sat again.

"I really would like to know what the hell is going on," Buoniconti said. Outside a breeze pushed the palms just enough so you could hear them. "But I'm going to deteriorate anyway, so do we go back to UCLA? I'm up in the air."

NOVEMBER 21–28, 2016

Football in America

America's Game is somewhere between a crossroads and an existential crisis. How do we feel about it now?

BY GREG BISHOP AND MICHAEL McKNIGHT

Chapter 1

Football is under attack, unfairly maligned, too big to fail or already failing. It's concussions and Colin Kaepernick-on-his-knee; it's declining youth participation and diminishing TV ratings. *It has peaked.* It's $4 billion NFL franchise valuations, $60 million high school stadiums and $100 million player contracts. *Still peaking.* It's oversaturated, unwatchable and fragmented, too expensive to watch and too dangerous to play. *Peaked.* It's the lifeblood of small towns, the front porch of universities, by far the country's most popular and profitable sport. *Forever peaking.*

Football's place in American culture in 2016 can be debated from thousands of competing vantage points. Which is why SPORTS ILLUSTRATED dispatched two writers to traverse the U.S., hitting 30 states over the course of October, conducting hundreds of interviews with NFL owners, high school coaches and Pop Warner parents; Uber drivers, dancers, veterinarians and teachers....

All those disparate voices, all their conflict, all their angst, led to 345 Park Avenue in Manhattan on the day after Donald Trump was elected the 45th president of the United States. Trump had said that he would fire the NFL's commissioner if he won. Yet here is Roger Goodell on Nov. 9, in his sixth-floor office at league headquarters, past the lobby adorned with glass-encased Lombardi trophies and an American flag. The NFL's insignia, its famous shield, is splashed everywhere. The NFL Network—not one iota of election wrap-up—plays on an array of TVs.

Goodell sits at an oak conference table. A framed print of falling confetti hangs on the wall behind him, near another Lombardi trophy. He leans back in a brown leather chair, sipping from a water bottle cradled in his left hand. He's asked about the election, and if he sees any parallels between the country and its favorite sport—citizens and fans who want change, who don't trust polls or ratings numbers, who think America has gone soft. "You guys are better to determine that than I am," he says. "Listen. What's going on in the country right now, we see it. It's out in front of us. People are looking for change and improvement, and that's our constitutional right."

He pauses briefly and adds, "But I'm happy to talk about football."

Three days ago he attended the Eagles-Giants game in New Jersey, and he says the fans he spoke to at various tailgates gave him an earful—but not in the way anyone who's worried about the game and its health and the safety of its players might expect. He says those fans spoke mostly about their teams, their favorite players and the various ways in which they consume football. They called the game an "escape"—like the Cubs winning the World Series. America needs those sporting diversions, Goodell says, now more than ever.

He's asked how often he hears about concussions and player activism in his travels. *He must, right?* "The fans are more interested in football," he says. "We are the ones who make safety a priority. They support that because they want to see their players play." But, he adds, "I'd be fooling you if I don't say: I hear guys that say, Just let them play."

The conversation unfolds this way for almost an hour, Goodell defending his sport and deflecting most of the criticisms lobbed its way with increasing furor. Take head injuries, for example. Goodell mentions that his twin 15-year-old daughters play lacrosse; how there's a debate in his household over whether they should wear helmets. They don't, he says, because lacrosse officials are afraid that would change the game, that it will become more aggressive. "O.K.," he says, "but I want my daughters to be as safe as possible...and [at the same time] I want our kids to take risks."

Goodell comes across at times like a job applicant who's saying that his biggest weakness is "taking on too much." *Everything is perfect. Under control. Nothing to see here.* But that's not how the vast majority of Americans that SI spoke to felt. They said, en masse, that they think concussions are a serious problem. SI polled fans at airports and stadiums and restaurants and classrooms, and in a formal survey found that 94% of respondents believe head injuries in football are a "serious problem." To this, Goodell points out that the NFL made 42 rule changes focused on player safety in the last 14 years. "The 94% is [reflective] of our effort to make the game safer," he says. "The NFL has been a leader in this area. What we've found is that people don't truly understand all the things we've done to make it safer."

The ratings drop? That's the result of a number of factors, Goodell says. Games that went head-to-head with presidential debates. The unpredictable competitiveness of certain matchups. The new ways in which young people watch. "Any theory or any consideration—we look at all that," he says. "There are still the same number of folks—maybe even slightly more—actually watching. We're reaching them [in ways other than through broadcast television], and they're engaging with football."

He says at least half a dozen times—in response to questions about perception and domestic violence and player discipline and approval ratings—that the league will do everything it can to grow football in the long term. That's everything from studying the length of commercial breaks to how long it takes officials to review instant replay calls, from streaming games on Twitter to growing football internationally. "Listen, I understand there are a lot of opinions," Goodell says. "What we really try to do is get beyond just the opinions and get to what we're doing to address the issues that have real substance to them."

Rain falls outside his windows on the Manhattan streets. "Football unites people," Goodell says. "It brings the country together."

That's one take on football in 2016, delivered from a perch high above Park Avenue where one of the sport's most powerful figures directs the country's most powerful league. Football in America? From the street level, it's far, *far* more complicated.

It's Sunday afternoon, Oct. 2, outside Mons Venus in Tampa—one of 10 profitable game days the renowned strip club will enjoy in 2016. The Buccaneers and the Broncos are about to kick off a mile down the six-lane urban highway that hums nearby. Manager Bernadette Notte isn't a football fan, but she knows the Bucs' schedule by heart. "In the late summer I put it up on the bulletin board in back so the girls can see it," she says in a smoker's rasp. She has spent the week reminding the dozens of dancers in her employ that the place will be packed today with football- and nudity-loving fans and their wallets.

A dancer named Josie approaches. Young and waifish, with a whiff of Goth to her look, Josie makes clear that she and her coworkers are independent contractors; they come and go as they please. "There's no schedule." Which means Josie can come in for the pregame rush, leave and do something else for a few hours, then return later. In total this evening there will be 30 to 40 girls dancing for hundreds of patrons, a collision of football and vice that results in what Notte estimates is a 50% spike in business.

"Depends on who [the Bucs are] playing, what city [the guests] are from," Josie says. Green Bay games mean plenty of loot for everyone. "The Cheeseheads are the best fans who come in here," Notte interjects. "They're amazing." Saints fans too. "I'll dance for beignets," Josie says with a giggle that is drowned out by an apocalyptic rumble overhead—a fleet of choppers from nearby MacDill Air Force Base is rattling over Raymond James Stadium in a tribute to football and country.

Across the street at 2001 Odyssey, manager Shawn Douglas, a South Carolina native, likes the Gamecocks and the Panthers, but he *loves* when Carolina's NFC South rivals win down the street. Home games increase his club's usual Sunday haul by "50 to 100%—easy," he says.

Inside Odyssey's main door, visitors are greeted by an assault of deafening music and plasma TVs that right now show the Bucs' offense hurling itself in vain at the Broncos' defense. The stage is empty. Five performers work the sparse mid-game crowd. A dancer named Shannon sits in a private "champagne room" the size of a minivan's interior. She is physically beautiful in the ways that most heterosexual men measure such things, but "my last game day I only walked out with $100 for about eight hours [of work]," she says. Shannon is in her 30s and has been doing this since she was 18.

"Denver is really far away, so I don't expect too many of their fans here tonight," she says, nodding to the plasma above the stage. "Dallas is usually good. Green Bay. New Orleans. Atlanta—those guys like to spend money.... Every girl knows when every game is. Most of us have little pocket calendars."

Shannon is a football fan, albeit a conflicted one. "I'm definitely a firm believer in this whole CTE movement," she continues, clad in nothing whatsoever. "It's like the military—there should be more aftercare. Does the NFL cover them for life?"

No. "They should."

"Football is an American institution," she continues. "I don't think you can have an America without football. If there were more rules to protect the players, I don't think it would make it any less manly or fun to watch—or any less American."

A man hands Shannon a $100 bill. Her lips unveil perfect teeth. ZZ Top's "Got Me Under Pressure" comes on, and the lyrics might well have been written about the sport flickering silently across the room.

She's about all I can handle.

It's too much for my brain.

Later Shannon will point out that she's a successful small-business owner who works here "because it's an ego boost." She says she's concerned about her younger coworkers, who she says are uneducated and "express themselves poorly.... I wonder what their exit plan is." The club has its Adam Vinatieris, too. "We have a girl who works at night who is 52. Gorgeous. Little bit of fillers around her eyes, but not gross looking."

Shannon has a teenage son who played football until high school. Despite his broken nose and separated shoulder, "I didn't mind it at all," she says. "We have good insurance!...My parents always told me to try anything I wanted."

She might get out a nightstick
And hurt me real, real bad
By the roadside in a ditch.

A blonde dancer about half Shannon's age writhes expertly on the pole while, in an upper corner, Tampa Bay defensive tackle Gerald McCoy kneels near midfield, wincing, gripping a freshly injured leg that has ended his day and will keep him out of next week's game too. The tableau evokes something Bernadette said earlier, about managing the roiling turnover on her roster of entertainers: "We get new girls every day."

Up the street, halftime of that Broncos-Bucs game features a 10-minute Pop Warner exhibition, as dozens of NFL games do each fall. But in this game a 10-year-old player named Charlee stands out in the areas of foot speed and physicality, not to mention for the brown ponytail that flaps behind Charlee's helmet.

Charlee Nyquist is a girl, but the most important things to know about her have more to do with her speed and tenacity. The naked eye shows her to be faster than most boys on the field. An outside linebacker, she engages, sheds and swims past blockers despite a thin build and a face that *American Girl* magazine would kill to put on its cover.

"Because I'm a girl," Charlee says, "people think, *She just wants a touchdown—that's why she's playing.* That's not why I'm playing. I play because, first off, I want to be a role model for other girls. I want girls to get playing." Her second reason for playing, she says matter-of-factly, is "hitting. It's something that girls think of as scary and just...not normal. But I think it's cool."

Wearing her grass-stained jersey, without shoulder pads, Charlee sits in an empty concourse inside Raymond James Stadium. A lightning delay has interrupted the fourth quarter of what will ultimately be a 27–7 Broncos win. A mesh bag containing her helmet lies next to her pink-socked feet.

"I'm pretty fast, so next year I might be playing running back," she says, "but I like hitting because it's just"—she laughs—"I just think it's fun. You get this feeling of excitement. Everyone is like, *Yeeeah!*"

Charlee's dad, Eric, stands nearby, arms folded, beaming. He's a NASCAR executive, but the most important things to know about Charlee's dad are that he loves whatever his daughter loves and that he hardly misses a second of it. He isn't delusional about her dream of playing college football. If anything, he's frustrated. When Charlee's out of earshot, Eric, 45, says, "Lingerie football is the only outlet for women who want to play tackle football. That's ridiculous. Those women are amazing athletes, and there are lot of them. I bet every one of them loves playing the game." How does this key player in a pro sports juggernaut, a businessman whose first job out of college was a two-year stretch as the NFL's manager of business planning, recommend this chasm be filled? "If the NFL takes this on, they gotta start somewhere like Orlando or Dallas, where there's enough collective mass [to sustain a women's league]."

"I almost had a sack out there," Charlee says later of her halftime performance, her little-girl lisp belying a confidence that makes her seem 20. "But he only got like a yard. And it [set up] second-and-long."

Does she ever think about getting hurt?

"Yeah, sometimes, because one kid broke his rib cage. And one of my own teammates—I was substituted out one play, and he went in and broke his arm. And I thought, That could have been me. But it's football. You're gonna get hurt; you're gonna get hit."

Over the course of 20 minutes Charlee says something along the lines of "I want to be a role model for other girls" 13 times. She lays out her plans to start a league for women and predicts that in 10 years she'll be the first female in the NFL, "because it would show women that they're as strong as men." Even her dad seems a little stunned by the world-changer he and his wife, Michele, have created. "Our thing is, 'kind and happy,'" he says. "We want our kids to be kind to others—and to be happy. That's it. All of this," he adds, waving a hand toward his child and the NFL stadium she just conquered. "All this is...."

He can only shrug.

About 550 miles due north of Tampa lies Presbyterian College, a small liberal arts school in Clinton, S.C., that offers a freshman class called The Religion of SEC Football.

Professors Terry Barr (English) and Michael Nelson (History) are fans of the Alabama and Arkansas football programs, respectively, although *fans* is probably too mild a word. So deep is their knowledge of those teams' three-deep depth charts, so committed are they to the Tide's and the Hogs' Saturday kickoff times and the three hours that follow, that these academics often find themselves perplexed by the scale of their own devotion. Hence the course, which in essence asks, *Why?*

"Two guests today," the tweed-coated Nelson says at the start of one class. "Dr. Sarah Burns is a PC graduate who went on to Tennessee to get her Ph.D. in psychology. She teaches in our psych department. And Dr. Doug Daniel, who teaches in the math department." For these two scholarly visitors, Tennessee football is their fixation. What follows is not unlike an AA meeting.

Burns's dad (last name: Connor) named his daughter so that her initials would be S.E.C. She accompanies her presentation with slides, including one that reads, "Jesus is a Volunteer, Galatians 1:4." The bearded Daniel reads aloud from a 10-page essay he wrote recently about his boyhood love for the Vols, which deepened even as he gathered postgraduate mathematics degrees. The harmonic analysis researcher points out that the mathematical chances of Tennessee completing the Hail Mary that beat Georgia four days earlier had been 0.23%.

"We invest more of ourselves into this sport than we do in our faith," Nelson, 46, points out. "*Sometimes our families.*" There are chuckles, but one listener disagrees. Burns, 37, cites her familial upbringing and the game's "regional associations"—the us-against-them of college football—as the sources of her addiction. She talks about the weekly ritual of it, about how "we structure our entire lives around Saturdays."

The class ends with a brief and sobering discussion about death threats recently directed at LSU's 21-year-old QB, Brandon Harris, who threw a costly interception against Wisconsin. As students gather their books and file out, the sky outside has darkened. The storm that will become Hurricane Matthew—and which will cause Florida's game that weekend against LSU to be rescheduled, which in turn will cause Florida's Nov. 19 date with Presbyterian to be canceled—is taking shape hundreds of miles to the south.

Barr, by email, will note weeks later that "[Presbyterian] is getting somewhere between $350,000 and $500,000 to not play Florida. Is there a price low or high enough to save us from that [beatdown]?...Divine intervention, that hurricane, comes through in the end! We are saved from ourselves!"

Spiritually, it's a long way from SEC country to the single-lane roads that traverse Scooba, Miss., with its two gas stations and its population of 716. Scooba is home to a Subway, a motel, a row of boarded-up storefronts and, notably, one of the best juco football programs in America, East Mississippi

Community College. Or, as the popular Netflix series filmed here calls it, *Last Chance U.*

Head west from those pump stations on Johnson Street, past the bank and the beauty salon, and there's the Lions' Sullivan-Windham Field, named after Bob "Bull" (Cyclone) Sullivan, EMCC's coach from 1950 through '52 and again from '56 through '69. (Lest you forget him, there's a 7'6" bronze statue outside the stadium of the dually nicknamed coach whom Frank Deford, in a 1984 Sports Illustrated cover story, pronounced "the toughest coach of them all.") Sullivan favored leather helmets without face masks long after most coaches. He conducted goal-line drills and sprints in a nearby pond, and when one lineman removed his new shoes so as not to ruin them, Sullivan ran him barefoot through blackberry vines and sticker bushes. Another player nearly drowned. "I've heard people say [Sullivan] couldn't coach today's athlete," says 60-year-old Nick Clark, who played for the Bull from '64 through '66 and who now works as EMCC's vice president for institutional advancement. "If someone was rolling around with a knee injury, he'd yell, *Boy, that damn knee is four feet from your heart! You ain't going to die!* If he did that today, somebody would probably sue him."

If Sullivan embodies the tough-love, no-water-breaks, what's-concussion-protocol? football generation, then the current program illustrates the way the game has changed. The Lions play on an all-weather turf field and wear eight different uniform combinations. For the last two seasons they've been chronicled on Netflix, whose cameras trail the players one October afternoon as the P.A. announcer leads a pregame prayer, asking God to watch over the teams and the country. There's no kneeling during this national anthem. Every single player, coach and fan holds hand to heart.

Between EMCC and its opponent this evening, Northwest Mississippi Community College, roughly 50 Division I–caliber football players take the field, including Lions quarterback De'Andre Johnson, who was dismissed from Florida State in July 2015 after a video surfaced showing him striking a woman at a bar. (He accepted a plea deal for misdemeanor battery last December, apologized to his victim on national TV and has since volunteered at a battered women's shelter. "This," he says, "is my second chance.") Fans with camouflage cellphone cases and American flag hats pack the stands as Johnson scores five touchdowns and accounts for 442 total yards in a 51–32 triumph.

Afterward, Netflix cameras roam the field, and Johnson takes a picture with his position coach, Clint Trickett. Like Johnson, Trickett, 25, never expected to settle in a one-stoplight town near the Alabama border. The son of a coach, one of three brothers who now work in football, he played at Florida State and West Virginia and then retired in 2014 after suffering five concussions in 14 months. The Johnson-Trickett snapshot is one of football in modern-day America: a QB kicked out of school after video of his crime went viral...a young coach who wants to stay in football despite his concussion history...a season chronicled for a popular reality TV show that is streamed over the Internet....

Trickett, though, retains some of Sullivan's tough-guy coaching ethos. "I hope it doesn't get to the point where we're being soft with [this game]," he says. "The second the softness takes away from the integrity of the game, you gotta draw the line."

"Look," he continues, "the good [of this sport] outweighs the bad a million to one. I'm fine. Football will be too."

That seems abundantly clear an hour west, on the campus of Clemson, which on a warm fall day provides a snapshot of a more traditional football player and program. Hunter Renfrow came here two years ago as a 155-pound walk-on wide receiver. Last January, at 175 pounds, he caught two touchdowns against Alabama in the national title game. He knows what it's like to be on top of the totem pole and at the bottom.

Right now the redshirt sophomore is sitting in a sunlit terrace high above Memorial Stadium wearing a purple-and-orange DREAM THE DREAM T-shirt. Behind him, in the distance, lies a vast construction site, where Clemson's new, $55 million training facility–palace is being built. The Tigers are unbeaten and ranked No. 3 in the country, but football's advances stop for no man.

Renfrow, 20, has scored seven touchdowns in his college career and, by his estimation, suffered about that many concussions since he began playing football in grade school. "I played some of my best high school games with a concussion," he says. "I was watching *Last Chance U* not too long ago, and Clint Trickett said football has given way more to him than concussions have taken away. I go along with that. I don't really worry about it too much."

What Renfrow sees as the biggest threat to college football has nothing to do with the game's physicality. He hates the idea of scouting combines and Rivals camps, where individual players are valued above their teams. "That's why some players don't care about the team." Clemson weeds out such players, he adds. "No one here thinks he's bigger than the team." The reason is "culture," Renfrow explains.

No one expounds on that notion better than Thad Turnipseed, who is one of Clemson coach Dabo Swinney's best friends, as well as his director of recruiting. More than any man but Swinney, Turnipseed is responsible for the palace being built adjacent to Death Valley. Today, huge tractors roll across the clay upon which the sprawling edifice is being built, forming orange clouds slightly darker than the jerseys Clemson wore three days earlier in an epic win over Louisville. Before you judge the building for its planned two-lane bowling alley, though, or its nap room, or the massive playground slide that connects the second floor to the ground floor, first listen to Turnipseed, 44, describe the philosophy behind it all. He doesn't deny that the building's biggest purpose is to attract recruits. It's what happens *after* those recruits arrive that he believes sets Clemson apart.

"Dabo's challenge to all college football programs is, We gotta start building better people and stop using kids," says Turnipseed, who likes to show recruits' parents the 38 surveillance cameras positioned throughout the property. ("This ain't gonna be *Animal House*.") He also shows them where the CU in Life program will be housed ("for training in life skills and community service") and the future homes of the Fifth Quarter initiative ("for professional development and job mentoring from our alumni") and the Tigerhood program ("How do you become a good man? How do good men think?"). "This is more about philosophy than facility," Turnipseed says, adjusting his hard hat amid the whir of power tools.

How does he respond to those who criticize a college football program with a planned 12 plasma panels in its main foyer and a football-shaped couch the size of an end zone? "Right, wrong or indifferent," he says, "the front door of your university, at this level, is the football team. There's no other avenue where you can have 30 to 50 million people engaged with your institution like we had at the national championship game. I'm not saying that's right. I'm saying that's reality.... It's not debatable whether a successful football team is good for a university.

"So that's how I'd answer that."

At the Residence Inn in Pensacola, Fla., the middle-aged white woman holding down the front desk considers Football in America, same as Trickett and Renfrow, but without the personal investment. "Football is like riding a motorcycle," she says. "There's only so much a helmet can do."

No one knows that better than 74-year-old James Andrews, who works across the Pensacola Bay at the Andrews Institute for Orthopaedics and Sports Medicine and whose cellphone rings nonstop at dawn on Monday mornings in the fall—20 calls one Monday, 45 the next. He puts the device on speakerphone and holds it inches from his face; it's always a general manager, athletic director, agent, coach.... *So-and-so hurt himself in our football game last weekend. Can we send you an MRI?*

"We're picking up the pieces from college and pro games that weekend," sports' busiest and most famous orthopedic surgeon says. "The wreckage." Games mean broken bones, torn ligaments.... Football, Andrews says, is not a contact sport, as it is often described. "It's a *collision* sport. If we started a new sport today and we wrote up the rules and regulations and we called it football, they probably wouldn't allow it."

On weekends Andrews attends games with Auburn, Alabama and the Redskins, all of whom he works for. Team doctors occupy an odd space in the sports universe. Many of the players they care for don't want to let on that they're injured; coaches don't want to remove their best athletes from the game; fans want championships; universities want revenue...and here's this doctor, whom nobody really trusts, trying to navigate a minefield where money matters most. Down the hall from Andrews, fellow orthopedic surgeon Steve Jordan, who previously worked as Florida State's team doctor for 24 years, says that the players he encountered in his past rarely talked about head injuries—except for how to navigate around them in order to remain on the field. One player, he recalls, was knocked down, hit in the head right in front of him. "You O.K.?" he asked. The player bounced up, yelled, "Yeah, it's my ankle," and ran back onto the field.

"Most [players] were dishonest—a majority," says Jordan, 60. "As a doctor, you felt the pressure from the player. You feel the pressure from the fans."

But a doctor's proximity to the NFL's best players doesn't mean he can easily connect with those directly responsible for their health. Back in April, Andrews sponsored a football-injury conference in Destin, Fla. He invited orthopedic surgeons, biomechanists, trainers, therapists...and coaches. Guess which group had the smallest numbers? "I've tried to get coaches to come and listen to injury prevention talks," he says. "You almost have to trick them to come." On the field, he says, "they have a taboo about even talking to the team doctor."

One group that will listen, undoubtedly: moms. An afternoon's drive to the northwest, in Atlanta, more than 100 of them—the majority of them African-American, all local—are running go routes behind Rich McKay as the Falcons' president and CEO explains the difference between the Moms Clinic he's hosting one October evening at South Cobb High and the slightly patronizing "Football 101" seminars that the NFL has largely moved on from. "[Football 101] went through the basics of what a first down is, the four downs, timeouts." McKay spreads his arms wide, revealing the squadron of mothers behind him. "This is all about health and safety, arming moms with information about the risks of the game and how to mitigate those risks. Then we let them have a little fun on the field."

The laughter and dropped passes and tackling drills in the background are a physical release for women who just spent an hour watching demonstrations on how to properly fit their sons' helmets and pads, how to navigate the confusing world of supplements and PEDs, how to balance academics against the statistically slim chance that their sons will play college ball.

Out on the field, clinic director Buddy Curry, a former Falcons linebacker, starts doing what he does best. "One!" he yells. Every mom, having just been coached on this, stomps into a half-lunge. "Two!" Their rear feet come forward, forming 100 squats. "Squeeze!" One hundred sets of shoulder blades retract. "Sink!" The squats deepen. "Rip!" Four hundred hands and hips fly forward with surprising synchronicity and speed, completing the tackle. "Break down!"

"*Hunnnh!*" The collective two-foot stomp and grunt is loud and visceral.

When the clinic is over, eye-black-wearing mom Marilyn Mason, whose 16-year-old plays for South Cobb, explains, "I came here to see football from my son's perspective. The first time he got tackled [in Pop Warner], I cried. He had a concussion last year that was very difficult. It hurts me to watch him play, but I know football keeps him disciplined and teaches him to be part of a group."

Adrienne Harden's three-year-old son scored his first flag football touchdown two weeks earlier for the Hiram Hornets. She came tonight "because this my baby, my three-year-old *baby*—"

"—Wait till contact," interrupts a friend.

Lavita King and Stephanie Green are the mothers of two South Cobb seniors. "The safety issues we talked about tonight," says Green, "I didn't know them like I thought I knew them." Learning about PEDs and hearing the surprising news that not every supplement at GNC is good for her son "was awesome, I needed that." Asked if the information they learned tonight arrived too late in their sons' lives, they exclaim, "Yessss!" Their chorus is joined by a third mom who works in a nearby hospital "that gets a lot of football injuries."

Green explains the feeling of watching her son play, calling the physical sensation "like a tightening."

"Dads can say 'just shake it off,'" says King. "But not us mamas."

It's 9 a.m. on a Sunday, and a mostly empty city smells like urine and stale cigarettes. Welcome to Bourbon Street. There's a street performer on the corner strumming a guitar, his case nearly empty. Between songs he declines to discuss the current state of football, waving dismissively as he talks. "What do I care about rich people destroying other rich people?"

An hour later, as kickoff between the Saints and the Panthers approaches, vendors hawk Mardi Gras beads and face-painting services on Poydras Street outside the Superdome. Scalpers work the area across the street from Champions Square. One recalls how his father resold tickets at the Superdome, back when fans wore paper bags over their heads. Times change, same as football. Fans pay more now, especially the visitors. "I don't watch football much," he says. "But I damn sure need the money."

Inside, the game kicks off, and in the top row of the stadium, in section 608, a middle-aged telecom exec leans against the wall and says his "interest has waned significantly the last couple years." He played lacrosse when he was younger, sustaining multiple concussions. An imaging scan recently revealed damage to his brain, he says. Both of his sons have dealt with head injuries. That concussions in football have always bothered him comes as little surprise. And yet there's that conflict. "They have to make the game safer or it's barbaric—but then when they make it safer, it's ruining the game," he says. "It's an unsolvable conflict, an unfixable problem."

Besides the Saints, he hardly watches football these days. ("How many gladiators do you watch anymore?" he asks, sighing.) He's aware of the decline in ratings and, like Goodell, thinks that results from many factors. In New Orleans, he says folks like his brother-in-law swore off the NFL after the Bountygate scandal. "There will always be football," he says, "but it has reached its peak."

The second half resumes, and he gets lost in a last-minute Saints victory. Afterward, New Orleans safety Roman Harper is told about the musician who doesn't care, the scalper who needs the dough and the fan in section 608. "I would tell them, Enjoy the product we put out there on the field," he says. "We sign up for this. I've been trying to kill and hit people since I was eight years old. That's my decision."

"The game," he says, "will change with the time. You can't be the dinosaur. You gotta be the crocodile."

The next morning, 80 miles northwest in Baton Rogue, Pulitzer Prize–winning author Jeffrey Marx considers the Saints and football over a shrimp-and-crawfish omelet. He's not conflicted. Never has been. "In my writing I've tried to explore my belief that sports are the most popular platform in America. Period," says Marx, 54. "Not just football—but football probably is the most powerful of sports in its ability to reach young people."

Marx became a Baltimore Colts ball boy when he was 11 and worked four summers for the team. Those experiences, he says, changed his life. Fast-forward to 2001, when the team's old venue, Memorial Stadium, was being torn down. Marx called as many of the players from his childhood as he could find. He stumbled upon Joe Ehrmann, a Colts D-lineman from 1973 through '82 who had become a minister and high school coach in Baltimore.

Ehrmann had started a mentoring program called Building Men for Others, and he attacked what he called fake masculinity in football. Instead, he emphasized emotions that one doesn't typically associate with athletes. Love. Empathy. Kindness. His coaches yelled, *What is our job?* and players responded, *To love us!*

In 2004, Marx wrote a book about Ehrmann and his program titled *Season of Life*. In the subsequent 12 years he says he's heard about the book's impact from someone every single day. He explains how a judge told him recently that he'd assigned a convict to read the book and then write about it. The essay partially determined his sentence. That's the kind of impact football can have, Marx says, why it will always exist, always thrive.

"Football is the most violent sport in America, and it's causing all sorts of problems," Marx admits. "It's equally a fact that when the sport is used in a strategic way, it can change lives, families, whole communities. I don't think those facts are mutually exclusive."

Chapter 2

The Grand Poobah of Football in America sips iced tea inside a conference room at his latest cost-be-damned sports palace. Jerry Jones, owner of the most valuable sports franchise in the world ($4 billion), arrived in Frisco, Texas, earlier this afternoon from Arlington, via an airbus H145 helicopter, at what he calls the Cowboys' "world headquarters." He sits down and gestures at his kingdom, which is named the Star and sponsored by Ford. "Before we're through here, we'll have spent almost $2 billion," Jones, 74, says with a shrug, dropping interview notes on a table, never to look back at them.

The topic: the current state of the nation's most popular sport. Jones is as responsible as anyone for a moment in football history that he calls "very unique," and if he's being honest, this moment snuck up on him. "We"—and by this he means himself and others in positions of power, at all levels of the game—"may have taken for granted that the decision-makers know that football is good for you," he says. "I've just assumed that everybody would get it and [the lessons] would get passed along.

"Football's not for everybody," he goes on. "I'm not complaining, but maybe I had blinders on when I bought the Cowboys [in 1989 for $140 million]. I didn't see that we needed to say any more until probably the last 10 years."

Jones takes another sip of tea and launches into his personal football history: four seasons as a fullback and guard at Arkansas, national championship in 1964, the thesis he wrote on the role of communication in football, the father who told him that with a career in sports he would "never amount to anything." This continues for half an hour—the lessons learned, the sacrifices made, how he wouldn't own a stadium and a helicopter if not for the game. "The point of that whole long-winded deal is this," he says, "I've had [football] in my blood."

Tears well in Jones's eyes. (*Misting*, he calls it.) Football provides myriad similar experiences, he says, especially for "the 70% of our players who have had no male role models apart from their coaches." Critics, he says, miss the point of it all: the community, the ties that bind generations...

The conversation winds to player safety and head trauma. Jones saw only clips of the movie *Concussion*. He knows that Jeff Miller, the league's senior vice president for health and safety policy, acknowledged on Capitol Hill last March a link between football and degenerative brain disorders such as chronic traumatic encephalopathy. Jones does not agree with Miller or the many doctors and studies that share the same view. He just believes it's too early to know anything definitively. "We're drawing conclusions so far out in front of the facts," he says. "I can live with that, as long as we understand that I've seen milk and red meat [debated] for the last 30 years, whether they're good for you or not."

He wants football to be safer—as safe, he says, as it can be. He wants studies, research, plans. He advocates making smaller face masks to "reduce the courage" of tacklers who are tempted to lead with their heads.

Another sip of tea and Jones says that what has surprised him most about being an NFL owner is how the league is expected to lead the way in combating domestic violence, promoting activism, advancing safety procedures. While many would argue the NFL has failed in those areas, especially when it has come to early research on concussions, Jones disagrees. "I'm going to carefully choose my words here," he says. "The game of football is *convenient* to involve in the discussion of head injuries. Anybody who stops and thinks for a few minutes will realize that many other sports involve contact with athletes' heads. Many other occupations do, as well.... I don't become unduly alarmed. We don't have the answers. There is no such thing as *the answer*."

After 90 minutes Jones is still talking, getting even more passionate. He's built a 12,000-seat indoor football stadium at the Star, and it is being used by eight high schools. It's a mini AT&T Stadium: same seat backs, same turf, same polish on the concourse floors. There's a VIP viewing area. Nike will outfit all the teams. Jones did this, he says, because he wants to reach parents directly. They'll ultimately decide if their kids play football, when they can play tackle, for how long. He calls his sparkling new headquarters an "oasis" connecting professional and amateur sports, and he sees harmony between the two going forward.

"Whether it be concussions, whether it be the issues with player behavior—take everything we're looking at," he says, "and then take what I saw in 1989 when I gave everything I had to [buy the Cowboys]. That was a bleak picture back then. This, today"—the billions of dollars being moved, the spot atop the American sports totem pole, the growing global footprint—"this looks like the clouds have parted compared to then."

How 'bout them *Cowboys*!? Clad in a silver-and-blue number 4 jersey, Phil Ebarb orders a Boudin sausage at a seafood kitchen in Grapevine, Texas. From where he sits, it's about a 20-minute drive to AT&T Stadium, where his nephew, Cowboys rookie quarterback Dak Prescott, is preparing to face the Bengals this afternoon.

Ebarb, 50, isn't hungry though. He's nervous. It's one thing to worry or scream or track a player's progress from vantage points removed—on a couch, on a fantasy app. But that's his *blood* out there on the field, the boy who wore an Emmitt Smith jersey growing up in western Louisiana. Before Ebarb's sister Peggy died of colon cancer in 2013, he promised her he would look after Dak, who chose number 4 because his mom was born on the fourth of September. She loved the contact in football, the way bigger defenders couldn't drag down her boy.

"It's emotional," Ebarb says. "Proud, first and foremost. You're concerned—worried this world is going to wrap him up, worried for his heart, worried about his health. And then there's the excitement. You *can't wait* to see it. You're ready. You're bewildered. It's surreal that this is reality."

Where Jones's eyes "misted," Ebarb's *pool* with conflicting emotions. "You don't reconcile them," he says. "You *navigate* them. You're the ball in the pinball machine—thrown here, pushed there. You feel all of that in the same minute, at the same time. It's...overwhelming."

Ebarb is a singer-songwriter who worked with James Brown and hung out with Willie Nelson; his band performs what he calls "musical gumbo," a mix of up-tempo country and rock. He'll soon require hip and knee replacements after all those years onstage. A fractured disk in his back during high school ended his basketball career, the same as knee injuries halted the professional football aspirations of Dak's father, Nathaniel, who was invited to an NFL training camp, and Dak's brother, Jace, who was once a top college recruit. "Twice the athlete Dak is," Ebarb says.

Yet Ebarb views all those injuries through the prism of sacrifice—the price men pay for what they love. "If you work at a school and some nutbag shows up and shoots at kids and kills teachers, do you quit?" he asks. "We have to do what we have to do. You can't stop livin', man."

He pulls up a text message he sent Dak yesterday. It reads, in part, "When you're smiling out there, it confirms for me you do this for the moments. That's why I play music. The moments that haunt. Create your moments. I love you."

"Let's don't get it messed up," Ebarb says. "Dak is a performer. This is an entertainment business. Football is a machine, man, and the machine rolls on."

That it does. Even as Ebarb watches from AT&T Stadium's lower level as Dak and the Cowboys dismantle Cincinnati 28–14, the high rollers in box seats feast on produce from an organic farm 25 miles to the southeast, the very spot where, just nine years ago, Paul Quinn College gave up its football program in favor of...agriculture.

Here, just south of downtown Dallas, rows of cucumbers, radishes, basil, tomatoes, jalapeños and bell peppers grow between two goalposts. One afternoon, three days after the Cowboys' win, tilapia swim in an aquaponics system that is 70 yards from a blank, antiquated scoreboard. Hens lay eggs near a cartoon rendering of an anthropomorphic radish in full Heisman pose.

The man responsible for this gridiron garden, school president Michael Sorrell, arrived here in 2007, shortly after an analysis from the Boston Consulting Group concluded that the private, historically black college could no longer afford NAIA football. Sorrell looked around—at the "food desert" surrounding campus, with so few healthy options; at his weight, which had ballooned by 15 pounds since his move; at the former football players, whom he could spot by the way they limped; at the Tigers' record, with just 11 wins from '00 through '06—and made what he describes as an easy and prudent choice. The We Over Me Farm opened in May 2010. The school saves about $600,000 annually by not having a football team.

The players didn't take it well. They tried to intimidate Sorrell and griped about losing a chance to play professionally. This went on until Sorrell challenged them to raise $2 million to save the team, promising to match that amount and open an endowment. No one raised a dime. Gradually, the complaints subsided. And now, with the Cowboys as the farm's top client, Sorrell says, "we've sent more kale to the NFL than football players. In reality, not having football saved our institution."

Sorrell's choice speaks to what he sees as football's inherent conflict. "You create an economic engine [with] this sport; that impact is extraordinary," he says. "But the reality is, you also sacrifice a few souls. Bodies will be racked and damaged for the benefit of many." He shakes his head. "I'm not sure if football isn't the banking system in 2008. It's too big to fail."

Here, though, is that conflict again: At 50, Sorrell remains a die-hard Bears and Cowboys fan. He respects the power of football's platform, in which a backup quarterback can kneel during the national anthem and spark debate, outrage, maybe change. "Athletes are breaking the code," he says. "The code used to be: *We paid you a bunch of money...do what we say.* It feels like the sport is changing."

Bigger change, transformative change, he says, will come from the mothers who can veto football as a choice, just as Sorrell and his wife did with their own son. In the end he brings the conversation back to the students who receive a $5,000 tuition credit by working Paul Quinn's farm. "I want them to understand that the surest way out of poverty is to be the guy who signs the front of the check, not the back," he says. "Jerry Jones is a genius—flat-out. He played football.

"But what side of the checks does he sign?"

There is a complete spiritual opposite of the We Over Me Farm a mere 45 minutes to the north, straight up I-75. With 18,000 seats and a 38-foot-wide video board, Allen High's $60 million Eagle Stadium is *Friday Night Lights* in middle age. It's all the excess of Texas high school football wrapped up in one place.

The Eagles jog onto the field through billowing smoke and a giant inflatable A, with the nation's largest high school band (almost 800 students) performing in Halloween costumes (Barney Rubble on trumpet, Dracula on drums), and Football in America is thriving. Allen's residents voted by a two-to-one margin in favor of a $119 million bond in 2009 to build the venue, along with a fine arts auditorium and a district service center. The Eagles then won state titles in each of their first three seasons in their new home, starting in '12 (though all of the '14 games were played on the road after district officials shut down Allen's stadium to repair extensive cracking).

Tonight fans are tailgating, wiping away meat sweats, spoiled by success. They're smoking brisket, grilling sausage, lathering ribs in barbecue sauce. One says he has watched Texas high school football every Friday for 55 years. Another notes how this stadium has become something of a novelty, with visitors from as far as Canada this season. "If you can't get fired up here," an older man in an Allen hat says, "then your wood's wet."

Near the front entrance, at a makeshift tent for the program's booster club, adults grumble about Colin Kaepernick and player protests and the NFL in general. Several say they're watching less professional football this season, if at all.

As Allen's band director (Waldo) leads a sea of instruments in song, Chris Tripucka, the 53-year-old owner of a football-souvenir shop, sees the Eagles take a 42–7 third-quarter lead on Guyer High. Tripucka's father, Frank, played at Notre Dame and then for eight NFL and CFL teams over 16 seasons, ending in 1963. (The Broncos retired his number 18 jersey this season.) In 2013 the man friends called the Tough Polack died at 85 from, Chris says, "a combination of Alzheimer's and dementia that I know was caused from all the hits to the head." Still, even as Frank's condition had worsened, the Tough Polack lamented the state of Football in America. He had played one game with a leather helmet and most of his career without a face mask. The game he loved had gone soft.

Chris played receiver at Boston College in the '80s, and he undergoes cryotherapy each week from a helmet shot he long ago took to the spine. His oldest son, Shane, is the punter for Texas A&M. Shane had also lined up at receiver for Allen, until he took a brutal hit one scrimmage and his coach decided he didn't want to jeopardize the kid's scholarship chances. Chris broke the news to Shane, who cried for an hour. Secretly, Chris was relieved. "Having played the game, I know what the risks are," he says. "Those risks didn't bother me as a player. But they bother me as a parent."

On the field Allen is running out the clock. Tripucka loves these Friday nights and what they mean to his community, how the lessons doled out on that field teach boys to become men. He hates that third-graders practice in full pads, and he hates how today's kids specialize in one sport before they hit puberty. He disdains those things—but he can still get behind Allen's $60 million stadium. The town needed it, he says. Besides: McKinney High, a school without Allen's gridiron tradition, is building a $70 million venue seven miles up the road.

The clock hits zero and fans stream toward the exits. "I look down on the field and I see that the numbers aren't quite what they normally are," Tripucka says, referring to what he sees as a dwindling player pool. "You're seeing a small impact.

"Even in Texas."

Five hours to the south, but still in the thick of Texas football country, the first of four San Antonio Colts youth football games are under way on a Saturday morning. The outfit fields four teams across age groups from four to 13 and has 104 participants altogether—players and cheerleaders—down from a high of 140 a few years back. They're drilled by 39 coaches, and, like the 50-odd other youth football organizations in San Antonio (part of the 270-plus that make up the Texas Youth Football Association), they play almost year-round. They take only January off.

Colts president Robbie Adame, 31, surveys the field as one flag player, four or five years old, grabs a handoff and runs the wrong direction. Other leagues in Texas, Adame says, start at three. "Too young."

During their 2013 and '14 seasons the Colts participated in the Esquire Network's reality show *Friday Night Tykes*. Their coach then, Marecus Goodloe, was suspended after the first season for using foul language, one of myriad abhorrent acts—screaming coaches, helicoptering parents—the series highlighted. After that aired, TYFA membership *climbed* 35%, to about 18,000 players. "People act a certain way on TV," says Adame. "When they approached us last year [about filming another season], I told them I'm ready to be back to normal. I don't need all that." The injuries, though, are all real. Adame says the Colts average "five or six" concussions each season. He even recalls one on the Colts' flag team. When the movie *Concussion* came out, he says "probably three parents" took their kids out of the league. One father still wanted his son to play, even after the boy suffered two head injuries in four months. "I need something that says *He's cleared*," Adame told the dad. "I can't have that on my conscience."

Two Midget teams, ages six and seven, sprint onto the field through a banner that says TIME TO POUND, past posters reading COLTS STRONG and BIG GAME and SLEDGEHAMMER. One parent wears a T-shirt with HIGHLY AGGRESSIVE splashed across the front. A coach sets up a video camera in the stands. They'll study the tape next week.

Wesley Vallejo, a locksmith who helped found the Colts in 2003, says they used to recruit each weekend. They'd set up a tent on the main drag near the field and hand out fliers, selling parents on the program. They fought to retain their best players, who were constantly courted by other teams. "Losing games," Vallejo says, "is equivalent to losing kids."

Later, as two Rookie teams of eight- and nine-year-olds take the field, Colts coaches yell, "Is everybody ready!?"

In unison, "Yes, sir!"

A Junior Barons linebacker slams a Colts running back, and the Barons' sideline erupts. Parents chest-bump. "Textbook, baby!"

"That's how you hit, boy!"

After the Junior teams (10 and 11) kick off, one Barons coach screams at his players. If they don't want to play hard, he says, he'll find someone who does. Later he disagrees with an assistant's play-call suggestion and tells the man to "go sit in the f------ stands with your wife." The assistant leaves.

A parent yells, "Hit somebody!" A Colts player is down. One dad walks onto the field and shouts, "Put him on his back!" Later, another Colt is down. Nearby, two bench players throw rocks at a tree.

Another injury and coaches wave with urgency at the medics, summoning five volunteers who've come from nearby military bases. There's an altercation between parents in the stands.

"Carolina is down," a mom declares. His banner hangs on the fence behind him: JAY$HAWN #1 CAROLINA. Four parents carry a tent onto the field to shield Carolina from the sun. Medics roll out the ice chest. An ambulance and two fire trucks arrive, and Carolina is carted off on a stretcher. Play resumes.

Colts coaches tell their players, who are down two touchdowns, to win this one for Carolina. One teammate walks over to Carolina's sign, clasps both hands together and prays.

Another teammate comes to the bench holding his head. His father, a coach, says, "That's part of football, son. I would have hit your ass too. That's the way it is. Lazy-ass football players get hurt."

Another child slumps on the bench with a sprained ankle and a mom declares, "We can't have somebody getting hurt every play."

A sixth injury in this one game. A fourth stoppage. A player limps off the field holding his left arm, and the medics, who arrived to find no medical supplies, fashion a splint out of an orange crate.

"This is crazy," says one medic, who identifies himself as PO3 Ross. "I've never seen anything like this. The parents are the worst. Some are worse than my drill sergeants."

The game ends.

"Jesus," PO3 Ross says. "It's done."

"Y'all gotta get some fight," one of the coaches tells the Colts. "We can't coach 'fight.'"

"At the end of the day, in football you're going to take bumps, bruises and broken bones," says one parent, who declines to give his name. "If you don't want to play football, go run track."

"Somebody gotta say it," he says, laughing.

Jessenia Quiñones isn't laughing. Every week dozens of NFL players lie flat on her massage table, their bodies dotted with black and brown and purple bruises, their fingers bent, their spines twisted. They've absorbed the impact of helmets to their hamstrings and braved the force of large men landing on their backs. That's football, they tell her. Contact on every play, injury as an occupational hazard.

Quiñones, 35, sits in a coffee shop back in Dallas, a day after treating several Cowboys players, one who hurt himself against the Bengals. "The doctor told him his neck is like he's in his 80s," she says.

A licensed massage therapist, the 5'3" Quiñones says MMA fighters come to her in the worst shape, but NFL players are a close second. No other sport approaches that level. The football players' biggest complaint, though, isn't the pain. It's that they don't get help, she says. "They're what we call *fakers at the facilities*," she continues. "They don't seek the attention they need. What makes me the saddest is that they're not able to tell their trainers, 'I'm really hurt.' Teams teach them how to talk to the media, how to manage their money. They don't teach them how to manage their bodies and their health."

These same players express no regrets. "The money keeps them there," Quiñones says. "They have a wife, and then they have a baby coming...." After they retire, she says, *then* they worry about their health. *Then* they never miss appointments. One retired NFL player whom she treated this week told her he regrets not taking her advice more seriously when he played.

Quiñones wishes more teams employed massage therapists, acupuncturists and holistic healers. "They pump these guys full of Vicodin," she says, "but that's *masking* pain, not taking care of it, camouflaging it so they can play again."

After years of working on athletes twice her size, Quiñones feels the impact of pro football. "I want to start getting out of it," she says. "It's murder on my hands.

"Football, it takes its toll."

Jerrod Black sure hopes so. "This is going to sound bad," he says from Christie's, a sports bar in Dallas's Uptown neighborhood where he's watching *Monday Night Football* over chicken wings and fries, "but I'm always looking for an injury."

A 27-year-old aspiring NFL nose tackle who benches over 500 pounds and squats more than 600 but who hasn't yet found a temporary roster spot (let alone a permanent one), Black is eyeing job openings. He is heartened tonight by Buccaneers running back Jacquizz Rodgers, a third-stringer seven days ago who, due to injuries, will get 30 carries against the Panthers. Suddenly John Hughes III, a defensive end whom Tampa Bay signed a week ago, is down, clutching his knee. "The universe is speaking right now," Black says.

The call will not come this week, or the next, and that is typical of life on the NFL periphery. For every Aaron Rodgers there are 400 NFL hopefuls like Black, though his example is extreme. Last December he was out of gas, out of options, parked outside the facility where he trained in Carrolton, Texas, when he asked himself, *Where am I going to sleep tonight?* Black was too proud to call his parents and too broke to pay for a motel room. He grabbed a pillow and a blanket and fixed a bed in his truck. He lived there for more than three months, spending his days in the training center and his nights in the parking lot, listening to crickets chirp.

On the fringe of professional football, he asked himself another question. *Dude, when are you going to stop and get a regular job?*

The answer, still, always: Not yet. Black grew up in Houston, was courted by the likes of Texas A&M and Nebraska, then went to Iowa State, where the forgettable Gene Chizik era ended when the coach bolted in mid-December 2008 for Auburn. Chizik told his team, "I always support the Cyclones." Then he walked out. Black says 16 members of his recruiting class transferred.

He landed at Southeastern Louisiana. He worked out for two NFL teams. He played indoor ball for the Green Bay Blizzard. He tore his right ACL. The Bucs called his agent, only to find out about the injury. The Cowboys brought him in for a visit in May 2014, then they signed someone else instead. Black's agent would call. *We might have something.* Always another tease.

He came to see how thin the margins were, the difference between the back end of an NFL roster and sleeping in his truck. Three of his Iowa State roommates, none of them stars, played in Super Bowls.

When one friend, former Giants safety Tyler Sash, was found dead of an accidental pain-medication overdose and then was discovered to have had CTE, Black began to worry more about concussions. And still he pushed on, reaching out to executives on social media, contacting reporters. "I'll give it until the end of this season" he says now as he finishes his fries.

Buoyed by a new partnership in an organic tequila company, Black is no longer homeless. He swears he had a dream recently in which he was playing for the Seahawks, wearing a blue jersey, walking out of the tunnel onto CenturyLink Field.

That dream, for now, sustains him.

Chapter 3

The tears start almost immediately, running down both cheeks as Jordan Shelley-Smith tries to explain how much football matters to him, how desperately he wanted to continue playing. It's killing him that he's sitting here while his Kansas teammates prep for Oklahoma State. Six weeks ago he was on that field with them, a starting left tackle with a shot at the NFL. Now he's just another former D-I player, a 22-year-old senior forced to retire because of concussions.

Inside the football communications office in Lawrence, Shelley-Smith's sentences start and stop as he wipes at droplets that say what his words cannot. That he misses football. That he's weaning himself off the high. "My dad told me to play with no regret," he says, "but this is all I've done, all I knew. My body just tapped out."

He leans forward, hands clasped, eyes still wet. The Jayhawks were one of just two winless teams in all of FBS last season, and in 2016 they were off to a 1–2 start when Shelley-Smith retired. But he deems his decision "the toughest call I've ever had to make. I have to deal with that every day for the rest of my life."

Shelley-Smith arrived at Kansas as a 6'5" tight end, converted to the line and played in 30 games. Then he sustained a concussion in October 2015 during a loss to Oklahoma State, and the headaches lingered into this fall. He got on the field only once this season, in a loss to Memphis on Sept. 17, after which the headaches became more frequent. The pain was worse than anything he'd ever felt. He was slow in practice, sometimes dizzy. "I noticed it most in the hitting," he says. "I felt...*off*."

He was cognizant of all the players, pro and college, who'd retired in recent seasons, their decisions, like his, colored by individual circumstances but sharing a similar theme—that the more players know about concussions, the more likely they are to leave the game early, faculties intact. Even though Shelley-Smith didn't care for the movie *Concussion*, even though he felt like the media had an antifootball agenda when it came to head injuries, he was more aware. *Everyone* has become more aware. So Shelley-Smith discussed the risks with his team's doctors, training staff and coaches, and with his fiancée. "The thing with your brain is, you really don't know," he says. "Ultimately, it came down to future health."

On Sept. 26 he told his teammates. On Sept. 27 he started to lose the weight he'd put on to play O-line. He was 302 pounds the day he retired but has shed 25 pounds since. He's taking classes to remain on scholarship after completing his degree in supply-chain management last spring. He works with his former teammates on their drills and in breaking down film, and he watches games from the sidelines. That has helped with the transition. In December he'll start working at a local retail outlet as an area supervisor.

He won't be alone. All over the country players like Shelley-Smith—players who love football, who learned discipline and earned college degrees on scholarship—will weigh the impact on their health from repeated head trauma. At Kansas, two of Shelley-Smith's teammates retired in recent seasons for similar reasons. One week after Shelley-Smith walked away, so did starting Oklahoma linebacker Tay Evans. That's Football in America, where it's becoming O.K. to say *No más*.

"Look, the more people talk about head injuries, the more people like me are open to making that decision," Shelley-Smith says. "More people understand what's at stake. Things are definitely changing."

So will Shelley-Smith let his son play football? Without hesitation: "Of course."

The six officials seated around a conference table at the office of the Parsons (Kans.) Recreation Commission can sympathize with the teary former footballer 130 miles to the north. They, too, weighed the impact of head injuries in football, and last summer switched their third- and fourth-grade tackle leagues to flag. Not everyone at the table agreed with that decision, but overall the town of 10,000 "was pretty welcoming of the change," says Gary Crissman, the PRC's executive director.

Maybe it helped that Shaun Hill, a former Parsons High QB who's now a backup for the Vikings, wrote an open letter to his hometown defending the commission's choice. Or perhaps the dangers of head injuries are just too obvious to ignore in 2016. Whatever the reasoning, there are 84 children playing flag football for the PRC this fall, more than triple the number who participated in tackle one season ago.

The six officials will oversee the playoffs tomorrow and so far report no major injuries. They're even considering changing their fifth- and sixth-grade leagues to flag. As they talk, a life-sized cutout of Hill smiles creepily in the background. He's a local hero, the son of former Parsons High assistant Ted Hill, who wouldn't let him play football until sixth grade. As a seventh-grader Shaun injured his neck; Ted made him sit out the next season.

Not everyone buys Shaun Hill's arguments in favor of flag football: players don't collide as much, their heads slam into the turf less often, they can spend more time on noncontact fundamentals. Emilio Aita, a longtime PRC coach, says that most studies about the benefits of flag aren't specific to *youth* football. Still, he left his children in the PRC's flag league, even as one asked him, "Daddy, can I just keep playing soccer until you let me hit somebody?"

Hill, meanwhile, hopes Parsons's switch will help eliminate one safety issue among many surrounding the sport. Asked by phone whether he's concerned about his own health, he says, "If I had any worries, I wouldn't still be playing."

Flag football? *Players retiring over concussions?* Good luck explaining such things to Gary Lothrop, a 59-year-old veterinarian and Nebraska fan who every week writes scathing emails about Cornhuskers football and fires them off to 500-plus eager readers. Eighteen hours before the Huskers host Purdue down the road at Memorial Stadium, he settles into a booth at Greenfield's Cafe in Lincoln and orders a club sandwich. He's weighing the risks-versus-rewards of Football in America, but he's coming to an altogether different conclusion from Shelley-Smith's or the PRC's.

"I always tell people, 'Jeez, I stick my arm up a cow's ass, up to my shoulder, for six bucks [as part of my job]. Sometimes I get crap in my ears.'" He sighs. "Everybody's [job] risk is different."

He's asked, Are players—particularly those at an FBS stalwart like Nebraska—taking an acceptable risk? Is football even a career choice they should have? "I don't know how to weigh in on that," he says, "but I do know: They have turned football into a game for people that should wear pink panties! They're a bunch of pansies!"

He mentions his three children, Nebraska fans all. His daughter suffered a concussion while playing youth soccer; his younger son sustained three concussions. Lothrop says he wishes the NFL hadn't "tried to bury" the issue of concussions but then adds, "I can assure you, 90,000 Nebraskans would not show up for flag football games."

The next morning, three hours before kickoff, Memorial Stadium's parking lots are already filling up. T-shirts read I SEE RED PEOPLE, hats are affixed with giant ears of plastic corn and one food truck displays a popular slogan: THROUGH THESE GATES PASS THE GREATEST FANS IN COLLEGE FOOTBALL.

Most of them, anyway. Before a game at Northwestern in September, three black Nebraska players knelt during the national anthem. One of them, senior linebacker Michael Rose-Ivey, was called a "clueless, confused n-----" on social media and told he should be kicked off the team, lynched or shot. One fan suggested the threesome be hanged the next time "The Star-Spangled Banner" played. Lothrop says he's embarrassed that a player received death threats, but he's not surprised.

That incident came four weeks after Kaepernick knelt during the anthem. That, too, struck a nerve in places like Lincoln. When the three Cornhuskers followed suit, Gov. Pete Ricketts called them "disgraceful" and "disrespectful"; two university regents echoed his thoughts.

In the lot before the Purdue game, fans like Greg and Vicki King share the regents' sentiments. Their son Jason, a senior, starts at left guard for the Boilermakers. Every week Greg, 59, and Vicki, 53, drive nine hours northeast from Little Rock to Purdue's campus in West Lafayette, Ind., where Greg fixes their son breakfast on Friday mornings. If the team travels that afternoon, so do they. "We've never missed a game," says Greg.

When Jason graduates, they're not sure how often they'll continue to watch the sport. "You can't ignore the players who are having personal issues with violence," Vicki says. "That's turning off a lot of people."

Greg nods. "When the right persons come back to represent football, it'll change. The ratings will go back up. Some of those guys on the forefront—Kaepernick, for instance—they're taking the audience away from football. Football is my release; it's like what some folks go to church for. I don't want to think about all that stuff at a game."

Even if most fans here agree that the game is not as healthy as it once was, they tend to peg football's ailments on someone else, something else, somewhere else. *Parents are too serious at youth games.... The NFL was ruined by big business.... Those damn millennials don't respect tradition....*

What fans want most is for their way of life—the romanticized way they see their own past—to remain unchanged. But it doesn't, and they're angry about that. So they drink beer. They scalp tickets. They hug their relatives. They try to hold on to a time that wasn't so confusing, a time that meant so much to them, before everything was different, before players knelt during the national anthem.

The Purdue game marks Nebraska's 352nd straight sellout. Afterward coach Mike Riley takes questions from reporters—mostly male, mostly white—who ask about the run game and the impact of special teams and his O-line woes. They, too, have lost themselves in football. On his way out Riley kisses his wife on the cheek, then he walks through a door that reads TRADITION OF TOUGHNESS and heads out into the night.

Halfway across the country Mike Riley's brother Edward, a professor of anesthesiology at Stanford and a former QB at D-III Whitworth University in Spokane, nurses an amber ale. He's seated in the back of Seattle's Zoo Tavern while one of the presidential debates plays overhead on the TVs. Patrons half-listen as they shoot pool and roll Skee ball.

Riley, 58, is here to weigh in on a different—but no less political—argument, one about football safety, concussions and a spate of former players who've committed suicide. He's a doctor, a healer, but his views align more closely with Gary Lothrop's than with Shaun Hill's.

Two years ago, when his youngest son expressed a desire to play football, Riley decided to study the medical literature available on head injuries. And after reading through the studies he concluded that concerns about the sport are "misplaced." Take one paper, Riley says, that examined nearly 3,500 former NFL players with at least five years of pension-credited seasons between 1959 and '88. That analysis looked at the league's highest-possible-risk subjects and found an incidence of neurodegenerative disease three times that of the general population. It also found the risk of death from neurodegenerative disease to be low for both groups—4.9% in former players, 1.5% overall. The way Riley reads it, that study shows that "the risk associated with a long NFL career is not insignificant—but it remains small."

It's too early, Riley says, to draw too many conclusions. Studies that have correlated the number of hits sustained by different position groups—more for, say, D-linemen than for QBs—with impaired cognitive function didn't measure the same function *beforehand*. Quarterbacks, he says, could have been higher-functioning to begin with. The pathologists who've found scars on the brains of dead players? They haven't yet done the clinical trials that would firmly establish a connection between repeated head trauma and brain damage, Riley says. "Typically, pathologists end their reports with stuff like 'clinical correlation needed,'" he continues. "We don't see that here. There's research, but it's early—and in the press, [doctors] seem to be stretching beyond what they normally would say."

While the beer drinkers around him mock the candidates on TV, Riley adds a disclaimer to his argument. He knows how this might sound, as if he's a doctor for Big Tobacco. He isn't saying football is safe, or risk-free. But he is saying the sport needs long-term epidemiological investigations that follow youth or high school players for 40 or 50 years, examining how they lived, where they came from and how they died.

Riley sustained concussions in his own football career; he once forgot his name when a doctor asked. Still, he says, "it should be a personal decision" whether or not to play. "People need to understand the risks—but the antifootball people need to realize they're involving their kids in other things that are even more risky than football. Like skiing. Equestrian jumping. There's no comparison there."

Both debates continue, two candidates arguing about America and Riley arguing about football's place in it. He mentions Todd Ewen, a hockey enforcer whose family believes he may have shot himself because he thought he had brain damage. An autopsy did not find CTE on Ewen's brain, which doesn't mean it wasn't damaged by playing hockey. "Suicides can develop contagions," Riley says. "It's called the Werther effect: Somebody famous commits suicide and kids copy it. What happened with CTE is it created a narrative for [football players] to have a fatalistic view of their lives."

He pauses, sipping at his beer. "We just don't know enough yet."

Midway through that debate Trump fields a question about gun rights and points out how in Chicago they have the toughest gun laws in the U.S., and yet, "by far, they have more gun violence than any other city." Eighteen hundred miles northeast of Las Vegas—2,000 from Edward Riley in Seattle—Larry Williams, the football coach at Chicago Vocational Career Academy, shifts on his stool at the President's Lounge bar on the South Side and raises a Red Stripe. "Here's to hope," he says. Hope for America. Hope for his team. Hope for his star running back as he recovers from multiple gunshot wounds.

Hope is what Williams, 43, has left. "The streets are winning the battle the coaches used to win," he says. "We can't compare to the streets. Nine times out of 10 players will choose the streets instead of coming to practice."

The Cubs are about to play Game 1 of the World Series in an hour, but Williams's mind is on Sept. 10. After his team's first loss of the season, he boarded a plane to Kansas to watch his son play junior college football. Hundreds of text messages pinged on his phone when he landed. *Everett was shot six times. Call me.*

A running back and defensive back who was drawing interest from mid-major colleges across the Midwest, Everett Henderson had accounted for 90% of Chicago Vocational's offense. Williams visited him that Monday, and not only had the 17-year-old survived six shots to his hands, buttocks and abdomen, but he was walking down the hospital halls with one of those bullets still lodged in his chest. Henderson told his coach what he remembered: He was sitting on his porch, sending text messages, when a man put a gun in his face. Henderson jumped off the porch, ran and heard *pop-pop, pop-pop, pop, pop.* As he bled on the ground, he says, the gunman stood over him and continued to shoot, even after running out of bullets. Then he walked off.

As Henderson recovered, Vocational's season collapsed. "We had to cancel our homecoming game because of death threats to Everett," Williams says. "Reporters kept asking, What gang was he in? I kept saying, He didn't exhibit that around the team." (Henderson has since been cleared to work out; police have not publicly I.D.'d a suspect.)

Patrons are buzzed into the President's Lounge, past signs reading NO WHITE T-SHIRTS and NO ONE UNDER 30. Williams sighs. He knows that the violence, the poverty, the fight for resources—it never ends. It's hard for him to get his players to school. Many walk through gang- and drug-infested neighborhoods. He spends $150 a week to get them bus passes, buys them meals, hands out Gatorade. "Out of my 25 kids, probably two of them [live] with their dads," he says. "We've got to teach them the basics, like hygiene, how to brush their hair—things a teenager should know."

Williams describes Vocational's locker room, its equipment and its stadium as "deplorable." Everything is outdated, broken, chipped or torn. He can hardly keep 25 players on his roster; sometimes he can't get enough kids to show up to hold practice. The school district, perhaps sensitive to all of these issues, wouldn't let him meet with a visiting reporter on campus, so here he is at a bar, three miles from his alma mater, winner of 11 city championships, where Dick Butkus once starred. CVCA used to teach 32 vocations; now it's only six. A building that can hold 4,000 students is now home to about 920.

Through it all Williams sees improvement in his players, who largely go to class and plan for college. "That's why football is so important, now more than ever," he says. "If I have 22 kids [on my team], that's 22 kids who won't be in somebody's gang, 22 kids that mothers won't have to bury. The gang violence in Chicago is uncontrolled; you can't stop it.

"But this is America. You have to try."

Crystal Dixon has a message for parents of kids under 14 who say they love football so much that they're willing to assume its risks, who say things like, *Everything is dangerous. You can get hurt walking down the street.*

"It's not worth it," she says. She's sitting in a coffee shop in Torrance, Calif., five years to the day after her 13-year-old son, Donnovan Hill, was paralyzed from the waist down during a Pop Warner game, and seven months after he died at age 18 following what should have been routine surgery. "I was one of those cheering parents," she says. "I loved football. My dad took me to Raiders games. But there was a lot I didn't know until Donnovan got hurt."

To those who point out how rarely injuries as severe as Donnovan's occur, Dixon says, "Last year 17 kids died from football-related injuries. A couple weeks ago a kid got hit in the stomach and died two days later." She pulls up a story on her phone about a Texas teen who died 48 hours before this meeting, following a JV game. "It *keeps* happening."

One of her most difficult realizations came after her son's death. "I didn't know Donnovan had a brain injury until we donated his brain to Boston University," she says. "They told me it was so bad they wanted to keep studying it. They'd never seen anything like it. Just from one hit."

Some collisions that cause catastrophic injuries can appear harmless. The headfirst, open-field tackle Donnovan attempted on Nov. 6, 2011, looked bad in every way. "Fourteen years old—high school—is the earliest a child should play tackle," Dixon says. "Donnovan [thought it should be] 12."

Dixon says her son's concern about the game, and his passion for it, coexisted after his injury. "After he got hurt, he didn't want to watch football. Then he started getting comfortable with what had happened, and it got easier. After that, he watched every Saturday." Oregon was his favorite team. The college game was his passion, which is why his mom can only watch pro games. Later today she'll catch the end of a matchup between the Broncos and her beloved Raiders.

"I have a love-hate relationship with football," she says. "I'm on the fence. I lost my kid to it, but I know how he felt about it. He still loved the game."

Nineteen-year-old Peyton Smith likes the sport that his famous father plays, but he *loves* a different one. He is the son of Ravens receiver Steve Smith Sr., one of football's toughest and most outspoken characters, hypermasculinity in shoulder pads. But while Peyton watches football and follows football, he does not *play* football. He's a freshman at DePaul, and he's here in Chicago on a soccer scholarship.

Smith took up the so-called beautiful game when he was four, displaying the speed, athleticism and shiftiness that has positioned his father as a potential Hall of Fame inductee. He tried football at 12, played the same position as his dad and wore his number, 89. "It was a lot of pressure," he says, "and I definitely wasn't as good at it as soccer."

Peyton wears a red N.Y. hat turned backward and black-framed glasses as he emphasizes that he's not *antifootball*. He grew up watching as his 5'9" dad built a fearless reputation by traversing the middle of the field, even before rules began to discourage targeting. Sixteen seasons of hit after hit. "Always entertaining, but definitely nerve-racking," Peyton calls it. "Especially for my mom. She freaks out *a lot*."

Peyton was at the game when his father tore his Achilles last season. Three months later Steve was there, beside his son at the dais, beaming, when Peyton signed his DePaul letter of intent after piling up 30 goals and 28 assists as a senior at Carmel Christian in Matthews, N.C. The scene highlighted soccer's growing popularity. Peyton, like most of his friends, wakes up early on weekends to watch the English Premier League. His viewing options for both sports have multiplied in recent years. He watches soccer online and catches football on Twitter every Thursday.

Football's critics, Peyton says, overlook the physicality in soccer. He sustained a concussion when he collided with an opponent at 12. He cites a former teammate who missed more than a year following a head injury; now he plays college soccer, but he's not allowed to head the ball.

As for his dad's sport, "it will always be pretty big," Peyton says. "But head injuries are definitely a factor now; people are concerned about it." He pauses, considering the future. "Soccer is a good option," he says, "but I don't think it'll surpass football. I don't think football will ever die."

Anyone bold enough to imagine the death of Football in America might as well make the three-hour drive north from DePaul, hugging the shores of Lake Michigan, to Green Bay. In Titletown, there are more pro football players than there are Uber drivers, which says as much about the size of the city (pop. 105,000) as it does about the outsized importance of the game in the heart of Packerland. Those drivers are often called upon to drop visitors off at Packers landmarks, their rides consumed by conversations about what the game means here.

Take Jason Murphy, a 911 dispatcher who drives for Uber in his spare time and who let his previous ride off at the Packers Hall of Fame. "I was explaining how football is so rooted here that you almost take it for granted," says Murphy, in a camouflage Green Bay hoodie. "Like, Lambeau Field is two miles from my house."

He steers his Subaru Legacy past a house door painted with the likeness of Brett Favre, past fences decorated to honor the team's 27 division titles. He describes this season as "a little sketchy," what with all the injuries at running back and the inconsistency from Aaron Rodgers. "We're spoiled," he says of a town that's grown fat on football. "Two weeks ago the Packers were booed at home. I understand...."

He trails off, leaving unsaid what seems obvious, that Football in America is changing, even in Green Bay. Strangers still wave as cars pass through the neighborhoods around the stadium. Fans still hang green-and-gold bird-feeders on their porches. Tourists still stop by the statues of Vince Lombardi and Curly Lambeau for photos. But that quaint, small-town vibe now competes with the chaos of construction. The Packers are building a Titletown District on 34 acres of land just west of Lambeau. The plans call for a sledding hill, an ice skating trail, a playground and a hotel, plus "commercial and retail elements"—less Titletown, more Titletown, Inc. The total cost: between $120 million and $130 million, $65 million of which comes from the team's initial investment.

"It's a trade-off; you can't keep the true small-town feel [if you want to] have revenue," says another Uber driver, Larry Pongratz, as he pilots his Ford Fusion down a street named after current coach Mike McCarthy. "Look what they're doing—they're taking over an entire city block."

He's in a philosophical mood: "They'll get it sorted out. Same as on the field. I miss the bone-jarring hits. There seem to be less of them. But I might be a little bloodthirsty, too." Pongratz sighs. "We'll always have tradition."

You want tradition? Meet David Baker, whose voice booms as he recalls Trump visiting his workplace in September. The Republican presidential nominee was in Canton, Ohio, and wanted to see the Pro Football Hall of Fame, where Baker is the president.

The two men discussed the crisis the sport faced in 1905, when at least 18 people died playing football, and how President Theodore Roosevelt famously stepped in, encouraging safety changes and the forward pass. Roosevelt, Baker says, "saved football" and the "values that it teaches."

But now? Now "the whole game is so screwed up," Trump told one rally in Reno. He promised to make America great again. Football, too, presumably.

"We may be at another Teddy Roosevelt moment," Baker, 63, says now. "The game has been under attack. Because of concerns over concussions or the violence in the game, it has somehow become politically incorrect to speak out *for* football.

"I believe there is an incredible silent majority out there that loves this game, that think it's valuable," he continues. "If you ever tried to take it away from them, they would stand up for it."

A *pro*-football faction? Baker thinks such a group could rise up to save the sport—but he's not waiting to find out. Instead he's spearheading the development of a Hall of Fame Village in Canton, where football and its greatest players will be celebrated. It will have a revamped museum and sports complex, a hotel and conference center, restaurants and retail stores, a virtual-reality area and an assisted-living facility for former NFLers. *All for just $500 million*—and right in time for the NFL's 100th season, in 2019.

From 1996 to 2008, Baker was the commissioner of the Arena Football League, where he grew attendance, TV ratings and revenue. Two of his sons played college football, at USC and Duke. The one at USC, Sam, won 35 consecutive games and played in the NFL; the son at Duke, Ben, lost 22 straight and now works for NASCAR. Sam's wife is African-American. In the 1970s, David's father wouldn't let him bring an African-American teammate into their house in Mississippi.

The village, these grand plans—Baker says they should reinforce the lessons his sons learned through the game. "The world today is a challenging place," he says. "Children need to have some values, some toughness in them, some nobility."

They'll find all that in football, he says, as long as those who value the sport speak as loudly as its critics. "This world, with social media, is becoming more and more narcissistic," he says. "It's becoming more money-driven. Football and its values are timeless and universal.

"We need that now more than ever."